# Origin of the Anglo-Saxon Race

*A Study of the Settlement of England and the Tribal Origin of the Old English People*

By Thomas William Shore

**PANTIANOS
CLASSICS**

Published by Pantianos Classics

ISBN-13: 978-1-78987-159-3

First published in 1906

# Contents

# Preface

THIS book, which is the outcome of many years of close research and careful study, was practically complete at the time of the author's death, and he had intended its early publication. Some portions of the manuscript had been revised for printing, some of the chapters had received numerous additions and alterations in arrangement even until within a few days of his death, and others still needed their final revision. From time to time portions of the subject-matter of this work had formed the text for papers read before various archæological societies, notably the series of three papers on Anglo-Saxon London and its neighbourhood, published by the London and Middlesex Archæological Society. The editors' task has been that of revising and editing the manuscript, and seeing the work through the press. The order of the chapters and the general scope and plan of the book are as the author left them. In discharging their task, the editors have made as few alterations as possible, and only such as they felt sure the author would have himself carried out; but the work necessarily suffers from the lack of that final revision which the author alone could have given it. Every endeavour has been made to see that the information is as exact as possible, and most of the references have been verified. The index of place-names and the general index have been made by Blanche Shore, the author's daughter.

T. W. SHORE, M.D.,
Kingswood Road,
Upper Norwood.

L. E. SHORE, M.D.,
St. John's College,
Cambridge.

*April, 1906.*

# Chapter One – Introduction

IF we had no contemporary information of the settlement, for instance, of the State of Massachusetts, and nothing but traditions, more or less probable, concerning it until the middle of the nineteenth century, when an account of that settlement was first written, we should scarcely be warranted in regarding such a narrative as veritable history. Its traditionary value would be considerable, and there its value would end.

This supposed case is parallel with that of the early account of the Anglo-Saxons and the settlement of England as it went on from the middle of the fifth to the middle of the seventh century. That which Bede wrote concerning his own time must be accepted as contemporary history, and for this historical information we venerate his memory; but the early settlements in England were made six or eight generations before his day, and he had nothing but tradition to assist him in his narrative concerning them. We may feel quite sure that he wrote his best. Many of the old chroniclers who copied from him, and some of the historians who followed them, have, however, assigned a greater value to Bede's early narrative than he himself would probably have given to it. In this work it will be our aim to gather what supplementary information we can from all available sources, and among the more important subjects that will be dealt with are the evidence of ancient customs and the influence of family organization as shown by the survival of many ancient place-names.

Anyone who departs from the beaten track, and attempts to obtain some new information from archæological and other research bearing on the circumstances of the Anglo-Saxon settlement, will find many difficulties in his way, and that much time is required to make even small progress. Here and there, however, by the comparison of customs, old laws, the ancient names of places, and other archæological circumstances, with those of a similar kind in Scandinavia or Germany, some advance may be made.

It is to tribal organization and tribal customs that we must look for explanation of much that would otherwise be difficult to understand in the Anglo-Saxon settlement and the origin of the Old English race. Many of the ancient place-names can be traced to tribal origins. Others, whose sources we cannot trace, probably had their origin in tribal or clan names that have been lost. Many of the old manorial and other customs, especially those of inheritance, that survive, or are known to have prevailed, and the variations they exhibited in different English localities, were probably tribal in their origin. The three national names, Angles, Saxons, and Jutes, denoting the people by whom England was occupied, were not the names of nations, as nations are now understood, but convenient names for confederations of tribes. The dialects that were spoken by the English settlers were probably mutually intelligible, but were not, until the lapse of centuries, one speech. Their variations have not yet wholly passed away, as the differences in grammar, vocabulary, intonation, and pronunciation of English dialects still show. It is to the ancient tribes of North Germany and Scandinavia that we must look if we would understand who were the real ancestors of the Old English people, and in comparison with the Germanic element, the Scandinavian has probably not received the attention to which it is entitled. The old place-names in England, except along the Welsh border and in Cornwall, are almost all of Teutonic origin, but we cannot say what they all mean. It is easy to guess, but not easy to guess rightly, for the Northumbrian and Mercian speech of the earliest periods have been almost lost,[1] and the early West Saxon dialect during the later period was not what it was during the earlier. The names of places appear in perhaps the majority of cases to have been given them from topographical considerations. Some of these, derived from hills, fords, woods, and the like, may be of very early date, but most of them are probably later. The place-names derived from tribes or clans are, however, as old as the settlement, whether they arose from a kindred of people or from one man of a particular race. In considering this subject the earliest forms of local government must not be ignored. In the primitive settlements the customary law was administered by families or kindreds. It at first was tribal, and not territorial. The communities must have been known by names they gave themselves, or those by which the neighbouring communities commonly called them. Probably in most cases the names which survived were those by which their neighbours designated them. As regards the disappearance of Anglo-Saxon names, nothing is more striking in one county of Wessex alone—Hampshire, the original Wessex—than the large number of boundary names and names of places mentioned in the Saxon charters that now are lost or are beyond identification.[2] There are, however, mixed with the Teutonic names of places all over England, others denoting natural features, which must be ascribed to an earlier period even than the Anglo-Saxon. In the work of reading the great palimpsest exhibited by the map of England the philologist claims to have the last word. He tells us of declensions and conjugations, of vowel changes and consonant shiftings, and much more that is valuable, assuming to give authoritative interpretations; but, as Ripley says,[3] 'Because a people early hit upon the knowledge of bronze, and learned how to tame horses and milk cows, it does not follow that they also invented the declensions of nouns or the conjugations of verbs.'

As regards the names of places that were called after the names of their occupants or the descendants of some early settler, those in which the Anglo-Saxon patronymic termination -ing—denoting son of, or descendants of—occurs are the most important. This patronymical word -ing has been shown by Kemble [4] to have been used in place-names in several ways. In its simplest form at the end of a name it denotes the son or other descendant of the person who bore that name. Another use of it, as part of a plural termination, was to denote the persons who lived in a particular place or district, as Brytfordingas for the inhabitants of Brytford. It is also sometimes used in another form, as in Cystaninga mearc, the mark or boundary of the Cystanings or people of Keston in Kent,[5] and in Besinga hearh, the temple of the Besingas, probably in Sussex.[6]

The word *ing* in combination was also sometimes used as practically an equivalent of the genitive singular. Examples of this usage occur in such names as Æthelwulfing-land and Swithræding-den, now Surrenden in Kent, which are equivalent in meaning to Æthelwulfes land and Swithrædes den, or wood.[7]

In the Anglo-Saxon charters, or copies of them which have been preserved, many names ending in the word -*ingas,* denoting people of a certain clan or ga, are mentioned. Of these, about 24 are in Kent, 11 in Sussex, 5 in Essex, 7 in Berks, 8 in Norfolk, 4 in Suffolk, 12 in Hants, and 3 in Middlesex.[8] Many more clans no doubt existed, whose names may probably be inferred from existing place-names. On this, however, I lay in no stress. The termination -*ingahem* in place-names occurs in a large group in the North-East of France, where an early Teutonic colony can be traced. Local names ending in -*ingen* are scattered over Germany, most numerously in South Baden, Würtemberg, and along the north of the upper course of the Danube, and it was to these parts of Germany that people closely allied to the Old Saxons migrated. They moved south-west, while many who were kindred to them in race passed over into England, and hence the similarity in the endings of their place-names.

Anglo-Saxon names of places are almost universally feminine nouns ending in -*e*, and forming the genitive case in -*an*. When connected with other words they generally appear as genitives, but sometimes combine with these words, and form simple compounds without inflection.[9] Of these many examples will appear.

The Old English place-names of which the words *men* or *man* form part, and which do not appear to be names derived from inflected words, are somewhat numerous, and most of them may probably be regarded as the tribal names by which the settlers at these places were first known. Of such names, Normanton, Eastmanton, Blackemanstone, Hunmanbie, Osmenton, Ockementone, Sevamantone, Salemanesberie, Galmentone, Walementone, Elmenham, Godmanston, are examples. It is hardly possible that such names as these could attach themselves to places, except as the abodes of men described. These, or nearly all of them, are Old English, and occur in the Charters or in Domesday Book. Brocmanton is also met with in the thirteenth century,[10] and may probably be traced to a tribal Brocman.

The philological evidence bearing on the subject of this inquiry is of two kinds (1) The evidence of the old names in use during the Saxon period; (2) the evidence of the old dialects.

The anthropological evidence is also of two kinds, viz.: (1) The evidence of human remains, chiefly skulls from Anglo-Saxon burial-places, and that of similar remains of the same period from old cemeteries on the Continent; (2)

the racial characters of people in various parts of Northern Europe and in parts of England at the present time.

The archæological evidence that will appear is not only that relating to objects found, but also to customs that prevailed, especially those relating to inheritance, which are among the most persistent of early institutions. In several parts of England accounts have come down to us in the folk-lore or traditions and in historical references of a clan-like feeling between people of adjoining villages or districts. Traces of dislike or jealousy between village and village have been reported in several counties, notably in Hampshire and Cambridgeshire.[11] In the latter county Conybeare mentions the rivalry between the men of Barrington on the Mercian side of the Cam and those of Foxton on the East Anglian side. He shows that this rivalry was of ancient date, and quotes a reference to a faction fight between the two villages in July, 1327. Even in that great district which forms the borderland between Yorkshire and Lancashire stories are still current of the reception which the inhabitants of the Yorkshire valleys sometimes met with when they crossed the moorlands into Rossendale in Lancashire. The traditional reception of such a stranger was to call him a foreigner, and to 'heave a sod at him.' Such an old local tale conveys to us an idea of the isolation that must have prevailed among some at least of the neighbouring settlements of the Old English, especially when inhabited by people descended from different tribes, and not comprised within the same hundred or area of local administration. Thorold Rogers tells us that in the Hampshire Meon country the peasantry in one village, West Meon, had an open and hearty contempt for the inhabitants of the two neighbouring villages which, in the case of one, was almost like the dislike of the Southern French for the Cagots. There was, he says, a theory that the inhabitants were descended from the ancient Britons, whom the Jute settlers had failed to drive out of their morasses.[12]

On this subject of strangers in race settled near each other Seebohm says: 'The tribal feeling which allowed tribesmen and strangers to live side by side under their own laws (as with the Salic and Ripuarian Franks) was, it would seem, brought with the invading tribes into Britain.'[13] In the cases in which strangers in race lived near each other there was little under ordinary circumstances to bring them into social intercourse, and the sense of estrangement was not altogether removed after many generations. It is difficult to see the occasions on which the people of different primitive settlements some miles apart would have opportunities of meeting if they were not included within the same hundreds or wapentakes.

Bearing in mind these circumstances, we cannot wonder if it should appear that the original Anglo-Saxon settlers in some instances called their neighbours in the next settlement, if they were of a different tribe, by the tribal name to which they belonged, or one expressive of the sense of strangers or foreigners. Such a meaning is apparently conveyed by the use of the Anglo-Saxon prefix *el*, other, strange or foreign.[14] Angles, Saxons, Jutes, Frisians, Danes, Norse, and Wends, comprised people of many various tribes, speaking many various dialects, some of which must have been less intelligible to people who as English settlers lived near them than their own vernacular speech. In this sense they would be more or less strangers to each other, and such a line of cleavage would be more marked in those cases in which different local customs prevailed in neighbouring townships. In some parts of England we may still find here and there traces of old place-names denoting, apparently, the idea of other, or strange, people. Such Anglo-Saxon names as Elmanstede,[15] now Elmstead, in Kent, and Elmenham,[16] now Elmham, in Norfolk, probably had this original signification. They can hardly be words derived from inflected names. These and other similar names express the sense that the inhabitants in these hams, steds, worths, beorhs, and tons, were other men or strangers to the people living near them, who probably gave the places these names. It is difficult to see what other meaning can be attached to such names as Elmanstede and Elmenham. They apparently point to conditions of early settlement somewhat similar to those under which townships are formed in many instances in the western parts of the United States and Canada. There emigrants of various European nations are forming their new homes in separate communities of their own people, while others in neighbouring townships who are doing the same are of other races, and are strangers to them. The newer Anglo-Saxon race is being rejuvenated on American soil, as the older stock was by similar conditions formed in England. The isolation of many of the earliest villages in England may probably be seen in the traces we find of the primitive meeting-places for exchange of commodities—i.e., the earliest markets. These are not in the towns, but on the borders or marks of the early settlements, where people of neighbouring places appear to have met on what was perhaps regarded as neutral ground. Some of these old border places may still be recognised by the name *staple*, although by the rise of newer villages they may be border places no longer. Thus, in Hampshire we have Stapler's Down, south of Odiham; Stapeley Row, Ropley; Staple Ash, Froxfield; Stapleford, Durley; Staple Cross, Boarhunt; and Stapole Thorn, a name that occurs in a Saxon charter on the south of Micheldever.[17] An example on the border of two counties is that of Dunstable, and another is the Domesday place Stanestaple, in Middlesex.

Even as late as the time of Henry I. there are orders that neighbours are to meet and settle their differences at the boundaries of their land, and there are many traces of the meeting-places of courts having been at the boundaries of ancient settlements.

The settlers who became the ancestors of the Old English race were people of many tribes, all included within the later designation Anglo-Saxon. They were not exclusively Teutonic, for among them was a small minority of people of various Wendish tribes, the evidence of whose immigration will appear in subsequent pages. In regard to speech, there must have been many dialects at first, and we can trace, more or less, the use in England of three classes of them—viz., the old Germanic, whether Old Frisian or Old Saxon; the Old Norrena, now represented by the Icelandic; and the Old Slavic speech of the Wends—the Wendish, of course, only to a very limited extent. The oldest examples of the Old Northern language are not, however, to be found in the Icelandic, but in the names and words graven on stones in runic characters in Scandinavia, Denmark, and Britain. This method of attempting to read some of our disguised or altered place-names appears to be reasonable to the archæologist, who looks not merely to the historical statements of the old chroniclers and the names for his evidence, but also to the surviving customs, to anthropological and archæological discoveries, to folk-lore, and all other sources from which information bearing on the settlement may be gleaned. The value of the information that may be gathered from these sources to the historian or philologist is great. We can see on the Ordnance map of England many names whose origin goes back only to recent centuries, but we find also in every county many others of extreme antiquity. If we could fully understand them we should know much relating to the Anglo Saxon period of our history of which we are now ignorant. Even the different ways in which the homesteads in different parishes or townships are arranged, whether they are scattered or clustered in groups, give information by which the archæologist is able to assist the historian. The scattered homesteads may in some districts be as old as the British period, or in others may have been formed first by emigrants who came from some old Continental areas where the Celtic arrangement survived. There are many other and more numerous areas where nucleated villages exist, in which the homesteads are collected, some arranged on the plan of having roads radiating from them—*i.e.*, the star-like way, similar to the German type common between the Elbe and the Weser. In other instances we find collected homesteads of an elongated, rounded, or fan-shaped form enclosing a small space, around which the original houses were built. These resemble the village types east of the Elbe, in the old Slavonic parts of Germany, and the type was in all probability brought to this country by some Wends or Germanized Slavs. If a few villages here and there are of a Wendish rather than of a purely Germanic type, we may reasonably look for traces of Slavonic influence in the customs, folk-lore, and in some at least of the names of the district.

From the circumstance that various old dialects were spoken in England during the Anglo-Saxon period, it follows that we may look for the origin of some of our place-names in the Old Norrena of the northern runic writing, or in the Icelandic tongue, as well as in those of old Germanic origin, and perhaps in some few instances in the Old Slavic dialect that was spoken by the Wends, of whose settlement in England evidence will appear. It was from these elements, with some admixture of the Celtic, that the Anglo-Saxon language was formed on English soil.[18]

In the Hundred Rolls of A.D. 1271 there are many people mentioned who bore the surname of Scot, which was no doubt originally given to them or their forefathers because they were Scots who had settled in England. Unless we are to believe the existence of the mythological ancestors of various tribes, such as Angul, the eponymous ancestor of the Angles; Saxnote, of the

Saxons; Dan, of the Danes; Gewis, of the Gewissas, and so on, we must allow that the earliest individuals who were called by a tribal name derived it in some way or other from that of the tribe, as those first called Scot did from the early Scots. Such names as Scot, Welsh, Breton, Cornish, Frank, Fleming, and others, were apparently given to the individuals who bore them by people of other descent near whom they lived, because those so designated were people of the nations or tribes denoted by these names. We may also trace such mediæval names as Pickard, Artis, and Gascon, to natives of Picardy, Artois, and Gascony.

It is not easy to see how such a personal name as Westorwalening, which occurs in Anglo-Saxon literature,[19] could have arisen except as the designation of a man belonging to the tribe of Westorwealena, or Western Welshmen.

The older names, Goding, Godman, Waring, Quen, Fin, Hune, Osman, Osgood, Eastman, Norman, Saleman, Alman, Mone, Wendel, Winter, and others, may also he traced to the names of the corresponding ancient tribal people, or to the countries whence they came. It is very difficult, for example, to see how the name Osgood was applied to a person, except that, having migrated from the homeland of the tribe to which he belonged, his neighbours, finding it necessary to designate him among themselves by some name, called him Osgood or Ostrogoth, because he came from Ostergotland in Sweden. These tribal settlers were all included under the general designations of Angles, Saxons. and Jutes, but have in many instances transmitted their tribal names to us in those of the places they occupied.

In considering this part of our subject, it is important to remember that the nations and tribes of Germany and Scandinavia were in many instances known by more than one name. The people sometimes mentioned as Sassi and Swæfas were Saxons, or very closely connected with them. Those known as Hunsings, Brocmen, and Chaukians, were Frisians, or their close allies. The Dacians were Danes, and the Geats and Gutæ were Jutes. The Rugians and Wilte were tribal people among the Wends, and these, by Scandinavians, were called Windr or Wintr.

Some of the Danes were called after the names of their islands, and some of the Goths after the names of portions of ancient Gothland. In looking for traces of these races among our ancient place-names, it is clear, therefore, that the old tribal designations cannot be disregarded. Another important consideration is that, for one man who bore a tribal name which has survived, there may have been many others of the same race called by other names, or whose names did not become attached to any place, and so have not come down to us. The testimony which names afford must, however, be considered with caution, for it is certain that they do not always imply what they seem to imply. From the archæologist's point of view, modern place-names, without their most ancient forms as a guide, or without circumstantial evidence showing a reasonable probability what their most ancient forms were, are almost valueless. The Anglo-Saxon names, however, are of great value. Many instances are known of places which have two names, both of them apparently old, and it is probable that instances of this double nomenclature which have not been recorded, or which have not come down to our time, were much more numerous. As already mentioned, many places must originally have got their names from the people who lived in them, or from people who were their neighbours. Possibly, in some cases, people in neighbouring settlements some miles away in one direction called a place by one name, and those some miles away in another direction called it by another. If these neighbours spoke different dialects, as they may have done on the borders of the primitive districts or States, the use of such double names would be more likely, and perhaps in some cases probable. The tendency to give nicknames, or ekenames, to both people and places has also to be taken into account. The tendency of people to turn names the meaning of which they did not understand, or which had become lost as the language became modified or changed, into familiar animal or other names. such as Camelford from Gavelford, when the meaning of the primitive name had ceased to be remembered, must also be recognised. The alteration in some place-names may be traced also to another cause—the influence of humour. Of such names. whatever may be the exact date of its origin, is that of the vale of Catmouse in Rutland. It occurs on some old maps as Catmose, and whatever may have been its ancient significance, it is certain that it could have had no reference to cat and mouse. In some parts of England the old local name Mousehole occurs. This is probably also a humorous name, derived in some instances at least from mosshole—*i.e.* the place where moss or peat was formerly dug. Such names as Sawbridgeworth, the Domesday name of which was Sabrixte-worde, and Hungriweniton are examples of the same kind. Market Jew, the popular name for Marazion, is said to have come from the old name Marghaisewe, meaning a Thursday market.[20]

Ekenames or nicknames were also used by the Anglo-Saxons, and were often those of animals. Such a name is that of Barrington in Cambridgeshire, as cited by Skeat, the name denoting the ton of the sons of Bera (bear).[21] Barrington, as already mentioned, was a frontier village. The use of ekenames or nicknames is certainly as old in this country as the period of the Anglo-Saxons. Our earliest literature affords evidence of it. They were not only applied to individuals, but to communities or places. It is perhaps impossible to say at the present time, in regard to numerous old place-names that still remain, which are original names or survivals of them. and which are ancient nicknames or survivals of them; but it is probable that there are many ancient eke- or nicknames the meanings of which we cannot interpret. A philologist who undertakes to explain English place-names by the rigid rules of modern philology, without taking into account the human element connected with the subject, the tendency of people to modify names into more familiar forms, or to modify their sound for the sake of change and variety alone, will find himself in difficulties with a considerable number of them. The oldest forms of those place-names that are also tribal names are important evidence, which will not be invalidated if in many instances the name has been derived from the personal name of the head of a family rather than from the people of a community. The early customary ties of kindred among the Anglo-Saxons were very strong. With a chieftain, some of his kindred commonly lived under a primitive form of family law. A chief or headman named Hundeman or Huneman by his neighbours around the Anglo—Saxon place Hundemanebi, now Hunmanby in Yorkshire, may reasonably be considered to have been a Frisian of the Hunni or Hunsing tribe, and the people who settled with him to have been of his family or kindred. Similarly, where we find a place named after the Wends or Vandals, it may have derived its name from the Vandal chief alone, or from the community of kindred people under him. Such an Anglo-Saxon name as Wendelesworth in Surrey could hardly have been derived from any other circumstance than the settlement on the south bank of the Thames of a man named Wendel, because he was of the Vandal or Wendish race, or from a kindred of Vandals. The name of this place appears much earlier than that of the stream of the same name. It matters little whether the name arose from the Wendish chief or from his people. The name Wendel was probably given to him or them, because of his or their Wendish or Vandal origin, by the people of adjoining settlements in Surrey or Middlesex, who were of another tribal origin.

This case of Wandsworth is interesting, not only because its old name points to a Wendish origin, but also on account of its custom of junior inheritance, which was of immemorial usage and came down to modern times. On the manor of Wandsworth the youngest son inherited his father's land, a custom of peculiar interest in reference to Wendish researches. The Wends who took part in the Anglo-Saxon settlement were Slavs of such a mixed Slav descent that they had retained a custom, that of junior right, which was the ancient law of inheritance among the Slavs, and it is very difficult to avoid the conclusion that the Wendish origin of the name is confirmed by the survival of the custom. We are not now, however, considering the settlement in any one district, but the general evidence of a mixture of people of many tribes in different parts of the country, by the formation of communities of people of various races near each other. In connection with this inquiry the survival of names of places derived from the names of well-known tribes among the ancient Germans and Scandinavians, and the survival here and there, notwithstanding the changes likely to have occurred in the course of many centuries, of manorial customs which are known to have been ancient customs, or to closely resemble customs which in ancient time prevailed in parts of Germany and Scandinavia, are most important considerations. Customs of family inheritance, where they can be traced, are in many instances of as much value as contemporary historical information. It does not appear that there is any county in England where the surviving place-names are exclusively of Saxon, Anglian, Jutish, Danish, or Norse origin. If, for example, we consider those in the great areas to which the natural entrances from the sea are by the Humber, the Wash, the Thames, and the Southampton Water, with its adjoining estuaries, we shall find evidence of names of various origins, pointing to settlements of people of distinct races or tribes. In all parts of our country we find that during the last thousand years men have left in their architecture survivals of the period in which they lived. Tribal customs among our forefathers had an earlier origin than their arts, and we may recognise in their survival proof of the settlement of people of several different tribes.

Like a stream which can be followed up to many sources, the Anglo-Saxon race may be traced to many tribal origins. It is not the purpose of this book to describe the conquest of England, but rather its settlement by the conquering tribes and races. With this object in view, it is necessary to give attention rather to the sites of settlements than the sites of battles, to the arrangements of villages rather than the campaigns by which the districts in which those villages are situated were opened to settlement. It is not within its scope to ascertain the number of conquered British people slain on any occasion, but rather to find the evidence which indicates that some of them must have been spared in parts of the country, and lived side by side with their conquerors, to become in the end blended with them as part of a new race. It is within its scope to show that in various parts of England people of diverse tribes became settled near to each other, in some districts one tribe preponderating, and in some another, a preponderance which has produced ethnological differences that have survived to the present time, and has left differences in dialects that bear witness to diversities in their origin.

[1] Skeat, W. W., 'Principles of English Etymology,' p. 490.
[2] 'Codex Diplomaticus Ævi Saxonici,' edited by Kemble, Index.
[3] Ripley, W. Z., 'The Races of Europe,' p. 456.
[4] Kemble, J. M., *Philological Soc. Proc.,* iv.
[5] 'Codex Dipl.,' No. 994.
[6] *Ibid.,* No. 1,163.
[7] Kemble, J.M., *loc. cit.*
[8] Kemble, J. M., 'Saxons in England.'
[9] Guest, E., 'The English Conquest of the Severn Valley,' *Journal Arch. Institute,* xix. 197.
[10] 'Testa de Nevill,' 62*b*, 68.
[11] Conybeare, E., 'History of Cambridgeshire,' 139.
[12] Rogers, Thorold, 'Economic Interpretation of History,' 284.
[13] Seebohm, F., 'Tribal Custom in Anglo-Saxon Law,' 498.
[14] Bosworth and Toller, 'Anglo-Saxon Dictionary.'
[15] 'Codex Dipl.,' Index.
[16] *Ibid.*
[17] 'Liber de Hyda,' pp. 86, 87, A.D. 1026.
[18] Marsh, G. P., 'Lectures on the English Language,' First Series, 42, 43.
[19] Sweet, H., 'The Earliest English Texts,' 489.
[20] Courtney, M. A., *Folk-Lore Journal,* v. 15.
[21] Skeat, W. W., Cambridge Antiq. Soc, Oct. pub., xxxvi., p. 18.

# Chapter Two - The Saxons and Their Tribes

WE have so long been accustomed to call some of the English settlers Saxons that it is with some surprise we learn none of them called themselves by this name. As far as England was concerned, this was the name by which they were commonly called by the Britons, and it was not generally used by the people themselves until some centuries later. Nations and tribes, as well as individuals, must always be known either by their native names or by the names which other people give them. They may, consequently, have more than one name. The name Saxon, although not used by the tribes that invaded England in the fifth and sixth centuries as their own designation for themselves, is more ancient than this invasion. Before the end of the Roman rule in Britain it was used to denote the part of the English coast from the Wash to the Solent and the Continental coast of North-Eastern France and Belgium, both of which were known as the Saxon Shore. This name apparently arose from the descent of pirates who were called Saxons. On the other hand, there is evidence leading to the conclusion that there were early settlements of people known as Saxons on these coasts. Both these views may be right. for the piratical Saxons, like the Northmen of later centuries, may first have plundered the coasts and subsequently settled along them. In any case, a Roman official or admiral, known as Comes litoris Saxonici,[1] Count of the Saxon Shore, was appointed to look after these shores. After the departure of the Roman legions the partly Rornanized Britons naturally gave the name Saxon to invaders from Germany, as this name had come down to them from the Roman period. for after the time of Constantine the Great all the inhabitants of the coasts of Germany who practised piracy were included under the Saxon name.[2] It is a curious circumstance that the parts of England in which the Saxon place-names. such as Sexebi and Sextone, survived at the time of Domesday survey are not in those counties which were comprised within either of the Saxon kingdoms of England. In considering the settlement, the name Saxons comes before us in a wider sense than that of a tribe, as denoting tribes acting together, practically a confederacy. In this sense it was used by the early British writers, Angles, Jutes, and people of other tribes. all being Saxons to them, and the settlers in all parts of England were known as Saxons by them, as well as the people of Sussex, Essex, and Wessex. In this wider sense the name Saxonia was used by Bede, for though an Anglian, he described himself as an office-bearer in Saxonia. The settlers in Hampshire, who after a time were known in common with those in neighbouring counties as West Saxons, did not call themselves Saxons, but Gewissas, and the most probable meaning of that name is confederates, or those acting together in some assured bond of union.[3] Their later name of West Saxons was apparently a geographical one.

The name Saxon was no doubt found a convenient one to describe the tribal people who migrated to England from the north coasts of Germany, extending from the mouth of the Rhine to that of the Vistula, but among themselves these Saxons were certainly known by their tribal names. Saxons from older Saxony were no doubt largely represented among them, but the singular fact remains that in England the name Saxon was used, at first, only by the British chroniclers as a general designation for their enemies, while the incoming people were clearly known among themselves by their tribal names. At various periods people called Saxons in Germany colonized other lands besides England. Some migrated eastward across the Elbe into the country of the Wends, and began that process of gradual absorption under which the Wendish people and their language have now been completely merged into the German. Others migrated to the south.

The early reference by Cæsar to a German nation he calls the Cherusci probably refers to the people afterwards called Saxons. Some German scholars identify the god of these people, called Heru or Cheru, as identical with the eponymous god of the Saxons, called Saxnot, who corresponded to the northern Tyr, or Tius, after whom our Tuesday has been named.[4] The Saxon name was at one time applied to the islands off the west coast of Schleswig, now known as the North Frisian Islands, and the country called by the later name Saxland extended from the lower course of the Elbe to the Baltic coast near Rugen. The earlier Saxony, however, from which settlers in England came was both westward and northward of the Elbe. There were some Saxons who at an early period migrated as far west as the country near the mouth of the Rhine, and it was probably from this colony that some of their descendants migrated centuries later into Transylvania, where their posterity still preserve the ancient name among the Hungarians or Magyars.

As regards the Saxons in England, it is also a singular circumstance that they were not known to the Northmen by that name, for throughout the Sagas no instance occurs in which the Northmen are said to have come into contact in England with people called Saxons.[5] One of the names by which they were known to the Scandinavians appears to have been Swæfas.

The Saxons are not mentioned by Tacitus, who wrote about the end of the first century, but are mentioned by Ptolemy in the second century as inhabiting the country north of the Lower Elbe.[6] Wherever they may have been at first located in Germany, it is certain that people of this nation migrated to other districts from that occupied by the main body. We know of the Saxon migration to the coast of Belgium and North-Eastern France. and of the special official appointed by the Romans to protect these coasts and the south-eastern coasts of Britain. On the Continental side of the Channel there certainly were early settlements of Saxons, and it is probable there were some on the British side. These historical references show that the name is a very old one, which was used in ancient Germany for a race of people, while in England it was used both in reference to the Old Saxons and also in a wider sense by both Welsh and English chroniclers. In Germany the name was probably applied to the inhabitants of the sea-coast and water systems of the Lower Rhine, Weser, Lower Elbe and Eyder, to Low Germans on the Rhine, to Frisians and Saxons on the Elbe, and to North Frisians on the Ryder.[7]

In considering the subject of the alliances of various nations and tribes in the Anglo-Saxon conquests, it is desirable to remember how great a part confederacies played in the wanderings and conquests of the northern races of Europe during and after the decline of the Roman Empire. The name Frank supplies a good example. This was the name of a great confederation, all the members of it agreeing in calling themselves free.[8] Hence, instead of assuming migrations (some historically improbable) to account for the Franks of France, the Franks of Franche-comte, and the Franks of Franconia, we may simply suppose them to be Franks of different divisions of the Frank confederation—*i.e.*, people of various great tribes united under a common designation. Again, the Angli are grouped with the Varini, not only as neighbouring nations on the east coast of Schleswig, but in the matter of laws under their later names, Angles and Warings. Similarly, we read of Goths and Vandals,[9] of Frisians and Chaucians, of Goths and Burgundians, of Engles and Swæfas, of Franks and Batavians, of Wends and Saxons, of Frisians and Hunsings; and as we read of a Frank confederation, there was practically a Saxon one. In later centuries, under the general name of Danes, we are told by Henry of Huntingdon of Danes and Goths, Norwegians and Swedes, Vandals and Frisians, as the names of those people who desolated England for 230 years.[10] The later Saxon confederation is that which was opposed to Charlemagne but there was certainly an earlier alliance, or there were common expeditions of Saxons and people of other tribes acting together in the invasion of England under the Saxon name.

In view of a supposed Saxon alliance during the invasion and settlement of England, the question arises, with which nations the Saxon people who took part in the attacks on Britain could have formed a confederacy. Northward, their territory joined that of the Angles; on the north and west it touched that of the Frisians, and on the east the country of the Wendish people known as the Wilte or Wilzi. Not far from them on the west the German tribe known as the Boructarii were located, and these are the people from whom Bede tells us that some of the English in his time were known to have been derived.

During the folk-wanderings some of the Suevi migrated to Swabia, in South Germany, and these people, called by the Scandian nations the Swæfas, were practically of the same race as the Saxons, and their name is sometimes used for Saxon. The Angarians, or Men of Engern, also were a tribe of the Old Saxons. Later on, we find the name Ostphalia used for the Saxon country lying east of Engern, now called Hanover, and Westphalia for the country lying west of this district. Among the Saxons there were tribal divisions or clans, such as that of the people known as the Ymbre, or Ambrones, and the pagus of the Bucki among the Engern people.[11]

This pagus of the Old Saxons has probably left its name not only in that of Buccingaham, now Buckingham, but also in other English counties. In Norfolk we find the Anglo-Saxon names Buchestuna, Buckenham. and others. In Northampton the Domesday names Buchebi, Buchenho, Buchestone, and others, occur. In Huntingdonshire, similarly,we find Buchesunorth, Buchesworth, and Buchelone; in Yorkshire Bucktorp, in Nottinghamshire Buchetone, in Devon Buchesworth and Bucheside, all apparently named after settlers called Buche. If a settler was of the Bucki tribe, it is easy to see how he could be known to his neighbours by this name.

The Buccinobantes, mentioned by Ammianus,[12] were a German tribe, from which settlers were introduced into Britain as Roman colonists before the end of Roman rule in Britain.[13] The results of research render it more and more probable that Teutonic people under the Saxon name were gradually gaining a footing in the island before the period at which the chief invasions are said to have commenced. In the intestine wars that went on in the fifth century the presence of people of Teutonic descent among the Britons might naturally have led to Teutonic allies having been called in, or to have facilitated their conquests.[14]

Ptolemy is the first writer who mentions the Saxons, and he states that they occupied the country which is now Holstein; but between his time and the invasion of Britain they probably shifted more to the south-west. to the region of Hanover and Westphalia, some probably remaining on the north bank of the Elbe. He tells us of a people called the Pharadini, a name resembling Varini or Warings, allies of the Angles, who lay next to the Saxons. He mentions also the three islands of the Saxons, which are probably those known now as the North Frisian Islands, north of the coast where the Saxons he mentioned are said to have lived. This is the country that within historic time has been, and still is in part, occupied by the North Frisians. The origin of the name Saxon has been a puzzle to philologists, and Latham has summed up the evidence in favour of its being a native name as indecisive. There was certainly a god known in Teutonic mythology as Saxnote or Saxneat, but whether the name Saxon was derived from the god, or the god derived his name from the people who reverenced him, is uncertain. We find this Saxnote mentioned in the pedigree of the early Kings of Essex. Thunar, Woden, and Saxnote are also mentioned as the gods whom the early Christians in Germany had to declare publicly that they would forsake,[15] and the identity of Saxnote with Tiu, Tius, or Tyr, is apparent from this as well as from other evidence.

During the Roman period a large number of Germans, fleeing from the southeast, arrived in the plains of Belgium, and the names Flamand, Flemish, and Flanders were derived from these refugees, who in some accounts are described as Saxons, and the coast they occupied as the well-known *litus Saxonicum*, or Saxon shore.[16] This is an important consideration in reference to the subsequent settlement of England, for it shows that there were people called Saxons before the actual invasion occurred, located on a coast much nearer to this country than that along the Elbe. In the time of Charlemagne the lower course of the Elbe divided the Saxons into two chief branches, and those to the north of it were called Nordalbingians, or people north of the Elbe, which is the position where the Saxons of Ptolemy's time are said to have been located. One of the neighbouring races to the Saxons in the first half of the sixth century in North Germany was the Longobards or Lombards. Their great migration to the south under their King Alboin, and their subsequent invasion of Italy, occurred about the middle of the sixth century. This was about the time when the Saxons were defeated with great slaughter near the Weser. by Hlothaire, King of the Franks. Some of the survivors are said to have accompanied the Lombards, and others in all probability helped to swell the number of emigrants into England. It is probable that after this time they became more or less scattered to the south and across the sea, and in Germany the modern name Saxony along the upper course of the Elbe is a surviving name of a larger Saxony. The Germans have an ancient proverb which is still in use: 'There are Saxons wherever pretty girls grow out of trees'[17]—perhaps a reference to the fair complexion of the old Saxon race, and to its wide dispersion.

The circumstance that the maritime inhabitants of the German coasts were known as Saxons before the fall of the Roman Empire shows that the name was applied to a seafaring people, and under it at that time the early Frislans were probably included, The later information we obtain concerning the identity of the wergelds, or payments for injuries, that prevailed among both of these nations supports this view. The Saxon as well as the Frisian wergeld to be paid to the kindred in the case of a man being killed was 160 solidi, or shillings.[18]

There are two sources, so far as our own island is concerned, whence we may derive historical information concerning the conquest and settlement of England—viz., from the earliest English writers and from the earliest Welsh writers. Bede is the earliest author of English birth, and Nennius, to whom the 'Historia Britonum' is ascribed, is the earliest Welsh author. The veracity of the 'Historia Britonum' is not seriously doubted—at least, the book under that name of which Nennius is the reputed author. Its date is probably about the middle of the eighth century, and we have no reason to suppose that the learning to be found at that time in the English monasteries was superior to that in the Welsh. Nennius lived in the same century as Bede. but wrote about half a century later. His information is of value as pointing to a large number of German tribes under the general name of Saxons, rather than people of one nationality only, having taken part in the invasion and settlement of England. Nennius tells us of the struggles which went on between the Britons and the invaders. He says: 'The more the Saxons were vanquished, the more they sought for new supplies of Saxons from Germany, so that Kings, commanders, and military bands were invited over from almost every province. And this practice they continued till the reign of Inda, who was the son of Eoppa; he of the Saxon race was the first King in Bernicia, and in Cær Ebranc (York).'[19]

In reference to Cæsar's account of German tribes, it is significant that he mentions a tribe or nation called the Cherusci as the head of a great confederation. It is of interest to note also that, as long as we find the name Cherusci used, Saxons are not mentioned, but as soon as the Cherusci disappear by name the Saxons appear, and these in a later time also formed a great confederacy. The name Gewissas, which was that by which the West Saxons were known, included Jutes—*i.e.*., in all probability, Goths, Frisians, Wends, and possibly people of other tribes, as well as those from the Saxon fatherland.

The Saxons of England were converted to Christianity before those of the Continent, and we derive some indirect information of the racial affinities between these peoples from the accounts of the early missionary zeal of priests from England among the old Saxons. Two of these, who are said to have been Anglians, went into Saxony to convert the people, and were murdered there; but in after-centuries their names were held in high reverence, and are still honoured in Westphalia. We can scarcely think that they would have set forth on such a missionary expedition unless their dialect or language had so much in common as to enable them as Anglians from England to make themselves easily understood to these old Saxons.

The question who were the true Saxons—*i.e.*, the Saxons specifically so called in Germany—has been much discussed. The name may not have been a native one, but have been fixed on them by others, in which case, as Beddoe says, it is easier to believe that the Frisians were often included under it.[20] They may have been, and probably were, a great martial and aggressive tribe, which spread from the country along the Elbe over the country of the Weser, after conquering its previous inhabitants, the Boructarii, or Bructers. Such a migration best accounts for the later appearance of Saxons in the region which the Old English called Old Saxony, and erroneously looked upon as their old home, because their kindred had come to occupy it since their separation. The Saxonia of the ninth century included Hanover, Westphalia, and Holstein, as opposed to Friesland, Schleswig. the Middle Rhine provinces, and the parts east of the Elbe, which were Frisian, Danish, Frank, and Slavonic respectively.[21] Among the Saxons of the country north of the Elbe were the people of Stormaria, whose name survived in that of the river Stoer, a boundary of it, and perhaps also in one or more of the rivers Stour, where some of the Stormarii settled in England.

William of Malmesbury, who wrote early in the twelfth century, tells us that the ancient country called Germany was divided into many provinces, and took its name from germinating so many men. This may be a fanciful derivation, but he goes on to say that, 'as the pruner cuts off the more luxuriant branches of the tree to impart a livelier vigour to the remainder, so the inhabitants of this country assist their common parent by the expulsion of a part of their members, lest she should perish by giving sustenance to too numerous an offspring; but in order to obviate the discontent, they cast lots who shall be compelled to migrate. Hence the men of this country made a virtue of necessity, and when driven from their native soil have gained foreign settlements by force of arms'[22] He gives as instances of this the Vandals, Goths, Lombards. and Normans. There is other evidence of the prevalence of this custom. The story of Hengist and Horsa is one of the same kind, The custom appears to have been common to many different nations or tribes in the northern parts of Europe, and points, consequently, to the pressure of an increasing population and to diversity of origin among the settlers known as Saxons, Angles, and Jutes in England.

The invasions of England at different periods between the fifth and tenth centuries, and the settlement of the country as it was until the end of the Anglo-Saxon period, were invasions and settlements of different tribes. It is necessary to emphasize this. Bede's list of nations, among others, from whom the Anglo-Saxon people in his day were known to have descended is considerably longer and more varied than that of Jutes, Saxons, and Angles. During the centuries that followed his time people of other races found new homes here, some by conquest, as in the case of Norse and Danes, and others by peaceful means, as in the time of King Alfred, when, as Asser tells us, Franks, Frisians, Gauls, Pagans, Britons, Scots, and Armoricans placed themselves under his government.[23] As Alfred made no Continental conquests, the Franks, Gauls, and Frisians must have become peaceful settlers in England, and as the only pagans in his time in Europe were the northern nations—Danes, Norse, Swedes, and Wends—some of these must also have peacefully settled in his country, as we know that Danes and Norse did largely during this as well as a later period. Men of many different races must have been among the ancestors of both the earlier and later Anglo-Saxon people.

In the eighth and ninth centuries three kingdoms in England bore the Saxon name, as mentioned by Bede and the Anglo-Saxon Chronicle—viz., Essex, Sussex, and Wessex—and one province, Middlesex. As will be seen when considering the evidence relating to the settlers in various parts of England, it does not follow that these several parts of our country which were called after the Saxon name were colonized by people known as Saxons in Germany. The customs that prevailed in these parts of England were different in many localities. The relics of the Anglo-Saxon period that have been discovered in these districts present also some distinctive features. It is certain from the customs that prevailed, some of which have survived, from the remains found, from the old place-names, and from the variations in the shape of the skulls discovered, that the people of the Saxon kingdoms of England could not have been people of one race. The anthropological evidence which has been collected by Beddoe[24] and others confirms this, for the skulls taken from Saxon cemeteries in England exhibit differences in the shape of the head which could not have resulted from accidental variations in the headform of people all of one uniform race or descent.[25] The typical Saxon skull was dolichocephalic, or long, the breadth not exceeding four-fifths of the length, like those of all the nations of the Gothic stock. Goths, Norwegians, Swedes, Danes, Angles, and Saxons among the ancient nations all had this general head-form, as shown by the remains of these several races which have been found, and from the head-form of the modern nations descended from them; but among these long-headed people there were some with variations in the skull and a few with broad skulls.

The Saxons must have been nearly allied to some of the Angles. This is shown by the probability that the so-called Saxons are located by Ptolemy in the country north of the Elbe, which by other early writers is assigned mainly to the Angles. His references to the tribe or nation known as the Suevi point to the same conclusion, the Suevi-Angli mentioned by him[26] being apparently another name for the people of the country which, according to others, was occupied by Saxons, and these Suevi or Suabi are mentioned as at Saxon pagus in early German records.[27] The Scandian peninsula, so remarkable for early emigration, was probably the original home at some very remote period of the ancestors of the nations known in later centuries as Saxons, Suevi, and Angles. The racial characters of all the Teutonic tribes of North Germany, as of their modern representatives, were fair hair and eyes. and heads of the dolichocephalic shape. These characters differentiated the northern tribes of Germany from the more ancient occupants of Central Europe, as at the present time they distinguish them from the darker-haired South Germans of Bavaria and Austria, who have broader skulls than those of the north. The skulls which are found in ancient burial-places in Germany of the same age as the Anglo-Saxon period are of two main types—viz., the dolichocephalic or long, and the brachycephalic or broad. In the old burial-places at Bremen, from which 103 examples were obtained, only 5 typical broad skulls were found, against 72 typical long skulls and 26 which were classed by Gildemeister as intermediate in form.[28] These 26 he regarded as Frisian, and gave them the name Batavian. In the South of Germany graves of the same age yield a majority of broad skulls, which closely correspond to those of the peasantry of the present time in the same parts of the country. From this it may be inferred that during the period of the English settlement people with long skulls were in a great majority in North Germany, and people with broad skulls in a majority in the southern parts of that country, certainly in these districts south of Thuringia. Bede tells us that the people of England were descended from many tribes, and Nennius says that Saxons came into England from almost every province in Germany. Unless we are to entirely discredit such statements, the probability that some of the settlers whom Nennius calls Saxons may have been broad-headed is great. That various tribal people under the Saxon name took part in the invasion and settlement of England is probable from many circumstances, and, among others, the minor variations in the skulls found in Anglo-Saxon graves corresponding to the minor variations found to exist also among the skulls discovered at Bremen. Of these latter Beddoe says: 'There are small differences which may have been tribal.'[29] The same author remarks also of these Bremen skulls, that there are differences in the degree of development of the superciliary ridges which may have been more tribal than individual.[30]

Of 100 skulls of the Anglo—Saxon period actually found in England, and whose dimensions were tabulated by Beddoe, the following variations were found, the percentage of the breadth in comparison with the length being expressed by the indices:[31]

| Indices | | | | | Number of Skulls. |
|---------|---|---|---|---|-------------------|
| 65-66 | .. | .. | .. | .. | 1 |
| 67-68 | .. | .. | .. | .. | 1 |
| 69-70 | .. | .. | .. | .. | 8 |
| 71-72 | .. | .. | .. | .. | 14 |
| 73-74 | .. | .. | .. | .. | 33 |
| 75-76 | .. | .. | .. | .. | 21 |
| 77-78 | .. | .. | .. | .. | 14 |
| 79-80 | .. | .. | .. | .. | 6 |
| 81-82 | .. | .. | .. | .. | 2 |
| | | | | | 100 |

From this table it will be seen that 8 of the 100 have a breadth very nearly or quite equal to four-fifths of their length—*i.e.*, they are the remains of people of a different race from the typical Anglo-Saxon.

The typical Saxon skull is believed to have been similar to that known as the 'grave-row' skull on the Continent, from the manner in which the bones were found laid in rows. Thcse occur numerously in Saxon burial-places in the Old Saxon and Frisian country, their mean index being about 75—*i.e.*, they are long skulls.

The variation in the skulls from Anglo-Saxon graves in England, as will be seen from the table, is very considerable, but the majority have an index from 73 to 78–*i.e.*, they resemble in this respect those commonly found in the old burial—places of North Germany. The variations have been attributed by some writers to the racial mixture of Saxons with the conquered Britons.[32] Since, however, similar variations are seen in skulls obtained from the graves at Bremen and other parts of North Germany, it is probable that the so-called Saxons were not a people of a homogeneous race, but comprised tribal people who had variations in head-form, a small percentage being even broad-headed. The migration of such people into England among other Saxons would explain the variations found in the Anglo-Saxon head-form, and, moreover, help us to explain variations in custom that are known to have existed within the so-called Saxon kingdoms of England.

[1] 'Notitia Utriusquo Imperii.,' 'Mon. Hist. Brit.' xxiv.
[2] Camden, W., 'Britannia.' i., ci.
[3] Stevenson, W. H., *English Hist. Review*, xiv. 36.
[4] Wagner, W., 'Asgard and the Gods,' translated by Anson, 9, 10.
[5] du Chaillu, 'The Viking Age,' i. 20.
[6] Ptolemy, 'Geography,' lib, ii., chap. x.

[7] Latham, R. G., 'Germania of Tacitus,' cxv.

[8] Latham, R. G., 'Germania of Tacitus,' Epilogomena, lix.

[9] Paulus Diaconus.

[10] Huntingdon's Chron., Bohn's ed, 148.

[11] 'Monumenta Germaniæ,' edited by Pertz, Scriptures i., 154.

[12] Latham, R. G., *loc cit.*, Epilegomena, lxxxii.

[13] Stephens, G., 'Old Northern Runic Monuments,' i. 61.

[14] Stephens, G., 'Old Northern Runic Monuments,' i. 62.

[15] 'Monumenta Germaniæ,' edited by Pertz, i. 19.

[16] Réclus, E., 'Nouvelle Géographie Universelle,' iv. 81, 82.

[17] Manzel, W., 'History of Germany,' Bohn's ed., i. 117.

[18] Seebohm, F., 'Tribal Custom in Anglo-Saxon Law,' 213.

[19] Nennius, 'Historia Britonum,' Bohn's ed., p. 409.

[20] Beddoe, J., 'Races in Britain,' 41.

[21] Latham, R. G., 'Handbook of the English Language,' 23.

[22] William of Malmesbury's Chronicle, ed. by Giles, Book I., cl.

[23] Asser's 'Life of Alfred,' edited by Camden in 'Anglica Scripta,' p. 13.

[24] *Loc. cit.*

[25] Haddon, A. C., 'The Study of Man,' quoting Beddoe, 'Histoire de l'Indice céphalique.'

[26] Latham, 'Germania of Tacitus,' 27. quoting Ptolemy.

[27] 'Monumenta Germaniæ,' edited by Pertz, i. 368.

[28] Beddoe, J., 'Races of Britain,' 43, quoting Gildemeister, *Archiv für Anthropologie*, 1878.

[29] Beddoe, J., 'Races of Britain,' 46.

[30] *Ibid.*

[31] Haddon, A, C., *loc. cit.*, 85.

[32] Haddon, A. C., *loc. cit.*, 85.

## Chapter Three - The Angles and Their Allies

THE Angles are first mentioned by Tacitus under the name of Angli in connection with another tribe, the Varini. From the third to the fifth century we hear nothing of the Angli. In the time of Bede they reappear as the Angles in a new country.[1] The part they are said to have played in the settlement of England is very large, all the country north of the Thames, except Essex, being supposed to have been occupied by Angles. The district in North Europe that bore their name is very small—Anglen, a part of Schleswig. There is evidence, however, that they were more widely seated, occupying a large part of the south of the Danish peninsula, some at least of the Danish islands, and part of the mainland of Scandinavia. The Angles were certainly closely connected to, or in alliance with, the Warings, the Varini of Tacitus, and this was long continued. In the time of Charlemagne we read of a common code of laws sanctioned by that King, called 'Leges Anglorum et Werinorum,' the laws of the Angles and Warings. The Angle country on the mainland of Northern Europe touched the Frisian country on the west, that of the Saxons on the south, and that of the Wendish tribes of the Baltic coast on the east. Their immigration into England was so large, and the area of the country they occupied so much greater in extent than their Continental homelands, that we are led, as in the case of the Saxons, to look for a confederacy, or an alliance of some kind, under which people of various tribes joined the Anglian expeditions.

That the names Saxons and Angles were understood in a composite sense in the time of Bede is evident from his writings. In narrating some events connected with missionary undertakings, he says: 'About that time the venerable servant of Christ and priest, Egbert, proposed to take upon himself the apostolic work to some of those nations that had not yet heard it, many of which nations he knew there were in Germany, from whom the Angles and Saxons who now inhabit Britain are known to have derived their origin, for which reason they are still called Germans by the neighbouring nation of the Britons. Such are the Freesons, Rugians, Danes, Hunni, Old Saxons, and the Boructarians.'[2] From this we learn that some of the people who settled in England under the names Angles and Saxons were of Danish origin. The country of the Continental Angles was close to the Danish islands, and, independently of any historical statement of the fact, it would be reasonable to suppose that the confederacy of which the Angles formed the chief part would for the purpose of their settlement in England include some of their neighbours, the Danes. Bede's statement shows that this actually was the case, and is proof that there were Danes settled in England under the name of Angles or Saxons before the Danish invasions began about the end of the eighth century. In considering Bede's reference to Germans, we should remember also that the name Germany in his time was understood probably in that wider sense in which it was understood by King Alfred—viz.; as extending from the Danube to the White Sea.

The Warings, whose name is coupled with the Angles by the early writers, were a people located on the south-west coast of the Baltic. From the first mention of them to the last we find them associated with the Angles, and as these accounts have a difference in date of some centuries, we may feel sure that the connection was a close one. Procopius tells us of Varini who were seated about the shores of the northern ocean, as well as upon the Rhine, so that there appears to have been a migration at an early date.[3] Beddoe has remarked that 'the limits of confederacies like those of the Franks, Saxons, Frisians, and Angles, who seem sometimes to have included the Warini, varied from time to time, and by no means always coincided with the limits of the dialects.'[4] This is an important consideration, for we find in the Frank confederation Franks who spoke a German tongue and others who did not, and it may have been the same in the confederated Angles and Warings. The Angles were a Teutonic race, and the Warings were probably a mixed one. In one of the Sagas they are mentioned as Wærnas or Wernas.[5] Tacitus, who does not appear, however, to have visited their country, mentions them as a German nation.[6] The Warings were one of the early commercial nations of the Baltic, and traded to Byzantium, going up the rivers of Slavonia in small barks, and carrying them across from river to river. The last mention of them is in 1030. By the early Russians they were known as Warings, their country as Waringia, and the sea near it as the Waring Sea. In Byzantium they called themselves Warings. They were in later centuries much mixed up with the Norsemen, and this infusion became stronger and stronger, until they disappeared as a separate nation.[7] It was chiefly men of this race who in the eleventh and twelfth centuries enlisted in the military service of the Byzantine Emperors, and were known in Constantinople as the Varangian guard, and in this corps there were also some Old English, a circumstance that points to connection in race. The Billings are said to have been the royal race of the Warings,[8] and it is probable that under this designation some of these people may he traced among the old place-names in England. The western part of Mecklenburg was long known as the Mark of the Billings. The name Wæring occurs in Scandinavian runic inscriptions. In one found at Torvic, Hardanger, Norway, the inscription reads, 'Læma (or Læda) Wæringæa'[9]— i.e., 'Læma (or Læda) to Wæring,' as if intended to be a monument to one who bore the Waring name.

The district called Anglen in the time of the Saxons is on the south-west of Sleswig, and is bounded by the river Slie, the Flensborger Fjord, and a line drawn from Flensborg to Sleswig. This district is small, not much larger, as Lutham has pointed out, than the county of Rutland.[10] Bede tells us that it had by the emigration of its inhabitants become deserted. Such a small district alone was not, however, likely to have been the mother-country of a large emigration across the North Sea for the occupation of a conquered country so large as England. Of course, the Anglen of Sleswig must have been a part only of the country from which the Angles came. That a population sufficiently strong to have largely conquered and given a name to England, and sufficiently famous to have been classed by Ptolemy among the leading nations of Germany, lived in so small an area is extremely unlikely. We must therefore conclude that the Angles extended over a larger area and that in the invasion and settlement of England their name was used as that of a confederacy which included Warings. There remains, however, the statement of Bede concerning Anglen. Its abandoned condition at the time he wrote is not improbable, but there is another explanation, as Latham has pointed out, which helps to account for its deserted state—viz., because it was a frontier land or march between the Danes and Slavonians (or Wends) of the eastern half of Holstein.[11] Many frontier lands of a similar kind have become deserted from a similar cause, and examples of this may be found in modern as well as ancient history. King Alfred. describing the voyager's course in his geographical description of the Baltic, mentions Denmark and Gothland, also Sealand, and other islands, and says:—'On these lands lived Engles before they hither to land came.'[12] This extract makes it quite clear that at the time he wrote it was understood in England that the Angles came partly from Old Denmark and Gothland, on the Scandinavian coast, and partly from Sealand and the Danish islands. as well as from Sleswig. This identification of Gothland and the part of Old Denmark in Scandinavia, also the Danish islands, as

26

lands from which the Anglian settlers in England partly came is of much importance. It helps us to understand the circumstance that a greater extent of England was occupied by Angles than by Saxons; that the predominant people gave their name to the country; and shows that there was a Scandinavian immigration before the eighth century. Our chroniclers have assigned a large territory in North Germany as the fatherland of the Saxons, but only Schleswig as the fatherland of the Angles. In this they certainly overlooked the statement of King Alfred, who had no doubt the best traditions, derived from the Northern countries themselves, of the origin of the race in assigning Gothland, Scandinavian Denmark, and the Danish isles as their homes. as well as the small territory of Anglen. Ancient Gothland occupied a larger part of Sweden than the limits of the modern province of the same name, and Scandian Denmark comprised Holland and Scania, now in Sweden. This great extent of country, with the Danish islands and the mainland coasts, would be sufficient to afford a reasonable explanation of the numerical superiority of the Angles among the English settlers. They were clearly people who formed a confederacy, as has been shown was the case of the Saxons, and these confederate invaders took their name from those who were the leaders of it. Even as late as Edward the Confessor's time the names Angles and Danes were considered as almost the same. His laws tell us of the counties which were under the laws of the Angles, using the name Angles for Danes. That the name of the earliest Angles comprised people of various tribes is also certain from the words used by Bede in his reference to them as the peoples of the old Angles. His actual words are 'populi Anglorum.' These words occur in the account he wrote of the names of their months, and may be seen in chapter xv. of his 'De Temporum Ratione.' Bede has thus put it on record that there were among the ancestors of Northumbrian Anglians of his time peoples or tribes of Angles. That some of them were of Scandinavian origin is clear from the evidence already stated It is also practically certain from the information Bede gives us concerning the date at which these peoples of the ancient Angles began their year. This was the eight Calends January, or December 25, the night of which, Bede says, was called by them 'Modranichte,' or the 'Night of Mothers,' an ancient pagan name, the origin of which he tells us he did not know. The ancient Anglians thus began their year at midwinter, as the Scandinavians did. The old Germanic year, on the other hand, began at the beginning of winter, or November 11, later on known as St. Martin's Day.[13] From this difference in their mode of reckoning as compared with the Germans, and their agreement with the Scandinavians, it is very difficult to avoid the conclusion that the ancient Angles must have been more Scandian than Germanic, That the Angles and Danes were probably connected in their origin is shown also by the statement of Saxo, the Danish historian, who tells us that the stock of the Danes had its beginning with Dan and Angul, their mythological ancestors.

Runic inscriptions are an important source of evidence in tracing the migrations of the Northern Goths, and of the neighbouring nations who acquired their knowledge of runes from them. In Sweden, Denmark, and Norway there are on fixed objects thousands of inscriptions in this ancient alphabet. Similar records are scattered over the regions which were overrun and settled by the Scandian tribes.[14] They have been found, on movable objects only, in the valley of the Danube, which was the earliest halting-place of the Goths on their Southern migration. They have been found also on fixed objects in Kent, which was conquered by the so-called Jutes, in Cumberland and other northern parts of England, Orkney, and the Isle of Man, where Norwegians formed settlements.[15] They are found in Northuniberland, where the Anglians settled at an earlier period than that of the later Norse invaders. Runes may be classed in three divisions—Gothic, Anglian, and Scandinavian. The oldest may date from the first or second century A.D., and the latest from the fourteenth or fifteenth century. The runic alphabet is called the Futhorc, after the word formed by its first six letters. The Anglian runes are used on the Ruthwell Cross, and several other Northumbrian monuments of the seventh and following centuries. One of the earliest examples is on a sword found in the Thames near London,[16] now in the British Museum. The Old English inscribed runic coins are scarce, and run from about the seventh to the first half of the ninth century, those solely in runic letters being outnumbered by others in which runic and Roman letters are mixed.[17] From the circumstance of the discovery of inscriptions in runic characters in parts of England which were settled by Angles and Jutes, and not in those parts which were settled by Saxons, we are able to draw two conclusions: (1) That the settlers in Kent must have been near in race or allied to the Anglian settlers of Northumberland and other Anglian counties; and (2) that there must have been an absence of any close intercourse or communication, and consequently a considerable difference, between the Scandinavian Angles and the Saxons, seeing that the Angles were acquainted with the runes and the Saxons were not, as far as appears from the total absence of such inscriptions on stones or other fixed monuments in Germany, and in Wessex, Sussex, or Essex. The runic inscriptions found in England are marked by the Anglian variety of the letters.

From their original home in the North, the Goths went southwards, and carried their art of runic writing with them, leaving examples of it here and there in inscriptions on portable articles found in the valley of the Danube, written in characters which mark the identity of the people with those of Northern Gothland. From their Northern home across the North Sea went also the Anglians, neighbours and allies of the people of Gothland, and they also carried with them the art of runic writing, which they had learnt from the Goths in the North, to their new homes in England. Across the same sea went also the Jutes or Goths to Kent, and left there examples of the same general evidence of the Northern lands whence they came and of the race to which they belonged.

From the circumstances mentioned, it will appear that Anglen, on the east coast of Denmark, could have been only a small part of the country inhabited by the people called by the Anglian name at the time of the English settlement. As Stephens says, the names Engelholm and Engeltoft, on the Scandinavian coast or mainland, still remind us of the ancient Angles. That name, he says, was, as regards the English settlement, the first under which the Scandians were known. Later on they were called Vikings or Northmen, or Normans. They carried with them to their new homes their native civilization and many advantages in the knowledge of arts and arms.[18] Stephens says that no runic characters have ever been discovered in any original German or Saxon manuscript. It appears certain that no runic stone or other fixed runic inscription has ever been discovered on German or Saxon soil. The ornaments of a personal kind which bear runic letters have been found by hundreds in the Northern lands, and those which have been found in Germany and other parts of Europe must have been carried there.[19] Since the Anglian inscriptions found in England are in characters earlier than those which are called Scandinavian, they must have been written by people who came during the earlier immigration, or by their descendants. The Scandinavian runes discovered in England are chiefly inscriptions on objects belonging to, or made by, the men who came in during the so-called Danish or Viking period.[20]

Many hundreds of inscribed stones have been found in ancient Germany, but they bear Roman inscriptions. The runes, consequently, afford us evidence in connection with the settlement of Angles in Britain of a kind which is wholly wanting in connection with the Saxons. As the total absence of runes on fixed monuments in Germany may be considered conclusive evidence that they were unknown to the German tribes, it is clear that these tribes could not carry them to England, and, as might be expected, there is, in the parts of England which were mainly settled by German tribes, a similar absence of runic inscriptions to that which exists in Germany. There is, however, a trace of some early inscribed stones in Wiltshire, which. according to Aubrey, were in existence until the year 1640. This is not improbable, but if Aubrey's statement is correct the occurrence of such inscriptions may be explained by the existence of a settlement of Goths or other Scandians there, and we find other evidence, which will be stated later on, of such settlements in Hampshire, Dorset, and Wiltshire. On this subject Stephens quotes Sir R. Colt Hoare, who says: 'At a place called the King's Grave, where is now the Sheep-Penning of West Amesbury, Aubrey writes, "here doe appear five small barrows at one corner of the Penning. At the ends of the graves were stones which the people of late (about 1640) have fetch't away, for stones, except flints, are exceedingly scarce in these partes. 'Tis said here there were some letters on these stones. but what they were I cannot learn." '[21]

The inscriptions in runic characters of an earlier date than the ninth century which have been found in England cannot have been due to the invasions of the Danes and Northmen, and consequently they must have been the work of earlier Goths and Angles. That on the sword or knife discovered in the Thames near London has been assigned by Stephens to the fifth century.[22]

This points to the period of the settlement of Kent, and the earliest invasions of the Goths and Angles. A gold ring, which was found near Cöslin, in Pomerania, in 1839, and which bore a runic letter of a specially Anglian or English type, is, according to Stephens, of the same period—viz., A.D. 400-500. He ascribes this rune (ᛇ) to English work, the letter being a variation of the Gothic rune (ᛋ), and its equivalence being the sound *yo*. With this single exception, this rune has only been found in England.[23] This discovery, in conjunction with the inscription on the sword found in the Thames, tends to show that there was a connection between the early Gothic and Anglian settlers in England and the inhabitants of the Baltic coasts in the fifth century. The evidence afforded by the finding of runic letters of this early date at Cöslin does not stand alone; it is supported by that of the objects which were discovered with it. The ring was found with a bracteate bearing runic characters, five other bracteates without runes, and two Roman golden coins, one of Theodosius the Great (A.D. 379-395), the other of Leo I. (A.D. 457-474). This latter coin, therefore, assists in confirming the date of the objects as about the end of the fifth century. Stephens says:[24] 'This is one of the few golden bracteates we can date with some certainty from a comparison of the other gold pieces with which it lay.' As is well known, the golden bracteates belong to a unique class of northern remains, and chiefly date from the early Iron Age in Scandinavia. They were generally shaped like coins, but were not used as coins, being intended for suspensory ornaments. They are of no common pattern, but differ much in size. weight. and other features.[25] As they differed much in their design, so they differed in regard to having runes or not. The most important hoard of them found in England was discovered at Sarr, in Thanet, in 1863. These, however, had no runic letters on them. The evidence that Goths and Vandals or Wends were often allied cannot be disputed, and that there was some alliance and consequent intercourse between their respective countries and the settlements of the Goths in England the discovery of these objects with Anglian or English runes on the Wendish coast ncar Cöslin in the fifth century is good evidence. The discovery of an English runic inscription of such an early date in Pomerania is important from another aspect. It was found in what was Gothic and Vandal territory, and the connection of the Vandals with the Anglo—Saxon settlement rests on strong evidence of another kind. Cöslin, where the ring was found, is on the Baltic coast, east of Rügen Island, and nearly opposite to the island of Bornholm. This coast was in the third century of our era near the country of the Burgundians, before their great migration to the south—western part of Germany and to France. During the third and following century the Goths and Vandals acted together as allies in various expeditions. The Isle of Gotland, as proved by the immense number of Roman coins of the later Empire discovered there, was even at that early period a great commercial centre. The Vandals were also great navigators, and the so-called Angles were in all probability a branch of the Gothic race, certainly of Gothic extraction. There must have been communications between the Gothic northern ports and the English settlements, and the discovery on the sword in the Thames, and a similar discovery of English runes on a ring found near the Baltic coast of Pomerania, is not, considering all these circumstances, a matter for wonder.

In order to realize the full significance of the evidence afforded by the runic inscriptions and their connection with the settlement of England, it is necessary to look at it from several points of view: First, that runes were of Northern Gothic origin, and the Gothic Futhorc or alphabet is the earliest; secondly, that the Anglian Futhorc consists of similar characters varied from the Gothic; and, thirdly, that the Scandinavian has later additions. The evidence shows that Goths and Angles introduced the art of runic writing into England before the end of the fifth century. It is interesting to consider also the probable origin of the runic letters themselves. Isaac Taylor has proved[26] that the early Gothic runes were modifications of the letters of the Greek alphabet, and were developed in Northern Gothland as a result of the commercial intercourse of the Goths across Eastern Europe with the Greek traders of the Levant. The Byzantine coins found in the island of Gotland certainly point to a trade of this kind at a sufficiently early period. Lastly, we have to consider the very interesting fact that when the runic letters which had been modified from the Greek were introduced into Britain by the Goths, these modified Greek characters which had come across Europe to the north, and thence to England, met there the letters of the Celtic or Romano-British alphabet. also derived from the Greek, but which had come there across Gaul from the Mediterranean[27] through Roman influence.

The Warings, who were such close allies of the Angles, were certainly much concerned with the early commerce of the Baltic and the overland trade between the dominions of the Greek Emperors and the Baltic ports. Nestor, a monk of Kiev, who wrote in the eleventh century, mentions Novgorod as a Varangian city, and it is therefore concluded that there was at that time at large settlement of Varangians in that part of Russia. We learn, also, that there were Gotlanders in early Russia,[28] and we know that the Isle of Gotland has revealed abundant traces of an ancient overland trade across that country. Another fact of interest concerning the later Warings is their possible connection with the Isle of Rügen, which, in the life of Bishop Otto, is mentioned as Verania and the population as Verani, who were remarkable for their persistent paganism.[29] These references point, without doubt, to the connection of Rügen with Slavonic paganism, and to the Warings of that time as associated with it. There is, as already mentioned, another more ancient reference to them by Ptolemy, under the name of Pharadini, the root syllable *Var* or *Phar* being almost certainly the same. Their name also appears in that of the old river-name Warina, the Warna, which gives its name to Warnof, and in Warnemünde, both on the Baltic coast. Procopius mentions the Warings, and tells us of the marriage of a sister of one of the Kings of the East English with one of their Kings. These allies of the ancient Anglians have left their mark on the subsequent history of Eastern Europe. Their influence among the old Slavs of what is now Russia was great, owing to their settlements among them and the commerce through their territory with Byzantium. In Constantinople itself the Varangian body-guard of the Greek Emperors was of political importance. The tall stature of these men and their fair complexions excited wonder among the Greeks and Asiatics of that city. Their name in Constantinople became the Byzantine equivalent for soldiers of a free company. The body of Huscarls organized by Cnut in England was a counterpart of the Varangian guard. In physical appearance their allies the Angles must have resembled them. Even at the present day the stature of the people in the least disturbed districts of England that were settled by Angles is above the average. It was, however, among the old Slavs that their influence was greatest, for the Slav, moulded by the Varangian, and converted to the Greek Church through Byzantine influence, became the Russian.[30]

The custom of disposing of the dead by cremation is so different from that of interment that where both prevailed there must in ancient time have been people of different races or tribes living in such a district. One fact which excavations in Anglo-Saxon burial-places proves beyond doubt is the contemporaneous practice of cremation and burial in various parts of England. In Norfolk, Cambridgeshire, Northamptonshire, and Gloucestershire, evidence has been obtained that both practices went on.[31] In some parts of Norfolk, Suffolk, and Derbyshire, cremation appears to have been the sole observance,[32] as at Walsingham, and at Kingston near Derby. In the cemeteries of Kent and Sussex burial appears to have been almost the exclusive practice. Derbyshire is peopled by descendants of Anglians, according to the present physical race-characters of the people. A passage in Beowulf furnishes evidence of the practice of cremation among the Angles,[33]—'To make a mound, bright after the funeral fire, upon the nose of the promontory, which shall be for a memorial to my people.' The pagan Anglians appear, from these discoveries and this passage, to have burnt their dead, as the pagan Esthonians did at a later period in the time of King Alfred.[34] The custom among the Teutons thus appears to have been a Northern one, and Anglian rather than Saxon. From the evidence which has been obtained, cremation appears to have been practised in Jutland and the western part of the Danish isles about the time of the Anglian migration, while burial prevailed at the same time in Zealand and part of Funen Isle.[35]

[1] Latham, R. G., 'The Ethnology of the British Isles.' p. 151.
[2] Boda, 'Ecclesiastical History,' edited by J. A. Giles, book v., chap. ix.
[3] Pracopius, 'de Belle Gothico,' iv. 20; Latham, 'Germania of Tacitus,' Epilegomena, cvi.
[4] Beddoe, J., 'Races in Britain,' p. 39.
[5] 'The Soap, or Gleeman's Tale,' edited by B. Thorpe.
[6] Latham, R. G., 'Germania of Tacitus,' Notes, pp. 143, 144.
[7] Clarke Hyde, *Transactions of Ethnalogiacal Society*, vii. 65-76.
[8] *Ibid.*, 64, and 'Traveller's Song.'
[9] Stephens, G., 'Old Northern Runic Monuments,' iii. 407.

[10] Latham, R. G., 'Handbook of the English Language,' p. 70.

[11] Latham, R. G., 'Handbook of the English Language,' p. 70.

[12] King Alfred's 'Orosius,' edited by H. Sweet, p. 16.

[13] Tille, A., *Transactions if Glasgow Arch. Soc.*, iii., part ii., 'The Germanic Year.' quoting Wienhold.

[14] Taylor. Isaac, 'History of the Alphabet,' pp. 210-215.

[15] *Ibid.*

[16] Taylor, Isaac, *loc. cit.*

[17] Stephens, G., *loc. cit.*, ii. 515.

[18] Stephens, G., 'Runic Monuments in England and Scandinavia,' i. 360.

[19] *Ibid.*, i. iv.

[20] *Ibid.*, i. 360.

[21] Stephens, G., 'Runic Monuments in England and Scandinavia.' i. 360. quoting Sir R. Colt Home and Aubrey.

[22] Stephens, G., 'Old Northern Runic Monuments,' i. 124-130.

[23] Stephens, G., 'Old Northern Runic Monuments,' vol. ii., p. 602.

[24] *Ibid.*, 542.

[25] *Ibid.*, ii. 509.

[26] Taylor, I., *loc cit.*

[27] *Ibid.*

[28] Morfill. W. R,, 'Russia,' p. 19. quoting Nestor.

[29] Latham, R. G., 'Ethnology of the British Isles,' 154.

[30] Rambaud, A., 'History of Russia,' i. 24.

[31] Akerman, J. Y., 'Remains of Pagan Saxondom,' Introduction, xiv.

[32] *Ibid.*

[33] *Ibid.*, xv.

[34] 'Orosius,' edited by Bosworth, J., 54.

[35] Englehard, C., 'L'ancient âge de fer en Séland.'

# Chapter Four - The Jutes, Goths, and Northmen

THE Jutes, who, according to the English chroniclers, were one of the three nations by which England was settled, are but little mentioned under that name by early historians of Northern Europe. Bede calls them Jutes, so that we may conclude that at the end of the seventh century this was the name by which these people were known in England. In early records relating to Germany and the North they appear to have been called by many names—Vitungi or Juthungi, Jutæ, Gætas, Gothi, Gothini, Gythones, Guthones, Gutæ, Gautæ, Vitæ, and Gæta.[1] The name Geats they derived from Geat, a mythological ancestor of Woden, according to the West Saxon genealogy, and Asser tells us that Geat was worshipped as a god.[2]

Tacitus mentions Goths under the name Guthones, and states that they occupied the country east of the Vistula. He says also that the Goutai lived in the island of Scandia, and we may identify the locality with the Swedish province of Gothland.[3] The people around the Gulf of Riga at the present day, including the Livonians, are partly of Teutonic origin, and may in part be descendants of those ancient Gothic people who are known to have lived east of the Vistula.

The Jutes who settled in England had much in common with the Frisians; so also had the Goths. In the mythological genealogies given in the Anglo-

33

Saxon Chronicle and elsewhere, Godwulf appears as the father of Fin, which probably refers to a very remote connection between the Frisians and the Goths, for later on the name Fin occurs as a representative of the Frisian nation.[4] The languages, as far as Frisian and the Mœso-Gothic are concerned, point to a similar connection. There is evidence of a large Frisian immigration in various parts of England, and much of the country was evidently settled by them under the names Saxons and Angles. As Goths and Frisians were connected in their mythological names, and the great mythological Frisian is Fin,[5] his name perhaps refers to an ancient link also with the Fin race, thus faintly transmitted through some remote connection. The accounts which the Frisians have of the expedition of Hengist are similar to those which we possess of him among the Jutes of Kent.

The Jutes, like the Angles, in all probability, were originally located in Scandinavia, for Ptolemy, writing in the second century of our era, places the Gutæ in the south of that peninsula. In Bede's time Jutland was known by its present name, and no doubt took it from the Jutes, but the time of their settlement in Kent and that of Bede are separated by nearly three centuries, and during this interval the Jutes may have become located also in Jutland. There is neither contemporary history nor tradition that a people so called were there before Bede's time. His statement that those who settled in England came from Jutland is, as Latham has pointed out, only an inference from the fact that when he wrote Jutes, Angles, and Saxons were in contact in the Danish peninsula and the adjoining part of North Germany, and also in contact in England. Under these circumstances it was a logical inference that the Angles came from Anglen and the Jutes from Jutland, but this is probably only true in part. Jutland may have been a Jutish colony like Kent and the Isle of Wight, and probably an earlier one, seeing that it is so much nearer to the original homeland of the Gothic race in Scandinavia, but that would not necessarily imply that all the Jutes came from Jutland.

Whatever may have been the origin of their name, it is probable that they were, like the modern Danes, men of more than average stature. It has been commonly assumed that during the inroads into the countries that were provinces of the Roman Empire, and the settlement of people who gave rise to new nations therein, only Britain was attacked by bands of Saxons, Angles, and Jutes. We do not read of conquests by these nations elsewhere. Some of the Saxons are, indeed, said to have accompanied their neighbours, the Lombards, in their great Southern expedition and invasion of Italy, but little is known of this alliance.

Apart from the statement of Bede, whose list of tribes from which the Old English of his time were known to have descended, is not repeated by the later chroniclers, it would seem improbable that, in the general rush for new territory, two or three German tribes or nations should have had left to them the island of Britain as a kind of exclusive territory for conquest and settlement. Bede, the earliest Anglo-Saxon historian, wrote, no doubt, according to the best information current in his day, and his statement concerning the many German tribes from which the English were descended is supported by modern research. Tradition cannot be altogether neglected. In all old countries there comes a time when history dawns, but men lived and died before that dawn, and only traditions concerning them came down to the historic period. Many such traditions are no doubt based on actual occurrences, the details of which have become more or less hazy, and in some instances distorted by the additions acquired through their narration by word of mouth from age to age. The story of Hengist may be a tradition of this kind.

As already stated, Nennius, in the 'Historia Britonum,' gives one name to all the invaders of Britain, that of Saxons, and does not attempt to distinguish them under the national or tribal names by which they were known among themselves. It was sufficient for his purpose as a British historian to describe these enemies of his countrymen by one general name.

In the passage of Bede in which he refers to some of the tribes from which his countrymen were known to have descended, we obtain a glimpse of those wider views of the origin of the Old English race which were known in his time, and were probably well recognised by existing tribal differences in dialect, customs, and even in the physical appearance of the people at the time he wrote.

In the passage of Nennius in which he mentions that among the early invaders of Britain there were some who came from almost all the provinces of Germany, we have corroboration of Bede's statement and another glimpse of the current knowledge in Britain at that time, and of the wider origin of the Old English than the later chroniclers have transmitted to us.

The general names Saxons, Angles, and Jutes were no doubt at first used as comprehensive terms for people of various tribes, but as time passed an, and the chroniclers omitted all references to the tribal names mentioned by Bede, these three names came to be regarded in a more limited sense as the names of the actual nations from which alone the Old English sprang. The omission of Frisians is especially remarkable. It has been shown that under the name Saxons the Frisians must have been included, and it will also be shown that they must be included among the Anglian settlers. It has also been shown that the Angles were allied to the Warings seated on the southwest of the Baltic coast. As Bede mentions the Danes in his list, it is also practically certain that the early Danes were allies of the Angles. The list, therefore, of the nations and tribes from whom the English of the end of the seventh century were descended becomes enlarged. Frisians, Danes, Hunni or Hunsings, Rugians, and Boructers, must certainly be numbered among them.

Moreover, when we consider Bede's list by the light of modern research, we arrive at the conclusion that some of the Franks probably took part in the settlement of England, for he mentions the Boructarii or Bructers, and these are known later on to have been part of the Frank confederation.

It is difficult to avoid the conclusion that the Goths must have been allies of the Angles. They were also close allies of the Vandals or Wends, of which nation the Rugians formed part. The commerce of the Baltic during the period of the Anglo-Saxon settlement was largely in the hands of the Goths. It is impossible to overrate the commercial importance of the Isle of Gotland at this time and for many centuries later. The ruins of Wisby, the chief port of ancient Gotland, are to this day the greatest wonder of the Baltic, and Öland Isle was another seat of ancient Gothic trade. There is some connection between the ancient trade of the Goths and the settlement of them and their allies in England. The most remarkable native commodity which came in ancient days from the Baltic was the fossil-gum known as amber. The trade in amber can be traced almost as long as any in Europe. It was known to the Greeks and Romans, and came from the North to the South by the old trade routes across the Continent. The Goths were known only too well to the later Roman Emperors. Long after the Romans had left Britain that country was still recognised as one of the provinces of the Empire, and as late as A.D. 537 Belisarius, in the name of the Emperor, granted it to the Goths,[6] which seems to show that the Byzantine Emperor of the sixth century knew quite well that Goths were already settled in our country.

The ancient people on the coast of the Baltic who collected amber and exchanged it for other commodities were called the Guthoncs and the Æstyi. There were two routes by which amber could reach the South of Europe in the time of the Empire—one through Germany, the other by the route further eastward through the countries known as Sarmatia or Slavonia. The double name for the people near the mouth of the Vistula probably arose in this way, from their being known to the Germans as the Æstyi, and to the Slavonians who traded across to the Black Sea as Guthones. These Guthoncs were Goths of the same race or descent as the islanders of Gotland, and as the people of East and West Gothland in Sweden. That the Reid-Goths—at least, some of them—lived in the Scandian peninsula is proved by a runic inscription on a stone at Rök in East Gothland, in which a chieftain named Waring is commemorated, and in which he is said to have increased their power.[7] This inscription also connects the Waring name with the eastern or Ostrogoths of Sweden. Amber was certainly used as an ornament among the Anglo—Saxons at a very early date. It has been frequently found in the form of beads and other articles in cemeteries in many parts of England, and its use at this early time in England points to an early trade with the Baltic. Its common use in the manufacture of beads and other personal ornaments may perhaps also point to a custom of personal decoration which was introduced into England by settlers from the Baltic. These amber traders were commonly known in England by their German name of Eastman, the Æstyi of the early writers.

The names Estum and Estmere are mentioned by King Alfred in connection with the Vistula in his description of the relative situation of Veonod-land—*i.e.*, Wendland, Vitland, and other countries on the southern coast of the Baltic Sea. The Æstyi are mentioned by Pliny and Tacitus, the former of whom locates them in 'Æstuarium Oceani.' an expression which, as Latham has pointed out, probably arose through the name Est-ware or Eastmen being misunderstood to have reference to an estuary.[8] Pliny connects the Æstyi with the amber country, and Tacitus, in following the coast-line of the Baltic, comes to their country. The locality of these people of the amber district was therefore the coast in which amber is found at the present day. To the north of it is the Isle of Gotland, and this island in the time of the Romans and during the Anglo-Saxon period was the greatest commercial centre in the North of Europe. The proof of its trade with England and overland with Eastern countries is complete. The evidence of its early trade during the Roman period is shown by the large number of Roman coins which have been found in the island. Thousands, indeed, of the Roman and early Byzantine periods have been discovered there. Similarly. during the Viking Age, the coins found in Gotland show that the island stood foremost as the commercial centre of the North. It kept its supremacy for ten or twelve centuries.[9] In addition, thousands of Arabic coins have been found there; also silver ornaments, to which the name Kufic has been given, showing that the old trade route with Gotland extended at one time as far eastward as Bokhara, Samarcand, Bagdad, and Kufa.[10]

Another source of evidence concerning the eastern trade of Gotland, and more particularly with the Eastern Empire, is that derived from certain weights of the Viking period found in the island, and now in the museum at Stockholm. These relate to the weights of gold and silver, and their unit is exactly the same as that of the Eastern stater,[11] thus pointing to a common weight in use for purposes of exchange between Goths of the Baltic and Greeks at the Levant.

It is of interest to note this influence of eastern trade in the monetary computation introduced into England by Danish and Scandian settlers. The ora is mentioned in the treaty between Alfred and Guthrum, in subsequent laws, and in Domesday Book. The marks and oras of the Danes were the computation in use in England within the Danelaw until after the Norman Conquest.

Although it is not probable that Danish marks and other coins were used as coins in England, money computations were often made in them: In Domesday Book the Danish money is mentioned as the computation in which customary payments were made in various boroughs and manors outside the Danelaw—Bristol, Dorchester, Wareham, Bridport, Shaftesbury, Ringwood, some manors in the Isle of Wight,in North-East Gloucestershire, and elsewhere, being among the number, thus clearly pointing to Scandinavian settlers.

The pounds and shillings of Wessex were Roman in their origin. The marks and oras of the Danish districts in England had an Eastern equivalence. As regards their value, they had their origin in the Eastern Empire and in the monetary exchange that prevailed along the Eastern trade route from Byzantium to the Baltic. More than 20,000 Anglo-Saxon coins have been found in Sweden and the Isle of Gotland, ranging in date from Edward the Elder to Edward the Confessor. Many of them are preserved in the Royal Collection at Stockholm.[12]

These remarkable discoveries,and especially the Roman coins on the one hand and the Anglo-Saxon on the other, show that the great trade of Gotland was continuous from the Roman period to the later Saxon time in England. Its commercial prosperity as the chief centre of maritime trade in the North of Europe must consequently have extended over the whole period of the attacks on Britain by the Saxons, Angles, Jutes or Goths, and Danes. There can, indeed, be little doubt that such a maritime centre as the island was during the fifth and succeeding centuries furnished ships for the invasions and settlement of England by Goths and their allies. Gotland was no ordinary island, and Wisby, its great part, was no ordinary seaport. It must have exercised no ordinary influenue on maritime affairs in Northern Europe during the time it flourished, and this influence certainly extended to England. The Goths and other Teutonic people of the Baltic are brought under very early notice by Pytheas, the renowned navigator of Marseilles, in the fourth century B.C. He tells us that he sailed up the Baltic in search of the amber coast, rounding the cape of what is now called Jutland, and proceeding about 6,000 stadia along the coasts of the Guttones and Teutones. As the date of this voyage was about 325 B.C., the account shows that Goths and Teutons at that early time were known names for Northern races.

The relations of the Goths and the Vandals is important, and must be fully considered in reference to any part of Europe that was conquered and settled by the former nation, which was more advanced in civilization and the arts than their allies. The Goths invented runes, and so established among Northern races the art of writing, and they were skilled metallurgists and gilders. The Vandals of the Baltic coast whom they conquered were a less advanced people, but a lasting peace appears to have been formed between them, and to have been subsequently remembered in Northern mythology. The conflict of the Æsir and Vanir is a Northern myth, which, considered ethnologically, may be regarded as founded on the wars carried on between the Teutonic and Slavonic races. That between the Goths and Vandals was a war of this kind, and it resulted in peace and a lasting alliance. The myth of the conflict of the Æsir and Vanir also terminated in a lasting peace and the exchange of hostages between the contending races. The alliance between the Northern Goths and the Vandals and their combined expeditions can be traced in the Anglo-Saxon settlement and in the present topography of England. In many parts of our country Gothic and Wendish place-names survive near each other, side by side with Gothic and Wendish customs, There is, indeed, in England very considerable evidence afforded by the ancient place names that two of the great nations of the North in the fifth and sixth centuries—the Goths and Vandals—who played such an important part in the destruction of the Roman Empire and the occupation of large provinces elsewhere, took part in the invasion and settlement of this country. This evidence is confirmed by the survival of customs among the English settlers, some of which have come down to our time, and for their remote origin may be traced to Goths, or to Vandals. Both these Northern nations were maritime people. The Baltic Sea was called in ancient time the Vendic Sea, after the Vandals, as the Adriatic Sea is called the Gulf of Venice after them to the present day. The conclusion, therefore, appears unavoidable that, under the general names of Saxons, Angles, and Jutes, some Goths and Vandals, as will be shown more fully in succeeding chapters, took a considerable part in the invasion and settlement of England. Later on, during the Viking Age, the Vikings of Denmark and Norway often acted in alliance with the Wendish Vikings of literature, and the occurrence in close proximity, in various parts of England on or near the coast, of Wendish place-names and Scandinavian place-names, which mark the settlements of these allies. Not infrequently, also, near such places the survival of characteristic Norse and Wendish customs can be traced.

There is evidence of the large immigration of settlers of various tribes from Scandinavia to be found in remains of their speech. The dialects which the Northmen introduced into England, both during the earlier settlements of Goths and Angles and the later settlements of Danes, certainly formed the basis from which some of the dialects spoken in many parts of England were formed. Skeat has pointed out that when Icelandic became a written language in the eleventh century, an interesting statement in regard to English and the language of the Northmen was made by Snorri Sturluson, the author of the Icelandic alphabet and its earliest literature. 'Englishmen,' he says, 'write English with Latin letters such as represent their sounds correctly. Following their example, since we are of one language, although the one may have changed greatly, or each of them to some extent, I have framed an alphabet for us Icelanders.' There is a statement also in the Saga of Gimlaugr Ormstunga that there was the same tongue used at the time the Saga was written—the eleventh century—in England, Norway, and Denmark.[13] This was the age of William the Conqueror, who was desirous that his own son Richard should learn the Old Danish language, no doubt with some political or administrative object in view, and we are told that he sent him for this purpose to Bayeux, where the Old Northern speech still lingered, although it had died out at Rouen.[14]

As the Jutes who settled in England were neither Norse nor Danes, as known at a later period, they must, by the evidence of the runic inscriptions found in Kent, have been either of the Anglian[15] or Gothic stock. In the time of Pytheas—fourth century B.C.—and in that of Ptolemy—second century A.D.—the Goths, as already mentioned, occupied a region on the east of the Baltic. Their name is lost there, but survives in Gotland Isle and Gothland in Sweden. Tradition ascribes the Baltic area as their original home, and in any case they must have been settled along its coasts at a very early period. The old name Uuitland for a part of the east coast of the Baltic reminds us of the Jutes, for Uuit is probably a modified form of Jute or Jewit, and in the Jutish parts of England, as in Hampshire, we meet with Uuit or Wit names, as Wihtland for the Isle of Wight. The identity of some of the Jutes with the Goths is shown by the similarity of the name, and its ancient occurrence on both sides

39

of the Baltic Sea; in the similarity of customs, as will be described later; and in historical references, such as that of Asser, who, in telling us that King Alfred's mother was descended from the Goths and Jutes, practically identifies them as being at one race. In the survival of monuments with old Gothic runes in Kent we have corroborative evidence.

Beddoe refers to the similarity of the place-names in many parts of England, and says:[16] 'The patronymical names and other place-names in Kent and other parts of England forbid us to imagine an exclusive Jutish nationality.' The evidence of Goths and Frisians in Kent, and of settlers of the same nationalities in many other parts of England, appears to afford a solution of the question who the people called Jutes in Kent or in Hampshire really were—i.e., mainly Goths or of Gothic descent.

The part which the nations of the Baltic took in the conquest and settlement of England has been underrated. With such a great centre of commerce and shipping as existed at Wisby, although smaller than it afterwards became, it is unreasonable to doubt the connection of the Goths with many of these maritime expeditions, if only as carriers. The time of the settlement of the Isle of Gotland is lost in antiquity. The only record of its remarkable history is the 'Gotlands lagaene,'[17] which is thought to be a supplement to the ancient laws of the country. This is supposed to have been written about A.D. 1200, and preserves in the old Gotlandish language laws that are apparently of a much earlier date. The discovery of so many Roman coins in the island shows that its commercial history is older than the time of the English Conquest. Whatever it was at that time—and relatively to most other ports it must have been great—Wisby became in the tenth and eleventh centuries a place of almost fabulous wealth. As regards the ancient homelands of the Goths in Sweden, the evidence of communications with Anglo-Saxon England is direct. In the south of the Scandian peninsula is a province now called Carlscrona, whose ancient name was Blekinge, under which name it is mentioned by King Alfred in his 'Orosius.' Stephens tells us of runic stones that have been found in Bleking, and on the authority of Elias Fries of Upsala he states they are said to be in Anglo—Saxon.[18] When we consider that there is historical evidence of the missionary labours of Englishmen among the heathen Goths of the South of Sweden, it will not appear surprising that inscriptions in Anglian runes should be found there. The church of Lund, the mother—church of that part of the country, was founded by Englishmen early in the eleventh century, according to Adam of Bremen.[19] Lund was the capital of this part of the peninsula, a city of great extent, of great antiquity, and one which enjoyed a high prosperity as early as the ninth century. Blekinge is mentioned as Blecinga-ég, or the Isle of the Blekings, by King Alfred, repeating the description of Wulfstan of his voyage up the Baltic. 'We had,' he says, 'first Blekinge, and Möen and Eowland, and Gothland on our larboard (bæc-bord), and these lands belong to Sweden; and Wendland was all the way on our starboard as far as the mouth of the Vistula.'[20] These on the larboard were, without doubt, homelands of some of the early people of the Jutish or

Gothic race. There is other evidence of early communications between England and Scandinavian. At Skaäng, in Södermanland, Sweden, there is a runic inscription on a stone of peculiar interest, from its association with England. It has the English sign (⍰) for the word *and*. This, Stephens tells us, is distinctly English, and only English, in its origin, so that inscriptions having it show English influence of some kind.[21] In considering this he regards it as evidence of early literary communications between the English settlers and their Continental kindred. We should remember also that this Old English sign abounds in Domesday Book. Stephens says: 'The Saxon and German pagans got their writing-schools as well as their Christianity and culture of movements, direct and indirect, chiefly from England and Anglo- Keltic lands, whose missionaries carried their runes with them, partly for secret writing, and partly for use in Scandinavia.' It is the evidence of the runes that shows the Scandian origin of the Anglians who settled in Northern England. Stephens' last words on this subject are: 'I beg the reader carefully to ponder the following remarkable and interesting and decisive facts in the list showing the numerical result (of runic discoveries) in every class up to June, 1894. It is: in Scando-Anglia, 10,423 runic remains; in Germany, Saxony, and elsewhere, 19 as wanderers.'[22]

The Northmen of the Anglo-Saxon period were certainly people of many tribes. The name included all the inhabitants of the Northern peninsula as well as the Danes. It was not confined in its meaning like the later name Norse. In Sweden there were the ancient provinces of Hallaud, Skäne, Bleking, Smaland, Södermanland, Nebrike, Vermland, Upland, Vestmanland, Angermaneland, Helsingland, Gestrickland, Delarna, Eastern and Western Gotland, and others. Vermland, which had been part of Norway, was added to Sweden after 860. In Norway there were the tribal provinces or districts of Nordrland. Halgoland, Ranmerike, Heredaland, Hadeland, Rogaland, Raumsdel, Borgund, Viken, and others.

People of these provinces or tribal districts were all Northmen, as understood by the early settlers in England. and in the parts of our country where Scandinavians made colonies some of these tribal names may still be traced, It is certain also that the inhabitants generally of the coast of Norway and the shore of the Baltic were called Lochlandach or Lakelanders,[23] and traces of them may perhaps be found in England under names derived from this word. 'Few and far,' says Stephens, writing of the tribes of Scandinavia, 'are the lights which glimmer over the clan lands of our forefathers. . . . We may learn a little more in time if we work hard and theorize less. But whatever we can new master as to the Old Northern language we have learnt from the monuments. Those, therefore, we must respect at all hazards, whatever systems may have to give way, even though the upshot should be that much of our boasted modern philology. with its iron laws and straight lines and regular police-ruled developments, is only a house built upon the sand.'[24]

The Northern dialects, as introduced into England from the fifth and tenth centuries, may have differed, in some respects, from the Icelandic or Old

Northern tongue as written in the eleventh century. Hence the great value of the earliest runic inscriptions as evidence, so far as they go, of the earliest meanings of some words that afterwards were used in Old English. In considering this probable change, Stephens tells us that the only corruptors of dialects he knew were those 'who improve Nature, by writing them not as they are, but according to their nations of what they ought to be—*i.e.*, in accordance with rules of grammar derived from other languages—for instance, the peculiar and comparatively modern Icelandic, with which they may be acquainted.'[25]

As the name Northmen was a general one, which included the different tribal people of Scandinavia, so the name Eastman appears to have also been a general name for the people of the Baltic region on the opposite shores to those of Sweden. With the Angles and Goths of the early period of the Anglo-Saxon settlement some people of the Norse race, afterwards so called, may well have been included. The earliest English coins found in Norway are of the period when the Norse began their Viking expeditions to the British shores. They comprise coins of Kewulf of Mercia, 796-819, Ceolwulf his son, 819-821, and Northumbrian coins of about 803-840.[26]

From the results of the researches of many archæologists, historians, and philologists, both English and Scandinavian, we are led to the conclusion that the Northmen of various tribes and nations had a greater share in the settlement of England than has commonly been attributed to them. Stephens assigns them a very large share indeed, and his great work on the 'Old Northern Runic Monuments' attests his vast research. He says: 'Anglic Britain was chiefly planted by Northmen in the second and following centuries, and was half replanted by them in the ninth and tenth.'[27] Whatever may have been the date of their earliest settlements, Northmen were certainly among both the earlier and later ancestors of the Old English.

[1] Latham, R. G., 'Germania of Tacitus,' Epilegomena, cxiv.
[2] Asser, 'Life of Alfred.'
[3] Taylor, Isaac, 'Greeks and Goths,' p. 46.
[4] Lappenberg, J. M., 'History of the Anglo-Saxon Kings,' i. 24, note.
[5] 'The Traveller's Song.'
[6] Church, A. J., 'Early Britain,' 88.
[7] Stephens, G., 'Old Northern Runic Monuments,' i. 228.
[8] Latham, R. G., 'The Germania of Tacitus,' Notes.
[9] du Chaillu, 'Viking Age,' ii. 218.
[10] *Ibid.*, II. 219.
[11] Seebohm, F., 'Tribal Custom in Anglo-Saxon Law,' 236.
[12] du Chaillu, *loc. cit.*, ii. 219.
[13] Skeat, W. W,, 'Principles of English Etymology,' 455.
[14] Ellis, G., 'Early English Metrical Romances,' Introd., p. 6.
[15] Taylor, I., 'History of the Alphabet,' 210-215.
[16] Beddoe, J,. 'Races in Britain,' 42.
[17] du Chaillu, P. B., 'The Land of the Midnight Sun,' 1. 304.
[18] Stephens, G., *loc. pcit.*, i. 359.
[19] Adamus Bremen, 'Hist. Eccles.,' lib. ii., chaps. xxix. and xxxviii.
[20] King Alfred's 'Orosius,' edited by H. Sweet, p. 20.
[21] Stephens, G., *loc. cit.*, iii. 24.

[22] Stephens, G., 'The Runes, Whence they Came,' Preface, 1894.

[23] Stephens, G., 'Old Northern Runic Monuments,' iii. 10.

[24] Stephens, G., 'Old Northern Runic Monuments,' iii. 396.

[25] *Ibid.*, iii. 24

[26] du Chaillu, 'Viking Age,' ii. 221.

[27] *Loc. cit.*, iii., Foreword.

# Chapter Five - The Frisians: Their Tribes and Allies

THE ancient Frisians are but poorly represented by their descendants on the coast of the North Sea at the present time. The greater part of Holland was at one time occupied by them, as the northern part still is. Their coast has undergone greater changes within the range of history than any other in Europe. An old map of the twelfth century shows that Texel and Vlieland, and the other islands now forming a crescent along the coast, were joined to the mainland. The river Ysel at that time passed into the sea through the narrow channel between Texel and the promontory of North Holland. The Vlie similarly had its outlet through a channel north of the present Vlieland. In the middle of the old northern province of Holland the Lake of Flevo was situated. This was an inland water of the same kind as the Frisian broads at the present time. As the result of a great flood in the autumn of 1170 the lowlands along the rivers began to disappear, and in the course of the next two centuries nearly a million acres of land had become submerged. By the middle of the fifteenth century there was left the Zuyder Zee of the present time, with the islands, to mark the great encroachment of the sea on the old Frisian country. Before the time when their history began the Frisians extended westward to the old Rhine, whose outlet is at Katwijk, and much farther to the northward, where their descendants still occupy the North Frisian Islands and the opposite coast of Schleswig. They and the Goths of the Baltic coasts were the greatest maritime nations of Northern Europe in the early centuries of our era. The old Frisian settlements, indeed, extended into the Baltic, where they came into contact with the Goths, Danes, Wends, and other nations. This was the direction of their early trade, by which they were brought into commercial connection with the Eastern trade route. The Scandinavian ratio of the value of gold to silver—1 to 8—which prevailed in ancient Frisia in the payment of the gold wergelds of the district near the Weser in a silver equivalent,[1] appears to be satisfactory proof of this commercial intercourse. It was without doubt from the Frisian coast that many expeditions started for the coasts of Britain, that resulted in the conquest of the country and the settlement of new races of people in it. Much has been written about the Anglo-Saxon settlement, but little has been told of the part which the Frisians played in this great migration. Some English historians only tell us of their settlements on the Scotch coast in the Firth of Forth and around Dunfries at the head of the Solway Firth. The evidence is, however,

43

abundant that the part they played in the settlement of England was hardly second to that of any race. They were probably included in the designation Saxon within the confederacy of the Saxon invaders, and as they were the chief maritime nation of North Germany at that time there can be no doubt that Frisian ships were used.

The settlement of some Frisians on the east coast of Britain in the time of the Empire is probable from Ptolemy's reference to the Parisi in the Holderness district, and the Teutonic equivalent of this name, Farisi.

Procopius also, the Greek historian of the sixth century,[2] says that three very populous nations occupied Britain—the Angles, the Britons, and the Frisians. Their migrations across the North Sea certainly began at an early date. By the middle of the sixth century there were scattered colonies of Angles and Frisians occupying districts of the east coast of Britain from the Tees to the Forth, and the kingdom of Bernicia was formed by Ida, the capital, Bamburgh, being placed on a headland not far from the Tweed.[3] The selection of such a site for the seat of government of a kingdom founded by a maritime people was characteristic. The Frisian country itself was a coast country, not extending far inland beyond easy access to and from the sea. It was natural, therefore, that the new settlements which such a people founded should be grouped so as to reproduce as much as possible facilities for communication similar to those to which they were accustomed. Their communications were kept up mainly by the sea, and the position of Bamburgh, as the seat of government for the settlers along the coast, points to this as well as to the site being chosen for defence. These were not the earliest of their race that came to Britain, and probably not the earliest settlers, for in the later Roman period we have a record of some colonies of Frisians and other German tribes introduced for military purposes.

Procopius mentions the inhabitants of Britain under the names 'Angeloi, Phrissones, and those surnamed from the island Brittones.' He thus calls the same people Angles and Frisians, whom Welsh authors, writing about the same date, call Saxons.

The Frisian occupancy of the coast of North Germany was probably continuous from North Holland to South Denmark, and there must be assumed to have been a fringe of them along the whole seaboard of Hanover and Holstein.[4] They were the neighbouring nation to the Angles, the Frisians lying west and the Angles east. The approach of the two people towards identity of race or origin is probably near, but there is no proof of any Frisian calling himself an Angle or *vice versá*. Both may have been called by the same name by a third nation, or both may have been called Saxon.[5] This consideration is important in reference to the use of the names Angles and Saxons as those of allied peoples and not merely of tribes or nations.

The Frisian people, both in Schleswig and in Holland, are an example of an ancient race in the last stage of gradual absorption by the more vigorous nations with which they are in close contact. Other races which were much concerned with the conquest and settlement of England as parts of confederacies have similarly become absorbed in the nationalities of their more vig-orous neighbours, and their languages have entirely disappeared. Of this, the case of the Wends, who occupied the coast of Pomerania, is an example. The Old Saxons, also, were relatively greater than the Saxons of Germany at the present day, and their language has been absorbed in the German. One of the most remarkable dissapearances of any ancient race is that of the Lombards or Longobards, who were neighbours of the Saxons. All that remains to re-mind us of them is the name Lombardy. The race and their language have entirely disappeared, and been absorbed by the Italian. A similar disappear-ance is that of the Burgundians. Their original home was in the East of Eu-rope, in and near the Isle of Bornholm in the Baltic and on the adjacent coasts, but as a result of their southern migration the race has been ab-sorbed, and the names Bornholm and Burgundy alone remain to tell us of their existence in North-Eastern Europe and in Eastern France.

At the present time the North Frisian area, which is separated by along stretch of coast from East Friesland, comprises the western part of Schleswig and the islands opposite. The North Frisian area comprised the parts about Husum, Bredsted, and Tondern, on the mainland of Schleswig, where the Fri-sians were distributed over some thirty-eight parishes, which, along with the inhabitants of the islands, gave a population in 1852 of about 30,000, In this northern province of Germany, as in Holland, the same process of absorption is going on, and more rapidly perhaps in Schleswig than in East Friesland. In these disappearing Frisians we may see the last remnants of a vigorous an-cient nation, largely concerned in the conquest and settlement of England, and numerously represented among the ancestors of the English people.

Several dialects of the Frisian language still survive, and a characteristic suffix for their place-names is the termination -um. This is the equivalent of the English -ham and the German -heim. In Friesland itself the places with names ending in -um are abundant. Within a few miles of Leeuwarden six-teen out of twenty-four places have this characteristic ending.[6] In Northum-berland many place-names terminate in -ham, but this suffix is in almost all instances pronounced -um.

Latham says that there are one or two names ending in this Frisian suffix in the Danish isles of Fyen and Sealand and this may be a trace of former set-tlements on the Baltic. Their trading voyages certainly led them there, and they were so closely connected with the Goths and Angles in alliance, and probably in early commerce, that Frisian settlements on the Western Baltic coast probably existed. They were also in communication and in alliance, at least from time to time, with the Wends or Vandals of the south coast of the Baltic. Alliances, indeed, played a very important part in the earlier conquest of England by the Anglo-Saxons, and in its later conquest by the Danes. In both of these conquests the Frisians took part. Some came in the former pe-riod under the name of Angles or Saxons, in the latter under the name of Danes or Vikings. Our early chroniclers had more accurate traditions of who the Danes were than modern historians have fully recognised. Henry of Huntingdon, in the passage in which he mentions the impiety of the Anglo—Saxons some time after their conversion, says: 'The Almighty therefore let loose upon them the most barbarous of nations, the Danes and Goths, Norwegians and Swedes, Vandals and Frisians.'[7] It will be noticed that he couples the Vandals with the Frisians, as if they were acting together in alliance.

Among the ancient Frisian books which exist is one known as the 'Keran fon Hunesgena londe,' or Statutes of the Country of the Hunsings, the date of which is about A.D. 1252, but the origin of the statutes is of a far earlier period. There is also another old law-book in existence, known as the 'Littera Brocmannorum,' or written law of the Brocmen.'[8] The chief part which remains of old Frisia is the country of the meres and broads of North Holland, but in assigning a locality to any ancient Frisian tribe, we must remember the great destruction of the land which has occurred within the range of history. The Brocmen certainly formed an old tribal division of the race, of sufficient importance to have laws of their own as distinct from their neighbours, and they, or some of their tribe, may have occupied part of East Friesland and probably some of the submerged country. Their country was also known as Brocmonnelond and Brockmerland.[9] The Frisian author Halbertsma tells us that the pagus of the Brocmen was in East Frisia. Among the Frisians there were certainly distinct tribes. Even as late as the twelfth century William of Malmesbury alludes to these ancient tribes in the expression, 'all the Frisian nations.'[10] We may probably trace three of them, of which the Hunsings would be one, in the three different amounts of tribal wergelds or compensations for injuries that prevailed in the ancient Frisian territory westward of the river Weser.[11]

The close relationship between the Anglo-Saxon and Frisian languages has been shown by Halbertsma and by Siebs among Continental scholars, and by philologists in our own country. This philological evidence supplies additional proof of the large Frisian element in the Anglo-Saxon settlement, in the comparison of the Frisian with the Old English or Anglo-Saxon language. On this subject Sweet says that the treatment of the letter *a* is almost identical in the two languages. In Frisian we find *mon* and *noma* alternating with *man* and *nama* (name). We find the same exceptional *o* in *of*, *nosi* (nose)—(O.E. *nosu*)—and the same change of *a* into *æ*; that in Frisian, which has no *æ*, is written *e*, as *ik brec*, *bec*, *kreft*, corresponding to the Old English *bræc*, *bæc*, and *cræft*. These changes, he says, do not occur in any of the other cognates, and could not, except by a most extraordinary coincidence, have been developed independently in English and in Frisian. They must therefore have already existed in Anglo-Frisian.[12] Frisian throws important light on the formation of the peculiar English diphthongs *æ* and *œ*. In the older Anglo-Saxon texts, including West Saxon, *a* is only diphthongised before *r*, and not before *l*, so that we have the typical forms *ald* and *heard*. In the oldest glossaries *hard* for *heard* is exceptional; but in a few old Northumbrian fragments *hard* predominates. The Frisian language similarly agrees in preserving *a* before *l* in *al*, *half*, *galga*, etc., while before *r* it is written *e*, doubtless for *æ*, as *herd* for

46

*hærd*, the Anglo-Saxon *heard*. The change of the word *hard* into *hærd* is parallel to that of the change of *bac* into *bæc*.[13] The resemblances to be found between the language still spoken by the scattered remnants of the ancient Frisian nation and that of our Saxon forefathers are many, and leave no room for doubt of their very close connection. One remarkable word they hand in common, and which has not been found in any other old Germanic language, is *sunnstede* for the solstice. The Frisian and Old English also evolved earlier than German their common term for equinox, Anglo-Saxon *evenniht*, Frisian *evenaht*.

We can trace various tribes of ancient Frisians—viz., the Hunsings, the Brocmen, the Huntanga, and the Chaucians or Hocings, and others. These people appear all to have been designated at times as Frisians, and at other times by their own special or tribal names. The Chaucians, however, were a populous race, and may be regarded in some respects as a separate nation in close connection with, and never in opposition to, the Frisians. They were seated in the country between the Weser and the Elbe. The name Cuxhaven at the mouth of the Elbe is one which was probably derived from the Chaucians, and has come down to us as that of a place situated in their old country. The Hunsings were the same people as the Hunni mentioned by Bede[14] as one of the tribes by which England was settled. The country they occupied was a district in the province of Gröningen, in the North of Holland, where the river Hunse flows from the south past Gröningen towards the sea. A part of this country is, or was within the last century, known by its old name as the 'District of Hunsing.'[15] The 'Hundings' also are alluded to in the 'Traveller's Song,' Hundingum being mentioned as if the people were a separate tribe. The Phundusii, also mentioned by Ptolemy, were prob-ably the same people at an earlier date, although located by him further to the north.[16] Hunnaland and Friesland are mentioned among the countries the Norse Vikings ravaged.[17] The pagus of the Huntanga, apparently, was located between the River Hunte in Oldenburg and the province of Grönirigen.[18] The name *Hun*, *Hüne*, or *Hunni* is one which in the sense of giant prevails in the popular traditions of North Germany. Grimm[19] tells us that it is especially characteristic of the prehistoric traditions of Westphalia, and that it extends as far westward as the Gröningen country and the river Drenth in Holland. Barrows and dolmens, known as giant hills and giant tombs, are also called in these parts of Europe *hünebedde* and *hunebedden*, 'bed' being commonly used for 'grave.' Another country of the Hunni has been identified by some Northern writers with the northern part of Jutland, where a few place-names that contain the word *Hüne* still survive. As the Frisians formerly extended much further north than their present limit in Schleswig, the occurrence of these names may be quite consistent with the later connection of the name with the Frisian Hunsings. It is quite certain that the name is a very ancient one, probably as old as that of Frisians themselves.

From these circumstances and references we may see that the *Hüne* or *Huni* name was probably applied to some of the inhabitants of Schleswig, as

47

well as to some in East Friesland. In the eighth century we read of the boundaries of the Hune in the south part of Denmark.[20] There is a reference also to the forest which separates Hunaland[21] from Reidgotaland, the latter name having been identified as referring to Jutland. In the province of Drenthe in Holland, where the river Hunse has its source, there still exists a remnant of a more ancient population than the old Frisian. These people are of different physical characters from their neighbours. They are broad-headed, while the true Frisians are long-headed. They are brown in aspect, while the Frisians are fair, and they are supposed to be descendants of a remnant of the very ancient brown race of Europe who were left when their country was overrun at a remote period by people of the Gothic or Germanic stock. We have no knowledge of the physical characters of the Hunsings or Hunni mentioned by Bede, but as these brown people of Holland who are to be found in Drenthe and Overijssel occupy the country which was in part occupied by the Hunsings, there may have been some connection between them.

Among the tribes or allies of the Frisians the most important was the Chauci or Chaucians. Tacitus mentions them as living on both sides of the Weser. Those settled between the Weser and the Elbe he called *Chauci majores;* and those on the west of the Weser, but higher up the river, *Chauci minores.*[22] His description of them is that of a considerable nation. He says that the land from Hessia was under the dominion of, and inhabited by, Chauci. He has left two accounts of them somewhat different, but that in his 'Germania' is believed to have been written later than that in his 'Annals,' or 'History,' and it may well have been that before writing his later account he had had opportunities of learning more about them and correcting his previous statements. He says that the Chauci never excited wars nor harassed their neighbours, and that they wished to support their grandeur by justice. This description agrees with the character of the Frisians, and may perhaps be taken to refer also to them.[23] The accounts which Tacitus gives of the German people between the Rhine and the Elbe are of more value than that of those beyond the Elbe, for in the former case he wrote from information collected from people who had actually travelled through the countries, which in the latter was probably not the case, as the countries were further removed from the Roman influence.[24]

The question may here suggest itself: What have these Chauci or Chaucians to do with the English settlement? I see no reason to doubt that they had a considerable share in it. Kemble found near Stade, in the part of ancient Frisia occupied by the Chaucians, and also far up the Weser, certain mortuary urns of a kind that is rare or unknown in other parts of Germany, but known to occur in Suffolk, Warwickshire, Derbyshire, the Isle of Wight, and other parts of England,[25] and the Chaucian name apparently survives in many old English place-names.

Ptolemy's account of these people agrees in regard to their locality with that of Tacitus. He says that they were contiguous to the Frisii, and, like them, extended along the coast, but also further inland. He tells us also that the Frisii lay in front of the Angrivarii, who, as we have seen, were a tribe of the Saxons, for these Angrivarii of the earlier centuries were the same as the Angarians or Engern people of Carlovingian time. Ptolemy says that the Chauci reached to the Elbe.[26] The survival of such a name as Cuxhaven in their old country is significant, the first syllable *Cux* having come form *Chauc.* This etymology, which has generally been adopted,[27] is important in reference to the traces of the Chaucians which may be found in England. Here in an ancient Chaucian region a survival of the old tribal or national name exists in the form *Cux.* In various parts of England where Frisians settled we shall also find it.

The name under which the Chaucians are mentioned in the Sagas is that of Hocings. In Beowulf we read of them under this name. Word for word, says Latham, this word Hocing is held to be that of Chauci by all, or most, who have written on the subject. Hocing. however, with its suffix *-ing*, means not so much a Chaucus as of Chauch blood.[28] The identity of the names is established by the ancient sound of *ch* being equivalent to that of *h.* This identification will be of use in endeavouring to unravel the threads in the tangled skein of information which has come down to us relating to the people concerned in the English settlement. The Chauci as a nation have long since disappeared, and were probably absorbed by the Franks of Germany. Some of them, no doubt, migrated to England, where they were absorbed in the Old English race. If we look for traces of them in England through the names by which they were known in their Continental home, we shall discover many parts of the country in which small colonies of them probably settled. As regards their alternative name Hocings, philologists give us several examples of the equivalence of the early *ch* and *h* sounds in these tribal or national names. South of the Chauci another great tribe of German people known as the Chatti were situated, from which, according to German philologists, in which others concur, the name Hesse has been derived. The Hessians are the descendants of the ancient Chatti or Hatti. They are mentioned under the names Chattuarii, Attuarii, and Hetware. In the name Attuarii, as Latham has pointed out, the *ch* sound disappears altogether. The name Hesse also, says Latham, word for word is Chatti.[29] The Old Frisian *ch* was equivalent to the Anglo-Saxon *h.*[30] We may therefore accept the identity of the sounds *chauc-* and *hoc-* in the names Chauci and Hocings, and this will be of interest in reference to traces of them in England. At some time during the period of the growth of the Frank confederation the Chaucians assumed the name of Franks, and their name disappeared from history.

Pliny's description of part of Frisia and the condition of some of its inhabitants may be overdrawn, but there is in it a sufficient element of truth to warrant the belief that foreign expeditions, with a view to settlements in a land more favoured by Nature, could not have been unpopular among them. Two or three days' sail would bring them to the coasts of Britain, where, if they could form colonies sufficiently strong to resist attacks, they could at least find a better subsistence, with more favourable conditions of life than those

Pliny describes. He says: 'In this spot the wretched natives occupying either the tops of hills or artificial mounds of turf raised out of the reach of the highest tides build their small cottages, which appear like sailing-vessels when the water covers the circumjacent ground, and like wrecks when it has retired. For fuel they use a kind of mud taken up by hand and dried rather in the wind than the sun, and with this earth they heat their food and warm their bodies, stiffened by the rigorous North. Their only drink is rain-water collected in ditches at the thresholds of their doors.' The reference to peat-digging, which is still extensively carried on in Friesland, the mounds on which their houses were built, and the appearance of the country, shows that this was a description of an eye-witness. The terp mounds on which the ancient habitations in the meres of Old Frisia were constructed have been shown to be composed largely of deposits due to accumulations under ancient pile dwellings, and many of them have been removed for manure and agricultural purposes.[31]

As already mentioned, the original home of the ancestors of the Frisians, Jutes, and Danes appears to have been in the Scandian peninsula, which Ptolemy, the geographer of the second century, understood to have been an island. He places the nations called the Phiresii, Gutæ, and Dauciones all within Scandia. The migration of the Phiresii south-westward has left its traces in certain parts of Jutland, and appears to have been such a very early one that it occurred before the invention of runes by their neighbours the Goths, for no fixed runic monuments have ever been found in any part of Old Frisia. The Daucones were the Dacians or Danes, and they migrated, apparently, after the invention of runes, for fixed monuments with runes are found in Denmark. As already pointed out, one of the strongest proofs of the Scandian connection of the Angles of Northumbria is that they took with them to England a knowledge of runic writing, and have left examples of their runic inscriptions on fixed stone monuments. Not so the Frisians, who, though allied with the Angles, were behind them in the knowledge of letters. The physical appearance of the Frisians at the present-day bears witness to the Northern origin of their race, Beddoe says: 'They are an extremely fair and very comely people. I found the Frisians from the Zuyder Zee through Gröningen (a Saxonised district) to beyond Ems, a taller, longer-faced, more universally blonde and light-eyed folk than the Saxons, the latter being often very hazel-eyed, even when their hair is light.'[32]

Among the indications that communication between the early Saxon people and those of the same races from whom they sprang was not wanting is the story of the early missionary work of the Old English Christians. The Frisians were pagans long after the conversion of those of their race who were descended from the early Frisian settlers in England. The Frankish monks had endeavoured in vain to convert them, and failed, perhaps through difficulties with their language. The Anglo-Saxon missionaries, being more allied in race, met with some success[33] William of Malmesbury tells us how their final conversion was brought about. He says: 'The ancient Saxons and all the Frisian nations were converted to the faith of Christ through the exertions of King Charles,'[34] but we know that in the conversions which followed the conquests of Charlemagne the sword was the chief instrument. It was by far different means that some hundred and fifty years earlier the band of Anglo-Saxon missionaries, of whom Wilfrid was the first, began their journeys into Germany, impelled by Christian zeal, and it can hardly be doubted by the sentiment also of common racial descent. They turned their energies to the conversion of their Frisian and Saxon cousins to the faith which the English people had themselves so lately adopted.

Wilfrid and Willibord, his pupil, Winirith or Boniface, Leofwine, the converter of the Saxons, Willehad of Northumbria, and the brothers Willibald and Wunibald, are but names to the political historian of the Continental nations from which the Anglo-Saxon race sprang. They stand out prominently, however, in the early ecclesiastical history of Northern Germany, where they are, even to the present day, as honoured as those of Augustine, Birinus, and Paulinus in England.

From such a country as ancient Frisia was, emigration, as the population increased, was a necessity. The story of Hengist and the custom of the expulsion of a number of the young people of his country may have reasonably prevailed in Friesland. Whether they settled in England under the names Angles and Jutes, or under tribal names of their own, it is certain that large numbers of Frisians must have become English colonists under the Saxon name. The old chroniclers are, indeed, at a loss whether to make Hengist a Frisian or a Saxon. One of them says:

'Ein hiet Engistus een Vriese een Sas
Die vten lande verdruen was.' [35]

[One was named Engist a Frisian or a Saxon, who was driven away out of his land]

There is direct evidence of early communication between ancient Frisia and England in the discovery in Friesland and Holland of movable objects with inscriptions on them in early tunic characters peculiar to England. At Harlingen, in Friesland, a bracteate was found which has on it large clear runes, the type of the A ( F ) being provincial English, which Stephens assigns to the fifth century. He says it was doubtless struck in England, or by an English workman in Scandinavia.[36] In Holland an English runic coin has also been found.[37]

The establishment of Frisian colonies on the north-eastern coasts of England and the south-east of Scotland during the early centuries of our era, before the end of the Roman rule in Britain, is supported by circumstantial evidence so strong that it cannot be doubted. It will be summarised in the chapters on Northnmbria. With the early Frisian colonists there must have been others of Anglian descent, among whom a knowledge of runic writing was known, as proved by inscriptions still existing.

In all countries of which early records exist we find traces of the custom of giving to people the same names as those of the tribes and clans to which they belonged. Many instances may also be found of men, when they lived as foreigners among people of another race, being known by the name of their own nation. Some of these old tribal clan or national names have come down as surnames to modern times. During the period of the Anglo-Saxon settlement it could scarcely have been otherwise in our own country. Men must have been commonly designated by their tribal or clan names if they lived among neighbours of another tribe who were unacquainted with the names by which these men called themselves. Such names are descriptive of the individuals to whom they were applied, and as in the early Anglo-Saxon period a *tun* or a *ham* was commonly named after that of the head of the family living in it, it is difficult to avoid the conclusion that many of the names of these early *tuns* and *hams* must be the same as the tribal and clan names of their first occupants. Personal names derived from those of tribes are older than those derived from countries or districts in which tribes settled. To call a man after the name of his tribe or clan in the time before the tribal wanderings of the German and Northern people had ceased was the most natural way of distinguishing him. The occurrence of so many names of people called Hun and Hune, or compounds of them, in Anglo-Saxon literature points to tribal people at that name having taken part in the settlement of England. The Hunsings and the people of the Huntanga tribe we can connect with the settlement, and with the Hunni mentioned by Bede. Many persons bearing Hun or Hune names are very frequently mentioned in Anglo-Saxon records— *e.g.*, Hunfrith fifteen times, and Hunred twelve times. Hunman and Huneman both occur. Huna, Hunes, Hune, Hungar, Hunbeorht, Hunni, and Hunding, are some of the forms of these personal names. Some of them are probably ancestral names repeated. There are more than 150 known instances of designations of this kind.[38] Even if we suppose that some persons who bore them obtained them from some other origin than that of the tribal name or that of an ancestor, the number which in all probability was originally derived from the tribal names of the Hunsings or the Huntanga will still be large. The people of these tribes were Frisians, and their settlements in England were both early and late. The last of their ancient immigrations, or of people of the same descent, into England took place in the twelfth century, when, as a result of inundations, many were obliged to seek new homes. It was early in that century that Flemings settled in parts of South Wales, where they were absorbed among the English settlers, and their language became lost in the English speech, as did that of the settlers centuries earlier.

The discovery of a large number of skulls at Bremen, of the same period as that of the Anglo-Saxon, has been referred to. Those intermediate in length were named Batavian or Frisian. Beddoe, in summarising the evidence of these ancient skulls in connection with the light they throw on the racial characters of the Old English people, says that the Frisian or so-called Batavian skulls have characters that resemble those of the Anglo-Saxons. 'John

Bull.' says Beddoe, 'is of the Batavian type,'[39] an opinion from so distinguished an anthropologist which is valuable evidence in support of the conclusion that there must have been a very large Frisian admixture in the Old English race.

[1] Seebohm, F., 'Tribal Custom in Anglo-Saxon Law,' 207.

[2] Procopius, 'De Bell. Goth.,' lib. iv., 20.

[3] Skene, W. F., 'Celtic Scotland,' i. 151.

[4] Latham, R. G., 'The Germania of Tacitus,' p. 242.

[5] Latham, R. G., loc. cit., p. 241.

[6] Van Langenheuzen's Map, 1843, quoted by Latham, R. G., 'Germania,' Notes, p. 119.

[7] Henry of Huntingdon's Chronicle, Bohn's ed., p. 148.

[8] Bosworth, Joseph, 'Origin of the English, Germanic, and Scandinavian Languages,' p. 61.

[9] Halbertsma, J. H., 'Lexicon Frisicum.'

[10] Malmesbury's Chronicle, book i., chap. iv.

[11] Seebohm, F., 'Tribal Custom in Anglo—Saxon Law,' 199.

[12] Sweet, H., 'Dialects and Prehistoric Forms of Old English,' Trans Philol. Soc., 1875-1876, p. 562.

[13] Sweet, H., 'Dialects and Prehistoric Forms of Old English,' Trans. Philol. Soc., 1875-1876, p. 563.

[14] Bede, 'Hist. Eccles.,' v.. chap. ix.

[15] The Frisians: Their Tribes and Allies.

[16] Ptolemy's Map of Germany, reproduced in Elton's 'Origin of English History.' second ed.

[17] du Chaillu, 'Viking Age,' i. 503.

[18] Monumenta Germaniæ, Script. ii. 38.

[19] Grimm, J., 'Teutonic Mythology,' 523.

[20] Monumenta Germaniæ, i. 34.

[21] Kemble, J. M., 'Saxons in England,' quoting Sögur, i. 495.

[22] Latham, R. G., 'The Germania of Tacitus,' Map.

[23] Bosworth, Joseph, loc. cit., p. 48.

[24] Latham, R. G., loc. cit., 'Prolegomena,' xv.

[25] Beddoe, J., 'Races in Britain,' p. 46.

[26] Ptolemy, ii. 2.

[27] Latham, R. G., loc. cit., 242.

[28] 'Germania of Tacitus,' edited by R. G. Latham, 243.

[29] Latham, R. G., 'The English Language,' 5th ed., p. 242.

[30] Ibid., 93. Also Maetzner, E., 'English Grammar,' i. 146-148.

[31] Proc. Soc. Ant. Scot., xxiii. 98-100.

[32] Beddoe, J., loc. cit., pp. 39, 40.

[33] Bosworth, J., loc. cit., p. 94.

[34] William of Malmesbury's Chronicle, book i., chap. iv.

[35] Maerlant, quoted by Bosworth, 'Origin of the English, German, and Scandinavian Languages,' p. 32.

[36] Stephens, G., 'Old Northern Runic Monuments,' ii. 555.

[37] Ibid., ii, 568.

[38] Birch, W. de Gray, 'Index Saxonicus,' and Searle, W. G., 'Onomasticon Anglo-Saxonicum.'

[39] Haddon, A. C., 'The Study of Man,' 84, quoting Beddoe.

# Chapter Six - Rugians, Wends, and Tribal Slavonic Settlers

THE name Wends was given by the old Teutonic nations of Germany to those Slavonic tribes who were located in the countries east of the Elbe and south of the Baltic Sea. It is the same as the older name used by Ptolemy,[1] who says that 'the Wenedæ are established along the whole of the Wendish Gulf.' Tacitus also mentions the Venedi. There can, therefore, be no doubt that these people were seated on the coast of Mecklenburg and Pomerania before the time of the Anglo-Saxon settlement. That there were some differences in race between the Wends of various tribes is probable from the existence of such large tribes among them as the Wiltzi and Obodriti, who in the time of Charlemagne formed opposite alliances, the former with the Saxons, the latter with the Franks. The Wends who still exist in Lower Saxony are of a dark complexion, and are of the same stock as the Sorbs or Serbs of Servia. They are Slavonic, but many tribes of Slavonic descent are fair in complexion. Procopius tells us that those Vandals who were allies of the ancient Goths were remarkable for their tall stature, pale complexion, and blonde hair.[2] It is therefore by no means improbable that the ancient Slavic tribes of the Baltic coast were distinguished by differences in complexion.

As the identification of Vandal or Wendish settlers with various parts of England is new, or almost so, it will be desirable to state the evidence of their connection with the origin of the Anglo-Saxon race more fully than would otherwise have been necessary.

The Vandals are commonly thought to have been a nation of Teutonic descent like the Goths, but there is certain evidence that the later Vandals or Wends were Slavonic, and there is no reason to doubt that these later Vandals were descended from some of the earlier. Tacitus mentions the Vandals as a group of German nations, the name being used in a wide sense, as British is at the present time. The most important reason for considering the early Vandals to be Teutonic is that the names of their leaders are almost exclusively Teutonic, as Gonderic, Genseric, etc.[3] This reason would be valid if there were nothing else to set against it. Leaders of a more advanced race, however, have led the forces of less advanced allies in all ages, and the Goths were a more advanced race than the Vandals, whom they conquered, and who subsequently became their firm allies. Among the collection of Anglo-Saxon relics in the British Museum axe a number of Vandal ornaments from North Africa, placed there for comparison with those of the Anglo-Saxon period. These are apparently rough imitations of those of the same age found in Scandinavia and in England—*i.e.*, imitations of Gothic work.

Of all the people in ancient Germania east of the Elbe whom Tacitus mentions as Germans, not a single Teutonic vestige remained in the time of Charlemagne. Poland and Silicia were parts of his Germania. When the Germans of Charlemagne and his successors conquered the country east of the Elbe there was neither trace nor record of any earlier Teutonic occupation.[4] Such a previous occupancy rarely occurs, as Latham has pointed out, without leaving some traces of its existence by the survival here and there of descendants of the older occupants. In Germany, east of the Elbe, no earlier inhabitants than the Slavonic have been discovered, excepting those of a very remote prehistoric age. At the dawn of German history no traces are met with of enthralled people of Teutonic descent among the Slavs east of the Elbe, and there are no traditions of such earlier occupants, while the oldest place-names are all Slavonic. If there were Germans, strictly so-called, east of the river in the time of Tacitus—*i.e.*, long-headed tribes—their assumed displacement by the Slavs between his time and that of Charlemagne would have been the greatest and most complete of any recorded in history[5] Ethnology and history, therefore, alike point to people of Sarmatian or Slavic descent—*i.e.*, brachycephalic tribes—as the earliest inhabitants of Eastern Germany, and indicate some misunderstanding in this respect by the commentators of Tacitus.[6] In Eastern Germany place-names survive ending in -*itz*, so very common in Saxony; in -*zig*, as Leipzig; in -*a*, as Jena; and in -*dam*, as Potsdam. All these places were named by the Slavs.[7]

The statement of Bede that the Rugini or Rugians were among the nations from whom the English were known to have descended was contemporary evidence of his own time. The Rugi are also mentioned by Tacitus.[8] Their name apparently remains to this day in that of Rügen Island, situated off the coast which they occupied in the time of the Roman Empire.

As Ptolemy tells us of the wenedæ seated on this same Baltic coast, and as they were Sarmatians or Slavs, it is clear that the Rugians must have been of that race. Some of the nations mentioned by Tacitus were, he says, of non-Germanic origin. Rügen Island was the chief place of worship for the Wendish race, the chief centre of their religion. On the east side of the peninsula of Jasmund in Rügen are the white chalk cliffs of Stubbenkammer, and on the north side of the island is the promontory of Arcona, where in the twelfth century we read of the idol Svantovit, and the temple of this Wendish god. No traces of Teutonic worship have ever been found in Rügen. They are all Slavonic. Saxo tells us at the worship of Svantovit at Arcana with the tributes brought there from all Slavonia.[9]

The probability of some very early settlers in Britain having been Wends, and consequently that there was a Slavic element in the origin of the Old English race, is shown in another way. The settlement of large bodies of Vandals in Britain by order of the Emperor Probus is a fact recorded in Roman history. The authority is Zosimus,[10] and this settlement is said to have taken place in the latter part of the third century of our era, after a great defeat of Vandals near the Lower Rhine. They were accompanied by a horde of Burgundians, and as they were apparently on the march in search of new homes, it probably suited them as well as it suited the Romans to be transported to Britain. Unless it can be shown that the Vandal name is to be understood to mean only certain tribes of Teutonic origin, this arbitrary settlement of Vandals in Britain is the earliest record of immigrants of Slavic origin. It is not possible to ascertain the parts of the country in which they settled, but as they were known to Roman writers by the names Vinidæ and Venedi, it is possible that the Roman place-names in Britain—Vindogladia in Dorset, Vindomis in Hampshire, and others—may have been connected with their settlements. It is possible also that during the time between their arrival and that of the earliest Anglo-Saxon settlers some of their descendants may have maintained their race distinctions apart from the British people, as descendants of some of the Roman colonists apparently did in Kent.

The defeat of the Vandals by Probus near the Rhine occurred in A.D. 277,[11] so that their settlement in Britain was not more than two centuries before the arrival of the Jutes and Saxons. As it is probable there were some so-called Saxons already settled on the eastern coast of England, with whom those of a later date coalesced, it is not impossible that some of the Vandal settlers in Britain in the time of Probus may have preserved their distinction in race until the invasion of the Saxons, Angles, and Jutes began.

The names in the Anglo-Saxon charters which apparently marked settlements of Rugians in England are Ruanbergh and Ruwanbeorg, Dorset; Ruganbeorh and Ruwanbeorg, Somerset; Ruwanbeorg and Rugan dic, Wilts; Rugebeorge, in Kent; and Ruwangoringu, Hants.[12] These will be referred to in later chapters.

The chief Old English names which appear to refer to them in Domesday Book are Ruenore in Hampshire, Ruenhala and Ruenhale in Essex, Rugehala and Rugelie in Staffordshire, Rugutune in Norfolk, and Rugarthorp in Yorkshire. Close to Ruenore, in Hampshire, is Stubbington, which may have been an imported name, as it resembles that of Stubnitz in the Isle of Rügen.

In its historical aspect the Anglo-Saxon settlement may be regarded as part of that wider migration of nations and tribes from Eastern and Northern Europe into the provinces of the Roman Empire during its decadence. In its ethnological aspect it may be regarded as a final stage in the westward European migration of people of the Germanic stock. As the history and ethnology of the Franks in Western Germany afford us a notable example of the fusion of people of the Celtic with others of the Teutonic race, so the history and ethnology of Eastern Germany afford an equally striking example of the fusion of people of Teutonic and Slavonic origins. It began at a very early period in our era, and the present irregular ethnological frontier between Germans and Slavs shows that it is still slowly going on. The eastward migration of Germans in later centuries has absorbed the Wends. The descendants of the isolated Slavonic settlers near Utrecht and in other parts of the Rhine Valley have also long been absorbed. The ethnological evidence concerning the present inhabitants of these districts and the survival of some of their old place-names, however, supports the statement of the early chroniclers concerning the immigration of Slavs into what is now Holland.

The part which the ancient Wends, including Rugians, Wilte, and other Slavonic people, took in the settlement of England was, in comparison with that of the Teutonic nations and tribes, small, but yet so considerable that it has left its results. During the period of the invasion and the longer period of the settlement, the southern coasts of the Baltic Sea were certainly occupied by Slavonic people. Ptolemy, writing, as he did, about the middle of the second century of our era, mentions the Baltic by the name Venedic Gulf, and the people on its shores as Venedi or Wenedæ. He describes them as one of the great nations of Sarmatia.[13] the most ancient name of the countries occupied by Slavs, but which was replaced by that of Slavonia. Pliny, in his notice of the Baltic Sea, has the following passage: 'People say that from this point round to the Vistula the whole country is inhabited by Sarmatians and Wends.'[14] Although he did not write from personal knowledge of the Wends, this passage is weighty evidence that they must have been located on the Baltic in his time.

During the time of the Anglo-Saxon period the Slavs in the North of Europe extended as far westward as the Elbe and to places beyond it. On the east bank of that river were the Polabian Wends, and these were apparently a branch of the Wilte or Wiltzi. This name Wiltzi has been derived from the old Slavic word for wolf, *wilk*, plural *wiltzi*, and was given to this great tribe from their ferocious courage. The popular name Wolfmark still survives in North-East Germany, near the eastern limit of their territory. These people called themselves Welatibi, a name derived from *welot*, a giant, and were also known as the Hæfeldan, or Men of Havel, from being seated near the river Havel, as mentioned by King Alfred. The inhabitants of the coast near Stralsund, who were called Rugini or Rugians, and who are mentioned by Bede as one of the nations from whom the Anglo-Saxons of his time were known to have derived their origin,[15] must have been included within the general name of the Wends. As these Rugians must have been Wends, the statement of Bede is direct evidence that some of the people of England in his time were known to be of Wendish descent. This is supported by evidence of other kinds, such as the mention of settlements of people with Wendish or Vandal names in the Anglo-Saxon charters, the numerous names of places in England which have come down from a remote antiquity, and the identity of the oldest forms of such names with that of the people of this race. We read also that Edward, son of Edmund Ironside, fled after his father's death 'ad regnum Rugorum, quod melius vocamus Russiam.'[16] It is also supported by philological evidence. As a distinguished American philologist says: 'The Anglo-Saxon was such a language as might be supposed would result from a fusion of Old Saxon with smaller proportions of High German, Scandinavian, and even Celtic and Slavonic elements.'[17] The migration of the Wilte from the shores of the Baltic and the foundation of a colony in the country around Utrecht is certainly historical. Bede mentions it in connection with the mission of Wilbrord. He says: 'The Venerable Wilbrord went from Frisia to Rome, where the Pope gave him the name of Clement, and sent him back to his bishopric. Pepin gave him a place for his episcopal see in his famous castle, which, in the ancient language of those people, is called Wiltaburg—*i.e.,* the town of the Wilti—but in the French tongue Utrecht.'[18] Venantius also tells us that the Wileti or Wiltzi, between A.D. 560-600, settled near the city of Utrecht, which from them was called Wiltaburg, and the surrounding country Wiltenia.[19] Such a migration would perhaps be made by land, and some of these Wilte may have gone further. The name of the first settlers in Wiltshire has been derived by some authors from a migration of Wilte from near Wiltaburg,[20] and the name Wilsætan appears to afford some corroboration. It is certain that Wiltshire was becoming settled in the latter half of the sixth century, and such a migration may either have come direct from the Baltic or the Elbe, or from the Wilte settlement in Holland.

It must not be supposed that there is evidence of the settlement of all Wiltshire by people descended from the Wilte, but it is not improbable that some early settlers of this time were the original Wilsætas. The Anglo-Saxon charters supply evidence of the existence in various parts of England, as will be referred to in later pages, of people called Willa or Wilte. There were tribes in England named East Willa and West Willa;[21] and such Anglo-Saxon names as Willanesham;[22] Wilburgeham, Cambridgeshire;[23] Wilburge gcmæro and Wilburge mere in Wiltshire;[24] Wilburgewel in Kent;[25] Willabyg in Lincolnshire;[26] Wilmanford,[27] Wilmanleáhtun,[28] appear to have been derived from personal names connected with these people. I have not been able to discover that any other Continental tribe of the Anglo-Saxon period were so named, except this Wendish tribe, called by King Alfred the men of Havel, a name that apparently survived in the Domesday name Hauelingas in Essex. The Wilte or Willa, tribal name survived in England as a personal name, like the national name Scot, and is found in the thirteenth-century Hundred Rolls and other early records. In these rolls a large number of persons so named are mentioned—Wiltes occurs in seventeen entries, Wilt in eight, and Wilte in four entries. Willeman as a personal name is also mentioned.[29] The old Scando-Gothic personal name Wilia is well known.[30]

The great Wendish tribe which occupied the country next to that of the Danes along the west coast of the Baltic in the ninth century was the Obodriti, known also as the Bodritzer. From their proximity there arose an early connection between them and the Danes, or Northmen. In the middle of the ninth century we read of a place on the boundaries of the Northmen and Obodrites, 'in confinibus Nordmannorum et Obodritorum.'[31] The probability of Wendish people of this tribe having settled in England among the Danes arises from their near proximity on the Baltic, their political connection in the time of Sweyn and Cnut, historical references to Obodrites in the service of Cnut in England, and the similarity of certain place-names in some parts of England colonized by Danes to others on the Continent of known Wendish or Slavonic origin. Obodriti is a Slavic name, and, according to Schafarik, the Slavic ethnologist, the name may be compared with Bodrica in the government of Witepsk, Bodrok, and the provincial name Bodrog in

Southern Hungary, and others of a similar kind. In the Danish settled districts of England we find the Anglo-Saxon names Bodeskesham, Cambridgeshire; Bodesham, now Bosham, Sussex; Boddingc-weg, Dorset;[32] the Domesday names Bodebi, Lincolnshire; Bodetone and Bodele, Yorkshire; Bodehā, Herefordshire; Bodeslege, Somerset; Bodeshā, Kent; and others,[33] which may have been named after people of this tribe.

The map of Europe at the present day exhibits evidence of the ancient migration of the Slavs. The Slavs in the country from Trient to Venice were known as Wendi, and hence the name Venice or the Wendian territory.[34] Bohemia and Poland after the seventh century became organized States of Slavs on the upper parts of the Elbe and the Vistula. The Slavonic tribes on the frontier or march-land of Moravia formed the kingdom of Moravia in the ninth century. Other scattered tribes of Slavs formed the kingdom of Bulgaria about the end of the seventh century; and westward of these, other tribes organized themselves into the kingdoms of Croatia, Dalmatia, and Servia.[35] In the North the ancient Slav tribes of Pomerania, Mecklenburg, Brandenburg, and those located on the banks of the Elbe, comprising the Polabians, the Obodrites, the Wiltzi, those known at one time as Rugini, the Lutitzes, and the Northern Sorabians or Serbs, became gradually absorbed among the Germans, who formed new States eastward of their ancient limits. These have long since become Teutonised, and their language has disappeared, but the Slavonic place-names still remain.

What concerns us specially in connection with the settlement of England and the Vandals is that these people were Slavs, not Teutons or Germans, as is sometimes stated. They are fully recognised as Slavs by the historian of the Gothic race, who tells us that Slavs differ from Vandals in name only.[36] It is important, also, to note that the Rugians mentioned by Bede were a Wendish tribe. Westward of the Elbe the Slavic Sorabians had certainly pushed their way, before they were finally checked by Charlemagne and his successors. The German annals of the date A.D. 782[37] tell us that the Sorabians at that time were seated between the Elbe and the Saale, where place-names of Slavonic origin remain to this day.

Those Wends who were located on the Lower Elbe, near Lüneburg and Hamburg, were known as Polabians, through having been seated on or near this river, from *po*, meaning 'on,' and *laba*, the Slavic name for the Elbe.

The eastern corner of the former kingdom of Hanover, and especially that in the circuit of Lüchow, which even to the present day is called Wendland, was a district west of the Elbe, where the Wends formed a colony, and where the Polabian variety of the Wendish language survived the longest. It did not disappear until about 1700-1725, during the latter part of which period the ruler of this ancient Wendland was also King of England.

During the later Saxon period in England the Wends of the Baltic coast had their chief seaport at Julin or Jomberg, close to the island called Wollin, in the delta of the Oder. Julin is mentioned by Adam of Bremen as the largest and most flourishing commercial city in Europe in the eleventh century, but it was destroyed in 1176 by Valdemar, King of Denmark,[38] Its greatest rival was the Northern Gothic port of Wisby in the Isle of Gotland. Whether Jomberg surpassed Wisby as a commercial centre, which, notwithstanding the statement of Adam of Bremen, is doubtful, it is certain that these two ports were the chief ports respectively of the Wends and the Goths of the Baltic. Both of them, even during the Saxon period, had commercial relations with this country, or maritime connection of some sort, as shown by the number of Anglo-Saxon coins and ornaments with Anglian runes on them found either in Gotland or Pomerania.

The connection of the Slav tribes of ancient Germany with the settlement of England is supported also by the survival in England of ancient customs which were widely spread in Slavonic countries, by the evidence of folk-lore, traces of Slav influence in the Anglo-Saxon language, and by some old place-names in England, especially those which point to Wends generally, and others referring to Rugians and to Wilte. The great wave of early Slavonic migration was arrested in Eastern Germany, but lesser waves derived from it were continued westward, as shown by the isolated Slav colonies of ancient origin in Oldenburg, Hanover, and Holland. The same migratory movement in a lesser degree appears to have extended even into England, bringing into our country some Slavonic settlers, probably in alliance with Saxons, Angles, Goths, and other tribes, and some later on in alliance with Danes. The existence of separate large tribes among the Wends is probable evidence of racial differences, and the alternative names they had are probably those by which they were known to themselves and to their neighbours. The remnant at the present time of the dark-complexioned Wends of Saxony, who called themselves Sorbs, shows that there must have been some old Wendish tribe of similar complexion, from which they are descended. As the country anciently occupied by the Wiltzi included Brandenburg and the district around Berlin, it joined the limits of ancient Saxony on the west. There is evidence, arising from the survival of place-names in and near the old Wendish country, to show that these Wilte have left distinct traces of their existence in North-East Germany—for example, Wiltschau, Wilschkowitz, and Wiltsch are places in Silesia; Wilze is a place near Posen; Wilsen in Mecklenburg-Schwerin; Wilsdorf nenr Dresden; Wilzken in East Prussia; and Wilsum in Hanover.[39] Similarly, names of the same kind which can be traced back to Saxon time survive in England. If the existence of these Wilte place-names in the old Wendish country of Gennany is confirmatory evidence of the former existence in that part of Europe of a nation or tribe known as the Wiltzi or Wilte, the existence of similar names in England, dating from the Anglo-Saxon period, cannot be other than probable evidence of the settlement in England of some of these people, for no other tribe is known to have existed at that time which had a similar name. This tribal name has also survived in other countries, such as Holland, in which the Wilte formed colonies. The Polebian Wends or Wilte were located on the right bank of the Elbe, where some ships for the Saxon invasion must have been fitted out. There were Saxons on the left bank and Wilte on the right. At a later period they were in close alliance, and unless there had been peace between them, it is not likely that a Saxon expedition to England would have been organized.

Under these circumstances, if we had no evidence of Wilte or other Wends in England, it would be very difficult indeed to believe that some of them did not come among the Saxons. The general name of the Wends survives in many place-names in the old Wendish parts of Germany, such as Wendelau, Wendemark, Wendewisch, Wendhagen, and Wendorf.[40]

It is difficult to avoid the conclusion that the old Slavonic tribes not only comprised people of different tribal names, but of different ethnological characters, seeing that at the present time there are dark-complexioned Slavs and others as fair as Scandinavians. No record of the physical characters of the ancient Wends appears to have survived, but observations on the remnant of the race, who call themselves Sorbs, in Lower Saxony have been made by Beddoe. The Wendish peasants examined by him and recorded in his tables[41] showed the highest index of nigrescence of any observed by him in Germany. These observations have been confirmed by the results of the official ethnological survey of that country.[42]

The coast of the Baltic Sea as far east as the mouth of the Vistula, and beyond it, is remarkable for having been what may be called the birthplace of nations. Goths were seated east of the Vistula before the fall of the Roman Empire. and Vandals appear to have occupied a great area of country around the sources of the Vistula and the Oder. In the middle of the fifth century the Burgundians were seated in large numbers between the middle courses of these rivers, while the Slavic tribes known as Rugians were located on the Baltic coast on both sides of the Oder. The name Rugini or Rugians thus appears, at one time, to have been a comprehensive one, and to have included the tribes known later on as Wiltzi.

In the Sagas of the Norse Kings, Vindland is the name of the country of the Wends from Holstein to the east of Prussia, and as early as the middle of the tenth century we read of both Danish and Vindish Vikings as subjects of, or in the service of, Hakon, King of Denmark.[43] In this century the Wends were sometimes allies and sometimes enemies of the Danes and Norse. There is a reference to interpreters of the Wendish tongue in the Norse Sagas.[44] The Wends were sea-rovers, like their neighbours, and comprised the largest section of the ancient association or alliance known as the Jomberg Vikings.[45] An alliance was made between the Danes and the Wends by the marriage of Sweyn, King of Denmark, to Gunhild, daughter of Borislav, a King of the Wends. Cnut, King of England and Denmark, was actually King of ancient Wendland, and the force of huscarls he formed in England was partly composed of Jomberg sea-rovers who had been banished from their own country. The evidence of Wendish settlers with the Angles, Saxons, and Jutes in England rests, as far as the Rugians are concerned, on Bede's statement, and generally on the survival of customs, place-names, and folk-lore. It is certain that large colonies of Vandals were settled in Britain before the end of the

Roman occupation, and some of them may have retained their race characters until the time of the Saxon settlement. It is certain, also, that there was an immigration in the time of Cnut. The evidence of a Wendish influence in the English race, arising from these successive settlements, extending from the Roman time to the later Anglo-Saxon period, cannot, therefore, be disregarded.

The Anglo-Saxon charters[46] tell us of Wendlesbiri in Hertfordshire, Wendlescliff in Worcestershire, Wændlescumb in Berkshire, and Wendlesore, now Windsor—all apparently named from settlers called Wendel, after the name of their race.

In such Old English place-names the tribal name lingers yet, as similar names linger in North-East Germany; and in the names Wilts, Willi, Rugen, Rown, or Ruwan, and others, we may still, in all probability, trace the Wilte and Rugians—Wendic tribes of the Saxon age. In the old Germanic records the Rugians are mentioned under similar names to those found in the Anglo—Saxon charters, Ruani and Rugiani.[47]

Some manorial customs, and especially that of sole inheritance by the youngest son, may be traced with more certainty to the old Slavic nations of Europe than to the Teutonic. Inheritance by the youngest son, or junior preference, was a custom so prevalent among the Slavs that there can be little doubt it must have been almost or quite the common custom of the race. The ancient right of the youngest survives here and there in parts of Germany—in parts of Bavaria, for example—but in no Teutonic country is the evidence to be found in ancient customs or in old records of the identification of this custom with the Teutonic race as it may be identified with the Slavic. In the old Wendish country around Lubeck the custom of inheritance by the youngest son long survived, or still does, and Lubeck was the city in which during the later Saxon age in England the commerce of the Wends began to be concentrated.

There is evidence of another kind showing the connection of Wends with Danes or Northmen. At Sondevissing, in Tyrsting herrad, in the district of Scanderborg, there is a stone monument with a runic inscription stating that 'Tuva caused this barrow to be constructed. She was a daughter of Mistivi. She made it to her mother, who was the wife of Harald the Good, son of Gorm.'[48] The inscription has been assigned to the end of the tenth century, and Worsaae says: 'We know that there existed at this period a Wendish Prince named Mistivi, who in the year 986 destroyed Hamburg, possibly the same as in the inscription.' This refers to a generation earlier than that of Cnut, to the time of Sweyn, who married the daughter of Borislav, King of the Wends. During the period of Danish rule in England there are several historical references to the connection of the Wends with England. In 1029, Eric, son of Hakon, was banished by Cnut. Hakon was doubly the King's nephew, being the son of his sister and the husband of his niece Gunhild, the daughter of another sister and of Wyrtgeorn, King of the Wends.[49] There was at this time an eminent Slavonic Prince who was closely connected with Cnut, and spent some time with him in England—viz., Godescalc, son of Uto, the Wendish Prince of the Obodrites, whose exploits are recorded in old Slavonic history. The Obodrites were the Wendish people whose warlike deeds are still commemorated at Schwerin. Godescalc waged war against the Saxons of Holstein and Stormaria, but was taken prisoner. After his release he entered the service of Cnut, probably as an officer of the huscarls, and later on he married the King's daughter.

There is another trace of the Wends in an English charter of A.D. 1026, which is witnessed by Earls Godwin, Hacon, Hrani, Sihtric, and Wrytesleof. The name of the last of these is apparently Slavonic.[50] There is also a charter of Cnut, dated 1033, by which he granted to Bouige, his huscarl, land at Horton in Dorset.[51] Saxo, the early chronicler of the Danes, tells us that Cnut's Wendish kingdom was called Sembia, and it was in the Wendish war under Cnut that Godwin, the Anglo-Saxon earl, rose to distinction. As Wendland was actually part of Cnut's continental dominions,[52] the migration into England of Wendish people during his reign is easily accounted for.

There is additional evidence of the intercourse of the Wendish people of Pomerania with the people of Anglo-Saxon England in the objects that have been found. The gold ring which was found at Cöslin, on the Pomeranian coast, in 1839, Stephens says was the first instance of the discovery of a golden bracteate and Northern runes on German soil.[53] The inscription is in provincial English runes, the rune ( ᛡ ), *yo*, a slight variation of ( ᛄ ), being decisive in this respect, for, as Stephens says, it has only been found in England. The ring must be a very early one, for it contains the heathen symbols for Woden and also for the Holy Triskele (**Y**). Stephens states that it cannot well be later than the fifth century, and that it had been worn by a warrior 'who had been in England, or had gotten it thence by barter.' The style is that of six centuries earlier than the eleventh or twelfth centuries, when the Germans came to Pomerania. The well~preserved characters on the ring point to its loss at an early date after its manufacture, and thus to early communication of some kind between England and Pomerania. It may have been the much-prized, rare ornament of a Wendish chief, brought or sent from England. In any case we know that the Wends, who had no knowledge of runes, must have prized ornaments such as this, whose construction was beyond their skill, for the relics of Vandal ornaments we possess from other countries where Vandals settled are clearly in many respects rough imitations of those of the ancient Goths.[54] With this English golden finger-ring there were also two Roman golden coins, one of Theodosius the Great (379-395), and the other of Leo I. (457-474), thus fixing the probable date of the ring as the fifth century. At that time the Goths were settling down in Kent, with some Wends, probably, near to them. They can be traced in both Essex and Sussex. The coast of the Baltic, it should also be remembered, was not only Wendish in the parts nearest to the Elbe, but also Gothic in those beyond the Vistula. The discovery of this ring in old Vandal territory with the Roman coins, and especially with the very early English runic characters upon it, assists in proving that the early Goths who settled in Kent were of the same stock as those who overran so large a part of Europe during the decline of the Roman Empire. In considering this, it should also be remembered that inscribed stones discovered at Sandwich, which are marked with very early runes, and are ascribed to the same early period, still exist in Kent.[55]

The evidence we possess relating to the connection of ancient Wendland with both the earlier and later Anglo-Saxons thus points to a continued intercourse between that country and our own. It is known to have been very considerable in the time of Cnut, who was the King or overlord of the Baltic Wendland. A large discovery of coins was made at Althofthen on the Obra, in the province of Posen, not far from Brandenburg, in 1872. From sixty to seventy Anglo-Saxon coins of Æthelred and Cnut, and an Irish one of Sithric, were found in this hoard. These Anglo-Saxon coins bear the mint marks of Cambridge, London, Canterbury, Shaftesbury, Cricklade, Oxford, Stamford, Winchester, York. and other places—twenty in all.[56]

The local traces of Wendish settlers in various English counties will he stated when considering the evidence of tribal settlers in different parts of England. Among these local traces are customs and folk-lore, which were of great vitality among these people of Wendland. On this subject Magnus, the historian of the Goths and Vandals, gives us positive information. He says: 'For, as Albertus Crantzius reports of Vandalia, "great is the ove men bear to their ancestors' traditions." '[57]

[1] Morfill, 'Slavonic Literature,' 36, quoting Ptolemy.
[2] Procopius, 'Wars of the Vandals' (Greek ed., 1607). book i., p. 92. and Greek-Latin ed.. iii. 313.
[3] Latham, R. G., 'Germania of Tacitus,' Eplleg. lxxxix.
[4] Latham, R. G., loc. cit., Prolegomena, xxvii.
[5] Ibid., Prolegomena, xxvii.
[6] Ibid., xxvi.
[7] Ripley, W. Z., 'Races of Europe,' 239.
[8] Germania, Sect. xliii.
[9] Saxa Grammaticus. translated by O. Elton, 393-395.
[10] Zosimus, i., c. 68.
[11] Hodgkin, T., 'Italy and her Invaders,' 217.
[12] Codex Dipl., Index.
[13] Bunbury, E. H., 'Hist. of Ancient Geography,' ii. 591.
[14] Pliny, 'Hist. Nat.,' iv., chap. xxvii., quoted by Elton, C. I. 'Origins of Engl. Hist.,' 40.
[15] Beda, 'Eccles. Hist.,' edited by J. A. Giles, book v., chap. ix.
[16] Cottonian Liber Custumarum, Liber Albus, vol. ii., pt. ii., 645.
[17] Marsh, G. P., 'Lectures on the English Language,' Second Series. p. 55.
[18] Beda, loc. cit., book v., chap. ii.
[19] Hampson, R. T., 'The Geography at King Alfred,' p. 41.
[20] Schafarik, 'Slavonic Antiquities,' quoted by Morfill, W. R., 'Slavonic Literature,' 3·35.
[21] Cart. Sax., edited by Birch. i 416.
[22] Codex Dipl., No. 931.
[23] Ibid., No. 967.
[24] Ibid., Nos. 641 and 387.
[25] Ibid., No. 232.
[26] Ibid., No. 953.
[27] Ibid., No. 1205.

[28] *Ibid.*

[29] Hund. Rolls, vol. ii., Index.

[30] Stephens. G., 'Old Northern Runic Monuments,' iii. 122.

[31] Monumenta Germaniæ, Scriptores ii. 677, A.D. 851.

[32] Codex. Dipl., Index.

[33] Domesday Book, Index.

[34] Menzel, 'History of Germany,' i. 242.

[35] Rambaud, A., 'History of Russia,' i. 23.

[36] Magnus, J., 'Hist. de omn. Goth. Sueon. reg.,' ed. 1554, p. 13.

[37] Monumenta Germaniæ, Ann. Einh., edited by Pertz, i. 163.

[38] Mallet, M., 'Northern Antiquities,' Bohn's ed., p. 139.

[39] Rudolph, H., 'Orts Lexikon von Deutschland.'

[40] Rudolph, H., *loc. cit.*

[41] Beddoe, J., 'Races of Britain,' 207.

[42] Ripley, W. Z., 'Races of Europe,' Map.

[43] 'The Heimskringla,' translated by Laing, edited by Anderson, ii. 12.

[44] *Ibid.*, iv. 201.

[45] Mémoires de la Société Royale des Antiquaires du Nord, 1850-1860, p. 422.

[46] Codex Dipl., Nos. 826, 150, 1283, 816.

[47] Monumenta Germaniæ, iii. 461.

[48] Worsaae, J. J. A., 'Primæval Antiquities of Denmark,' p, 118.

[49] Freeman, E. A., 'Hist. of the Norman Conquest,' i. 475.

[50] Freeman, E. A., *loc. cit.*, i. 650.

[51] Codex Dipl., No. 1318.

[52] Freeman, E. A., *loc. cit.*, i. 504, Note.

[53] Stephens, G., *loc. cit.*, ii. 600.

[54] Collection, British Museum.

[55] Stephens, G., *loc. cit.*, ii. 542.

[56] Warne, C., 'Ancient Dorset,' p. 320.

[57] Magnus, O., 'Hist. omn. Goth.,' quoting Albertus Crantzius, lib. ix., chap. xxxvii.

# Chapter Seven - Our Darker Forefathers

ONE of the facts concerning the colour of the hair and eyes of the people in different counties of England at the present time, brought to light by scientific observations, is that there is a higher percentage of people of a mixed brown type living in Hertfordshire, Buckinghamshire, Wiltshire, and Dorset, than in most other counties. Except those in Cornwall and on the old Celtic borders, the inhabitants of these counties are the darkest. This is usually explained on the supposition that in the process of the Saxon settlement at British population was allowed to remain in these parts of England, which in the course of centuries became mixed with the inhabitants of Anglo-Saxon descent, and consequently the present population is more marked than those of pure descent by brown, hazel, or black eyes, with brown (chestnut), dark-brown, or black hair.[1] The counties of Hertford and Buckingham have people as dark as Wales. All investigation goes to show that this brunette outcrop is a reality. Beddoe found that the area in which there is a larger percentage of brown people in England extends from the river Lea to the Warwickshire Avon. In dealing with the circumstances of the settlement, these ethnological facts must receive consideration. The survival of a British population is a possible explanation, and the one which appears to be the most natural. As there are some difficulties in this conclusion, the question arises, Is there any other way in which the origin of these mixed brown people, surrounded by others of a somewhat fairer complexion, can be explained? An alternative explanation is that people of a darker race may have come with the Angles, Saxons, or Danes, and have settled largely in these parts of the country. There is circumstantial evidence that people of a brown or dark complexion did come into England during the time of both the Saxon and the Danish settlements, and this may now be summarised.

First, we have the evidence that Wends were among the settlers either during the early period or later in alliance with the Danes. The Wends, specifically so called by the Germans, included some tribes much darker than the Saxons and Angles, as the remnant of the race still called Wends living on the border of Saxony and Prussia at the present time shows. They are the darkest people in Northern Germany, according to the official census. From 26 to 29 per cent. of the children of the Wendish district of Lusatia, south of Dresden, were shown by this census to be brunettes, notwithstanding the admixture of race with the much fairer people of Teutonic descent which has been going on along this borderland since the dawn of history. All the Slav nations are not dark. Some are as fair as the Scandinavians, while others, such as the Wends and the Czechs of Bohemia, are dark.

The Wendish place-names in Buckinghamshire and on its borders help to show that some people of this race probably settled in that county. Huntingdon tells us that during the later Saxon period they formed part of the Scandian hosts.[2] They were in alliance with the Norwegians, Danes, Swedes, Goths, and Frisians, or, in any case, people of these races were acting together in the Danish expeditions against England. It is likely, therefore, that when permanent settlements were formed adjoining townships would be occupied by people of this alliance. This consideration helps us to identify Wendlesbury in Hertfordshire.[3] Wendover and its neighbourhood in Buckinghamshire, the Anglo-Saxon Wendofra,[4] and Windsor, anciently Wendlesore,[5] close to the southern border of that county, were probably named after settlers who were Wends.

If British people were left, as suggested, like an eddy between the main lines of the Anglo-Saxon advance east and west of these counties, would it not be very surprising that the advancing Saxons should make no use of the existing Roman roads—the Watling Street, Ikenield Street, and Akeman Street—which passed through parts of these shires, while the Ermine Street also went through Hertfordshire? To suppose that invaders and subsequent settlers would have forsaken the excellent roads which the Romans had made, and in their advance would have passed through the more difficult country east and west of them, thus leaving undisturbed a British population. is most unlikely.

Secondly. these counties are not specially marked by the survival of Celtic place-names, nor by a dialect containing words of Celtic origin. In Anglo-

Saxon times there was, however, a place named Wealabroc, in Buckingham-shire.

Thirdly, it should be remembered that the western border of Buckingham-shire was at one time the western frontier of the Danelaw, which comprised fifteen counties known as Fiftonshire, until after the Norman Conquest, and that Danish law survived for more than a century after the Conquest east of this frontier.[6] This fact points to a population largely Scandian. There is, in addition, evidence that points to Norwegians of a brunette appearance as another source whence brown-complexioned people may have come into England. On the south-east coast of Norway, and here and there on the coast farther north, a population is met with which differs from the usual Norwe-gian type, and this has been referred by anthropologists to a very ancient settlement there of the pre historic brown race that survives in the highlands of Central Europe, and is known as the brown Alpine race.[7] This race is be-lieved to have extended before the dawn of history much further northwards in Germany. The brown people of Norway are well seen in Joderen, where Arbo found the blonde and really dark-haired people about equally repre-sented. The Norwegian brunettes differ from the typical blondes of that country in two other particulars. First, they are broad-headed, while the blondes, which comprise the bulk of the nation, are long-headed; and not only are the broader-headed people of these coast-districts darker as a whole, but in them the broad-headed individuals tend to be darker than the other type, as Arbo has clearly shown.[8] Secondly, the broadest-headed peo-ple of these localities in Norway incline to shortness of stature below that of the typical Norwegian.

From Huntingdon's statement concerning Vandals as Danish allies and these considerations, there appeals to be evidence to account for the greater percentage of brunettes, or the greater tendency to the brunette type, that prevails in Hertfordshire and Buckinghamshire over the adjoining counties, without necessarily concluding that such an ethnological phenomenon can only have been caused by a remnant of the British population. It is, indeed, an unlikely district for Celtic people to have been left in large numbers. On the contrary, in view of its excellent communications, it is a country where the conquest by the early settlers might be expected to have been most thor-ough. Whether the Hertfordshire and Buckinghamshire brunettes are partly due to the settlement of Wends and Norwegians of the dark type, as now suggested, or to some other cause, the British theory as a complete explana-tion. in view of the facts, appears improbable. The chief lines of the Anglo-Saxon advance during the early settlement were the navigable rivers and the Roman roads. The Scandian advances into the country during their con-quests and later settlements must have been along the same lines of commu-nication. On one occasion, at least, we read of the Danish host presumably using the Ikenield way, on the march from East Anglia into Dorset.[9]

This consideration of the probable origin of the great proportion of bru-nettes in two of the south midland counties of England leads us to that of colour-names as surnames and place-names, which may probably have been derived from their original settlers. For example, there is the common name Brown. This has been derived from the Anglo-Saxon *brun*, signifying brown. It is not reasonable to doubt that when our forefathers called a man Brun or Brown, they gave him this name as descriptive of his brown complexion. The probability that the brunettes were common is supported by the frequent references to persons named Brun in Anglo-Saxon literature. Brun was a name not confined to England in the Anglo-Saxon and later periods. On the contrary, we find that it was a common name in ancient Germany.[10] The typical place-name Bruninga-feld occurs in a charter of Æthelstan dated A.D. 938, 'in loco qui Bruninga-feld dicitur.'[11] Brunesham, Hants, is mentioned in a charter of Edward the Elder about A.D. 900.[12] Brunesford is another suggestive name[13] Brunman is mentioned as a personal name in Anglo-Saxon records of the eleventh century, and examples of the name Bruning are somewhat numerous in documents of the same period.[14] At the present time old place-names, of which the word *Braun* forms the chief part, such as Braunschweig or Brunswick, are common in Germany.[15] The custom of calling people by colour-names from their personal appearance, or places after them, was clearly not peculiar to our own country. It is probable that the name Brunswick was derived from the brown complexion of its original inhabitants. The map published by Ripley, based on the official ethnological survey of Germany, shows that parts of the country near Brunswick have a higher percentage of brunettes than the districts further north. Beddoe also made observations on a number of Brunswick peasantry, and records some remarkable facts relating to the proportion of brunettes among those who came under his observation.[16]

In view of this, and the evidence relating to the use of the Anglo-Saxon word *brun* in English place-names, we are not, I think, justified in deciding that all English names which begin with *Brun*, modernized into *Burn* in many cases by the well-known shifting of the *r* sound, have been derived from *brun*, a bourn or stream. rather than from *brun*, brown. Such names as Bruninga-feld[17] and Brunesham point to the opposite conclusion, that Brun in such names refers to people, probably so named from their complexions. If a large proportion of the settlers in the counties of Buckingham and Hertford were of a brown complexion, it is clear that they would have been less likely to have been called Brun or Brown by their neighbours than brunettes would in other counties, where such a complexion may have been rarer, and consequently more likely to have attracted the notice of the people around them. It is not probable that people who were originally designated by the colour-names Brown, Black, Gray, or the like, gave themselves these names. They most likely received them from others.

The evidence concerning brown people in England during the Anglo-Saxon period which can be derived from the place-name Brun is supplemented by that supplied in at least some of the old place-names beginning with *dun* and *duning*. Dun is an Old English word denoting a colour partaking of brown and black, and where it occurs at the beginning of words in such a combination as Duningland,[18] it is possible that it refers to brown people or their children, rather than to the Anglo-Celtic word *dún*, a hill or fortified place.

As regards the ancient brown race or races of North Europe, there can be no doubt of their existence in the south-east of Norway and in the east of Friesland.[19] There can be no doubt about the important influence which the old Wendish race has had in the north-eastern parts of Germany in transmitting to their descendants a more brunette complexion than prevails among the people of Hanover, Holstein, and Westphalia, of more pure Teutonic descent. We cannot reasonably doubt that, in view of such a survival of brown people as we find at the present time in the provinces of North Holland, Drenthe and Overijssel, which form the hinterland of the ancient Frisian country, numerous brunettes must have come into England among the Frisians. It would be as unreasonable to doubt this as it would to think that during the Norwegian immigration into England all the brown people of Norway were precluded from leaving their country because they were brunettes, or that the Wends, who undoubtedly settled in England in considerable numbers, were none of them of a brunette type.

The survival of some people with broad heads and of a brown type in parts of Drenthe, Guelderland, and Overijssel appears unmistakable.[20] They present a remarkable contrast in appearance to their Frisian neighbours, who are of a different complexion in regard to hair and skin, and are specially characterized as long-headed.

It was in Gelderland that ancient Thiel was situated, and the men of Thiel and those of Brune were apparently recognised as different people from the real Frisians, for in the later Anglo-Saxon laws relating to the sojourn of strangers within the City of London it is stated that 'the men of the Emperor may lodge within the city wherever they please, except those of Tiesle and of Brune.'[21]

The evidence concerning the origin of the broad-headed Slavonic nations connects them with the broad-headed and still older Alpine brown race of Central Europe. The most generally accepted theory among anthropologists as to the physical relationship of the Slavs is that they were always, as the majority of them are to-day, of the same stock as the broad-headed Alpine race.[22] This old race has sometimes been called the Celtic, but it is perhaps more accurate to say that it is the very ancient stock from which the old Celtic race of the British Bronze Age was an offshoot. This curious circumstance, consequently, comes before us in considering the Anglo-Saxon settlement of England. If the brunette character of the people of any part of England at the present time is due to a survival of the race characters of the Celts of the British Bronze Age, and if this same character has been caused partly by people of a darker complexion and broad heads settling as immigrants among the fair-haired and long-headed Teutons in other parts of England, this racial character in both cases can be traced along different lines to the same distant source.

The consideration of the evidence that people of brunette complexions were among the Anglo-Saxon settlers in England leads on to that of people of a still darker hue, the dark, black, or brown-black settlers. Probably there must have been some of these among the Anglo-Saxons. for we meet with the personal names Blacman, Blæcman, Blakernan. Blacaman, Blac'sunu, Blæcca, and Blacheman, in various documents of the period.[23] Blæcca was an ealdorman of Lindsey who was converted by Paulinus; Blæcman was the son of Ealric or Edric, a descendant of Ida, ancestor of Ealhred. King of Bernicia, and so on.[24] The same kind of evidence is met with among the oldest place-names. Blacmannebergh is mentioned in an Anglo-Saxon charter;[25] Blachemanestone was the name of a place in Dorset,[26] and Blachemenestone that of a place in Kent[27] Blacheshale and Blachenhale are Domesday names of places in Somerset, and Blachingelei occurs in the Domesday record of Surrey. The name Blachemene occurs in the Hertfordshire survey, and Blachene in Lincoln. Among the earliest names of the same kind in the charters we find Blácanden in Hants and Blácandon in Dorset. The places called Blachemanestone in Dorset and Blachemenestone in Kent were on or quite close to the coast, a circumstance which points to the settlers having come to these places by water rather than to a survival of black people of the old Celtic race having been left in them.

Among old place-names of the same kind in various counties, some of which are met with in later, but still old, records, we find Blakeney in Gloucestershire; Blakeney in Norfolk; Blakenham in Suffolk; Blakemere[28] an ancient hamlet, and Blakesware, near Ware in Hertfordshire. This Hertford name is worthy of note in reference to what has been said concerning the brunettes in that county at the present time. Another circumstance connected with these names which it is desirable to remember is the absence of evidence to show that the Old English ever called any of the darker-complexioned Britons brown men or black men. Their name for them was Wealas. So far as I am aware, not a single instance occurs in which the Welsh are mentioned in any Anglo-Saxon document as black or brown people; on the contrary, the Welsh annals mention black Vikings on the coast, as if they were men of unusual personal appearance.[29]

There is another old word used by the Anglo-Saxons to denote black or brown-black—the word *sweart.* The personal names Suart and Sueart may have been derived from this word, and may have originally denoted people of a dark-brown or black complexion. Some names of this kind are mentioned in the Domesday record of Buckinghamshire and Lincolnshire. These may be of Scandinavian origin, for the ekename or nickname Svarti is found in the Northern Sagas.[30] Halfden the Black was the name of a King of Norway who died in 863. The so-called black men of the Anglo-Saxon period probably included some of the darker Wendish people among them, immigrants or descendants of people of the same race as the ancestors of the Sorbs of Lausatia on the borders of Saxony and Prussia at the present day. Some of the darker Wends may well have been among the Black Vikings referred to in the Irish annals,[31] as well as in those of Wales,[32] and may have been the people who have left the Anglo-Saxon name Blacmanne-berghe, which occurs in one of the charters,[33] Blachemenestone on the Kentish coast, and Blachemanstone on the Dorset coast. As late as the time of the Domesday Survey we meet with records of people apparently named after their dark complexions. In Buckinghamshire, Blacheman, Suartinus, and others are mentioned; in Sussex, one named Blac; in Suffolk. Blakemannus and Suartingus; and others at Lincoln. The invasion of the coast of the British Isles by Vikings of a dark or black complexion rests on historical evidence which is too circumstantial to admit of doubt. In the Irish annals the Black Vikings are called Dubh-Ghenti, or Black Gentiles.[34] These Black Gentiles on some occasions fought against other plunderers of the Irish coasts known as the Fair Gentiles, who can hardly have been others than the fair Danes or Northmen. In the year 851 the Black Gentiles came to Athcliat[35]—i.e., Dublin. In 852 we are told that eight ships of the Finn-Ghenti arrived and fought against the Dubh-Ghenti for three days, and that the Dubh~Ghenti were victorious. The Black Vikings appear at this time to have had a settlement in or close to Dublin, and during the ninth century were much in evidence on the Irish coast. In 877 a great battle was fought at Lock-Cuan between them and the Fair Gentiles, in which Albann, Chief of the Black Gentiles, fell.[36] He may well have been a chieftain of the race of the Northern Sorbs of the Mecklenburg coast.

There is still another way in which men of black hair or complexions may have come into England—viz., as thralls among the Norse invaders. In his translation of 'Orosius,' King Alfred inserts the account which Othere, the Norse mariner, gave him of the tribute in skins, eiderdown, whalebone, and ropes made from whale and seal skins, which the Northern Fins, now called Lapps, paid to the Northmen. Their descendants are among the darkest people of Europe, and as they were thralls, some of them may have accompanied their lords. The Danes and Norse, having the general race characteristics of tall, fair men, must have been sharply distinguished in appearance from Vikings, such as those of Jomborg, for many of these were probably of a dark complexion. There is an interesting record of the descent of dark sea-rovers on the coast of North Wales in the 'Annales Cambriæ,' under the year 987, which tells us that Gothrit, son of Harald, with black men, devastated Anglesea, and captured two thousand men. Another entry in the same record tells us that Meredut redeemed the captives from the black men. This account in the Welsh annals receives some confirmation in the Sagas of the Norse Kings, one of which tells us that Olav Trygvesson was for three years, 982-985, King in Vindland—i.e., Wendland—where he resided with his Queen, to whom he was much attached; but on her death, whose loss be greatly felt, he had no more pleasure in Vindland. He therefore provided himself with ships and went on a Viking expedition, first plundering Friesland and the coast all the way to Flanders. Thence he sailed to Northumberland, plundered its coast and those of Scotland, Man, Cumberland, and

Bretland—*i.e.*, Wales—during the years 985-988, calling himself a Russian under the name of Ode.[37] From these two separate accounts there can be but little doubt, notwithstanding the differences in the names, of the descent on the coast of North Wales at this time of dark sea-rovers under a Scandinavian leader, and it is difficult to see who they were if not dark-complexioned Wends or other allies of the Norsemen. It is possible some of these dark Vikings may have been allies or mercenaries from the South of Europe, where the Norse made conquests.

As regards the evidence concerning black-haired settlers in England at a still earlier date, there is the story of the two Anglian priests named the Black and Fair Hewald, who, following the example of Willibord among the Frisians, went into Saxony as missionaries, and on coming to a village were admitted to the house of the head man, who promised to protect them, and send them on to the ealdorman of the district. They devoted themselves to prayer and religious observances, which were misunderstood by the pagan rustics, who apparently were afraid of magical arts. At any rate, these strange rites, so novel to them, aroused suspicion among the people, who thought that if these Angles were allowed to meet the ealdorman they might draw him away from their gods, and before long draw away the whole province from the observances of their forefathers. So they slew both the Black and Fair Hewald, whose names in subsequent Christian time were, and still are, held in high honour in Westphalia.[38] It is a touching story, and one that tells us more than the devotion, inspired by Christian zeal to risk their lives, which these missionaries showed for the conversion of men of their own race; for, as their names indicate, they bore in their different complexions evidence of the existence of the fair and dark people among the Anglo-Saxon stock.

As already mentioned, the name Brunswick appears to be one of significance, and the Wendish names in that part of Germany, Wendeburg, Wendhausen, and Wenden, may be compared with the Buckinghamshire Domesday names Wendovre, Weneslai, and Wandene, and with Wenriga or Wenrige in Hertfordshire. The probable connection of the Wends—some tribes of whom, such as the Sorbs, are known to have been dark—with parts of Germany near Brunswick, and with parts of Herts and Bucks, is shown by these names. Domesday Book tells us of huscarls in Buckinghamshire, and of people who bore such names as Suarting, Suiert, Suen, Suert. and Suiuard, among its land-holders, and it is difficult to avoid the conclusion that such names refer to people of dark complexions. Among the lahmens of Lincoln, a very Danish town, there were also apparently some so-called Danes of a dark complexion, for Domesday Book mentions Suartin, son of Gribold; Suardine, son of Hardenut; and Suartine Sortsbrand, son of Ulf.

In view of the facts pointing to settlements of Wends and dark-haired people in the counties of Hertford and Buckingham, the survival of the custom of junior inheritance at Cheshunt and Hadham in Herts is of interest. In cases of intestacy the land in the eastern part of Cheshunt,[39] or 'below bank,' which

72

is by far the greater part of the parish, descends to the youngest son by ancient custom, and that custom, traced to its most probable home, leads us to Eastern Germany, and to the old Slavic tribes which once occupied it, as will be fully considered in a subsequent chapter.

From the evidence mentioned, the impression left on the mind is that our Old English forefathers could not have been men of three ancient nations only, Jutes, Saxons, and Angles. These names, in reference to the conquest and colonization of England, were but general names for tribal people in alliance, generally the name of the largest section of such allies. They were no doubt convenient names, but cannot be regarded as ethnological designations. This has become apparent from the skulls and other remains found in Anglo-Saxon burial-places. The shapes and special characteristics of these skulls, whether from the so-called Anglian districts or Saxon parts of England, present such marked contrasts that anthropologists are unable to ascribe them all to one race of people. A minority of those found in ancient cemeteries in Sussex, Wiltshire, and the Eastern Counties, present such typical differences from the majority in each district as to leave no doubt that they represent a variety of race or people descended from a fusion of races. The easiest explanation of this is, of course, to turn to the ancient Briton, and generally the remote Briton of the Bronze Age known as the Round Barrow man. Where in early cemeteries Saxon or Anglian skulls have been found presenting characteristics which are clearly not of the Teutonic type, the early British inhabitant of the Bronze Age has usually been called in as an ancestor. The typical old Teutonic skull is dolichocephalic, the skull of the British people of the Bronze Age in brachycephalic. The inference that there was a fusion of race between the Saxons and Angles and people descending from men of the Bronze Age is easily drawn. There is, however, one difficulty. The Britons of the Bronze Age lived about 500 B.C., a date which may fairly be taken to represent the time of the Round Barrow men. The Angles and Saxons are usually said to have come here not earlier than about 500 A.D. There are, therefore, a thousand years between the two periods, and in that interval was the period of the Roman rule, during which men of almost every Roman province served with the legions in Britain, and in many recorded cases some of them settled here, and presumably left descendants. In view of this racial fusion which must have gone on, it is difficult to believe that the Romano-Briton of the early Anglo-Saxon period possessed the same skull characteristics as the much more remote man of the Bronze Age, who may not have been his ancestor at all. Moreover, the Welsh also, who may be supposed to be descended from this later British stock, are not broad-headed.

From what has been said of the presence of broad-headed people of a brunette type in parts of Norway, among the much more numerous long-headed people of a fair complexion who formed the bulk of the Norwegian nation, it will be seen that the facts point to an early broad-headed brown race, some of whom settled on the Norwegian coast, the long-headed fair race of the typical Norse variety having perhaps subsequently conquered them. In any case, we find evidence sufficient to justify the inference that probably the early broad-headed people were brown. The same result is obtained by the study of the broad-headed people of Central Europe at the present day, the descendants presumably of the old Alpine brown race. The same evidence is afforded by the remnant of the Wends, whose skulls are broad, and whose complexions are more or less brown at the present day, notwithstanding their fusion with the Germans. We have thus existing in Norway and parts of Germany at the present time people whose ethnological characteristics appear to agree with those of a section of the Anglo-Saxon people in England. It does not, of course, admit of proof that the broad-headed skulls, which occur in a small minority in Anglo-Saxon cemeteries, were the skulls of people of a brunette complexion. Similarly, we are unable to prove that the people who are called Brun, Brunrnan, or Bruning, in Saxon charters or other documents were broad-headed; but in view of the ethnological survival to the present day in various parts of North Europe, from which our Anglo-Saxon forefathers came, of broad-headed people of the brunette type, we can point in England to the fact that broad skulls are found in Anglo-Saxon graves, and to the historical fact that there were brown people in England during the Anglo-Saxon period, and there the evidence must be left. It may, however, be borne in mind that as brown passes into dark brown or black, the literary evidence concerning brown Anglo-Saxons is strengthened by that relating to the black men, or to those desgnated by the old brown-black word *sweart*, and in some cases, perhaps, even by the old word *dun*.

The evidence of brown people of the Wendish race may, however, be carried further by the comparison of surviving names in North-East Germany with similar surviving names in England. Those of Wendlesbury, Wandsworth (Wendelesworth), Windsor (Wendlesore), find their parallels in names in the old Wendish country of Mecklenburg, where similar names are to be found—such as Wanden, the name of a province and place on the border of ancient Wendland, and similar names in Brunswick, to which some of the Wends probably migrated. The name Wendland also survives in Hanover, where a remnant of the Wendish language died out only two centuries ago. In these names we discern a connection of the places with the Wends, who are at the present time the darkest people of Northern Germany. They were Slavs, whose line of migration in some far-distant era was from the country around the sources of the river Oder, down the wide valley of that river in Silesia to the Baltic coast of Mecklenburg and Pomerania.[40] This migration is marked at the present time by a greater percentage of people of the brunette type[41] in this district than prevails on its eastern or western sides, where fusion with other fairer-coloured races has been going on since the dawn of history. Whereas the country east and west of the valley of the Oder was found by the German Ethnological Survey to contain from 5 to 10 per cent. of brunettes among the present population, the country which marks the migration of the ancient Wends to the Mecklenburg coast contained 11 to 15 per cent. From this evidence and that of the complexion of the Wends of Saxony at the present time we are warranted in considering the ancient Wends to have been brunettes, or to have comprised tribes who were. It is on account of this historic migration, says Ripley, that Saxony, Brandenburg, and Mecklenburg are less purely Teutonic to-day in respect to pigmentation than they once were[42] Not only is there a greater percentage of brunettes in these parts of Germany than is shown in the purely Teutonic parts of that country, but the whole East of Germany contains a population which is broader-headed, shading off imperceptibly into countries where pure Slavic languages are in daily use. The connection with our own country, in its subsequent consequences, of this great migration of people having broad heads and dark complexions through Silesia into Mecklenburg is one of the most interesting considerations indirectly concerned with the Anglo-Saxon race.

[1] Ripley, W. Z., 'The Races of Europe,' p. 323, and Haddon, A. C., 'The Study of Man,' pp. 38, 39.
[2] Henry of Huntingdon's Chronicle, Bohn's ed., p. 148.
[3] Codex Dipl., 826.
[4] Dipl. Angl. Ævi Sax., by B. Thorpe, 527.
[5] Codex Dipl., 816.
[6] Cottonian Liber Custumarium in Liber Albus, ii. 625.
[7] Ripley, W. A., loc. cit., p. 206, and Map, ibid., quoting Arbo.
[8] Ibid., p. 208.
[9] Asser's 'Life of Alfred,' Bohn's ed., 263.
[10] Monumenta Germaniæ, edited by Pertz, Indices.
[11] Dipl. Angl. Ævi Sax., p. 186.
[12] Ibid., 146.
[13] Codex Dipl., Index.
[14] Searle, W. G., 'Onomasticon Anglo-Saxonicum.'
[15] Rudolph, H., 'Orts Lexikon von Deutschland.'
[16] Beddoe, J., 'Races in Britain,' 207–211.
[17] Dipl. Angl. Ævi Sax., 186.
[18] Codex Dipl., No. 283.
[19] Réclus, E., 'Nouvelle Géographie Universelle.' iv. 252.

[20] Réclus, E., loc. cit., iv. 252.
[21] Liber Albus, ii. 63, and ii. 531.
[22] Ripley, W. Z., loc cit., 355.
[23] Searle, W. G., loc. cit.
[24] Ibid.
[25] Codex Dipl.. No. 730.
[26] Domesday Book, i. 84 b.
[27] Ibid.
[28] Chauney, Sir H., 'Historical Antiquities of Hartfordshire,' 265.
[29] Annales Cambriæ, A.D. 987.
[30] 'Corpus Poeticum Boreale,' by Vigfusson and York Powell, Index.
[31] Chronicum Scotorum, edited by W. M. Hennessy, 151, 167.
[32] Annales Cambriæ, A.D. 987.
[33] Codex Dipl., No. 730.
[34] Chronicum Scotorum, p. 151.
[35] Ibid.
[36] Ibid., 167.
[37] 'The heimskringla,' translated by S. Laing, edited by Anderson, ii. 110, 111.
[38] Bright, W., 'Early English Church History,' p. 384.
[39] Bone, J. W., Notes and Queries, Seventh Series, ix. 206.
[40] Ripley, W. Z., loc. cit., p. 244.
[41] Ibid.
[42] Ripley, W. Z., loc. cit., p. 245.

# Chapter Eight - Danes, and Other Tribal Immigrants from The Baltic Coasts

THE settlement of Danes in England, which began before Bede's time, went on apparently more or less continuously after the eighth century. They are mentioned by the name Dene in early Anglo—Saxon records and in the 'Traveller's Song,' and by various names, such as Dacians, Daucnnes, and Scyldings in other ancient writings. Some of them were also known by names derived from the islands they inhabited or their Scandinavian provinces, such as Skanians from the province of Skane.

One of the earliest traces of the Danish name in England is Deniseshurne, mentioned by Bede, apparently a place in Northumberland. Another early name of the same kind is Denceswyrth in Berkshire,[1] in a Saxon charter about A.D. 811. The Anglo-Saxon names Denesig, now Dengey, in Essex,[2] Denetun or Denton in Kent, and Densige, appear to have been derived from those of individuals or families who were Danes, while the name Dentuninga, now Dentun, in Northamptonshire, apparently denotes a kindred of the same race. The Domesday Hundred name Danais, or Daneis, in Hertfordshire, is also apparently derived from the same people.

Two English woodlands bore old Danish names—viz., Danes Wood, now Dean Forest, in Glouoestershire, and part of the Forest of Essex, which was called in Danish literature 'Daneskoven,' or the Danish Forest.[3] Some of the tribal names of the Danes are known—viz., South Dene, North Dene, East Dene, and West Dene. Another branch of the nation is called by the name Gar Dene, or Gar Danes. The poem of Beowulf begins with a reference to them:

'What we of Gar Danes
  In yore days
Of people Kings.
  How the Æthelings
  Power advanced
Of Scyld-Scefing
  To the hosts of enemies
To many tribes.'

Who these Gar Danes were cannot be with certainty determined. There is a trace of them to be found in England, as will be stated later on, and they are supposed to have derived their name from their distinctive weapon, the spear. There were Scandinavian people settled on the south and east coasts of the Baltic among the Slavs and Eastmen who were known by the name of Gardar.[4] In the tenth and eleventh centuries these colonial settlers in Russia were strong enough to maintain a Scandinavian kingdom, also called Gardar,[5] or Gardarike, the name being derived from the many castles and strongholds (gardar), probably earthworks, which they made for defence.

The migrations of Scandinavians certainly began long before the English Conquest, and their settlements on the east coast of the Baltic point to the probability of some Eastmen having been among the allies of the Danes, and perhaps of the Goths, in their invasions of England. Old Scandian colonies have been traced in Courland and Livonia by the discovery of sepulchres similar to those of the Iron Age in Scandinavia. In Esthonia, also, the names of places and of the islands off the coast point to such settlements—Nargö, Rogö, Odinsholm, Nuckö, Worms, Dagö, and Runö. The old Danish empire extended over all the countries bordering on the Skagerac, and hence Dane became synonymous in English with Scandinavian, and the old Norrena language was called the Dönsk, or Danish, tongue. The later Danish empire of Cnut comprised part of Mecklenburg as well as the Cimbric Chersonese.[6] He was thus King of the Wends as well as of the Danes. During the time of their supremacy in the Baltic, Danes were the natural leaders of any confederation of the Baltic tribes in warlike expeditions for conquests or foreign settlements, as the Goths and Angles were before them. Skane, Halland, and Blekinge, now provinces of Sweden, formed part of the kingdom of Denmark for 800 years until 1658, when they were united to Sweden.[7] From what has already been said concerning the lands in which the Angles lived before they came to England, it will be seen that the probability of some Danes having come into England with them is great. Bede affirms as a positive fact that some of the English in his time were descended from Danes, and the early place-names confirm his statement. They were a colonizing race, and it is probable that the Scandinavian settlements in the North-West of Russia began as early as the eighth century, which was that in which Bede lived.

The greater Denmark from which the early settlers came was that which was known to King Alfred. When sailing into the Baltic, Othere, the Scandinavian mariner, told the King that he had Denmark on his left, and Zealand and many islands on his right. This was the kingdom whose capital was Lund in Skane, in the south-east of what is now Sweden, and it must have been from that country that many of those settlers came who have left their traces in some old Danish place-names that still cling to their English homes, such as the Domesday Scen and Scan names, which are only found in England in the Danish settled districts. Others, such as the old places named Lund in Lincolnshire and the East Riding, are apparently derived from their former homes in Skane. As already stated, Dan and Angul are mentioned by Saxo, the twelfth-century Danish historian, as the mythological ancestors of the Danes, and of these he tells us that Angul gave his name to the Anglians.[8] In this tradition we may see the probability of some very close connection in their origin between the Anglian and Danish races. Although Zealand had become the centre of the Danish monarchy when Saxo wrote in the twelfth century, yet Skane still formed an important part of it, and the Skanians are very frequently mentioned by him. In the twelfth century there were no doubt many more historical runic inscriptions existing within the limits of the ancient

Danish kingdom than the few hundreds which still remain, for the Danes were certainly acquainted with runes.

Denmark was long divided into three States or kingdoms. and we find three principal monuments connected with the election custom of their Kings—viz., at Lund in Skane, Lethra in Zealand, and Viburg in Jutland.[9] It has been said that the Anglo-Saxon settlers were people of various tribes speaking a common language. This was no doubt the case to a very large extent, but as Skandians are proved to have been among the Jutish and Anglian settlers by the evidence of runic inscriptions, and as the names for many objects, persons, and tribes in the Old Norrena or Dönsk tongue are different from their names in the old Germanic languages, it would, perhaps, be more accurate to say that the dialects of the settlers were mutually intelligible. The many synonymous words which came into use in Old English are proof that the dialects of different tribes were blended into that speech. The old Dönsk tongue was the language of Northern England, and it, or something very like it, must have been the speech of the Northern Angles. It must have been the dominant language used on the coasts of the Baltic, and we may therefore look to allies of the early Anglian settlers in England, and of the later Danish ones, for traces of other immigrants from the Baltic coasts.

The earliest example of the language of the Old English, or one of the earliest, is the Saga and poem known as the 'Beowulf.' Its scenery and personages are Danish,[10] and by Danish we must understand that early kingdom whose seat was in what is now Sweden. Marsh says: 'The whole poem belongs, both in form and essence, to the Scandinavian, not to the Germanic School of Art. The substance of "Beowulf." either as a Saga or as a poem, came over, I believe, with some of the conquerors, and its existence in Anglo-Saxon literature I consider one of the many proofs of an infusion of the Scandinavian element in the immigration.' This poem in its written form is of about the eighth century.

The extent to which the dialects of the old Northern language were spoken in England during the Anglo-Saxon period has probably been underestimated. Wherever there were Northern settlers, some dialect of the Northern speech must have been used, and evidence will be shown in succeeding chapters of its use in other parts of England than the Northern and Eastern Counties. To how great an extent this was the language of the Northern Counties in the early part of the tenth century may be estimated from the statement in the Egils Saga that in the reign of Æthelstan almost every family of note in Northern England was Danish on the father's or mother's side.[11]

In the account of the early history of the Danes which Saxo gives us, we read of the part which other nations of the Baltic coasts took in the war between them and the Swedes. There were Kurlanders, Esthonians. Livonians, and Slavs,[12] from the eastern or southern coasts of the Baltic Sea engaged in that war, and it is by such alliances rendered probable that in expeditions against England the Danes or Northmen also had Eastmen of these maritime nations acting with them. If alliances could exist in the later Anglo-Saxon period, there is no reason why they might not have existed during the time when the Danes were fighting for new homes and largely settling in England, or that some of these Baltic allied people may not have settled in England with them under the Danish name. Under that name Fins also may have come among other so-called Danes, and there is evidence that a few of them did come. Finland, the most northern of the Baltic countries, inhabited by people allied to, or perhaps even descended in part from, the old Gothic and Scandinavian stock, has been through the range of history, and still is, more advanced in the arts of civilization than its Slavic neighbours, and its geographical position in ancient time brought it into commercial intercourse with Scandinavia and Denmark.

There are reasons for believing that the Finnic race occupied part of the Northern peninsula at an early period in the history of Scandinavia. At a remote time, which tradition places at the beginning of the Iron Age in that country, but which may have been much earlier, the country was overrun by people of a different race from its aboriginal inhabitants—*i.e.*, by tribes of similar racial characters to those of the early Gothic or Teutonic stock. These newcomers are supposed to have driven the aborigines, who are believed to have been of Ugrian descent, northwards, where a remnant still exists, and are known as Lapps. These were, however, in ancient time also called Fins, and the name Finmark as the boundary of their country has come down to our time. The Fins of the Baltic, the inhabitants of the present Finland, are, however, now a different race from the so-called Northern Finns or the Lapps, and although they have affinity in language,[13] they were known as distinct in the time of King Alfred.

The Fins of Finland are for the most part blonde, and a longer-headed race than the Slavs, like the long-headed Letts and Lithuanians, and, like them, are of mixed descent. They are apparently, from all the evidence available concerning them, an offshoot from the same trunk as the Teutons,[14] or at least of the Aryan stock.

The Fins, who called themselves Quains,[15] are the same people as the Cwæns, which was their native name mentioned by King Alfred. In his 'Orosius' Alfred mentions both Fins and Scride Fins or Lapps, and describes the locality of each race. After mentioning the country of the Swedes and the Esthonian arm of the sea, he says: 'To the north over the waste is Cwénland, and to the north-west are the Scride Finns, and to the west the Northmen.'[16] In the Anglo-Saxon times some of the Cwæns or Fins occupied part of the Scandinavian peninsula as far south as Helsingland, on the east of Sweden, opposite to Finland, where the name Helsingfors probably denotes some ancient connection with Helsingland. As the Lapps were called Skidfinnen by the Norse, and are still called Fins by them, some confusion has arisen in the use of this name. As applied to natives of Finland it is not a native name. We may, however, look for traces of them in England under the name Cwén or Quén, as well as Fin, as we may of the Wands under their Northern name of Vinthr. If any Fins took part in the colonization of England, it must necessarily have been as members of a body of settlers under another name, probably with Swedes or Danes. As the true Fins have a connection with the Teutons in race, some of them may have been included in the Anglian or Danish hosts, and without the alliance or friendship of these nations, who at different times were masters of the Danish islands, it is not likely that any of them would have left the Baltic. It is in some of those parts of England which were occupied by Danes that traces of Fins, Lechs, and other Eastmen from the Baltic are found, where they may well have settled as Danish allies.

Among European nations generally the skull is orthognathous—*i.e.*, the plane of the face traced downwards forms an angle more or less approaching a right angle with the plane of the base of the skull. Among some of the tribes of Russia, of Ugrian or Mongol descent, prognathous skulls—*i.e.*, with this angle less than a right angle, and consequently with the lower and upper jaw-bones projecting iorwards—may be observed, and to a less extent the same ethnological characteristic is met with among some of the Russian races of mixed descent, whose ancestors presumably were at one time nearer neighbours to the Mongol tribes. This characteristic of prominent jaw-bones is of some importance in considering the evidence of the migration of the Mongols and their admixture with other races, seeing that examples of prognathous skulls have been found in Britain, and a decided tendency to prognathism may still occasionally be observed in individuals of NorthernEuropean races.

The Esthonians of the Baltic coast south of the Gulf of Finland are a people more or less allied to the Fins on its northern shore. De Quatrefages, who examined some skulls of Esthonians, discovered that one in three under his observation showed a well-marked prognathism. He says: 'Orthognathism being considered one of the attributes of the white rice, the existence of a prognathism very frequent and very pronounced appears to me difficult to understand.' He goes on to say: 'It becomes easy if we admit that it (prognathism) was, if not general, at least very frequent in the race, which was the first people of Western Europe, and that it is still represented among us by their more or less mixed descendants.'[17] In order to explain the phenomena of the prognathous skull, he thus supposes the characteristic to be a most ancient one, and to have descended to individuals of the present European races from some very remote Mongol ancestors. These characters are still represented by certain Mongol tribes in Russia, who at a very early period may have extended further westward, or have been among the remote ancestors of the Esthonians and Fins, whose language at the present time is allied to the Ugrian.

This may be interesting to the ethnologist, but the ordinary reader may reasonably ask what it has to do with the Anglo-Saxon settlement. Eight skulls out of twelve from West Saxon graves were found by Horton-Smith[18] to be orthognathous, one was mesognathous, and the other three were on the border of meso- and prognathisrn. Horton-Smith found himself in a difficulty in being unable to see where the prognathous tendency could have come from. He rightly said that prognathism could not have been due to admixture of Saxons with the descendants of Celts of the round barrow type, seeing that these broad-headed Celtic people were almost orthognathous, and that the difficulty remained no nearer solution, inasmuch as there were no prognathous races in Britain at that time. Anglo-Saxon or Danish settlers with these facial characteristics may, however, have come in as individuals, partly of Finnish and partly of Ugrian descent. The Esthonians are closely allied to the Fins, and prognathism has been found to be a characteristic of some of their skulls. In dealing with this subject, we have only to consider it so far as it may be concerned with the question of the settlement of England, and that question is: Did the Fins, Esthonians, or other Eastman take any part in that settlement? A well-marked tendency to prognathism is also exhibited by certain skulls from Anglo-Saxon graves at Winklebury, Dorset, as described by Beddoe, as well as in those described by Horton-Smith. Beddoe says that the Saxon skulls found at Winklebury are, on the whole, more prognathous than the Romano-British skulls found in the same neighbourhood. The same prognathous characteristic may be observed rarely even now among English people individually, and these individual peculiarities must have been caused by some racial fusion. It may have been due to some ancestor in recent centuries marrying a prognathous Asiatic, or it may be a race-characteristic of a very remote ancestor, which, as is well known, often shows itself after many generations.

The existence of a physical character such as this in some of the Anglo-Saxon people cannot be passed by. On this subject Beddoe says: 'There are in my lists more than 40 persons who are noted as prognathous. Of these, 29 are English, 5 Welsh, and 11 Irish.'[19] This refers to individuals who actually came under his observations. He mentions also three skulls from the Phœnix Park tumuli, of which two are figured in the 'Crania Britannica,' and others from the bed of the Nore at Borris, figured in Laing and Huxley's 'Prehistoric Remains of Caitlmess,' which show the tendency to prognathism to be of remote date. These ancient examples, however, among the prehistoric people of Ireland and Caithness can scarcely account for the tendency to prognathism shown by the skulls from West Saxon graves. That characteristic would be more likely to have been brought—into some parts of England, at least—by settlers from Baltic lands in near proximity to prognathous people, than to have been derived from remote prehistoric people who may be traced in Ireland or Caithness. Great indeed must have been the time which separated the Anglo-Saxon period from the remote era when people of Mongol descent may possibly have inhabited parts of Western Europe.

That the Esthonians or Eastmen and Fins had some connection with the Anglo-Saxons appears probable from other circumstances, such as the similarity of the objects found in Livonia with those of the Anglo-Saxon period in England, and from a resemblance of certain incidents in Esthonian folklore to those found in Kent. Wagner also mentions the Ögishelm—i.e., the Helmet of Terror. the name being derived from the King of the Ocean. The front of this helmet was adorned with a boar's head, which yawned open-mouthed at the enemy. The Anglo-Saxons and Esthonians of the Baltic alike wore helmets of this sort.[20]

In considering the probability that there were some Fins among other Northern settlers, we must remember their ancient names, Cwéns or Quéns. There are some Old English place-names which have been apparently derived from this source, such as Quénintone and Quénintune, in separate hundreds in Gloucestershire. Both are mentioned in Domesday Book. Cwuénstane, also, is mentioned among the boundaries of Selsea, in Sussex, in a charter dated A.D. 975.[21] Quintone or Quenton, in Northamptonshire, occurs twice in Domesday Book, and other places of the same name are recorded in Wiltshire and Warwickshire. Quenfell in Westmoreland. Queningburgh in Leicestershire, and Quenhull in Worcestershire, are met with in later records.[22] Ingulf in his chronicle mentions a place called Finset, and similar names, such as Finborough and Finningham, occur in the eastern counties. Still earlier references to Finset and Finbeorh occur in the Saxon charters, the former in Northamptonshire, the latter in Wiltshire.[23]

As regards the more general name Eastmen, there are some very old names which apparently denote settlements of them. The 'regione Eastregena,' also called Eosterge—i.e., the present hundred of Eastry in Kent—is mentioned in a Saxon charter. In the same county there are other Domesday names apparently referring to Eastmen.

There is another aspect from which the probability of settlers from the east coast of the Baltic having been among the later colonists of England may be considered. Nestor, the historian of the early Slavs of Russia, tells us that the Swedes (Russ or Varangians), having become the dominant class on the eastern shores of the Baltic, were invited by the Slavonians about A.D. 862 to settle in Russia, in order to put an end to the internal strife in that country, a movement which led to the first foundation of the Russian State.[24] Nestor died about 1115, and wrote, consequently, comparatively near the date he mentions. Many Swedish inscribed runic stones tell of warriors 'who fell in battles in the East;' and in the interior of Russia, western coins have been found in barrows over chiefs, among which are Anglo-Saxon coins, part very likely 01 the Danegeld,[25] which the Anglo-Saxons paid, and which fell to the share of Danish allies from the east masts of the Baltic.

It appears from Nithard that there was a considerable infusion of the Slavonic element among the English inferior tenants called *lats;* and Othere, the Norse mariner, informed King Alfred that the majority of *gajol-geldas,* or tenants paying some kind of rent, among the Northmen in his days were Lapps of the so-called Finnish race.[26] Having this evidence in view. it seems very unreasonable to doubt that some of them were introduced into England among the Northmen who were their lords.

In considering the evidence which may point to the settlement in England of some people of other tribes ethnologically allied to the Fins from the eastern coasts of the Baltic, we must not forget that the Livonians of the Gulf of

Riga are a race partly of Teutonic extraction. Livonia is south of Esthonia, and near the Livs are the Letts and Lithuanians, who also are not pure Slavs. That the Livonians are of Teutonic affinity or descent receives support from the head-shape of the race at the present day. They are long-headed, as all purely Teutonic races are, their cephalic index ranging from 77·8 to 79.[27] There was an early settlement of Teutons on this part of the east coast of the Baltic, and their early civilization must have resembled that of the tribes which sent colonists to England and became the founders of the Anglo-Saxon race. Among the collection of Anglo-Saxon relics in the British Museum there are similar objects found in Livonia, placed among the English collection for comparison, and consisting of axe- and spear-heads, buckles, chains for the neck, and other personal ornaments, which resemble those of the Anglo-Saxon period. Anglo-Saxon coins, in date from A.D. 991 to 1036, were found with these objects,[28] thus proving some intercourse between England and Livonia. The south part of Livonia is within the area of Lettish territory. The Lettish language is spoken in Courland, and there are some Letts within Prussia at Koenigsberg.[29] From their race connection, some Livonians, Letts or Lechs, and other Eastmen, may well have come to England with Fins among the Angles, Jutes, or the later Danes. There can be no doubt, from the Anglo-Saxon coins found, of communication between England and their country. In numerous instances people from Scotland were called Scot by Englishmen among whom they lived, others were called Waring from the Waring tribe, and Fleming from the Flemings. Similarly, the persons called Lyfing, Livingus, and Leving, in the Anglo-Saxon records[30] may very likely have obtained their names from the ancient Livs or Livonians, a name as old as Anglo-Saxon times.

The place-names supply a few traces of Lechs, under which names Livonians, some of whom still speak Lettish, may have been included. These Lech names occur in only a few parts of England, and these where Danes and other tribal people from the Baltic settled. That some representatives of the Lechs and other tribes of the Baltic near them may have settled in England is not improbable. The records of St. Edmund's Abbey certainly tell us of an invasion of Britain by tribes from the Vistula,[31] and the Anglo-Saxon Chronicle tells us of an invasion in the year 1064 of Rythrenan, probably ancestors of the Ruthenians of Russia, into the country around Northampton.[32]

In Domesday Book there is a record of a man named Fin holding land at Cetendone in Buckinghamshire. Over his name the word 'dan' is written, apparently for explanation in the usual way that he was a so-called Dane. During the later Saxon period all the immigrants into England from Baltic countries probably came under the Danish name. and some of them may have been descendants of Baltic colonists of Danish origin.

It is difficult, therefore, to avoid the conclusion that the tendency to prognathism which certainly existed among some of the early Anglo-Saxons came into this country through people of a more or less mixed race from the Baltic coasts. The remarks of Beddoe on the Shetlanders[33] are of interest in connection with this subject. He describes them 'as probably the fairest people of the British Isles. Black hair, however, does occur, and not very unfrequently. It is usually found in persons of a decidedly Ugrian aspect and melancholic temperament. The same type may be found at Wick. These people may be relics of the Ugrian thralls of the Norse invaders, or possibly descendants of some primitive Ugrian tribe.' Having in view the traces of Fins, which have been stated, the question may be asked, Is it not probable that there were settlements here and there of Fins among our Old English forefathers? They were an ancient maritime race, as they are at present. They were closely connected with Sweden, and were at one time partly located in it. Their country did not cease to be Swedish until about a century ago. The ancient nations of the Baltic were all in maritime communication. Their increasing populations must have made new settlements or emigration as much a necessity in ancient times as in modern. The fitting out of expeditions against the British coasts by the Angles and Goths of the earlier period, and the Danes of the later, must have been known all along the Baltic coasts. Would it not have been surprising if, amidst such maritime activity and pressure of population urging them on, some Fins, Helsings, and, other Swedes, had not joined in these expeditions?

The parallelism arises between the Anglo-Saxon settlement in England and the greater Anglo-Saxon settlement that has gone on, and is going on, in the United States. There was a settlement of Fins among the Swedish settlers in America and another of Dutch people near the river Delaware in Pennsylvania in the seventeenth century.[34] These settlers were soon absorbed among the English-speaking colonists and their distinctive ethnological characters lost. So it must have been in England, the dialects of the tribal settlers from the Baltic and their ethnological characters became in a few generations absorbed in the Old English.

The Fins have left the name by which they were called by the Frisians, Saxons, and other Germans, in some Fin place-names in England, which are mentioned in Anglo-Saxon charters and other early records. Whether these places were so called after individual settlers called by the tribal name or after a community, the significance is the same. They have also left their own name, by which they were known to the Goths, Norse, and Danes who spoke the Old Northern language—the name Cwæn—in a number of English place-names which have a similar significance, but with this difference: where we find a place mentioned apparently as the abode of a Fin or Fins we may look for Saxon or German neighbours, and where Cwæn or Quen occurs as an equivalent, we may look for neighbours who were Scandians.

It should be remembered that King Alfred, in describing the voyage up the Baltic, gives some account of the Esthonians and their customs, thus leading us to suppose he must have thought this information would be of interest to his countrymen.

The ancient nations known as the Eastmen, on the east of the Baltic Sea and south of the Gulf of Finland—*i.e.*, the Esthonians, Livonians, Lechs, and

Lithuanians—were, without doubt, partly allied in race to those other old nations and tribes from which the bulk of the settlers in England came. Their ethnological characteristics of the present day, their dialects or language, and their folk-lore, all point to such a connection. As among all pagan Teutonic tribes, water-worship existed among the Eastmen, and still survives in these Baltic countries. In Livonia there is a holy rivulet whose source is in a sacred grove, within whose bounds no one dares to cut a tree.[35] Traces of water-worship also survive among the Lechs.[36] The heathen reverence for wells and fountains was one of the most persistent of Anglo-Saxon superstitions. As it could not be abolished, it was modified by the dedication of wells to Christian saints, and the existence of holy wells in all parts of England at the present time is evidence of the ancient reverence for them. The most re-markable custom, however, which the ancient Livonians had in common with the Scandinavians and Germans was a kind of pagan infant baptism, by which water was poured on the head of a new-born child and a name was at the same time given him.[37]

Some other remarkable customs which the Old English had in common with Fins and Esthonians were those connected with midsummer. It is scarcely possible for us to realize the full extent to which customs connected with the summer solstice prevailed among our tribal forefathers. Their vitali-ty caused them to survive in England for more than a thousand years. The midsummer fires were lighted in many parts of our country, as they were in numerous districts in Northern Europe. The customs connected with the sol-stice must have been most strongly adhered to, if they had not indeed origi-nated, in Northern lands. In the North of Britain, as in Finland, Esthonia, and the greater part of Sweden and Norway, the evening gloam of midsummer passes into the morning dawn and there is no real night.

It is from the Fins and Esthonians that we derive one of the most interest-ing of midsummer legends:

'Wanna Issi had two servants, Koit and Ammarik, and he gave them a torch which Koit should light every morning and Ammarik should extinguish every evening. In order to reward their faithful services, he told them they might be man and wife, but they asked Wanna Issi that he would allow them to remain for ever bride and bridegroom. Wanna Issi assented, and henceforth Koit handed the torch every evening to Ammarik, and Ammarik took it and extin-guished it. Only during four weeks in the summer they remain together at midnight. Koit hands his dying torch to Ammarik, but Ammarik does not let it die; she lights it again with her breath. Then their hands are stretched out, and their lips meet, and the blush on the face of Ammarik colours the mid-night sky.'[38] The interest of the legend is increased by the meaning of the names. Wanna Issi in Esthonian means the Old Father, Koit means the dawn, and Ammarik means the gloaming, in the language of the common people.[39]

The names Eastmen or Esterlings occur in early records as names referring in a general way to people coming into England from the East. The name Os-gotbi,[40] which is mentioned in two Saxon charters as the name of a place in

Lincolnshire, now Osgodby, is more definite. The name Osgotecrosse is mentioned in the Hundred Rolls of Yorkshire.[41] The name Osmington, or Osmenton, as that of an old place in Dorset, is mentioned in a Saxon charter and in Domesday Book. The Osgothi could scarcely be other than the Eastern Goths—i.e., the Goths on the eastern coast of Sweden, or east of the Vistula, or some people of that race. The purest remnant of the old Gothic stock are the Dalecarlians, sometimes called the Swedish Highlanders, who inhabit the secluded district that stretches westwards from the Silian Lake to the mountains of Norway. They have preserved comparatively unchanged the manners and customs of their Gothic forefathers, and, as Bosworth has pointed out, a peculiarity of the old Gothic language—viz., the aspiration of the letters *l* and *w*. By this they bear witness in their tongue to the present day of their descent, for these peculiarities are an infallible characteristic of the Mœso-Gothic, Anglo-Saxon, and Icelandic languages.[42] The Anglo-Saxon people must have derived this peculiarity from a Northern source, for Bosworth tells us that the Danes and Germans cannot pronounce these aspirated letters.

The history of the Goths and Swedes in the Scandinavian peninsula shows that the latter became the predominant race in the ninth century, and subsequently the two nations were gradually blended into one. During the period when England received so many settlers from the North, we must look for traces of Goths and Swedes under their own tribal or national names. One of these was the tribe known as the Helsingi, whose homeland was the east coast of the Baltic, opposite to Finland, and, as the name Helsingfors shows, must have been connected with the Fins. They were also known as the Heslengi,[43] and under the name Helsings are mentioned in the 'Traveller's Tale' in connection with Wade and his boat, a mythical hero, like Weland the Smith. As a Northern nation their name must have been familiar to the Old English. One of the peculiarities of the old dialect of the Gothic people of Dalecarlia that has survived is the transposition of syllables, as *jasel* for *selja*, and *lata* for *tala*.[44] The transposition of consonant sounds, as in Helsingi and Heslengi, is well known. The survival of the name of this ancient tribe in those of Helsingborg on the west coast of Sweden, Helsingfors on the coast of Finland, and Helsinore, or Elsinore, on the coast of Zealand, points to the probability of their having been a maritime people, and as such likely to have taken part in maritime expeditions. In England such names as Helsington, near Kendal, and others may possibly refer to settlements of them.

It is in that part of Scandinavia which was the old country of the Helsings that commemorative stone monuments abounded when O. Magnus wrote his history of the Goths and Swedes. He says that 'these pillars are found among the Heslengi in greater quantity than elsewhere in the North,' and that 'obelisks of high stones are seen nowhere more frequently than in the public highways among the Ostrogoths, the Vestrogoths, and the Sweons or Swedes.'[45] Some of the runic inscriptions on the stone monuments still existing in Sweden in which England is mentioned are of great interest. They tell us of men 'who died in England,' of a worthy young man 'who went to England,' and of others who set out for the same country, that being all, apparently, that was known of them after they left their native districts. In one case we read of a memorial set up by his children to an English settler: 'To their father, Feiri, who resided westward in England.'[46] In another, to one who had died in England, and 'Urai his brother set up this stone to his memory.'[47] The inscriptions mentioned prove that Swedes must certainly be included among English colonists and among the forefathers of the Old English race. Such Anglo-Saxon names as Suanescamp, Kent; Swanesig, Berks; Swanetun, Norfolk; Swonleah, Hants; and Swonleah, Oxfordshire, are probably traces of them.[48] In searching for traces of Swedes in England we must look for them in proximity to Goths, Norse, or Danes, with whom they probably migrated, and look for traces of their names under the names Svear, Sweon, Swein, and perhaps Swirl. The latter name appears in the Orkney and Shetland dialect to be a corruption of Swein.[49] In addition, Stephens tells us of the words *suin*, *suain*, and *suen* being used.[50]

There was another ancient Baltic nation that may well have sent emigrants to England, the Burgundians of Bornholm and the country near the Vistula. They were closely allied in race to the Northern Goths. The island of Bornholm, called Burgunda-ea[51] by Wulfstan in the time of King Alfred, was named after them. They were a tall, blonde people,[52] and we know that there is historical evidence of the Emperor Probus having transported a great number of them from the Continent to Britain. Some of these may have been among the ancestors of the English race, as well as others who may have come in with the Angles, Jutes, or Danes.

We read in the old chronicles of Danes and Northmen, but there are few references to Swedes. They must, however, have been among the Danish forces, and were probably included under the names of Danes or Northmen. The rare mention of the Swedish name points either to the relative weaker state of the Swedes at the period of the settlement of England, or to their expansion on the east side of the Baltic. At that time the Northern Goths were the more important race, but later on the Swedish tribes advanced in power, and the Goths in the Scandian peninsula declined in relative importance. The more study we give to the Anglo-Saxon settlement, the more clearly we see evidence of a greater part having been taken in that settlement by Baltic races than has been commonly ascribed to them. The oldest settlement was not all German. Even the poem of Beowulf, one of the oldest examples of Anglo-Saxon literature, the scene of which is largely in Sweden, bears witness to this, for its substance must have come over with the conquerors, and its existence in Old English literature is one of the many proofs of an early infusion of the Scandinavian element in the immigration.[53]

The old provinces of what is now Sweden, which extended along the Baltic coast or lay near the entrance of that sea, were Vestergotland, Halland (opposite to the Danish Isles), Skane, Blekinge, Smaland, Ostergotland, Sodermanland, Upland (which contained the city of Upsala), Gestrikland, Helsingland, and Angermanland. Names of places derived from the names of some of these old provinces or tribal districts are certainly to be found in England. There is also the old boundary-name near Lake Wetter, formerly called the Wedermark. This was the country of some of the Eastern Goths called Wederas, and their name apparently survived in England in those of the Anglo-Saxon names Wederingsete,[54] in Suffolk, Vedringmuth in Sussex, and others. The settlement of people who took their name from the head of a family named after his tribe may perhaps be inferred from the ninth-century place-name Bleccingdenn[55] in Kent, which closely resembles that of the old province of Blekinge in part of Scandinavian Gothland.

Stephens draws attention to the name Salua in a Northern inscription, which word he interprets as of the Sals, or of the Salemen, a clan or tribe of Northern people.[56] As an instance of the connection of these people with England he refers to the district of the Sælings in Essex. The personal name Saleman is found in the Hundred Rolls, and may be traced from the Anglo-Saxon period downwards. The name reminds us of the Danish Isle of Sealand, and of a number of old Sele and Sale names in our own country, such as the Domesday name Salemanesberie or Salmonesberie. There was also in Gloucestershire a hundred at the time of the Domesday Survey named Sale-mannesberie-Hundred, apparently after the same place as that called Sul-monnesburg on the upper course of the Windrush in a charter of Offa dated 779.[57] The four Danish islands Sialand, Mön, Falster, and Laland, at one time are said to have formed a separate kingdom called Withesleth, over which the mythical Dan was the first King, who by tradition was one of the three sons of a King of Svethia or Sweden.[58] The inhabitants of these islands were probably all known by separate tribal names, derived from the names of the islands, and some of them may perhaps be traced in England.

If we had no records of settlements in the United States during the last three centuries, the names of some of the settlements alone would tell us of the countries and places from which some of the colonists probably came. Of such are the old names New Sweden and New Netherland, and the existing names New York, New Orleans, Montpelier, New London, Boston, New Hampshire, Andover, Gloucester, Hampton, Bristol, New Milford, Newcastle, Barnstaple, Norwich, Belfast, Plymouth, Beverley, Lancaster, and many others. Some of these names at least were given to the settlements by the earliest colonists to keep fresh in their memories the countries and places they had left. Similarly, nearly a thousand years earlier, some Scandinavian and other settlers in England from the Baltic coasts appear to have called some of their new homes Lund, Upsale, Rugenore, Gilling, Rye, Dover, Grinsted, Linby, Risberga, Eldsberga, Billing, and others, after places in Denmark or other countries on the Baltic they had left. Human nature in regard to the memory of the fatherland has been much the same in all ages of the world. In the history of our own race the descendants of the Old English have in this respect shown evidence of a sentiment common to themselves and their remote Scandinavian forefathers.

[1] Chron. Mon. de Abingdon, i. 24.

[2] Dipl. Angl. by B. Thorpe, xxxix.

[3] Worsaae. J. J., 'Danes and Norwegians in England.' 14.

[4] Cleasby and Vigfusson, 'Icelandic Dictionary.' Preface.

[5] *Ibid.*, and Rydberg, Viktor, 'Teutonic Mythol.,' 24.

[6] Seehohm, F., 'Tribal Custom in Anglo-Saxon Law,' 340.

[7] Otté. E. C., 'Denmark and Iceland,' p. 69.

[8] Saxo Grammaticus, translated by O. Elton, book i., 15.

[9] Mallet, M., 'Northern Antiquities,' edited by Percy. p. 116.

[10] Marsh, G. P., 'Origin and History of the English Language,' 101.

[11] Cleasby and Vigfusson, *loc. cit.*, Preface.

[12] Saxo Grammaticus.

[13] Sweet, H., 'History of Language,' 113.

[14] Ripley, W. Z., 'Races of Europe,' 365.

[15] Latham. R. G., 'Germania of Tacitns.' xv.

[16] 'King Alfred's 'Orosius,' edited by Bosworth, 38, 39.

[17] De Quatrefages, 'Sur crânes d'Esthoniens,' *Bulletins de la Société d'Anthropologie de Paris*, ii. serie, tome i.

[18] Horton-Smith, R. J. *Journal Anthrop. Inst.*, xxvi. 87.

[19] Beddoe, J., 'Races of Britain,' p. 10.

[20] Wagner, W., 'Asgard and the Gods,' translated by Anson, 242.

[21] Cart. Sax. iii. 193.

[22] Cal. Inq., Post-mortem, Edward III.

[23] Codex Dipl., Nos. 66 and 468.

[24] Metcalfe, F., 'The Englishman and the Scandinavian,' p. 197, quoting Nestor.

[25] *Ibid.*, 202.

[26] Robertson, E. W., 'Scotland under her Early Kings.' i. 257, quoting Nithard. 'Hist.,' i. 4, A.D. 843.

[27] Ripley, W. Z., *loc. cit.*, p. 340.

[28] Bähr, J. C., 'Die Gräber der Liven.'

[29] Sweet, H, *Philological Soc. Trans.*, 1877-1879, p. 47.

[30] Codex Dipl., No. 956, and Searle, W. G., 'Onomasticon Anglo-Saxonicum.'

[31] 'Memorials of St. Edmund's Abbey,' edited by T. Arnold, Index, and ii. 113.

[32] Anglo-Saxon Chron., MS., Cott. Tib., book iv.

[33] Beddoe. J., *loc. cit.*, 239.

[34] Winsor, Justin, 'History of America.' iv. 452. 496, etc., and State Papers. Colonial Series, 1677–1680, p. 623.

[35] Grimm. J. 'Teutonic Mythology.' ii. 598.

[36] *Ibid.*

[37] Mallet, M., *loc. cit.*, ed. 1847, p. 206.

[38] Max Müller, 'Chips from a German Workshop.' iv. 191. quoting Grimm, etc.

[39] *Ibid.*

[40] Codex Dipl., Nos. 906 and 964.

[41] H. R., i. 129.

[42] Bosworth, J., 'Origin of the English, German, and Scandinavian Languages.' 159, 160.

[43] Magnus, O., 'Hist. of Goths, Swedes, and Vandals,' ed. 1658, p. 11.

[44] Bosworth, J., *loc. cit.*

[45] Magnus, O., *loc. cit.*

[46] Mémoires de la Société Royale des Antiquaires du Nord, 1845-1849. p. 333.

[47] *Ibid.*

[48] Codex Dipl., Nos. 38, 1276, 785, 556, and 775.

[49] Tudor, J. R., 'The Orkneys and Shetlands,' p. 344.

[50] *Loc cit.*, i. 24.

[51] Alfred's 'Geography of Europe,' p. 55.

[52] Ripley, W. Z., *loc cit.*, p. 144.
[53] Marsh. G. P., *loc. cit.*, p. 101.
[54] Codex Dipl., Nos. 904, 932.
[55] Dipl. Angl., edited by Thorpe, Index.

[56] Stephens, G., *loc. cit.*, ii. 697.
[57] Cart. Sax., i. 320.
[58] Chron. Erici reg. ap. Langeb., quoted by Latham, 'Germania,' cxxv.

## Chapter Nine - Customs of Inheritance

WE must now consider a subject of great importance to this inquiry. The customs by which lands and tenements in various parts of England are inherited in some way different from the general law of primogeniture are many and various. None of these have arisen through any legal enactment, but have all come down from a remote antiquity, and are of prescriptive origin. Their existence in some manors and boroughs can be traced back to the Anglo-Saxon period. In addition to these exceptional rules of succession which are so marked in many separate places, there are other customs that differ from the general law which either have, or had, by long usage all the force of law over great districts. Some old manors were so extensive as to have been large areas, including many parishes. Since the sixteenth century, however, the manorial system, as it came down from the Old English and later periods, has been passing away, and what remains of it marks only its extreme decay. For the purpose of our present inquiry it is of little importance whether a local custom is still in operation, or in a state of decay, or has entirely gone, provided that it can unmistakably be traced in a particular locality. As the settlers in England came from Continental countries, the comparison of customs prevailing in England with those that are known to have existed in the lands from which they migrated is important. for it is only reasonable to suppose that tribal settlers brought with them to England their old rules of family inheritance, whatever they may have been. These ancient laws of inheritance enable us to trace, with some degree of certainty, the settlement of people of different tribes or races in various parts of our country. It is certain that old customs, especially those of inheritance, were very persistent, and are exemplified by the survival until the present day of many ancient manorial usages. Various customs of inheritance on the Continent can be traced back to the most ancient legal codes which arose out of the primitive folk-laws, and some of these still exist. In only two of them is a distinction made between movable and immovable property—viz., in the Thuringian law and in the Salic law. Some of the early Thuringians were located on the lower Elbe,[1] near some of the Angles, and in the Thuringian law land was inherited only by males of the male stem, while personalty went first to sons, and failing these, to daughters. In the Salic law sons preceded daughters in succession, and daughters were excluded from succession to land, although they shared with sons in movables.[2] Among the Angles and the Saxons on the

Continent male inheritance was the rule. Among the Goths and Frisians daughters appear from an early period to have shared the inheritance with the sons.

The early writer on the laws and customs of England, Henry de Bracton, who lived in the thirteenth century, tells us that England in his day differed from other countries in regard to the following of old customs. He says: 'Whereas in almost all countries they use laws and written right, England alone uses within her boundaries unwritten right and custom. In England, indeed, right is derived from what is unwritten, which usage has approved.' He continues: 'There are also in England several and diverse customs according to the diversity of places, for the English have many things by custom which they have not by (written) law, as in divers counties, cities and boroughs, and vills, where it will always have to be inquired what is the custom of the place, and in what manner they who allege the custom observe the custom.'[3]

Another and still earlier legal author, Glanville, who wrote in the time of Henry II., tells us in his chapter on inheritance that primogeniture was the rule of common law. In reference to the land of a 'free socman,' however, he tells us that it has to be ascertained whether the land was partible by ancient custom. If so, the sons take equally, saving that the first-born has the chief dwelling-house on the terms of making recompense in value to the others. If the land is not partible, then, according to the custom of some, the first-born shall have the whole inheritance; according to the custom of others, however, the last-born is heir.[4]

If a man owning houses or tenements within the city of Gloucester at the present time dies intestate, his youngest son, and not the eldest, succeeds to the property. This is a remarkable survival, and a similar custom formerly prevailed, or still does, in Leeds, Derby, Leicester, Nottingham, Stafford, and Stamford.[5] It prevailed not only in these boroughs, but in many manors in various counties, especially in Sussex, Suffolk, Surrey, Essex, Norfolk, Middlesex, and in a special part of Somerset. It still exists, or has been shown to have existed, also, to a less extent, on some few manors in Hampshire, Nottinghamshire, Lincolnshire, Huntingdonshire, Hertfordshire, Northamptonshire, Oxfordshire, Kent, Devon, Cornwall. Rutland, Herefordshire, Berkshire, Shropshire, and Monmouthshire. In Sussex it prevailed on 140 manors, chiefly in the Rape of Lewes, where the custom was almost an exclusive one. This junior right or inheritance of the youngest son, or borough-English, as it has been commonly called, also prevailed in parts of Glamorganshire, where its occurrence will be considered in connection with the settlement of the English on the Welsh border. There is no trace of any similar custom under which the youngest son is the sole heir in the ancient laws of Wales.

It is certain that this custom could not have arisen spontaneously in so many places and districts widely separated from each other. It has probably come from some general race custom, and has been preserved in the localities where it has survived by the attachment of the people to the usages of their ancestors. Nothing is more remarkable in the history of mankind than the attachment of people of all races to the customs which have been handed down to them from their forefathers. That junior right was preserved in the boroughs and manors in which it survived through all the period of the Middle Ages, when the tendency was one ever growing stronger in favour of primogeniture, is remarkable testimony to its vitality, and the attachment to it of those who lived under it. If we can thus trace it, as we may, as far back as the Old English period, when people certainly were as tenacious of their ancient customs as their descendants were, it is reasonable to conclude that those who lived under it in the Saxon period also inherited it from some earlier forefathers. The custom of junior right is no more likely to have been invented here and there in certain early boroughs and manors of Saxon England than of Mediæval England. We must look for its origin in the Continental homes of our oldest English forefathers. Some of the evidence which shows that the Anglo-Saxons had forefathers of many different tribes has already been brought forward, and the survival on our manors of so many different examples of ancient customary inheritance points to the same conclusion. On the Continent we find that junior right existed in various degrees, ranging from the descent of the whole inheritance to merely articles of household furniture, in Picardy, Artois and Hainault, in Ponthieu and Vivier, in the districts round Arras, Douai, Arniens, Lille and Cassel, and in the neighbourhood of St. Omer. It has also been noted at Grimberghe in Brabant.[6]

Similar customs prevailed in a part of Friesland, the most notable of which was the 'Jus Theelacticum,' or custom of the Theel lands, doles, or allottable lands in East Friesland, not far from the mouth of the Ems. There an inherited allotment was indivisible; on the death of the father it passed intact to the youngest son, and on his death without issue it fell into the possession of the whole community.[7] This was an exception to the more general Frisian plan by which the inheritance was divided. Similar customs which are not superseded by the civil code existed in Westphalia and parts of the Rhine provinces, and also in the Department of Herford near Minden, where, so strong is the hold of the custom, that until quite recently no elder child ever demanded his legal obligatory share, and the children acquiesced in the succession of the youngest.[8] The same custom also prevailed in Silesia and parts of Bavaria, where the newer laws of inheritance failed to break down the time-honoured succession of the youngest, the rights being preserved by a secret settlement or by the force of opinion. Similar customs prevailed in the forest of Odinwald and in the thinly-populated district to the north of Lake Constance. Many examples may be found in Suabia, in the Grisons, in Elsass, and other Teutonic or partly Teutonic countries, where old customs of this kind still influence the feelings of the peasantry, although they have ceased to be legally binding.[9]

The youngest son has his privilege, also, in the island of Bornholm, and a similar right has been observed in the territory of the old Republic of Lübeck,[10] a district where a Slavonic people formerly lived. Junior right also prevails in Saxe-Altenburg, which has an agricultural population of Slavonic extraction.[11]

It may be noted from this list of localities that the custom in Germany, North-Eastern France, and Belgium, survives in separated districts rather than in whole territories, and it is not to be necessarily understood that it survives in all places in the districts named. In Germany also it should be noted that it survives where Slavonic influence has been felt, such as in Oldenburg, Saxe-Altenburg, parts of Bavaria, and in Silesia. The same custom survives in parts of Pomerania, mingled in other places with primogeuiture.[12]

Pomerania was Slavonic, Oldenburg had an intrusive Slav settlement, and Saxe-Altenburg and parts of Bavaria have in a similiar way had Slav immigrants, or preserved a remnant of the older race from which the Slavs probably descended. The custom of junior right is clearly not a Germanic institution. It prevails in parts of Germany indeed, but it can be traced to no old German code of laws or general custom, as far as I have been able to discover. On the contrary, Tacitus tells us that equal division among the sons was the custom of succession among the ancient Germans. Germany was undoubtedly in the early centuries of our era much influenced by the hordes of Slavs on its eastern borders, and received many intrusive colonies of that race. There is evidence to show that junior right spread through the parts of Germany where it prevailed, owing to the migrations of the Slavs, or people of mixed Slavic and Teutonic descent. No instances of this custom occur in Scandinavia, and at the same time no instances can be adduced of Slav settlements in that peninsula. The custom of junior right is found in the early Russian code, by which the inheritance of the father appears to have passed to males in preference to females. and the youngest son was always to take the paternal house.

This early Russian code of laws, known as "The Rousskaia Pravdá of Yaroslav," which is preserved in the Chronicle of Novgorod, shows that the early Slavs had much the same institutions, such as trial by ordeal and by wager of battle, compensations for injuries, etc., as prevailed among other European nations at the same time.[13] Primogeniture is alien to the Spirit of Slavonic institutions.[14] It was first introduced into Russian law by Peter the Great, but, having been found unworkable, was abolished by the Empress Anne. It was so far restored by the Emperor Nicholas in 1830 that a father was then allowed to make his eldest son his heir if he chose to do so.[15] The Slavs are essentially agriculturists, and the tendency of the race is in the direction of co-operation. The primary element of organization in Russia—the village community, or *mir*,[16] under which the youngest son has a preference—is a survival of the old tenure of village communities that at one time must have been widely prevalent in Europe. When first we meet with the Slavs in history, we find them living in communities. Having all these facts in mind, we may reasonably look eastward of Germany for the origin of the custom by which the youngest son inherits. Nowhere else in Europe, except among the

Slavs, can it be traced, so far as is known, in an early code of laws. It can indeed be traced still further eastward among the Mongols of Asia, but it is unnecessary to follow it so far, for it is possible that it may have been derived by the Slavs from the earlier broad-headed Alpine race, of which they were probably an offshoot.

If we turn now to our own country, and consider such a case as that of the manor of Merdon in Hampshire, although the name of the village has for many centuries been changed to Hursley, we find that inheritance by the youngest son is still a living custom among the copyholders, and this on a manor with a name identical in part with that of the primitive *mir*, which may be only an accidental coincidence. In Sussex, where of all the English counties junior right most largely survives, *mer*, as part of place names, is also most largely represented. Some of them in their old forms are Keymer, Angermer, Stanmer, Falmer, Jonsmere, Cuckmere, Bormer, Burgemere, Udimer, and Ringmer, and they will be again referred to. These names may be considered for what they are worth side by side with the existence of junior right in Sussex; they may be a coincidence, and no undue stress should be laid upon them. That *mer* or *mir* is, however, the name of a primitive agricultural community appears from the survival of the name in Russia, and it is certain that such communities came into England from Continental lands during the English settlement. All our available evidence, therefore, points to Eastern Germany, to old Slavic lands, and German territories which were influenced by Slavs, as the source or sources of English junior right. It was apparently a custom that, when once ingrained into the life of a tribe, would remain under more settled conditions of agricultural life, and be passed on from age to age and from country to country.

Turning now to the custom of primogeniture, it will help us in our inquiry if we bear in mind that the eldest son was nearly always preferred in the common law of Scotland,[17] and the Scotch along the east and south-east coasts are largely descended from Anglians and Norse. The eldest son had a preference by the common custom of inheritance in the Isle of Man, which was peopled by Norse colonists; and there, by the common law of the island, the eldest daughter, in default of brothers, succeeded to the inheritance.[18] Similarly, over a great part of Cumberland, which was colonized by the Norse, in default of sons the eldest daughter succeeded to the paternal estate.[19] Primogeniture was the rural custom of Normandy before the conquest of England. Bede tells us that in his time the eldest son had some preference or birthright in Northambria,[20] and, considering that Northumbria was occupied by Anglians, Frisians, and Norwegians, this is not surprising, for all these instances of rustic primogeniture point to Norway and the Scandian land as one of its homes. The Normans of Normandy originally came from these northern lands, and the Manx and Cumberland men came from Norway; where the custom of preferring the eldest daughter in default of sons[21] is an ancient one of the country. The evidence of south-eastern Scotland also points to Norway and the earlier Anglian lands, as does that additional evidence derived from isolated districts or manors in England in which, in default of sons, the eldest daughter succeeds to the paternal estate. The evidence of this eldest daughter custom is so strong that we shall probably be right in locating a Norwegian settlement in places where it prevails or has prevailed. It existed in Surrey at Chertsey, Beaumond, Farnham, Worplestn, and Pirbright; in Buckinghamshire at West Wycombe; in Berkshire at Bray; in Hertfordshire at Cashiobury and St. Stephens; in Northamptonshire at Middleton Cheney; in Herefordshire at Marden;[22] and in the great manor and hundred of Crondal in Hampshire.[23] close to the border of Surrey.

After the Norman Conquest, as is well known, under the Norman influence and the growth of feudalism, primogeniture overpowered the other customary rights of succession, and became the general law of the country; but before that time there existed, as these surviving instances show, a rustic primogeniture of remote origin, which, like the custom of Normandy, can be traced to Norway itself.

This succession by the eldest daughter in default of sons is a remarkable usage, and may be a survival in an altered form of an archaic rule, by which inheritances passed through the female in preference to the male line. S. Baring-Gould[24] has drawn attention to a custom that prevails in parts of the Black Forest, where land always descends through a female hand. It goes to the eldest daughter, and if there be no daughters, to the sister or the sister's daughter. The Black Forest is within the parts of Central Europe where descendants of the broad-headed Alpine race may be traced, and if this custom is pre-historic, which is extremely likely, its origin must probably be ascribed to that race. There are, however, in Norway traces of a broad-headed brown race, distinct from the Lapps, the existence of whom has been already mentioned, and they have been described by Ripley as probably of the Alpine stock. It is quite conceivable that this eldest daughter custom in Norway may have been derived from these older Norwegian people and preserved in its present form in parts of that country.

After the Norman Conquest the strict rule of Norman feudal primogeniture was deliberately applied by the Norman Kings wherever possible, not only to English military fiefs, but to agricultural holdings of all kinds. The urban customs of the French portions of Hereford and Nottingham appear to have been altered in this way. The rural primogeniture of Normandy and Picardy, however, long remained in an exceptionally vigorous form, which may, perhaps. have been due to the Scandinavian origin of the Normans, and to the vitality of their ancient customs among the people. It is certain also that this rustic primogeniture has survived over a wide area of Cumberland, of which the continued existence of the right of the eldest daughter, in default of sons, is sufficient proof. That this part of the custom, which is one of the marks that distinguishes it from the feudal primogeniture, survived at all in England is proof of its vitality, and evidence that it must have come with the Norse people of Cumberland from Norway, where it prevails to the present day.

and, so far as known, nowhere else in Northern Europe, except in similar ancient Norwegian colonies. It was a custom in parts of Saxon England, and helps us to trace the origin of the English people of these districts. Its absence elsewhere in England, where Norse settlements from other evidence can be shown to have existed, may be due to the rigour by which the newer primogeniture of the feudal type was enforced.

The earliest reference to the custom of dividing the inheritance among the sons which prevailed among the ancient German tribes is that of Tacitus. After the fall of the Roman Empire, the earliest reference, so far as known, is that of the time of Clothair, and is contained in his code of laws. It confirms the several customs of inheritance which at that time prevailed.[25] The date of this is about A.D. 560, which shows that at this time the customs of succession had become various. Between the time of Tacitus and that of this king the people of Germany must have become considerably changed, for Teutonic tribes had left it and pushed on to the South and West, while Slavonic tribes had migrated into it from the East. In one instance a whole nation had come—the Slavic Czechs—who had in the fifth century driven out their predecessors, the Teutonic Marcomanni,[26] from Bohemia, as these had previously driven out the old Celtic Boii. The old name Boii, however, remained, and became the German designation for a new race. The Wilte had probably come into Frisia, and had settled around Utrecht[27] and in other districts in the Rhine valley. Migrations of Saxons and other races had also occurred.

The ancient custom of inheritance generally prevailing in Frisia was one under which all the children alike inherited. It is so described in a work on Frisian jurisprudence written in the sixteenth century.[28] In Holland at the present day we may look almost in vain for large landowners, for under the Dutch law all children share their father's possessions.[29] Among the Frisians there were some communities, however, probably of mixed descent, who had apparently the custom of junior right already mentioned.

It may reasonably be conceded that where the Frisians settled in England they would be likely to take with them their own mode of inheritance. Similarly, we cannot doubt that those tribes which had a custom of junior right would continue it in the new land. One settlement may have had one custom, and the next another; but when, as was in some instances the case, a number of old settled villages became parts of one great lordship or manor, and a general custom for the whole manor or lordship was adopted, it may well have been a compromise between the two older customs, and in this way a system of partible inheritance, with preference to the youngest son in regard to the homestead, may have arisen.

Tacitus told his Roman readers that the Germans knew nothing of testament or the power of bequeathing property by will, but he said they had rules of intestate succession. The property set free by a man's death did not pass to any body of persons who stood in different degrees of relationship to the dead man, but the kinsmen were called to the inheritance class by class.[30] First the sons, if there were any; failing them, the brothers; and failing them, the uncles, divided the inheritance between them. This is the same custom that we find prevailed on manors in various parts of England. Partible inheritance in English custom was subject in different places to many variations in detail. In Kent it was mixed up with a preference for the youngest son, who by the Kentish custom claimed the paternal house, apparently by making compensation to his brothers. This corresponded to the custom of one part at Frisia.[31]

The three several systems of inheritance—the succession of the youngest to the whole estate; the succession of the eldest; and the partible custom by which all shared alike, whether sons only, or sons and daughters—stand out, however, as three well-marked ancient systems. Can we trace them to their primitive sources? Junior right, as far as the Teutonic nations are concerned, apparently came from the East, and rustic or primitive primogeniture from the North; but the question remains, From what source did the Germanic people derive their custom of partible inheritance? It prevailed among the Romans and the Greeks, but it is not at all probable that any custom of Germany beyond the pale of the Roman Empire could have been derived from the Empire and have been adopted by the German people. Bearing in mind that there was an ancient trade route between the Baltic and Greece by which Scandinavia was brought into commercial intercourse with the southeast of Europe, and the probable origin of the Old Northern runic letters from characters of the ancient Greek alphabet, it is possible that the Northern Teutons learnt this custom from the Greeks, as they did the basis for their runes. It is probable that the very earliest Teutonic home was the Scandian peninsula, and that for centuries there was a steady flow of fair-complexioned, long-headed people from Scandinavia into Germany. This migration began at an early period, before, indeed, the Northern runes were invented, as is shown by the absence of runic inscriptions on fixed objects in Germany. It is unlikely, therefore, that the custom of partible inheritance among Germanic people was derived from the Greeks. The custom of dividing the inheritance is one which may easily have arisen spontaneously from its fairness.

We search in vain for any ancient exclusive examples of junior succession on a large scale among the purely Teutonic nations. In Germany partible inheritance prevailed among both nobles and peasants, and even as late as the Middle Ages asserted its ancient right over primogeniture. The partible tendency in Germany resulted in the Middle Ages in a division of the principalities, which has left its mark on that country to the present day. As generations went on, Saxony was split up into Saxe-Weimar, Saxe-Eisenach, Saxe-Gotha, Saxe-Meiningen, Saxe-Coburg, Saxe-Römhild, Saxe-Eisenberg, Saxe-Saalfeld, Saxe-Hildburghausen, etc. Hesse, similarly, was divided into Hesse-Cassel, Hesse-Darmstadt, Hesse-Rheinfels, and Hesse-Marburg. Other parts of the country exhibit similar examples of subdivision, the Reusses being, perhaps, the smallest into which principalities were divided.[32] Primogeniture was adopted in Germany to save the princely families from extinction. The custom of parting the father's property was clearly based on a sense of justice to all the children alike. Its primitive form was probably that in which the sons and daughters all had their shares. This was the custom of Frisia, and apparently that of the Northern Goths, for we find that some of their descendants at the present time in Sweden have the custom, and cling tenaciously to it. In Dalecarlia, where the people are of the purest Gothic descent, land is divided equally among all the children,[33] and consequently the divisions have in some cases become very small. A farmer in Dalecarlia at the present time occasionally has 300 parcels of land over a district four miles square.[34] In Götaland, also, the land is partible, and in case of sale the relatives have the first right of purchase.[35] It is not difficult to understand how among a warlike people like the Saxons, or even the Goths themselves after they had left their Northern home, a modification of the partible inheritance custom of their ancestors might have been found necessary, and so that which in more ancient and perhaps more peaceful times had been shared by both males and females was limited under different conditions of life to male children only. This was the custom of the Germans as described by Tacitus. Male inheritance was the custom of the Saxons,[36] and in the custom of gavelkind, by which daughters shared only in default of sons, it was, and is still, the custom in Kent, which was settled by Goths and Frisians.

In the laws of the Visigoths land is stated to be hereditary property, and there is special reference to its division among co-heirs.[37] The rule of this code was equal division among sons and daughters alike.[38] Just beyond the present border of Göteborg, on the south-eastern frontier of Norway, the river Glommen flows into the sea, and on an island near the mouth of this river a remarkable inscription in Gothic runes was discovered on a stone weighing many tons.[39] The size and weight of the stone are sufficient to prove that this inscription was no wanderer. It could not have been carried from place to place or from country to country, as a ring or brooch with runic characters might have been. The inscription is in pure Gothic, such as Bishop Ulphilas wrote for the Mœsa-Goths who migrated from the north and settled near the mouth of the Danube. This inscription is not perfect, but what remains has been translated as follows:

'Three daughters shared . . . Wodarid st.
They the heiresses share the heritage.'

The daughters of the Gothic race still share the heritage in Dalecarlia, in Frisia, and, after the sons, they still share it by ancient custom in Kent and other parts of England. They did not share it in Norway, nor in Old Saxony, not among the Angles, nor in the tribes of Germany closely connected with them. Among the Continental Angle tribes the distinct feature of succession which can be most strongly traced is that of male inheritance. This is found in the laws of the Angles and Warings that were sanctioned by Charlemagne. Similarly, among the Continental Saxons the rule of inheritance gave the preference to descendants of males over those of females as far as the fifth generation.[40]

In England there is a reference to the descent of land being limited to male succession in a charter dated A.D. 963, relating to a lease, for three lives, of land at Cotheridge in Worcestershire. In this it is expressly stipulated that the land is to descend on the spear hand.[41] Still further back the Anglian custom of limiting the succession to males must have prevailed in parts of Mercia, for in A.D. 784 Offa made a grant of land in which the succession is limited to the male line.[42] The only places in the Midland counties where we can trace old customs of inheritance that give a reversion to females after males are those that were comprised within the Soke of Rothley in Leicestershire,[43] and Leicestershire apparently had some Gothic or Frisian settlers. The Mercian customs generally show a marked difference from the Kentish custom, and that which can be traced in parts of the South-Western counties.

The customs of rustic primogeniture, ultimogeniture, or succession by the youngest, and partible inheritance, all of them with some variations in detail, remain as witnesses before us of the three chief schemes under which the land of England in Anglo-Saxon time passed from the fathers to their successors; and the three systems can be traced to different parts of the Continent from which Angles, Saxons, and Jutes or Goths came. Of these, the partible custom was the widest spread in Germany, and probably in England and Scandinavia; rustic primogeniture in the North of England and Norway; and junior right on many English manors and scattered districts on the Continent, but on the east of the Elbe it prevailed as a custom over great territories.

The general absence of testamentary power among the Germanic tribes was long continued by their descendants who settled in England. It was not until a comparatively recent time that persons who held estates as manorial tenants, known as copyholders, could by their wills bequeath their lands and tenements to whom they wished. By the custom of many manors, however, they could devise their holdings by a process of surrendering them into the hands of the lord in his court. Those manors and boroughs, consequently, whose tenants and burgesses had the absolute right of bequeathing their estates without reference to their lords and their courts possessed a valuable privilege, which had come down from the remote time of the Anglo-Saxon period. This power was tended to all copyholders by the Statute of Wills passed in the reign of Henry VIII.[44] That such an Act was necessary in the sixteenth century shows what an exceptional privilege among the lower class of tenants the old customary right, where it prevailed, really was; and as it did not prevail among the ancient German tribes, its origin may perhaps be traced to settlers of Northern descent.

From the circumstance that the custom of dividing the father's lands prevailed among the socmen of the Danish districts in England during the later Saxon period, we may conclude that partible inheritance was a custom of Denmark. The two leading features of socage holdings were: (1) That it was certain both in tenure and the services due from the holder; (2) it was held by custom of the manor.[45] Socmen were thus freeman, and they are chiefly mentioned in Domesday Book in districts within the Danelaw. As Scandinavian settlements, however, can be traced in counties west of the great Danish districts in England, so many socmen or freemen of this kind are mentioned in Domesday Book outside the Danelaw in the central and western counties. It appears to be certain that much of the land which was held by socage tenure remained partible until some time after the Conquest.[46] The preference in the partition of land, according to the Norwegian custom, which the eldest son enjoyed has already been pointed out. A similar preference appears to have existed largely on the socage lands that were by custom divided in England, so that the change by which the eldest son became the sole heir, instead of the first of them, crept in by degrees, probably in imitation of feudal tenure, the owners of socage lands choosing rather to deprive their younger sons of their customary share than that the elder should not be in a position to keep up the family influence or dignity.[47]

[1] Droysen, G., 'Allgemeiner Historische Handatlas.'

[2] Lodge, H. C., 'Essays in Anglo-Saxon Law,' p. 137. quoting 'Lax Salica.' 59.

[3] Bracton, H. de, 'De legibus ct censuetudinibus Angliæ,' edited by Twiss. i. 45.

[4] Glanville, R. de, 'Tract. de leg. et cons. reg. Angl.,' lvii., and Pollock, F., 'Land Laws,' Appendix, 214, 215.

[5] Elton, C. I., 'Gaveikind,' Index; Ibid., 'Origins of English History,' 184.

[6] Elton, C. I., 'Origins of English History,' p. 190, note, quoting references.

[7] Ibid., 191.

[8] Ibid., 192.

[9] Elton, C. I., loc. cit., p. 193.

[10] Ibid., p. 193.

[11] Hall, H., Notes and Queries, Seventh Series, ix. 449.

[12] Ripley, W. Z., 'Races of Europe.' 248, quoting Baring-Gould.

[13] Morfill, W. R., 'Slavonic Literature,' p. 84.

[14] Morfill, W. R., 'Russia,' p. 192.

[15] Ibid. 284.

[16] Ibid., 350.

[17] Cecil, Evelyn, 'Primgeniture,' p. 6:, quoting Erskine, 'Inst.,' book iii., 8, 6.

[18] Ibid., pp. 66, 67.

[19] Elton, C. I., 'The Law of Copyholds,' p. 134.

[20] Beda, 'Life of St. Benedict,' s. 11.

[21] du Chaillu, P. B., 'Land of the Midnight Sun,' ii. 289. 290.

[22] Elton, C. I., 'The Law of Copyholds.' p. 134.

[23] Baigent, F. J., 'The Hundred and Manor of Crondall,' p. 163.

[24] Baring-Gould. S., 'Germany, Past and Present, p. 69.

[25] Monumenta Germaniæ, Legum, tome i., edited by Pertz.

[26] Morfill, W. R., 'Slavonic Literature.' 34.

[27] Bede, 'Eccles. Hist,' book v., chap. ii.

[28] De Haau Hettema, 'Jurisprudentia friesca,' Jahrh., ii., 100 ff.

[29] Meldrum, D. S., 'Holland and the Hollanders,' 26-28.

[30] Pollock and Maitland. 'History of English Law.' ii. 248, quoting 'Germania,' chap. xx.

[31] Robertson, E. W., 'Scotland under her Early Kings.' ii. 266.

[32] Cecil, Evelyn. 'Primogeniture,' pp. 120, 121.

[33] du Chaillu, P. B., loc. cit., ii. 255.

[34] Baring-Gould, S., loc. cit., 84.

[35] du Chaillu, P. B., loc. cit., ii. 336.

[36] *Vida* 'Iuris Provinci alis quod speculum Saxonum vulgonuncipatur Samosci.' 1502.

[37] Lex Visigothum, viii.

[38] Cecil, Evelyn, 'Primogeniture.' p. 153.

[39] Vigfusson, G., and York Powell, F., 'Corpus Poeticum Boreale,' i. 573.

[40] Lappenberg, J. M., 'England under the Saxon Kings,' ii. 120.

[41] Cart. Sax., iii. 339.

[42] Codex Dipl., Introd., xxxiii.

[43] *Archæologia*, xlvii. 97.

[44] Elton, C. I., and Mackay, H. J. H., 'Law of Copyholds,' 83.

[45] Vinogradoft, P., 'Villainage,' 197.

[46] Glanville, R. de, *loc. cit.*, lvii., chap. i.

[47] Elton, C. I., 'Gavelkind,' 17.

# Chapter Ten - Family Settlements and Early Organization

WITH the origin of any nation its early institutions must necessarily have been closely connected. Some of the most interesting traces of Anglo-Saxon life may he followed as far back as the time of the settlement. The changes which time has brought about in the early institutions that came into England with our tribal forefathers make it difficult to form an accurate estimate of them from the knowledge we have of the organization that prevailed during the later part of the Old English period. The later part of the period is historic, the earlier is prehistoric. We know that much which was concerned with the organization of settlers by families, with their local government and the administration of law, did survive from the earlier to the later period, but much must have been changed or modified. The earliest dialects show important variations from the language of the time of the last Saxon King. Similarly, we can trace developments by studying the various collections or codes of Anglo-Saxon law that have come down to us. The earliest are those of Æthelbert, King of Kent, about the beginning of the seventh century, and these are archaic compared with those of the later period. During the Saxon Age progress was going on, although but slowly. The dialects of the tribes became the language of a nation, the territorial organizations of Counties and hundreds were developed out of the tribal districts and the local organizations of the kindred or mægth. The laws developed so as to be better adapted to the increasing population and the new areas which were becoming gradually occupied. The courts by which they were administered grew in importance, and the general laws and customs of the areas that afterwards formed the later shires became more fully recognised. The collective responsibility of the kindred passed into the collective responsibility of the hundred, and changes in the territorial jurisdiction were probably in many cases made. Yet, with all these and other changes, there survived one great underlying principle which was a characteristic of the Anglo-Saxons in

101

their tribal state—the principle of local self-government. This can be traced to the German and Scandian fatherlands of the settlers, and was brought to English soil by our earliest tribal ancestors. The Anglo-Saxon people were of two classes—viz., those who were freemen, and took part in the government of their districts, and those who were not freemen, for whom their lords were answerable. As regards the freemen, the principle of local government appears in its origin to have been closely connected with the organization of people of the same kin. In early Anglo-Saxon institutions prominence is given to the kindred or mægth. People within the recognised degree of kinship were necessarily bound together as an organized body by their collective responsibility, that they all should be law-abiding. This kindred organization is the most natural to any people in a tribal state. It was certainly brought into England by the tribal Anglo-Saxons, but it was no doubt here previously among the Britons, since it survived among the Welsh in a special form for many centuries. The tribal people at the time of their settlement were organized locally, so that the kindred as a body were liable for the good behaviour of every member of that body, and, on the other hand, they defended each other against injury by others outside their organization. If one of their number had injury done him, the fine payable by another mægth or body of kindred was shared by them. They paid the fines or wergelds, and they received them. From this it follows that the family tie was the basis of all government, and the early settlements must have been communities of people of the same kindred. If the kindred had been much scattered they could not have retained their organization. These bodies of kinsmen united together formed a larger political unit of some kind. Thus, by a comparison with what is known to have existed among the German tribes in the early centuries of our era, and what can be traced to a remote period among the Scandian tribes, we can understand the early organization which settlers from these countries brought into England. As an American writer[1] has said: 'We can now trace the slender thread of political and legal thought, so familiar to our ancestors. through the wild lawlessness of the heptarchy and the confusion of feudalism, and can follow it safely and firmly back until it leads us upon the wide plains of Northern Germany, and attaches itself at last to the primitive popular assembly, parliament, law-court, and army all in one.' In our study of the English settlement it is this local administration of the law by the freemen of any district which comes prominently before us in the earliest assemblies or courts which we can trace, and in the organization of the later Hundred Court. This principle of local justice, which survived so long in England in a modified form, notwithstanding many political changes, has left the names of its courts in the names of some of the extinct hundreds, and surviving evidence of its legal power in the sites and names of its places of execution. Gallows and gibbet names are found on our Ordnance maps, and there are many others, which are known locally, still attached to sites where the most severe penalties of the law were carried out. The survival of many Continental tribal and clan names in all the Anglo-Saxon States, side by side with different manorial customary laws, is evidence of a great commingling in England of Continental tribal immigrants. The tribal traditions lived long on English soil. The early Kings were styled Kings of people and not of territories. As new tribal States were formed in England, the ealdormen, who were their viceroys, took their titles from their tribes and not from their States, such as the Ealdorman of the Sumersætas, the Hecanas, the Wilsætas, etc. After the conversion of the people to Christianity grants by early Kings of the power of administering justice in their territories to Abbots and other great men—*i.e.*, seignorial jurisdiction—certainly were made. The early charters of the Abbeys of Peterborough, Glastonbury, and others, show that in whatever words the power may have been conferred, it was a reality. It is this early delegation of judicial authority which imparts so great an interest to some of the sites which were the meeting-places of old courts, or some of the ancient places of execution. Cnut, in his laws, reaffirms the legal authority which the King has over all men in Wessex, unless, he adds, 'he will more amply honour anyone and concorde to him this worship.' It was in regard to the freemen only that the administration of the law was closely connected with the organization of the kindred. If an unfree man was accused of any crime, the oaths of his brothers, uncles, and cousins were not acceptable as evidence of his innocence, for by remote tribal custom, which prevailed for centuries after the early Anglo-Saxon settlement, such relatives had not the privileges of a free kindred. If a man was made a freeman he was still by tribal custom without kindred to answer for him, and the lord had to do this until after several generations his descendants had become a kindred.[2]

The unfree man could clear himself of the crime imputed to him by the ordeal, of which there were several kinds, such as the trial by red-hot iron and by boiling water, which after the conversion of the Old English people to Christianity were carried out in the churches as a religious service.[3] For the ordeal by hot water a fire was kindled under a caldron in a remote part of the church. At a certain depth below the surface of the water a stone or a piece of iron was placed. Strangers were excluded, and the accused was attended only by twelve friends. The priest said or sang the Litany, and at its conclusion a deputy from each side was sent to ascertain the heat of the water. On their declaration that the water was boiling, the accused plunged his naked arm into the caldron and brought out the stone or iron. The priest instantly wrapped the arm in a linen cloth and fastened it with the seal of the Church. At the expiration of three days, the fate of the accused was decided according to the appearance of the scalded arm. If the appearance of the arm was decidedly bad, the unfortunate man was led away to execution.

For the ordeal by hot iron the same precautions were observed in regard to the number of attendants, and the Mass appears to have been celebrated. As soon as it began a bar of iron of the weight of one or three pounds, according to the nature of the accusation, was laid upon the coals. At the last Collect it was taken off and placed upon a pillar. The accused instantly took it up with his hand, made three steps on the lines previously marked out to nine feet in length, and threw it down. The treatment of the, burn and the indications of guilt or innocence were the same as in the trial by hot water.[4] Such customs as these, modified by Christian usage, could only have had their origin among people in an archaic tribal condition.

It was from such a trial that a freeman accused of any crime could be saved by his kinsmen acting as his compurgators or oath-helpers, and taking oath that they believed him to be innocent. There can thus be no doubt that the principle underlying the structure of tribal society was that of blood relationship among the free tribesmen.[5] This was the basis of the old customary laws introduced by the early Anglo-Saxons. They brought their tribal law with them, being yet in a tribal state. The earliest local settlements we can trace are those of families, and these were very often called by the name of their head, by which the family and descendants were commonly known. Among the early Anglo-Saxon tribes every freeman had two mægths—that of his father or paternal kin, and that of his mother or maternal kin. These groups, entirely distinct before his birth. united in his person, and both had with him rights and duties of kindred, but in different degrees.[6] Those only were of kin and belonging to the mægth who had common blood originating from lawful marriage. In considering the rights and duties of a man's kindred, we can, therefore, see that marriages must in almost all cases have been limited to families or groups of kinsmen living at no great distance apart. The degrees of relationship within which the duties and rights of kindred were confined constituted what was called the *sippe*, which can be clearly traced in Germany, and of which some traces are still existing in England at the present day. This archaic institution is one of the most curious survivals of the Teutonic race. It survived in England in the law of cousinship, and traces of it may probably still be found in some place-names. Bracton, who wrote in the thirteenth century, tells us of the law of succession in his time. He says: 'Of kinship and of relationship some are upwards and others are downwards, and others are travers or sidewards. Ancestors succeed on failure of those below them. The computation does not go beyond the sixth grade or degree—*i.e.*, great-great-grandfather's great-grandfather, because such a computation would be beyond the memory of mankind.'[7]

The early German method of reckoning the degrees of side-relationships is described in documentary evidence of the thirteenth century.[8] but comes down from a much earlier time. It is explained by reference to the joints of the human body from the head to the tips of the fingers. There are thus to be observed seven joints in the human frame—viz, those of (1) the neck, (2) the shoulders, (3) the elbow, (4) the wrist, and (5, 6, and 7) the joints of the fingers. Then we read: 'Now mark where the sippe begins and where it ends. In the head it is ordered that man and wife do stand who have come together in lawful wedlock. In the joint of the neck stand the children, born of the same father and mother. Half-brothers and sisters may not stand in the neck, but descend to the next. Full brothers' and sisters' children stand in the joint where the shoulder and arm come together. This is the first quarter of the sippe which is reckoned to the maegen, brothers' and sisters' children. In the elbow stands the next; in the wrist the third; in the first joint of the middle finger the fourth; in the next joint the fifth; in the third joint of the middle finger the sixth; in the seventh stands a nail, and therefore ends here the sippe, and this is called the nail mage.'

All this is important in considering the influence of the mægth or kindred in connection with the English settlement and Old English life. The name constantly comes before us in records of the period. We read of the Mægasetas of Herefordshire and Gloucestershire, and the mægth name, the *g* sound having passed into *y*, probably appears in many Old English place-names. Nor is the end of the sippe wanting among our ancient topographical names. The *nail*, as the name for the limit of kindred, perhaps, still survives in those of Nailsworth, Nailsea, and the stream called Nailbourn in Kent. In a charter relating to land at Salwarpe in Worcestershire in 817 the Nælcsbroc is mentioned as a boundary stream.[9] These names are only curious surviv-als or dim shadows at the present day, but they were full of life and meaning to our Old English forefathers.

When a man committed a crime in Wessex, as we learn from the laws of King Alfred, two-thirds of the wergeld or fine had to be paid by his father's mægth, and one-third by his mother's mægth.[10] As the individual members of the mægth became powerful and wealthy, a tendency appeared on the part of the rich to discard their poorer kin. Thus, a freeman need not pay the wergeld of a slave or of one who had forfeited his freedom.[11] Moreover, as time went on, the tendency to weaken the tie of kinship was encouraged by the State, which had much to fear from the independence of powerful fami-lies, and whose peace was endangered by the continuance of the old system of private vengeance,[12] which was one of the old obligations of kinsmen if the wergeld was not paid them. King Edmund tried to break this down by permitting a mægth to abandon their kinsmen guilty of homicide. The influ-ence of the Church also tended to weaken the kindred tie in the case of reli-gious Orders, for those who became monks lost all the rights of kindred. In some cases, also. a man lost his family rights as a penalty. In the forty-second law of Alfred it is ordered that a man who should attack his foe after he had yielded should forfeit his right to the mægth. All these laws and customs re-lating to the mægth refer to one of the oldest of the Anglo-Saxon institutions affecting social life and the administration of law. The mægth and its organi-zations assist us in understanding the settlement of the Anglo-Saxons by families. All over England we find evidence of this in the Saxon place-names, many of which are tribal names, or derived from them. These family settle-ments made up the larger community of the mægth, whose existence as the basis of organization is evidence of the formation of villages or communities of people within the recognised degrees of kindred.

The term *sibscraft* for kinsmanship, and also *mægth* and *sippe*, denoting kindred, became disused at the close of the Saxon period. In many parts of England, however, it is probable that the name of the old mægth survives in the modern form *may* or *maid*. In the old country of the tribal Mægesetas there are two hills, May Hill near Ross, and another near Monmouth, whose names are probably examples. The numerous earthworks called Maiden Castle, many of them of Celtic origin, were probably used as defensive earthworks by the early mægths. Some of these, which comprised many families, were certainly large communities, and we know that the repair of local fortifications was one of the obligations of all Anglo-Saxons. The words *mæden* and *mægden-man* as variants of mægth are mentioned in the Anglo-Saxon laws. These *maiden* names have thus probably been derived from the mægth. The mægenstan, or boundary of the mægth, is mentioned in a charter relating to Ashbury in Berks in 856, and there are many instances in which the origin of such names as Maybury and Mayland may reasonably be traced to an old mægth. Maidenhead, originally Maydenhithe, Maidstone or Maydenstan, and similar names, are probably examples which in their old forms referred to a mægth.

The *sippe* name, modified in sound, probably survived in the Anglo-Saxon names Siberton in Northamptonshire, Sibbestapele and Sibbeslea in Worcestershire, Sibestun in Huntingdonshire, Sibbeswey and Siblingchryst in Hampshire.[13] The word *sibry* was also an equivalent for kinship, but while in our common tongue the latter survived, the former passed into disuse. Other old names, such as Sipson in Middlesex, Sibley Headingham in Essex, Sibsey in Lincolnshire, Sibthorp in Notts, Sibton Sheales in Northumberland, and Sibbertoft in Northamptonshire, appear to be names of the same kind. Another trace of the old word *sippe* for kindred may be found in the word *gossip*, which originally meant a godsip or god-parent, and was so used as late as the seventeenth century.

The sippe, as we have seen, included in all seven joints or degrees, and as a whole, therefore, nine generations, reckoned on the human frame thus: Head, neck, shoulder, elbow, wrist, first finger-joint, second joint, third joint, and nail. Within these nine generations it was possible for a family to form a large community, and some settlements were no doubt of one family descent only. There is an interesting reference to the sippe and its joints in the laws of Æthelstan relating to the degree of kinship within which marriages were not permissible. 'And let it never happen that a Christian man marry within the relationship of six persons of his own kin—that is, within the fourth joint.'[14] The fourth joint was the wrist. A similar reference occurs in the laws of Cnut. In old Frisian law relating to the next of kin, in the case where a man or woman dies and leaves no near relatives to divide the property, the *sibbosta sex honda* is mentioned—that is, their six next of kin, viz., father, mother, brother, sister, child and child's child.[15] The first instalment of the wergeld, called the healsfang, which the mægth or kindred, in the case where a member was killed or injured, was entitled to receive, was shared equally between the father, the children, brothers, and the paternal uncles. The rest of the fine was shared by the whole kindred,[16] but it does not appear that any record remains to show exactly how or in what proportions.

There is another aspect from which the mægth or kindred may be viewed, and that is in relation to oath-taking. It is not possible for us to realize fully the oath-taking that was carried on as a judicial system among the Old English and the tribes from which they sprang. If a man was accused of a certain crime, and he swore he was innocent, he had the right of proof, and called his oath-helpers around him. If they took oath that they believed his oath to be clean, and that he did not commit the crime, his acquittal followed as a matter of course. This was trial by compurgation, and much depended on which party had the right of proof. A man naturally looked to his kindred for his oath-helpers, and the wider his kindred, the more numerous were those he could generally gather for his defence. He had, no doubt, to convince them that he was innocent, and they would be ready to take oaths in his defence, for if he was proved guilty they would, as his kindred, be liable to pay his fine.

It is not possible to understand the circumstances of the settlement and life of the Old English people without realizing the great importance of the kindred tie. In the many instances in which we find old settlements named as the *tun* or *ham* of a man, the settlement was not only the *tun* or *ham* of a man, but also of his family and of some, at least, of his near kindred who assisted him in the cultivation of the land. The -*ing* terminal part of many place-names in south and south-eastern England had a wider significance than merely 'son of.' In many cases it included all the near kindred, probably in some cases all those who were liable as kinsmen. Viewed in this light, such place-names as Basing, Malling, Goring, Sonning, and Charing, and those ending in -*ingham*, -*ington*, and others of a similar kind, denoted bodies of kinsmen having an organization of their own. Such names may thus be traced to family settlements, comprising, as time went on, in some cases persons who were not only children or grandchildren of the original head of the family, but relatives within the limit of the sippe, to the seventh degree of relationship. As these settlements sent off some of their number to form other settlements in the forest-land or other unoccupied territory, their kinship to the parent stock would last until the nail had been reached—*i.e.*, the limits of the sippe had been passed—and the rural colonies had formed new kindreds of their own, the original kin or ken name given to them by the first settlers, or the parent stock whence they came, alone surviving to afford us a dim glimpse of their origin. It was one of the duties of the kindred, in the later Saxon time, at least, to see that the landless kinsman had a lord in the folk-gemot, otherwise they had themselves to become responsible for him to the State. This collective responsibility of the kindred survived in England as a tribal usage after many generations of occupation and settlement. It survived for centuries after the introduction of Christianity, which, from the sense of individual responsibility, was opposed to the principle of joint responsibility of the kindred. Nevertheless, this tribal custom, with its wergelds or fines, lasted long, and even the clergy placed themselves under it by claiming that a

Bishop's wergeld to be paid if he were killed should be that of a prince, and a priest's that of a thane.[17]

From what has been said, it will be seen that the probability of the Domesday names of some of the hundreds being the later names for still older tribal areas of administration is great. These older areas appear in some instances to be known in Anglo-Saxon time by a tribal name. Among such old Domesday hundred names are Honesberie in Warwickshire, Danais or Daneis in Hert, Godelminge and Godelei in Surrey, Estrei in Kent, Wandelmestrei and Bexelei in Sussex, Honeslaw in Middlesex, Salemanesberie in Gloucestershire, Wederlai in Cambridgeshire, Normanecros in Huntingdonshire, Weneslai and Wilga in Bedfordshire, Hocheslau in Northamptonshixe, Wensistren and Angre in Essex, Caninga in Somerset, and Hunesberge in Devon. In addition to these, whose names have apparently a connection with old tribes which we can identify, there are many others whose names, ending in -ga or -ges, seem to denote various clans or kindreds. Of such are Hapinga, Lothninga and Dochinga in Norfolk; Blidinga and Ludinga in Suffolk; Clauelinga and Rodinges in Essex; Wochinges in Surrey; Brachinges in Hertfordshire; and Mellinges and Staninges in Sussex.

We are not without evidence of the existence, even in the later Saxon time, of agricultural communities that were their own lords, nor without traces of the existence of these lordless villages to our own time. They existed apparently here and there within the Danelaw. or among settlers of Scandinavian origin. Thus, Domesday Book tells us, concerning Goldentone in Bedfordshire. that the land there was held by the men of the village in common, and that they had the power to sell it.[18] Similarly, at the present time in another Scandinavian district, at Ibthorpe, a manor in the parish of Hurstbourn Tarrant, in Hampshire, the inhabitants are lords of the manor, and have territorial jurisdiction over a rather extensive common.

In the time of the Empire one fact concerning Celtic, German, and Wendish tribes alike, which appears to have interested the Roman observer, who could find no parallel to it in his own country, was the custom of cultivating land in common.[19] Wendish immigrants would therefore bring with them, like their much more numerous Teutonic neighbours, a common system of agriculture.

On the other hand, it must be remembered that in the social life of our Old English forefathers no point is established by clearer evidence than the existence of people of all classes, from the great lord down to the slave who could be sold. Slavery was an Anglo-Saxon institution, and there are some early records relating to it. There is an account of a slave sold to a Frisian merchant in London in the seventh century. One of the laws of Ine is directed against 'those men who sell their countrymen,' and another of Æthelred orders that 'no Christian or uncondemned person be sold out of the country.' There were slaves among the Old English whom their lords could dispose of from the time of the earliest settlements. There were above them unfree men, who had certain rights and certain specified services to render to their lords. Above these were the freemen, who enjoyed the protection of their kindred, and thus formed a large privileged class. An old record says: 'It was whilom in the laws of the English that people and law went by ranks, and then were the witan of worship, worthy each according to his condition.'[20]

All freemen were bound under penalties to attend the local assemblies of their district, and these, later on, were the Hundred Court and Shire Court. They collectively administered the highest justice, and this part of their function was recognised as late as the time of William the Conqueror, in one of whose laws they are referred to in these words: 'Let those whose office it is to pronounce judgment take particular care that they judge in like manner as they pray, when they say "Forgive us our trespasses." . . . Whosoever promotes injustice or pronounces false judgment through anger, hatred, or avarice, shall forfeit to the King 40s., and if he cannot prove that he did not know how to give a more right judgment, let him lose his franchise.' The highest courts were the courts of the early primitive States, which afterwards were called shires, and the local courts were those of the smaller regions, afterwards called hundreds. These courts were commonly held in the open air at well-known meeting-places, as in Germany and Scandinavia. Even as late as the thirteenth century the States of East Friesland assembled under three large oaks which grew near Aurich,[21] and open-air courts of the hundreds survived in England to a later date.

The various tribal names that were in use in England before the origin of the present Shires either must have been brought by the original settlers from the Continent or have been newer designations that arose after their settlement. Such names as Engle, Waring, Gewissas, Ymbres or Ambrones, Wilsæte, Thornsæte, and others, are native names that no doubt came in with the settlers themselves. Others that are met with appear to have had their origin from topographical and other local circumstances. Few tribal names in use on the Continent survived as names for tribal areas of England, which shows that the provinces in England were not commonly settled by people of one tribe. New designations would thus become necessary for the people of various Continental tribes living in one English tribal area. These new names would thus become the collective names of people of various older tribal origins, and the older names would survive in England, if at all, not as tribal names, but as names of settlements, and in many instances of places that were called after the heads of families or small communities of people of the same kin. There is a list of Anglo-Saxon tribes preserved in the Harley MSS. known as the Tribal Hidage, the earliest of which is of the tenth or eleventh century, but refers to a considerably earlier date. Some of these tribal areas were large and some small, and others are known to have existed, for they are mentioned in early records. They will be referred to later under the several parts of the country of which they apparently formed a part.

All the German nations anciently acted upon the principle of judging every man by the laws of his native country, for which reason the Franks allowed the different tribes subdued by them to retain their own laws.[22] This general custom of the German tribes helps us to understand several matters concerning the Anglo-Saxons which would otherwise be very obscure. The existence of so many small hundreds in the South-Eastern and Eastern counties—and each hundred certainly had its own court—points to the settlement in these districts of many different tribes, each judged by its own customary laws. On the Continent, Franks, Burgundians, Alamanni, and others of whatever nation living in the Ripuarian country, were all judged, and dealt with if guilty, according to the law of the place of their birth.[23]

Ancient Norway was divided into districts called shires, and it is from this Scandinavian name the English divisional name was probably derived. The early shires or hundreds which are so clearly indicated in the North of England have left their traces also in other parts of the country. Among the probable survivals of their names are the old shires of Cornwall, and among others in old records are Pinnockshire, Blakebornshire,[24] and Kendalshire in the county of Gloucester; Upshire in Essex; and Chipshire in the north-west of Buckinghamshire. These primitive shires were early names of those districts afterwards called hundreds. The word *scir* in Anglo-Saxon nomenclature was also applied to ecclesiastical as well as to political divisions. Kirkshire in some parts of England appears to have been an early name for parish, and the possessions of the Archbishop of York are mentioned in Domesday Book as his scire. The name Sherborne survives in various parts of England. In Dorset the territorial district or diocese of the Saxon Bishop of Sherborne was called Selwoodshire.[25]

The districts of Northumberland, Yorkshire, and Lancashire which were in ancient time called shires, and in some cases still are locally so called, correspond to the hundreds or wapentakes of other counties. Wessex in the early period of its history comprised Hants, Wilts, Dorset, and Berks, and as time passed on, Somerset, Devon, and Cornwall were added to it. Mercia, however, if we are to judge by the number of its later shires, had more primitive states than Wessex. There is no more reason to suppose that when the shires of Mercia were first recognised as counties these territories were thus all arranged for the first time than there is to suppose that the states, called later on Wilts, Dorset, and Somerset, did not exist before they were called shires. In Mercia we read of ealdormen of the Hecanas before we read of Herefordshire, and of the Hwicci before we read of Worcestershire. Every early state which later on became a county had its viceroy. Mercia, having so many more states, would be likely to have more ealdormen or viceroys than Wessex on great occasions to witness the charters of the Mercian Kings. This is what we generally find by a comparison of the number of witnesses who sign as *dux* or *comes* in the charters respectively of the Kings of Mercia and Wessex. When the Kings of Mercia were overlords of Kent and Surrey the number of their viceroys would be increased, and later on, when the Kings of Wessex had acquired this supremacy, the number of their viceroys would be increased. In a charter by the Mercian King Kenulf in 814 relating to land at Chart in Kent,[26] there are sixteen witnesses who sign as *dux* or ealdorman.

In Kenulf's charter relating to the establishment of the abbey at Winchcombe in 811 there are eleven witnesses similarly described.[27] The occasion on which this charter was signed was a very important one, and many of the Mercian ealdormen were probably assembled. In another charter of the same King in 816, granting certain lands to the Bishop of Worcester, there are also eleven witnesses who are styled *dux* or ealdorman.[28] Some of these may have been the viceroys of more than one of the areas of administration or states, afterwards called shires or counties, but that eleven men of this rank should be witnesses of charters of the Mercian King shows that he had many of them, and as each had an area of administration, perhaps more than one, this number points to the existence in Mercian territory of more states than existed in Wessex. The greatest number of ealdormen who appear to have witnessed any charter by a King of Wessex is nine, and the occasion was the grant of land at Droxford in Hampshire in 826 by Egbert. He had, however, at that time become the overlord of much more of England than Wessex. Several of his charters concerning land in Wessex are witnessed by three ealdormen only, and important ones by Ethelwulf, his son, are witnessed by only six.[29] Although territorial changes were in some cases made, it is certain that the Old English counties arose from the primitive states.

One of the most important of the Old English local organizations connected with the shires and hundreds was that for defence. All freemen were under three general obligations. which were apparently of ancient date at the time when we first meet with them in records—viz.: (1) They were obliged to take their part in military service for the defence of their state or the kingdom of which it formed part, the levies being made in each state, afterwards known as the county; (2) they were under the obligation to assist in maintaining the local fortifications; and (3) they were similarly obliged to assist in the maintenance of bridges. The liability for military service in case of urgent necessity still exists in our Militia Act; the maintenance of bridges remains as a county charge; but the liability for the repair of local defences has passed away. It is, however, interesting to us when studying the remains of these ancient fortifications which still exist in most parts of England. Some of them are great mounds of the later Saxon period. but many of them are old Celtic earthworks which the Britons made, and the Saxons adopted for their own defences. In some parts of the country, as on two hills close to Burghclere in Hampshire, the remains of two great British camps may be seen, one of which, on Beacon Hill, was maintained apparently during the whole Anglo-Saxon period, and the other, on Ladle Hill, allowed to fall into disuse and decay, the banks being now almost obliterated, while the other is in a much more perfect condition. In the confirmation of Magna Charta by Edward I. we read that 'no town nor freemen shall be distrained to make bridges nor banks, but such as of old time have been accustomed to make them in the time of King Henry our grandfather, and no banks shall be defended from henceforth but such as were in defence in the time of King Henry our grandfather, by the same places and the same bounds as they were wont to be in his time.' All freemen among our Old English forefathers were trained to the use of arms, and were always ready to take the field or defend their fortifications. When the repair of these banks ceased there is, so far as known, no record, but from the above quotation it is certain that they must have been kept up as local defences to be used in case of need for at least two centuries after the Norman Conquest. It is no doubt owing to the ancient local obligation to repair them that so many remain in a fairly perfect state. Maiden Castle, near Dorchester; Uffington Castle in Berkshire; and Painswick Castle in Gloucestershire, are other examples of earthworks that were probably kept in repair until a late period.

[1] Adams, Henry. 'The Anglo-Saxon Courts of Law.' 'Essays in Anglo-Saxon Law,' Boston, 1876, p. i.

[2] Laws of Wihtræd, 8, and Seebohm, F., 'Tribal Custom in Anglo-Saxon Law,' 46.

[3] Lingard, J., 'History of the Anglo-Saxon Church,' ii. 135.

[4] Ibid., ii. 136.

[5] Seebohm. F., 'Tribal Custom in Wales,' 54.

[6] Young, Ernest, 'The Anglo-Saxon Family Law.' 'Essays in Anglo-Saxon Law,' 125.

[7] Bracton, H. de, 'De legibus et consuetudinibus Angliæ.' i. 553.

[8] Young, Ernest, loc. cit., quoting 'The Sachsenspicgel,' I. 3, par. 3.

[9] Cart. Sax., i. 501.

[10] Laws of King Alfred, 27.

[11] Laws of Ine, 74, par. 2; Æthelstan, vi. 12, par. 2.

[12] Young, Ernest, loc. cit., p. 140.

[13] Codex Dipl., Nos. 964, 209, 1094, 595, 589, and Dom. Bk.

[14] Laws of Æthelstan. vi. 1:. quoted by Ernest Young, 'Anglo-Saxon Family Law,' pp. 127, 128.

[15] Young, Ernest, loc. cit., p. 133.

[16] Young, Ernest, loc, cit., p. 144.

[17] Seebohm, F., 'Tribal Custom in Anglo-Saxon Law,' 385.

[18] Domesday Book, i. 213 b.

[19] Codex Dipl.. Introd., i., p. iv.

[20] Seebohm, F., 'Tribal Custom in Anglo-Saxon Law,' 367.

[21] Mallet, M., 'Northern Antiquities,' translated by Bishop Percy, ed. 1847, p. 511, note.

[22] Menzel, W., 'Hist. of Germany,' i. 162; Monumenta Germaniæ, edited by Pertz. i. 2.

[23] Seebohm, F., 'Tribal Custom in Anglo-Saxon Law,' 166, and Ripuarian Law, xxxi.

[24] Cal. Inq. Post-mortem. ii. 237.

[25] Ethelwerd's Chronicle.

[26] Cart. Sax., i. 481.

[27] Ibid., i. 473. I

[28] Cart. Sax., i. 498.

[29] Ibid., ii. 64, and ii. 94.

# Chapter Eleven - The Jutish Settlers in Kent

THE settlers in Kent are of special interest from several points of view. Known as Jutes since the beginning of our history, they can, without much difficulty, be traced as regards their origin to more than one of the ancient nations or tribes of Northern Europe, and as they alone of all the early colonists in the South of England adopted as the name of their kingdom its name in the Romano-British period, Cantium or Kent, we may reasonably look among them for a survival of some people from the Roman time. The name Gutæ appears on an ancient tunic monument in Scandinavia, about 400 A.D. being assigned to it by Stephens,[1] and one of the historians of the Goths tells us that Gothi, Gatæ, and Guthi are names for the same people,[2] so there can be no doubt that Guthi, or Jutes, were of the same race as the Northern Goths. Under this name, as in the case of Angles and Saxons, other tribal people also probably settled in Kent. Bede wrote of them all under the Jutish name, and as the later chroniclers copied from him, the name Goths ceased to be used for the most part in England, but not wholly so. Asser, for example, tells us that King Alfred on his mother's side was descended from the Goths and Jutes of the Isle of Wight. The Kentish Jutes are also mentioned in early Northern literature by the name of Æscings.

Bede tells us that the Jutes under Hengist and Horsa came to Kent in three long ships, and of this there was no doubt a tradition current in his time. As it bears a remarkable resemblance to a Gothic tradition of older date, we may perhaps see in it another gleam of light connecting the Jutes with the Northern Goths. The old Gothic story speaks of the migration of people of three tribes of that race from Scandinavia to the eastern side of the Baltic Sea. It tells us of Ostrogoths, Visigoths, and Gepidæ,[3] who passed from their old homes in Scandinavia across the Baltic in three vessels. In this case it is clear that, as the migrating people were of three tribes, the traditional number of vessels was made to correspond to the number of the tribes. Similarly, in the Kentish tradition the number of vessels may have been repeated from age to age to the time of Bede, and have had its origin in people of three tribes having been among the settlers.

There is a similar tradition in reference to Sussex, and another in which the invaders are said to have come in five ships for the conquest of Wessex, and these traditions may also denote separate tribal expeditions.

Kent possesses at the present time, and has possessed from a time beyond the memory of man, a remarkable custom in its law of inheritance in cases of intestacy—i.e., the custom of gavelkind. The principal incidents of it are the partibility of the inheritance, the right of the widow or widower, the freedom from escheat for felony, and the infant's right to 'aliene by feoffment' at the age of fifteen years.[4] It is a custom which is the most remarkable of all which are recognised by our common law, seeing that a whole county is thus marked off from the rest of England by a peculiar rule of inheritance. While primogeniture is the common law of succession in other parts of England, gavelkind, or partible inheritance, is the law in Kent. It has also been the custom to divide lands and other property in the same way as in Kent on a considerable number of large and small manors in other parts of the kingdom, but with this important difference: the custom is presumed by law to exist in all parts of Kent unless it is proved that the lands were disgavelled or changed in their tenure, while outside that county it must be proved to have existed as an ancient custom. The proof is not required in Kent, but is required outside of it. Relatively to the whole country, however, the custom prevails on comparatively few manors out of this county.

All the available evidence tends to show that Kent was settled chiefly by Goths and Frisians under the Jutish name. It is most probable that its peculiar customs were introduced into that part of England by the people who settled there, and were not a survival of old Celtic customs of the same kind. This could hardly have been the case, seeing that the word *wealh*, for a Welshman, does not occur in the ordinances of the Kentish Kings. Partible inheritance is a custom which was very widely spread in the ancient world, and it is only by considering the other customs which were incidental to it in any country or locality, and by a comparison of these incidental customs with those in other countries or localities, that its probable origin can be traced. As it existed in England, the custom was varied in many details. The partible inheritance or gavelkind of Kent, however, stands out distinct in some respects as the 'custom of Kent.' It differs from that which prevailed in Wales in three essential points: In Kent only legitimate sons were entitled to a share of the inheritance, in Wales all sons claimed their shares; in Kent daughters succeeded if there were no sons, in Wales they did not; in Kent the widow was entitled to half her husband's estate as dower, in Wales she had no such provision.

A parallel in custom may be found by comparing the law of Kent with the Jutish law of King Valdemar II. in the thirteenth century, both of which contain the provision that the son, in reference to the property of the deceased father, shall be considered of age in his fifteenth year. This usage, though on the one side in accordance with Danish laws, and on the other valid among the socmen in other parts of England, is probably not derived from the Saxons, but is rather to be referred to the immigration of the Jutes.[5] Such a comparison also assists the evidence, which tends to show that the numerous socmen were of Scandinavian rather than of Saxon origin. Among other early privileges of Kent was the custom of freedom from ordinary distress. There was a Kentish process of 'cessavit,' under which, if a tenant withheld from his lord his due rents and services, the custom of the country gave the lord a special process for the recovery of what was due to him.[6] A somewhat similar custom of freedom from ordinary distress prevailed in London in very early time, and in a few other parts of the country. Where rents could not be recovered by the ordinary process of distress they were called 'dry rents.' The value of the comparison of these customs becomes clear when it is remembered that the ancient Visigoth law prohibited distress,[7] and these Visigoth settlers in Western Europe probably brought it from their Northern home. As it was common alike to the Visigoths, the people of Kent, and those of London, it supports the evidence that the Jutes were mainly Goths, and that people of this race settled in sufficient numbers in Kent and in and around London to insure the continuance of one of their customary privileges.

The Kentish land tenure was also distinguished by the prevalence of family or allodial rights.[8] The land was more or less of the nature of family land, as it was in parts of Hampshire and other counties that can be connected with settlements of Goths or other people of Northern origin.

In the division of the father's land by the custom of Kent, the youngest son appears to have been entitled to the family hearth or homestead on making compensation to his brothers. This can also be traced among the Frisians.[9] Subject to this preference for the youngest in regard to the hearth, the partition by the gavelkind custom gave the eldest son the first choice of the divided parts of the land.[10]

Another of the incidental customs of Kent was the widow's right to half of her deceased husband's estate. This has survived with other gavelkind customs until modern times. By the old common law of England, a widow, unless debarred by some local custom, received one-third of her husband's estate as dower. In the case of the Sussex tenants on manors where borough-English survived, she was entitled to have for her life the whole of her husband's lands. On some manors in various parts of England her dower was only a fourth. It is of interest to find that this custom of a provision for widows prevailed among the Goths. Olaus Magnus, writing of the ancient Goths, tells us that 'among them a man gave a dowry for his bride instead of receiving one with her.' The earliest reference we have in England to the custom of the morning-gift, or endowment of the wife, is in the early laws of Kent, and the oldest race to which a similar custom can be traced is the Goths.

That Kent was largely settled by Goths is proved by the evidence of the runic inscriptions which have been found within it. The most important of them are those discovered on two large stones at Sandwich. These were fixed monuments, and the inscriptions must therefore be identified with the people who lived near them. These monuments could not have been brought from Gothland or any other Northern land, as personal ornaments with old runic inscriptions could. Stephens[11] says: 'These are evidently heathen stones. Such stones would not have been erected after Kent was christianised—say, A.D. 600 at latest. They could not have been raised over dead Vikings, for the High North had by this time cast aside the old Northern stave, and adopted the Scandinavian alphabet, or futhorc.' This opinion from the greatest writer on runic monuments is valuable as showing that the runic letters on the Sandwich stones are old Northern Gothic, and not the later Scandian; that these monumental inscriptions are pre-Christian, and consequently of a date not later than the end of the sixth century. This discovery, therefore, proves the settlement of Northern Goths on the east coast of Kent. As the runic monuments have been discovered chiefly in the east of the county, it was presumably there that the Goths mainly settled.

The people in some parts of Kent exhibit in many respects the typical Frisian race characters. Those observed in Friesland at the present time have been described by Lubach as 'a tall, slender frame; a longish oval, flat skull, with prominent occiput; a long, oval face, with flat cheek-bones; a long nose, straight or aquiline, the point drooping below the wings; a high under-jaw and a well-developed chin.'[12] Many years ago Macintosh drew attention to somewhat similar features prevalent among the people of West Kent. He says: 'The Jutian characters are prevalent about Tonbridge,' and are 'a narrow face, very convex profile, head narrow, rather elongated, and very much rounded off at the sides, very long neck, and narrow shoulders.'[13] These physical characters may still be observed in the county, and more particularly in its western parts.

The ancient Goths, one of the noblest of the old European races, have long since disappeared. Their identity has been almost entirely lost in the birth of new nations. If we seek for any remnants of the old stock, we shall find them, such as they are, in the Dalecarlians of Sweden, among whom the custom of partible inheritance still survives. The Goths were the people most advanced in civilization of the nations in the Scandian peninsula, and we must trace to the parent Gothic stock many of the qualities of the present races of Scandinavia and the northern parts of Germany. They have disappeared, but the newer nations which sprang from them have preserved until our own time their love of liberty. If we trace it to its ultimate source, England is Gothic by birth, and Kent pre-eminently so. The Kentish man's liberty was his marked characteristic in the Middle Ages—a characteristic which had come down to him from the earliest Kentish settlers. Descended partly from Frisians—who were themselves, as the remnant of their ancient language shows, also of the old Gothic stock—and strongly marked by their love of freedom, the people of Kent preserved, through all the changes of the Anglo-Saxon period and the later powerful influences of feudalism, their free institutions, the relics of which, in the customs incidental to the gavelkind land tenure, have come down to our time. There is, perhaps, no survival in the length or breadth of England that is as remarkable as this.

Under the laws of Æthelbert, the Kentish ceorl was a freeman, and we read of him later in the laws of subsequent Kings. It was the proudest privilege of birth in Kent in the Middle Ages that every man so born, or whose father was so born, was free from those obligations of personal service which inferior tenants in other counties were bound to fulfil. The Kentish man was free to move, and if he went into another county and some lord of the manor claimed villein services from him, it was a good answer in law if he pleaded his father's Kentish birth.[14] This privilege of personal freedom, which is now the birth-right of every Englishman, was only the birthright of the people of one of our present counties in the period of feudal domination—viz., the people of Kent. Many other people who were inferior tenants on manors elsewhere were more or less freemen. Their number collectively was great, but no other instance occurs of any county in which all the people born in it, or whose fathers were born in it, were personally free. In this respect there was, perhaps, only one other area of local government which could be compared to Kent with all its privileges, and that was the City of London. In London every man from the earliest time was personally free if born there.

116

One of the general conclusions which an examination of the Anglo-Saxon relics found in England leads to is the similarity that many of them exhibit in design and ornamentation to those of early date, before the later so-called Viking period, which have been discovered in the Scandinavian peninsula— the home of the Northern Goths. From whatever source they acquired their knowledge of iron-working and its accompanying arts of metallurgy and gilding, the Goths certainly introduced this knowledge and art into the Scandian peninsula. These arts were much practised by the Gauls until the fall of the Roman Empire, after which they were lost in the South; but as they had been acquired by the Goths of Scandinavia, they were preserved and developed by them in the North, where they were unaffected by the great wars which marked the decline and fall of the Empire in other parts of Europe.[15] These lost arts were thus recovered from the Goths, and were reintroduced into England by them. Some of the oldest English ironworks were those of the ancient Andredsweald forest district of Sussex and Kent. Among Anglo-Saxon relics there are well-known Kentish types, many examples of which have been found also in the Isle of Wight, South Hampshire, and other parts of England, in or near to which settlements of Goths can be traced.

The early laws of Kent appear to afford evidence of the survival in that State in the sixth century of descendants of some of the settlers introduced into Britain from the Continent before the end of the later Roman occupation. Such settlers in various parts of the Empire were known as Læti. In Kent these people were called Lætas. This is a fact of interest and importance, for these Lætas of Kent in King Æthelbert's time were probably descendants of some of the Burgundians, Alamans, Vandals, or others, who were settled in Britain by Probus and some of his successors, as already mentioned. Their number and influence in Kent must have been considerable, as special provision was accorded to them in one of the laws of Æthelbert—viz., that which says, 'If anyone slay a Læt of the highest class let him pay 80 shillings, if he slay one of the second class let him pay 60 shillings, and if of the third, let him pay 40 shillings.'[16] In considering, therefore, the possibility of the survival elsewhere in England of any descendants of the tribes introduced into Britain by the Roman Emperors, the evidence that in Kent some descendants of these people survived increases the probability that in other parts of the country, such as along the so-called Saxon shore, similar descendants of the barbaric settlers of the time of the Empire who had not been absorbed in the Celtic population may also have survived until the same period. In connection with the early settlement of Kent, this reference to the Lætas in the Laws of Æthelbert is of more historical value than the story of Hengist and Horsa. In the early history of France the Læti are known as soldiers of the Empire, or their descendants.

There is, however, another view by which the Lætas of Kent may be regarded. They were, as mentioned, of three classes, and were protected by Æthelbert's laws by three degrees of fine or wergeld, in case any one of them should be killed—the higher the class, the higher the fine. The name Lætas may have been used to denote freemen of this early time, as the name Læti was on the Continent. In the early laws of Scandinavia we read of three classes of men who had obtained their freedom—i.e., who had become freedmen—and they also were protected by fines or wergelds in the same proportion as those connected with the Lætas of Kent—viz., 80, 60, and 40 ores of silver.[17] The highest class of these was the man whose great-grandfather had been also a freedman, called in Scandinavia a leysing. As the evidence concerning the Jutes connects them with Scandinavia, this system of classing the freemen or freedmen of Kent may have been a Northern custom introduced into that part of England by them. The people so classed may therefore have been in part introduced by the Jutes, and in part have been descendants of the older Teutonic settlers introduced into Britain by the Romans, and for administrative purposes classed under this system.

That Frisians were largely represented among the settlers in Kent is generally allowed. The traces of Frisians in Kent, as elsewhere, may be looked for under the tribal designations by which people of that race were known, or called themselves. Bede mentions the Hunni as one of the tribes from which the people of England in his time were known to have descended, and these can be identified with the Frisian tribe known as Hunsings. The name Hunesbiorge occurs in a Kentish charter,[18] and Honinberg Hundred is mentioned in Domesday Book. Brocmen and Chaucians, and other Frisians of tribal names now lost, were probably represented among the settlers in Kent under the name of Jutes. Of these Jutes, the Goths were probably the more numerous, seeing that the name adopted for the Kentish people generally was a modified form of Gutæ, a name for their own race.

The traditional freedom of the people of this county, and the still older traditional freedom of the Frisians, confirm the other evidence, anthropological as well as philological, which connects Kent with ancient Friesland. The old laws of the Frisians declare 'that the race shall be free as long as the winds blow out of the clouds and the world stands.'[19]

The Frisians, with the Batavians of what is now Holland, came under the dominion of Charlemagne, who confirmed their laws and left them their native customs.[20] The personal freedom of the people of Kent was their most highly prized birthright, derived from their tribal ancestors, and has been commemorated by Dryden in the following lines referring to that county:

'Among the English shires be thou surnamed the free,
And foremost ever placed when they shall numbered be.'

This last line, about being placed first, refers to another remarkable Kentish custom or claim—viz., that of being marshalled in the van of the national army when being led to war. This claim was one of the warlike privileges of the men of Kent, and was recognised throughout the period of their early history. As will be shown later on, it was a claim which was also recognised and allowed to Kentish settlers in another part of England.

There may have been more than one Baltic homeland of the Jutes, and Witland, east of the Vistula, may have been one of them. Wulfstan, in narrating his voyage up the Baltic to King Alfred, says that Witland[21] was east of the Vistula, and appertained to Eastum or Eastland. The old form of the *w* in Witland is *uu*, and in this form Uuitland is close in sound to Jutland. It would, from this and other evidence, appear not improbable that Eastmen may have settled among the Jutes in Kent.

The remarkable collection of ancient skulls that formerly existed at Hythe were believed by some who examined them to have been the remains of men who fell in battle. Knox,[22] who examined them in 1860, thought that a large number of them were of the Celtic type, and the remainder of Anglo-Saxon type. Two of the skulls he believed to be those of Lapps. Another observer found broad skulls as well as long ones among them.[23] To account for the broad skulls, we must suppose either a survival in this part of Kent of descendants of the broad-headed men of the Bronze Age—for the later Celts were not of this type—or the arrival with the long-headed Teutonic invaders of some men of a broad-headed race.

In Romney Marsh and the neighbouring portion of the Weald, Beddoe's observations show that darker hues[24] prevail among the people, and it is near the coast of Romney Marsh that the Domesday place Blachemene-stone—now Blackmanstone—is situated. Such a name is unlikely to have been given to a place on the coast from a survival of dark Celtic people there. As a coast place, it is far more probable that it got its name from dark-haired settlers. This was the country of the tribe known in Saxon time as the Merscwara, and it must be concluded that, whether these people were partly of Celtic descent or not, there was probably some ethnological difference between them and the people in other parts of Kent. Two designations—'Men of Kent' and 'Kentish Men'—have come down to our time. They are certainly old, the former being the designation of the people in the east around Canterbury, and the latter that of those in the west of the county. The traditions relating to these names for Kentish people are apparently as old as the time of the settlement. The inhabitants of the eastern part of the county were certainly called 'Men of Kent,' and those in the western part 'Kentish Men.' In one of the early charters the words 'provincia orientalis Cantiæ,' or province of East Kent, occur.[25] The Anglo-Saxon Chronicle tells us, under the year 858, that the Danes fought with the Men of Kent (*mid Cantwarum*). Under the year 865, it states that they made peace with the Men of Kent. Under the year 902, we read of the Danes and the Cantwara, or Men of Kent. Similarly, in the same Chronicle we have some references to the West Kentish people. Under the year 999, we read of the Danish army going along the Medway to Rochester, and of the 'Centisce fyrd,' or Kentish military array, which is also mentioned as the 'weast Centingas,' or West Kentish men. Under the year 1009, the same Chronicle mentions the East Centingas, or people of East Kent. There appears, consequently, to be no doubt that the provinces of East and West Kent were well known in Saxon time, and little doubt that these corresponded with the diocesan divisions, or Dioceses of Canterbury and Rochester. As the runic monuments, which must be assigned to the Goths, have only been found in East Kent, it is possible that the two ancient divisions of Kent were ethnological divisions, and mainly, perhaps, between Goths in the east and Frisians in the west.

If further evidence were wanted to prove the settlement of Goths in Kent, it could be found in the earliest money that was used. Sceatts and scillings are mentioned in the Kentish laws, the sceatt being a small silver coin of a value somewhat equivalent to the later penny. In a fragment of Mercian law which has survived sceatts are also mentioned.[26] In the early Northumbrian metrical translation of the Book of Genesis, which is ascribed to Cædmon in the seventh century, the word *sceat* is used for the passage in which Abraham declares he would take 'neither sceat ne scilling' from the King of Sodom. Sceatts and scillings are mentioned in one of the Northern Sagas—'The Scald's Tale'—so that sceatts must have been known in the North of Europe, the original home of the Goths. That the coin was in use among the people of this race is shown by its name in the translation of the Gospels made in the fourth century by Bishop Ulphilas for the Mœso-Goths, who had migrated from the North and settled near the lower course of the Danube. In the passage 'Show me a penny,' etc., the Latin word *denarius* is translated *skatt* in two instances. Its occurrence in the Kentish laws thus points to Goths, and the use of a similar name in Mercia and Northumbria indicates a Gothic influence.

From the evidence that has been stated, the Scandinavian origin of the Jutes appears to be conclusive, and this is supported by the early monetary currency in the Kentish kingdom. The Kentish shilling differed greatly from those of Wessex and Mercia. It was much more valuable, and of the weight of a Roman ounce of silver, or 576 wheat-grains.[27] This was the same as the Scandinavian ora,[28] which was divided into smaller silver coins, each one-third of its weight and value, called the ortug, weighing 192 grains of wheat. This latter was of the same weight and value as the Greek stater of the Eastern Empire.[29]

In Kent, therefore, we find that the earliest shilling, which was worth 20 sceatts, or 1 ounce of silver, was the equivalent also of 3 Byzantine staters. Consequently, in this monetary equivalence we see on the one hand evidence of the Scandinavian connection of the Kentish Jutes or Goths, and on the other evidence of the Eastern commerce between the Goths of the Baltic regions and the Greek merchants of the Eastern Empire.

In its monetary system and reckoning the kingdom of Kent seems to have been peculiar from the first,[30] and to have continued peculiar for centuries, for its shilling was exactly equal in value to two of the small gold coins, known as tremisses, in circulation in North-East Frisia in Charlemagne's time,[31] the ratio between gold and silver at that time being 1 to 12. The evidence that Kent was occupied mainly by Goths and Frisians appears, therefore, to be established by the monetary systems of these ancient nations, which point to ancient commercial intercourse between them and Kent, or to racial affinity. This commercial connection between the Goths and Frisians is also supported by the earliest knowledge we have of the wergelds, or fines for slaying a freeman, paid to his kindred by Goths of the Isle of Gotland and by the East Frisians. It was 160 gold solidi, or shillings, in the case of each of these tribal people.[32]

As regards the shapes of villages and settlements, Kent affords examples, apparently, of both the isolated homestead system, which may be ascribed to Frisians, and of the collected homestead plan. The lone farmhouses in the county, which are called *tons*—such as Shottington, Wingleton, Godington, and Appleton—may be regarded as venerable monuments of the settlement in these instances having been by families and not by larger communities.

The influence of Kent in the origin of the Old English race has been underestimated. This early kingdom was a limited area, with no hinterland for expansion and for the settlement near it of its surplus population. As time passed on, its limits were found too circumscribed to accommodate the increasing number of its people, and colonies were sent out. We can trace some of these Kentish colonial settlements, as will be shown in later chapters, in some of the southern and western counties, in Essex, and in the upper parts of the Thames valley.

[1] Stephens, G., 'Old Northern Runic Monuments,' iii. 397.

[2] Magnus, J., 'Hist. de omn. Goth. reg.,' ed. 1554. p. 15.

[3] Kemble, J. M., 'Saxons in England,' i. 16.

[4] Elton, C. I., and Mackay, H. J. H., 'Law of Copyholds,' 1893, p. 8.

[5] Lappenberg, 'Hist. Anglo-Saxon Kings,' ed. 1884, i., 123, 124.

[6] Elton, C. I., 'Gavelkind,' p. 196.

[7] Maine, Sir H., 'Early Institutions,' 269, 270.

[8] Robertson, E. W., 'Scotland under her Early Kings,' ii. 264.

[9] *Ibid.*, ii. 266.

[10] Lambarde, W., 'Customs in Gavelkind: Perambulation of Kent,' 1570, ed. 1826, p. 519.

[11] Stephens, G., *loc. cit.*, i. 363.

[12] Beddoe, J., 'Races of Britain,' p. 40.

[13] *Trans. Ethnological Society*, vol. i., p. 214.

[14] Lambarde, W., *loc. cit.*, p. 511.

[15] Starkie-Gardner, J., 'Ironwork,' p. 37.

[16] Laws of Æthelbert, 26.

[17] Seebohm, F., 'Tribal Custom in Anglo-Saxon Law,' 485, 486.

[18] Cart. Sax., ii. 202

[19] Monumenta Germaniæ, and 'Laws of the Frisians,' quoted by Rogers, J. E. Thorold, 'Holland,' p. 4.

[20] Rogers, J. E. Thorold, 'Holland,' pp. 4, 5.

[21] King Alfred's 'Orosius,' edited by Sweet, H., p. 20.

[22] *Archæologia Cantiana*, xviii. 333-336.

[23] *Ibid.*, 334.

[24] Beddoe, J., 'Races in Britain,' 256.

[25] Codex Dipl., No. 256.

[26] Seebohm, F., *loc. cit.*, 445.

[27] *Seebohm, F.,* loc. cit., *pp. 448, 449.*

[28] *Ibid.*, 233.

[29] *Ibid.*, 233.

[30] Seebohm, F., *loc cit.*, p. 442.

[31] *Ibid.*, 454, 455.

[32] *Ibid.*, 231, 232.

# Chapter Twelve - Settlers in Sussex and Part of Surrey

SUSSEX still shows some remarkable traces of its early Anglo-Saxon people. The survival of the custom of borough-English, by which the youngest son is the sole heir to his father's estate, on about 140 manors in this county, is in all probability due to its having been the custom of some of the original settlers. It is most common in the Rape of Lewes, but exists also on manors elsewhere.

This custom of borough—English or junior right prevails more extensively in Sussex than in any county. While Kent is marked by a survival of partible inheritance, Sussex is marked in a similar way by the survival among the copyholders on a very large number of its manors of sole inheritance by the youngest son. These two customs resemble each other in one respect—the preference for the youngest. In Kent he was entitled to have the homestead on making an equitable compensation to his brothers, but in all other respects the inheritance was divided equally between the sons, so that in Kent the special recognition of the youngest son is only weak. On the contrary, in the Sussex custom the recognition of the claim of the youngest son was absolute, as he succeeded to the whole of the land to the exclusion of his brothers. As already shown, this custom can be traced more clearly to Eastern Europe than to any other source.

The following circumstances in reference to settlements in the South-East of England are important considerations: (1) The Goths, under the name of Gutæ or Jutes, were the chief settlers in Kent, as proved by historical statements, the existence of fixed monuments with Gothic runes on them, and the survival of gavelkind, with its incidental customs of freedom from distress and dower of widows which can be traced to a Gothic source. (2) The existence in Sussex over a large area of the custom by which the youngest son succeeded to the whole of his father's estate. (3) The existence in Kent of a recognition of the youngest son to a less extent, he being entitled to the paternal homestead. (4) The prevalence of junior right at the present day as the survival of an ancient custom of inheritance among some people in Friesland, and among the Slavs. (5) The Slavic origin of the old Vandal or Wendish tribes of the south coast of the Baltic Sea, close to the ancient seat of the Goths. (6) The survival of ancient Vandal or Wendish placenames in both Sussex and Essex.

Goths and Vandals, when allied in warlike expeditions, were commonly called Astings.[1] It may, of course, be accidental that a tribe called the Hæstingas was settled on the borderland between Sussex and Kent, but there is evidence of some commingling of the people of these counties near their border. The custom of partible inheritance, which is general in Kent, does not exist in Sussex, except at Rye,[2] where it may still survive in cases of intestacy, and Rye was only separated from Kent by Romney Marsh, now reclaimed. The largest of the Wendish tribes of North-East Germany was the Wilte, called also Lutitzer. The names of several of the hundreds of Sussex in Saxon time—viz., Wendelmestrei, Willingham, Welesmere[3]—are suggestive of Wends or Wilte. When we compare the name Wendelmestrei with the place-name Wendelstein in one of the old Wendish parts of Germany, we can scarcely doubt how the Sussex name arose, if considered in reference to the survival in Sussex of an old Wendish custom.

There are other Anglo-Saxon names of places in this county which may also have been derived from persons who were called by some tribal name, such as Bucgan-ora,[4] now changed to Bognor, and Buckingham, which may have come from the name of the pagus of the Bucki, in the Engern country of the Old Saxons. The name Bexwarena-land for the country around Bexley occurs also in a charter of Offa,[5] and, as it is written in the genitive plural, it must be considered to refer to a settlement of people known as Bexware.

In the extreme West of Sussex there is a place near Selsea called Wittering, which is mentioned in a charter of the tenth century as Wedering,[6] a name presumably derived originally from a settler called Weder, from his tribal name—that of the Wederas or Ostrogoths from the Wedermark, on the east of Lake Wetter. The name occurs in the boundaries of Selsea, another bound-ary-name of the same land being Cwuenstane.[7] This latter is much like Cwén, the Norrena name for a Fin. Another Fin settlement appears probable from the Sussex Domesday place-name Fintune.

Similarly, the Domesday name Angemare—the Angemeringum or An-gemæringtun of Saxon charters[8]—reminds us of the ancient Swedish prov-ince of Angermanland, on the west of the Gulf of Bothnia, opposite to Finland. As already mentioned, there are still existing in the north-eastern provinces of Sweden stone monuments with runic inscriptions to those who 'resided westward in England,' or who 'died in England.'[9] Eastmen or Ostrogoths were names used somewhat freely in ancient time for the same people, and it is possible that the two Domesday places in Sussex named Essete may refer to settlers who were Eastmen. There are four places in Sussex named Ga-ringes, and as g and w were interchangeable in sound, these may be equiva-lent to Waringes, and point to settlements of Warings.

Hunestan is a Domesday name apparently referring to the settlement of a family of Hunsings, as Sasinghā does to one which bore the Saxon name.

A trace of people who were in some way connected with Franks or Bur-gundians in Sussex is afforded by the discovery of a weapon known as the angon in a cemetery of the Anglo-Saxon period at Ferring. This weapon, al-most unknown in connection with ancient burials in England, is frequently found on the Continent in ancient graves of Franks and Burgundians.[10]

It is not suggested that all the manors in Sussex on which the custom of junior right prevailed were settled by Wends. That custom can be traced more fully to the Slavs than to any other race, but in ancient time, as well as in modern, the Slavs were settled close to, or even among, the Teutons, and it might have been adopted by some of the Saxon tribes or communities of mixed descent, and have been introduced into Sussex and other parts of England partly by Wends and partly by Frisians, Burgundians, or others who had adopted it. This supposition is supported by the survival of this old custom over considerable portions of North Germany at the present time, whereas generally among the Germans the mode of succession of the nobles, as well as the inferior tenants, was partible inheritance. As regards the inferior tenants, in parts of Germany the parcelling out of the land into smaller and smaller portions led to such impoverishment that the 'Minorat succession' was in modern time established so that the youngest son was constituted by law heir to the father's farms and lands, it being considered that the father was better able to portion off his elder children in his lifetime.[11] A community of mixed descent in contact with another which had the junior right custom might have adopted it in ancient time, as it was by German law in modern time.

The place-names in Sussex ending in the word -mer are suggestive. Grimm tells us that the older Slavs called the world mir and ves'mir.[12] Mir is also the name for peace, and seems akin to mira or mera, a measure. Among all the counties of England Sussex is remarkable for its place-names terminating in this word -mer, in some cases -mere. It appears to refer to a boundary or limit rather than to a marsh, for some of the names which have this ending are situated on high ground, such as Falmer—the Domesday Felesmere. Keymer, Angermer, Stanmer, Jonsmer, Cuckmere, Ringmer, Udimore (commonly pronounced Udimer), Tangemere, Linchmere, and Haslemere, on the county boundary, are other examples of the name. Some of these, like those of other ancient places and hundreds in Sussex, probably refer to people.

Among Domesday names of significance in reference to Frisians of the Chaucian tribe are Cochinges and Cochehā. As in some other counties in which there are traces of Wendish settlers, we find a place-name containing the root sem, probably derived from the old Slavonic word for land. It occurs in the Domesday place-name Semlintun.

The number of places in Sussex whose names bear a resemblance to Frisian names is remarkable. The terminal pronunciation of some of them in -um and -un also resembles the Frisian. In Friesland we find Dokkum, Workum, Bergum, Akkrum, Wierum, Hallum, Ulrum, Loppersum, Makkum, Bedum, and others of the same kind. In Sussex we find Horsham (locally pronounced Horsum and Hawsom), Hailsham (Helsum), Sedlecombe (Selzcum), Friston (Frissun), Cocking (Cokkun), Lillington (Linkun).[13] The indications pointing to Frisians in this county are sufficient to show that people of this nation must have settled among the South Saxons.

That there were among these Frisians tribal Hunsings and Chaucians is probable from such family names as Friston, Hunston, the Domesday names Cochehā, Cokkefeld, and the numerous similar names, Cuckmere, Cuckfield, Cocking, Cockhais, Cockshut stream, Cokeham (a hamlet of Sompting), and Cooksbridge, north of Lewes. These latter, which may be compared with

Cuxhaven in the old country of the Chaucians and similar names in various parts of England, point to family settlements of these tribal people.

The name Swanborough, the Domesday Soanberge, probably denotes the settlement of one or more families of Sweons or Swedes. Their connection with the Viking expeditions has been proved, and is not a matter of conjecture. In the original settlement of Sussex it must, however, be accepted that people of Saxon origin, including the Frisians, were in the majority, and so gave their name to the kingdom. The occurrence of the Domesday name Sasinghā, denoting a family of Saxon origin, in a county supposed to have been entirely settled by Saxons, may be explained by its possible use, in this instance, as a distinctive name for a Saxon settler in a district in which the neighbouring settlements were those of people who were not Saxons.

Sussex, like all English maritime counties, had its later Scandinavian settlements as well as those of the early Saxon period. At Framfield there were customary laws of inheritance of much interest, which point, in all probability, to settlers of more than one ancient race. These customs were the subject of a legal inquiry early in the seventeenth century, and were set forth by the Court of Chancery, 4 James I. There was at Framfield bondland and assartland, the former being in all probability that which was first under cultivation, and the latter that which was converted to arable land by some early forest clearing, possibly for a later settlement of Scandinavians. However this may have been, the custom was that if any man be first admitted tenant of any assartland and die seised of it, and also of bondland, then the eldest son should be admitted heir of all his land, and if he have no son, the eldest daughter should succeed. If, however, the tenant be first admitted to the bondland, also called yardland, the youngest son, and failing sons, the youngest daughter, should succeed to the whole of his land. If he left no children, the youngest brother; failing brothers, the youngest sister; and failing these, the youngest uncle or aunt or youngest cousin, males being preferred in each degree of relationship.[14] The custom by which the eldest daughter succeeded if there was no son makes it probable that there was a Norse settlement on the assartland at Framfield. We may find another trace of people of Norse descent in parts of East Sussex in the custom of 'principals,' by which the eldest son on some of the lands in Sussex belonging to Battle Abbey was entitled to certain heirlooms or articles in right of primogeniture.[15] The succession by the youngest seems to have been originally connected with the bondland, and follows the custom that so largely prevailed in the Rape of Lewes.

The eldest daughter custom at Framfield and the custom of 'principals' in reference to the eldest son, when compared with the customs of Norway and Cumberland, are so clearly of Scandian origin that we may look for other traces of the Northmen in Sussex. The name *rapes* for the county divisions appears to be of Scandinavian origin, and to be connected with Anglo-Saxon *rap*, *ræp*, and the Gothic *raip*, signifying a rope. In Iceland districts are called *hreppar* to the present day.[16] Scandinavian place-names may be recognised in Harlinges (an old place near Framfield), Bosham, Bosgrave, Thorney,

Angmering, Swanborough, Denton, Scale near Stenning, and Angleton, all ancient names which occur in their old forms in ancient records. There are two places named Blechington, one north of Brighton, and the other east of Newhaven. These family settlement names suggest some connection with Scandian people from Blekinge, the province in the South of Sweden. These ancient names, and the survival of the customs mentioned, so clearly point to Northmen that there can be no doubt that settlements of them, probably during the later Saxon period, took place on the Sussex coast.

At Rotherfield there were three kinds of heritable land—viz., farthingland, cotmanland, and assartland. The eldest son was heir of the assartland, and the wife was not entitled to dower. The assartland was that which had been reclaimed from some forest clearing, and, being new cultivated land, there was no customary mode of inheritance attached to it. Consequently, it followed the common law of primogeniture. The youngest son was heir of the farthingland and cotmanland, but, if there were no sons, there was this difference between the descent of farthingland and cotmanland: the former descended to the youngest daughter, while the latter was divided among all the daughters.[17] To this extent the cotmanland followed the custom of Kent, and the farthingland the custom of a great part of Sussex.

History is silent concerning Norse colonies on our southern coasts, but the customs and old place-names which have been mentioned point to a considerable settlement of Scandinavians in Sussex, and Sweons or Swedes among them. That Swedes came among the Vikings, as already mentioned, is proved by the runic monuments of their country. In the district of Vaksala (parish of old Upsala) there is still existing an inscription to Sigvid, 'the England seafarer.' In Vestermanland there is another 'to a worthy young man, and he had gone to England.' In Gestrikland, near Gefle, is another made by relatives to 'their brother Bruse when he set out for England.'[18] Some of these and other inscriptions may be memorials of actual settlers in our country. There is additional evidence relating to Northmen. The Domesday names Totenore, Sidenore, Venningore or Waningore, Icenore, and the other early names Cymenore, Kynnore, and Cotenore, show by their terminations traces of Scandinavian people. Among other Danish or Scandinavian traces in the oldest place-names are those beginning with *Sale*, which may refer to settlers from Sealand. These are the Domesday places Salecome and Salhert, now Salehurst, and Salemanneburn,[19] a name for one of the old hundreds. The conditions under which settlements were formed in Sussex must have been peculiar to it from the first. With a great extent of coast, and the country nearest to it being for long distances sparsely supplied with wood, the early settlers must have depended for that commodity on the forest district further north, or on woods which became common to certain hundreds or groups of village settlements. The Andredsweald forest was known as the 'Sylva communis' in the Anglo-Saxon period.[20]

There are still surviving a number of place-names ending in the word *-tye*, which probably denoted common lands or rights of some kind attached to various places. Berwick-tye, Bramble-tye, Horntye, Pilstye, Puckstye, Wroth-tye, also Tyes and Tyes Cross, Tye farm, and Tye hill, are examples.

The survival of borough-English on a considerable number of manors in the south of Surrey points to colonization from Sussex. The custom of succession by the youngest son not only survived until modern time in these places, but the division of the manors into so-called boroughs also survived. At Dorking there were four boroughs—viz., Chipping borough, comprising the greater part of the town; Holmwood borough, comprising the country on the south side of the town; Milton borough; and Westcote borough. There were, similarly, a number of rural boroughs in the manor of Croydon, where borough-English also survived. These arrangements for rural government, with a headman called the head-borough, are the same as existed in parts of Sussex, where succession by the youngest son was the custom. It is known that this custom prevailed on at least twenty-eight manors[21] in Surrey, including Dorking, Croydon, Reigate, and Bletchworth.[22] These places are all on, or quite close to, the lines of the old Roman roads which connected Sussex with London, and the survival of a Sussex custom at places in Surrey situated on these roads suggests migrations of people along them. Borough-English is also known to have prevailed in the following rural parts of Surrey: Weston Gumshall, Sutton (near Woking), Little Bookham, Wootton, Abinger, Padington, Towerhill, Nettley, Shere, Cranley, Compton-Westbury, Brockham in Betchworth, and Dunsford. The migration from Sussex into Surrey thus appears to have been considerable.

There is in the south-east of Surrey some evidence of the commingling of local colonists from both Sussex and Kent in this part of the Weald forest. It can be traced in the manorial and other local customs. At Lingfield the officials called head-boroughs were appointed for all the manors within this large parish, as was the case in Sussex on the manors where borough-English prevailed. Sterborough, one of the manors of Lingfield, bears this borough name. Part of this rural borough lay in Kent, and was subject to gavelkind. The tenants of the other part of this manor held their land subject to the payment of a heriot of the best beast on the death of the tenant.[23] This custom was probably introduced into England by Scandinavians, and is commonly met with in districts settled by them.

Blechingley had some customs which bore a strong resemblance to some of those incidental to gavelkind in Kent. The tenants paid no heriots, but one penny only, and no more, for admission to their lands. They could sell or alienate their lands, as the gavelkind tenants in Kent could. They could grant leases without their lord's license,[24] as Kentish tenants could. Part of Godstone was held of the manor of Blechingley, with presumably similar customs. At Reigate the free and customary tenants had the custom of borough-English, and held their lands and tenements in free and common socage,[25] which corresponded very closely to gavelkind in Kent. Similarly, at Limpsfield the copyholds descended to the youngest son,[26] like those held in the barony of Lewes.

In a previous chapter the development of the hundred as a division of the later English shires from the primitive districts that had their separate popular assemblies of freemen has been referred to. Sussex affords us examples of hundreds mentioned in Domesday Book that appear originally to have been districts of this kind. This is seen in the case of the hundred of Bexelei, the area of which probably was that mentioned in a charter in the time of Off a as Bexwarena-land.[27] These Bexware people thus mentioned as a district community no doubt had their local assembly or court, common to all Teutonic tribes, and it is difficult to see any other probable origin of the later hundred of Bexelei. The hundreds of Sussex were very numerous, and consequently for the most part small. No fewer than fifty of them are mentioned in Domesday Book, and they include those bearing the clan or tribal names Mellinges, Staninges, Ghestelinges, and Poninges, which are examples of small communities of people of the same kindred, and many similar names are mentioned in the Saxon charters. With the exception of Kent, Sussex contained a larger number of hundreds at the time of the Survey than any other county on the south-east coast. As we cannot suppose that all these comparatively small separate areas of administration arose in the later Saxon period, the conclusion appears unavoidable that the South Saxons were originally settled in small district communities, administered by their own local assemblies of the freemen.

Some evidence of variation in race among the South Saxons has been obtained by the examination of skulls from their cemeteries. Of fourteen, examined by Horton-Smith, found at Goring, near Worthing, thirteen were long and one broad.[28] The long skulls were very marked, the average index being 72. As the English skull at the present time has an average index of 78, it will be seen that the great majority of the settlers at Goring were characterized by having specially long heads. They correspond closely to the ancient German type found so numerously in an old burying-ground at Bremen, which has an index of 71 or 72. The skulls with this average characteristic index were found in that part of ancient Frisia inhabited by the Chaucians, and as some of the Sussex place-names point to Frisian settlers, the coincidence is suggestive. In reference to the broad skull, Horton-Smith supposes a fusion of race to have taken place between the Saxons of Sussex and some British descendants of the period of the Round Barrow or Bronze Age. He points out, however, an important difference in the height of the skulls—viz., that the height-index of the Round Barrow race, according to Thurnam, is 76, whereas that of the typical Saxon is 70. The settlement in Sussex of some broad-headed people with the long-headed majority, coming from a Continental area where people of both race characters are known to have lived, is probably a better explanation.

The survival of junior inheritance on so many manors in Sussex, and the discovery of differences in the skulls, suggest the inquiry, What evidence is there in Sussex of a typical Saxon race? The custom was foreign to the Continental Saxons. The settlers in Sussex must apparently have been tribal people of more than one race. They may well have been of three races, as perhaps is dimly remembered in their traditional arrival in three ships. The observations which were made half a century ago on the ethnology of the people of this county by Mackintosh are of interest. He says: 'In Sussex the Saxon type is found in its greatest purity in the area extending from East Grinstead to Hastings.' It is in this area that place-names ending in -ham, such as Withyham, Etchingham, Northiam, and Bodiam, occur. He says also that 'in Sussex the majority of the inhabitants would appear to belong to two races—the Saxon, and a race with harder and more angular features.'[29] The immigration of other settlers among the Frisians and Saxons probably explains this.

The village arrangements in Sussex show examples of both isolated and collected homesteads. In some parishes, as in Kent, there are old place-names apparently of early settlements, distinct from the name of the parish itself. Such names, which are now applied to hamlets or farms, were in many instances probably the names of settlements by families in isolated homesteads. This plan of village occupation, which prevails so largely in the country west of the Weser, may have been introduced into Sussex by Frisian settlers. It may, however, be a British survival which some of the tribal South Saxons found here, and adopted in the districts in which it can be traced. In other parts of the county that are marked chiefly by villages of collected homesteads the old Celtic arrangement appears to have been replaced by that observable between the Weser and the Elbe, occupied by the old Saxons, and in the country north and east of the Elbe, occupied respectively by Saxons and Wends.

One of the most interesting circumstances connected with early Sussex is the migration of a large body of Sussex people at the beginning of the eighth century, and the establishment by them of a colony in Somersetshire, which will be discussed in the chapter on the South-western counties. The early date of this migration, which can be proved, shows that the tribal people who brought with them the custom of junior inheritance into the Rape of Lewes must have been early settlers there, and it is quite certain they were not, strictly speaking, Saxons.

[1] Latham, R. G., 'Germania of Tacitus,' xviii.

[2] Elton, C. I., and Mackay, H. J. H., 'Robinson on Gavelkind,' p. 33.

[3] Domesday Book.

[4] Cart. Sax., i. 82.

[5] Ibid., i. 294.

[6] Ibid., iii. 193.

[7] Ibid.

[8] Codex Dipl., Nos. 314 and 1067.

[9] Mémoires de la Société Royale des Antiquaires du Nord, 1845-1849, p. 333.

[10] Read, C. H., Archæologia, liv. 369.

[11] Baring-Gould, S., 'Germany, Past and Present,' pp. 56-68.

[12] Grimm, J., 'Teutonic Mythology,' ed. by Stallybrass, ii., 793.

[13] Lower, M. A., 'History of Sussex,' vol. i.

[14] Corner, G. R., 'On Borough-English' Sussex Archæological Collections, vi. 175, 176.

[15] Encyclopædia Britannica, Ninth ed., 'Primogeniture.'

[16] Domesday Book, General Introduction, by H. Ellis, pp. 179, 180.

[17] Corner, G. R., *loc. cit.*, vi. 15.

[18] Mémoires de la Société Royale des Antiquaires du Nord, Copenhagen, 1845-1849, pp. 334-346.

[19] Placita de quo warranto, 749.

[20] Horsfield, T. W., 'History and Antiquities of Lewes,' p. 3.

[21] Corner, R. G., *loc. cit.*, 15.

[22] Elton, C. I., and Mackay, H. J. H., *loc. cit.*, 238.

[23] Manning and Bray, 'History of Surrey,' ii. 340.

[24] *Ibid.*, ii. 296.

[25] *Ibid.*, i. 281.

[26] *Ibid.*, ii. 394.

[27] Cart. Sax., i. 294.

[28] *Journal Anthrop. Inst.*, xxvi. 83.

[29] *Ethnological Society Transactions*, i. 214, 215.

# Chapter Thirteen - The Gewissas and Other Settlers in Wessex

THE settlement of people of more than one race in Hampshire under the name of Gewissas is historical. The evidence rests partly on the statement of Bede, who wrote within two hundred years of the probable date of the invasion of this part of Britain. His information was derived from Daniel, Bishop of Winchester, and the Bishop no doubt obtained it from people of more than one race distinctly surviving in Wessex in his time. The chief point in this historical evidence cannot be doubted—viz., that there were people settled in the Isle of Wight and the southern part of the county who were of different descent from those in other parts of the early kingdom of Wessex. The original kingdom was no doubt at first what is now called Hampshire, or the county of Southampton, but the small state soon grew in extent, so that before the end of the sixth century it comprised parts at least of what is now Dorset, Wiltshire, and Berkshire. The settlement of Hampshire, therefore, cannot be fully considered without reference to that of the counties which adjoin it on the west and north. According to the genealogy of the Kings of Wessex, Cedric was a great-grandson of Gewis,[1] but this genealogy is legendary, not historical. It may be accepted, however, as evidence of the antiquity of the tribal name Gewissæ, which long survived in this kingdom. In A.D. 766 Cynewlf, King of Wessex, gave a charter to the monastery of Wells, and in it he styles himself 'Cynewlphus Gewissorum rex.'[2] This is evidence of the survival of the name more than two centuries after the arrival of the Gewissas in Hampshire. The West Saxon Kings must have been proud of it to have retained it. Still later, in the year 825, Egbert used the same title 'rex Gewissorum'[3] in a charter in which he gave land at Alton to the Monastery of SS. Peter and Paul at Winchester. Eadred also, in the year 946, in a grant of land to the thegn Ethelgeard, describes the situation of this land as being at Brightwell, in the district of the Gewissi—*i.e.*, Brightwell, near Wallingford, in Berkshire, so described, probably, to distinguish it from another Brightwell in Oxfordshire.[4]

Even after the Norman Conquest, Ordericus Vitalis, writing in the twelfth century, mentions the district round Winchester as the country of the Gewissæ. The name evidently had great vitality, and must have been a common one to have been used by a chronicler at so late a date. When we consider its probable origin, we have first to note the occurrence of the name Gewis in the genealogy of the West Saxon Kings,[5] and, secondly, its probable meaning. Gewis would naturally arise at the time when the Anglo-Saxon genealogies were drawn up, from the tribal name Gewissæ or Gewissas being in common use. This name of the mythological ancestor of the royal house is certainly more likely to have been derived from the name of the tribe than that the tribal name should have had its origin from a mythological one.

Its meaning has recently been discussed by Stevenson,[6] who has stated the opinions of various writers. The most probable derivation appears to be that of Müllenhoff, who connects it with the Gothic *ga-wiss*—junction—and Gewissas are thus explained as confederates.

In the traditionary accounts of the occupation of Kent and Sussex, we read of invaders coming in three ships in each case. In the account relating to Wessex we read that they came in five, and this may have some reference to tribal expeditions of confederates. That the settlers who occupied Hampshire consisted of people of more than one race admits of no doubt. As will be shown, there is evidence within the limits of ancient Wessex of settlements by Goths or Jutes, Saxons, Frisians, and Wends. There is evidence also of later considerable settlements of Northmen. The interpretation of the name Gewissas as confederates is certainly confirmed by what can be discovered concerning the West Saxon people. Indeed, confederacies played such an important part in the settlement of England generally that it can be no matter for surprise to find sufficient evidence, even apart from the historical, to show that Wessex was colonized by people of various races. There were small confederacies as well as large ones among the ancient tribes of Germany, and it is possible that such names as Gewiesen, Gewissenruhe, and Gewissowice, which still exist in North-East Germany,[7] may have had their origin in clan confederacies of people of different tribes or kindreds.

As regards the Gothic connection of the word, it is of interest to note the occurrence of *gewiss*, used in the sense of 'assured' or 'certain,' in an inscription on one of the capitals of a column which still remains at Ravenna, and which commemorates the rule of Theodoric, the great Gothic King at that place. He, the greatest of the Goth rulers, was King over people of the same descent as the Northern Goths or Jutes, many of whom, without doubt, made for themselves English homes in Hampshire and the Isle of Wight, as members of a confederacy known as that of the Gewissas. These were apparently sworn or assured allies.

Among these Gewissas or confederates, Saxons and Frisians were probably the greatest in number. From what is known of their descendants on the Continent, they were people of a blonde complexion, so that the prevailing ethnological character of the people of Wessex agrees with that of the present inhabitants of Friesland and North Germany.

At the time Bede wrote contemporary evidence existed of the two chief tribes, who, under the name Gewissas, made up the West Saxon State. At that time the Isle of Wight was under its own chiefs or Kings, subordinate only to the Kings of Wessex; and there are some references which point to a government of the Meon country, or south-east part of Hampshire, at one time by Princes, apart from the direct rule of the Wessex Sovereigns. The Jutes of the Isle of Wight certainly, and those of the south-east part of Hampshire possibly, were under their own local administration at the time when Daniel, Bishop of Winchester, informed the Venerable Bede of the political condition of his diocese. There is no room for doubt concerning the accuracy of Bede's statement, for it has been proved by archæological and anthropological researches. The remains of the Saxon period which have been brought to light by the spade in the Isle of Wight, and much more recently in the Meon valley, are all of the Kentish type, and, like them, exhibit a distinct resemblance to similar relics which have been found in Northern countries from which the Jutes or Goths migrated—i.e., Gothland and some of the Danish isles, as well as Jutland.

One of the Danish isles at the present time is named Mön, or Moen, and as the Danish ö or oe is in sound like the French eu,[8] it is practically the same in sound as the Hampshire Meon, in the valley of which people from Moen were probably among the Jutish settlers. That the identity of the Jutes and the Goths, or the very close affinity between them, was known locally in Wessex as late as the end of the ninth century is proved by a statement made by Asser,[9] that King Alfred's mother was Osburga, daughter of Oslac, a Goth by nation, descended from the Goths or Jutes of the Isle of Wight. The name of Gutæ, as already mentioned, is found in very early Gothic runes in Scandinavia, and Stephens places their date as early as A.D. 400. The evidence of the connection of the Goths with the Isle of Wight is also supported by the discovery of a runic inscription within it. This is on the inner side of the scabbard mount of an iron sword found at Chessell Down about the middle of the nineteenth century, and is in the British Museum, where, many years after its discovery, it was taken to pieces to be cleaned. During this process the staves of the runes, which could not previously be observed, were seen to have been clearly, but not deeply, incised by a sharp instrument on the elegant silver mount. The words 'Æco Sœri,' which are clearly visible in runic characters, Stephens places between A.D. 500-600 in date, and interprets as an imprecation against the foe with whom the sword might come into contact.[10]

The Jutes of Hampshire are probably referred to in the old name Ytene, for the district which is now the New Forest. This word is apparently a later form of the Anglo-Saxon Ytena, genitive plural of Yte, a form of the word Jutæ used by Bede. This part of the county was known as Jutish for centuries. Florence of Worcester, writing at the end of the eleventh century, mentions the 'provincia Jutarum,' in which the New Forest was formed. The Goths occupied the south parts of the county east and west of Southampton Water, as well as the Isle of Wight.

We can have no doubt that Saxons of some tribe or tribes were largely included among the settlers of a district afterwards known to its neighbours as Wessex, or the kingdom of the West Saxons. Among these, in a country with good harbours, there can be little doubt that Frisians, who were the people among the so-called Saxons most given to maritime pursuits, were represented. Such names as Emsworth and the river Ems in the south-east of the county remind us of Emden and the river Ems, close to Eastern Friesland. It is among the present Frisians that traditions of Hengist survive, and it is only in connection with the Jutes and Frisians that this name occurs. It is of interest, therefore, to note that the name is mentioned in the West Saxon charters—Hengestes-geat in Hants,[11] and Hengestesrig[12] in Dorset.

The harbours of these counties were their ports of debarkation, and it was up the river valleys and along the old Roman highways that the country was settled. The valleys of the Itchen, Test, Avon, Stour, and others, afforded a passage into the interior and higher parts of the country, and there is evidence to show, more especially in Dorsetshire, that settlements by people of the same tribe were made in the same or in adjacent valleys. In Berkshire the lines of colonization appear to have been varied. The natural way into that county is not by Southampton Water, but up the valley of the Thames. Berkshire did not come under the rule of the Gewissas at such an early period as Hampshire, part of Dorset, and the south part of Wiltshire. It was separated from early Wessex by a wide forest, of which traces still remain in the nomenclature of the district. Many of the settlers in Berkshire probably came by way of the Thames, but after the extension of the West Saxon State they appear to have been known as Gewissas equally with the people of the original settlement.

That some of the Berkshire settlers followed the same route from the south as the West Saxon armies is shown by the ethnological evidence and by the dialects. Beddoe,[13] referring to the south of Hampshire, says: 'The Saxon and Frisian types undoubtedly spread from this centre far to the north and west, predominating in a great part of Berkshire and central Oxfordshire, and occupying in force the valleys which radiate from Salisbury among the Wiltshire Downs.' Referring more especially to the people of Wilts, he also says: 'I do not mean that the Wiltshire people are anything like pure Saxons or Frisians; I should be quite satisfied if it were granted that they were at least half Saxon.'[14] The prevalence of the blonde type in parts of Hants, Wilts, and Dorset is one of the chief points in the present physical characters of the inhabitants of these counties. Beddoe says: 'Hampshire bears witness that it was a starting-point of Saxon colonization by the blonde character of the population.' He also speaks of the 'blonde, smooth-featured Saxons about

Wilton,' and tells us that 'the blonde types are common from Wareham to Yeovil.'[15]

In Hampshire, however, we do not meet with a general blonde type. Of the New Forest district Mackintosh says: 'The New Forest is inhabited by a mixture of races which almost defy classification, the complexion in general being dark;'[16] and this prevalence of dark-complexioned people among the inhabitants of the New Forest district is still apparent, as it is in parts of Wiltshire and Dorset.

The same ethnological observer, Mackintosh,[17] also says: 'In the middle and north of Hampshire the people in general belong to a dark-complexioned race. I have heard the opinion expressed that they are Wends, or a Belgic tribe of Wendish extraction.' The present writer is not able to regard the dark-complexioned type as being quite so general, but in the central and north parts of the county it may still be found, although perhaps less strongly marked now than half a century ago. The darker complexion among some of the Hampshire people, as among those of Wiltshire and Dorset, may be due in part to their descent from people of darker hues, who were among the original Gewissas. The Goths were of a fair type, as has been already described in the chapter on Kent. The inhabitants of the Isle of Wight, although now a very mixed population, still show occasional conformities to the original Jutish type, and this may be observed in the face of the monumental effigy of one of the D'Orseys, an old Isle of Wight family, in the church at Newport. It may be seen among the people of the Meon district, and may be noticed among people who may be met in the streets of Winchester at the present time.

From what has already been said, it will be seen that the Kentish custom of partible inheritance can be traced to a primitive Gothic source, and the custom of junior right to a primitive Wendish or Slavonic source. As Hampshire was settled by colonists of various races, united under the common name of Gewissas, the people of the various tribes may be expected to have brought into this county some of their peculiar customs, as Goths did into Kent, and tribal Frisians and Wends probably did into Sussex. It will be desirable, therefore, to consider in some detail the various primitive customs of succession and land tenure which actually prevailed in Hampshire. No instance of exactly the same custom of partible inheritance that prevailed in Kent can be cited in this county, but a large number of cases can be quoted of land being held by parage or parcenary tenure, a custom in its nature very like gavelkind. The survival of this parage or parcenary custom was mainly in the old Jutish parts of the county—viz., in the Isle of Wight and the New Forest district. The manors in which this custom prevailed were each considered as one manor for the purpose of taxation, but were held jointly by more than one tenant, one of them being responsible for the payments. In some cases these co-parceners were brothers, and are so described in Domesday Book. The custom of gavelkind in Kent was very similar to this, the land being, indeed, actually divided, but taxed collectively. In Hampshire it was taxed as a whole, and held by parceners as a whole, without apparently being actually divided. Except in preventing minute subdivision, there was in practice very little difference.

In the adjoining county of Dorset partible inheritance of the Kentish type survived at the time of the Domesday Survey and long afterwards at Wareham and in Portland Island. In Hampshire at the time of the Survey the partible custom, which may have prevailed at an earlier period among the descendants of the Northern Goths or Jutish settlers, had apparently given place to a modified tenure, so that parceners inherited their shares in an undivided estate. Under the general law of the kingdom, apart from recognised local customs, none but females were able to hold an estate together.[18] By the custom of gavelkind this was different, for by it males might hold lands in parcenary, the descent being to all males equally.[19] Parceners took their estates by descent, and their very title or name accrued only by descent.[20] The parceners in the Jutish parts of Hampshire who are mentioned by name in Domesday Book are all males. Parceners do not take by survivorship, but lands descend to their issue as in gavelkind.[21] From these considerations there can be no doubt that we may see in the parcenary tenure which prevailed so largely in the Isle of Wight and the New Forest district, which are known to have been settled by Jutes, traces of inhabitants of the same race as that of the people of Kent, among whom gavelkind was, and is, such a strongly-marked characteristic custom. In this parage custom we may also see the survival of family influence in the ownership of land, as opposed to the manorial. The family tenure was the older, and had come down from the tribal era; the newer manorial system gradually supplanted it. The Domesday record of Hampshire thus affords examples of both the older and the later systems.

In addition to the earlier immigration of people of several races, there is in Hampshire evidence of later settlements of Danes and Northmen. Even as late as the Domesday Survey the tenants on the manors of Ringwood and Winston, and of Arreton in the Isle of Wight, paid their dues or rents by Danish reckoning, the ora being the coin for their computation. The prevalence of allodial tenure along the western border of the county is recorded in Domesday Book, and here Danish place-names such as Thruxton (Thorkelston) and Wallop, with the characteristic Norwegian termination -op, survive. Odal or allodial tenure was a family tenure, in which one of the family held the land, and is specially characteristic of Norway, although not in ancient time confined to it. The same custom survived until modern time in the old Norse islands of Orkney and Shetland. The odaller or udaller was a free tenant, and had certain rights which he transmitted to his descendants. If through poverty he was obliged to sell his land, his kindred had the right of pre-emption, or of redeeming it when able to do so.[22] This udal or allodial custom prevailed along almost the whole of the western border of Hampshire at the time of the Domesday Survey. It existed also on some manors in the Isle of Wight and elsewhere in the county. Its prevalence is another link in the chain of evidence connecting the settlers of early Wessex with Jutes or other people of a Northern race. Allodial tenure is recorded in Hampshire in the hundreds of Andover, Brocton or Thorngate, Fordingbridge and Christchurch, on forty-seven manors extending from Tidworth in the north to Sopley and Winkton in the south. This custom is only recorded in Domesday Book in the southern counties of Hampshire, Sussex, Surrey, Kent, and Berkshire, but it may have prevailed on manors elsewhere without being specially mentioned. It is referred to in the tribal laws of the Franks and of the Angles and Warings.[23] Its existence at the present time in Norway and its survival in the Norse islands of the Orkneys and Shetlands may afford a clue as to whence the Scandinavians, whether the earlier Goths or the later tribal settlers in England, came. The Danish conquerors of Wessex were probably to some extent supplied with lands within that State itself, and it is not improbable that depopulated Saxon manors and lands or forest clearings were given to them. We can scarcely think that Cnut, King of Denmark and King of Wendland, whose name is so much connected with Wessex, and who when in England chiefly resided within it, would fail to provide his followers with lands near the seat of his government at Winchester. The *thorpe* place-names in the old parts of Wessex, of which there are a considerable number, support this view. Other Norse names, such as Hurstbourn, formerly known as Up Husbond and Down Husbond, are clearly Scandinavian. The forest land around Up Husband or Hurstbourn Tarrant was called Wikingelega Forest,[24] or later Wytingley Forest, a name derived from Wikings.

These considerations open up the still larger question, What was the relationship of the Goths at the time the Gewissas settled in Hampshire to the people known as Northmen? The term Northmen had certainly a wider significance than its limitation to the Norse or people of Norway. All the four chief Northern nations of antiquity, Goths, Danes, Norse, and Swedes, spoke the old Norrena dialects or language,[25] of which the best-written example that exists is the Icelandic, the later representative of the language carried to Iceland by the colony of Northmen who settled there. The custom of partible inheritance among all the sons equally not only prevailed among the ancient Goths, but also among the ancient Northmen. It survives both in Gothland and in Norway to the present day. The system of udal or odal right is the foundation of the whole social system of Norway, and to it the people have tenaciously clung for long centuries, during all the political changes through which Norway has passed, or the political crises to which it has been subjected. One of the incidents of this odal right at the present time is that one of the sons has by custom the right to pay the others their share of the estate if they all agree. This one is also by custom the eldest.

The allodial tenure that existed at the time of the Domesday Survey on the manors along the western border of Hampshire and other parts of that county was apparently of the same nature as the odal right still in operation in Norway. It may have been introduced into Hampshire at the time of the settlement of the confederated invaders, the Gewissas, or by a later settlement after one or other of the Danish inroads. That this tenure existed in some parts of the county and not in others is not surprising when we consider that the original settlers were not all of the same race, but Gewissas, confederates, or assured allies of several tribes or nations. Wallop, close to the western border of the county, presents a good example of the equal right of sons to share their father's estate. A manor there was at the time of the Norman Survey held 'by four Englishmen, whose father held the land in allodium.' This appears to be a case exactly parallel to the custom of Kent, the father's land being divided equally between his sons, but yet the whole, land taxed collectively. We must also remember that parage or parcenary tenure, by which one tenant was responsible, but others shared with him, was not the same as allodial. The land was in both cases family land, held collectively in the former case, and by one of the family in the latter. This is clearly seen in the manors and tenures of the Isle of Wight, mentioned in Domesday Book, where twenty-one tenures in parage are named and thirty in allodium. Under this odal or udal tenure in Norway at the present time all the kindred of the udalman in possession are what is called *odelsbaarn* to his land, and have in the order of consanguinity a certain interest in it, called *odelsbaarn ret.*[26] Hence, if the udalman in possession should sell or alienate his land, the next of kin is entitled to redeem it on repaying the purchase-money, and should he decline to do so, it is in the power of the one next to him to claim his right and recover the property to the family or kindred. The effect of this custom is evidently, to a certain degree, to entail the land upon the kindred of the udalman. It affords us a glimpse of the probable operation of the early Anglo-Saxon mægth, which did not as a collective body of kindred own land, but everyone in the mægth or kindred had obligations to the others in the same mægth, with certain reversionary rights.

From the consideration of the historical evidence relating to the settlers of Hampshire, the survival for centuries of the term Gewissas as their original collective name, and the various customs and tenures which existed in so marked a way at the time of the Domesday Survey, it is difficult to avoid the conclusion that the Goths or Jutes must have had much in common with those afterwards known by the general name of Northmen, and from the evidence of the runes it is certain that there was a close connection between the Goths and Angles on the one hand and the Norse on the other.

The darker-complexioned people among the invaders and colonists of England during the Anglo-Saxon period were probably some of the Wendish or Northern Serbian race who were at that time in alliance with other Northern tribes. The ancient Vandals have left permanent traces of their extensive conquests more or less in alliance with the Goths. Their settlements extended from North Africa and Spain to the present Slav states of Eastern Europe, and thence northwards to the Baltic. Along this extended line of ancient Vandal occupation we find historical evidence or other traces of their allies, the Goths. If they were allies, at times, in other parts of Europe, there cannot be much room for doubt that they may also have been allies in England. The evidence of the settlement of some Wends among the Gewissas of Hampshire is derived partly from the county itself, and partly from traces of them in Wiltshire and Dorset. There are nine manors in Hampshire on which borough-English has been traced. The historical statement of Bede that Rugians were among the ancestors of the people of England living in his time cannot be explained away. In Bede's time there must have been a common knowledge that part of the English people were descended from Rugians, and these were Wends, the Isle of Rügen being the chief seat of Vandal worship in the North of Europe.

In the parts of South Hampshire which were occupied by the Goths we find the early names Ruwanoringa[27] in a Saxon charter and Ruenore[28] in Domesday Book for a place now called Rowner. The equivalence of the old *g* sound in such names as Rügen to that of the later *w* is proved by the oldest records of both Germany and England. These names of the Saxon period certainly appear to indicate a settlement of Rugians—*i.e.*, Wends or Vandals. Attention has already been drawn to the various names by which ancient tribes were known. The name Rugians is, perhaps, a native name, and used as their own designation by these people themselves. They were certainly called Wends by the ancient Germans, including Saxons and Frisians. By the Northern nations, including the Northern Goths, the Vandals were called Vindr or Vinthr, whence probably our tribal or personal name Winthr or Winter. In English localities with settlements of Goths and others speaking the same language, which had here and there also settlements of Vandals, these latter would naturally be known to their neighbours as those of the Winthr, and the bearing of this on English place-names will be fully discussed in the next chapter. In other localities where Frisians, Saxons, and others speaking German dialects had here and there similar Vandal settlements among them, these neighbours would be designated Wends or Wendeles. In other districts it is reasonable to suppose that Vandals may have retained their tribal names, such as Rugians or Wilte, and the latter appears in the early Saxon name of the Wilsæte or Wiltshire settlers. It is not suggested that all the people of Wiltshire were descendants of the Wilte, but the name Wilsætas may have arisen owing to an original settlement of these people in the south of the county.

One of the most remarkable boundary names which we meet with in Anglo-Saxon charters is that of *crundel.* The name survives as a village name in that of Crondall in the north-east of Hampshire, where the extensive ancient manor of this name formed the north-eastern boundary of the county. The name is now confined to the village and parish which still forms part of the county border, but in Saxon time Crundele was the name of the hundred or great manor which extended from Yateley in the north to Aldershot in the south, including both these places. It was this manor which King Alfred in his will bequeathed to Ethelm, his nephew. The name *crundel*, however, is met with frequently in Dorsetshire, Wiltshire, Hampshire, and Berkshire, in the boundaries mentioned in charters, and less frequently in Somersetshire,

Gloucestershire, and Worcestershire. The name is not a common one, and is practically confined to these counties as far as the Saxon usage of it is concerned, and where it occurs in the charters it is always as a boundary name.

The word as a boundary name may have come into use among the Anglo-Saxons from those people who were called Gewissas, for it is only found in Saxon charters relating to the counties which were settled by the Gewissas or colonised by them. Hampshire, Dorsetshire, Wiltshire, and Berkshire were the earliest counties they occupied, and after the conquests of Ceawlin and other kings, West Saxon settlers occupied parts of Gloucestershire, Worcestershire, and Somersetshire. The Thames forms a dividing line north of which the name crundel as a boundary does not occur in the charters. In Wiltshire the name is mentioned eighteen times, in Dorsetshire eleven times, Hampshire nine times, Berkshire fourteen times, Somersetshire four times, Gloucestershire once, and Worcestershire four times. On the Continent similar words occur in both Scandian and Slavonic countries, of which Carlscrona in Sweden and Kronstadt are apparently examples. In Central Europe the place-names beginning with the word *krain* occur chiefly in those parts that are or were Slavonic.[29] The occurrence of these crundel names in Wessex, and only in those counties in which Gewissas settled, appears to connect its use with these people.

As it existed at the time of the Domesday Survey, the extensive settlement of Crondall in the north-east corner of Hampshire was certainly Scandinavian, for among the customs of that great manor, which included Crondall, Yateley, Farnborough, and Aldershot, that of sole inheritance by the eldest daughter in default of sons prevailed,[30] as over a large part of Cumberland, and this is a peculiarly Norse custom.

[1] Grimm, J., 'Teutonic Mythology,' edited by Stallybrass, vol. iv., p. 1711.

[2] Cart. Sax., i. 283, 284.

[3] *Ibid.*, i. 543.

[4] *Ibid.*, ii. 595, 596.

[5] Grimm, J., *loc. cit.*, iv. 1717.

[6] *English Hist. Review*, vol. xiv.

[7] Rudolph, H., 'Orts Lexikon von Deutschland.'

[8] Warsaae, J. J., 'Danes and Norwegians in England,' Preface, v, vi.

[9] Asset, 'Life of Alfred.'

[10] Stephens, G., 'Old Northern Runic Monuments,' iii. 460.

[11] Codex Dipl., No. 648.

[12] *Ibid.*, No. 455.

[13] Beddoe, J., 'Races in Britain,' 257.

[14] *Ibid.*, p. 259, note.

[15] *Ibid.*, 257.

[16] Mackintosh, D., 'Ethnological Observations,' *Trans. Ethn. Soc.*, ii. 217.

[17] *Ibid.*, ii. 214.

[18] Reeve's 'History of English Law,' edited by W. F. Finlason, ii. 587.

[19] *Ibid.*

[20] *Ibid.*, ii. 589.

[21] Lyttleton's 'Tenures,' edited by Tomlins, ed. 1841, p. 326.

[22] Tudor, J. E., 'The Orkneys and Shetlands,' pp. 18, 19.

[23] Seebohm, F., 'Tribal Custom in Anglo-Saxon Law,' 151, 170, 226.

[24] Red Book of the Exchequer, A.D. 1155-1156, part, ii., p. 663.

[25] Cleasby and Vigfusson, 'Icelandic Dictionary,' Preface.

[26] Laing, Samuel, 'Journal of a Residence in Norway,' ed. 1851, p. 137.

[27] Codex Dipl., No. 1263.
[28] Dom. Bk., 45, *b*.
[29] Rudolph, H., 'Orts Lexikon von Deutschland.'

[30] Baigent, F. J., 'Records and Documents relating to the Hundred and Manor of Crondall,' 163.

# Chapter Fourteen - Wessex (*continued*), Wilts, and Dorset

IN the Southern counties, where the underlying strata are chalk and limestone, there are numerous streams whose upper courses are dry in summer and have water in them only in winter. In Dorset there are two streams called Winterborne, in Wiltshire three, in Berkshire one, and in Sussex one. In these counties there are also many streams which have water flowing in them in winter and not in summer, but which have not the word winter connected with their name. Why a few should have this and many others not have it has not been explained. There are also villages called Winterborne on the streams of the same name. In view of the fact that there is a winter flow of water in many streams not called by the name winter, the popular explanation of the origin of the name Winterborne may not be the correct one. The names are old, the earliest references to a place or district so called in Dorset being A.D. 942 and 949.[1] The possibility that they have been derived from a tribal name must be considered.

The evidence already stated shows that the earliest settlers in Hampshire could not have been all of one race, and that there were in that county very considerable settlements of Goths and other Scandinavians. There are also traces to be found in parts of Dorset and Wiltshire of early colonies of people of more than one race, and of later settlements of Northmen. Such old place-names in Dorset as Godmaneston,[2] Goderiston,[3] and Goderthorn Hundred,[3] point to settlers who were Goths, as also does the custom of partible inheritance of the Kentish type among sons, and failing sons, among daughters, that survived at Wareham and Portland. The dialects spoken by the Northern people, whether Goths, Danes, Norse, or Swedes, were some form of the old Norrena,[4] and we may consider it certain that if there were Wends settled among people of any of these races in Dorset and Wilts they would not call them Wends, but by the name by which they were known in their own language—viz., Windr, Winthr, or Wintr.

There is ancient evidence that Scandinavians used the word Winthr or Windr for Wends. The words of an old writer on early Northern history on this subject are: 'Wandali quos nos materna lingua vocamus Windir.'[5] Another Northern writer mentions the Western Slavs as 'Slavi occidentales, or Vestr Vinthr,' and the Eastern Slavs as the 'Slavi orientales, or Austr Vinthr.'[6]

For this explanation of the origin of the Winter place-names in these counties to be probable, or even possible, it is necessary to prove the settlement in them of people who spoke a Norrena dialect. The ancient topographical names, some of which are now lost, in both these counties supply this proof.

In Dorset we find Swanage, Purbeck, Shapwick, Ore, Witherston, Butterwike, Wichampton, East Holm, West Holm, Byrport (now Bridport), Candel (which may be compared with Candleshoe Wapentake in Lincolnshire), Ringstede, Farnham, Gillingham, Grimston, Swindun, and other names which can be most satisfactorily accounted for by the Northern dialects. The name Rollestone Barrow, on the border of Wilts and Dorset, near to the dyke known by the Scandinavian name Grimsditch, points to the same conclusion.

In Wiltshire we find Burdorp and Salthorpe near Swindon, East Thorp and West Thorp on either side of Highworth, Ramsbury (with the old Estthropp and Westhropp[7] on either side of it), Rollestone, Buttermere, Normanton, Maniford, Burbage, Scandeburn, Grimstede, Hardicote, Ulfcote, and others, clearly denoting settlements of Norrena-speaking people. In the north of the county also is a circle of stones round an old burial-place near Winterborne-Basset, and the Kennet long barrow, very similar to those of Scandinavia. The barrow at Kennet so closely resembles that in which one of the Danish Kings is by tradition said to have been buried at Lethra in Zealand that Fergusson tells us the age of the one must be the age of the other.[8] Similarly, in Berkshire we find places with old Scandinavian names around Winterbourne.

In Dorset we also find proof of a large Scandinavian settlement in the Danish money computation mentioned in Domesday Book at Dorchester, Wareham, Bridport, and Shaftesbury, and at Ringwood, near its border.

When did this settlement take place? History is silent in reference to it, but the proof is clear that some Scandinavians did settle in all the counties of Wessex. Some of these may be accounted for by Goths and other Northern settlers among the early Gewissas. A large number probably settled in Wessex after the wars of Ethelred I. and his brother Alfred. It is certain that a considerable proportion of the fighting men of the old counties of Wessex had become exterminated before the peace between Alfred and Guthrum, and they were probably succeeded in many localities by colonists of Scandinavian descent. History is silent for the most part concerning the Anglian and Danish settlements in Lincolnshire and Norfolk, but these settlements cannot be doubted, nor can the settlements of Goths and Northmen in Wessex, either among the original Gewissas or after the Danish wars of the ninth and tenth centuries. In any district in which Scandinavian freemen were settled at a subsequent date to that of the original settlers some changes in land tenure and in the customs of inheritance would be likely to follow, as well as a change in some of the local names, which may account for the disappearance here and there of some very early customs.

In Dorset the Domesday names Windresorie and Windelhā occur, and the old names Windleshor' Hundred and Windregledy also are known. These apparently refer to men who were Vandals, or Windr, as they would be called by Scandinavian Goths and others who spoke some dialect of the old Northern tongue.

This old name Windr for Wends used by the Northern nations is a link in the chain of evidence by which Wendish settlements may be traced in our country. The name Winter in place-names occurs most frequently in Dorset, but also in Wiltshire and some other counties. It is chiefly attached to the word *bourn*, but by no means exclusively, the place-names Winterstoke, Winterhead (anciently Wintret), and Winterburge, being known in the southern counties; also Wintrinton in Dorset, Wintringham in Huntingdonshire, Wintrington in Lincolnshire, and Winterset in Yorkshire.

The name Windresorie for the place now called Broad Windsor in Dorset had its origin apparently under similar circumstances to those which gave rise to the name Windlesore, now Windsor in Berkshire. Among other early Dorset names that may be connected with people known as Windr are Windrede-díc or Windryth-díc, a boundary ditch near Shaftesbury, and Windærlæh mæd, near the river Avon, on the Hampshire border, which are mentioned in Anglo-Saxon charters.[9] These cannot refer to winter, the season.

The connection of the name of tribal people with the name of the stream flowing through their territory is an old custom of topographical nomenclature. In the northern parts of Germany we find many old examples of this. Among the instances[10] are the Stur River and Stormari, or Stormar people in the south of Holstein; the Hasa River and the Hassi tribe near Osnaburg; the Havel River and the Havelli, or men of Havel, in Brandenburg, mentioned by King Alfred; the Suala River and the Swalfelda people; the Ambra or Emmer River (now the Ems), and the Ambrones or Emisga tribe; the Meisse and the people of Meissen in Wendish Saxony; the Warinna River and the Werini or Waring tribe; the Wandalus River, or Waal, and the Vandals who settled in Holland; the Hunse River and the Hunsing people in Friesland; the Hunte River and the Huntanga tribe, also in ancient Frisia.

Similarly, in England in Anglo-Saxon time we find the Wiley and the Wilsæte, the Meon and the Meonwara, the Arrow and the Areosetna in Warwickshire; the Collingbourn[11] and the Collinga people in the east of Wiltshire. Further instances of the same kind may be traced in the Old English river-names Swanburne,[12] Honeyburn,[13] Broxbourn, Ingelbourn,[14] Coquet, and others.

With this evidence before us, both from ancient Germany and England during the Anglo-Saxon period, the probability that the streams called Winterborne may have been named after people called Wintr living on their banks is strong.

In Dorset the traces of Scandinavian and Wendish settlements abound, especially in the valley of the ancient Stur. This is a Northern name, a well-known example of it being that of Snorri Sturluson, the earliest Icelandic author. If we consider the names of the streams which are the feeders of the Stour, and the names of places along the course of that river and its tributaries, we may recognise the Scandinavian origin of nearly all of them. The Cale, the two Loddons or Liddons, and the Winterborne, are tributaries, while there are two places named Stourton, three places named Stour, and two named Sturminster. The name Stur is also significant in another way. There was a river Stör which was one of the boundaries of Stormaria, north-east of Hamburg, and that was a Wendish tribal district. This leaves little room for doubt concerning the Scandian or Wendish origin of some place-names in the valley of this Dorset river. Gilling is a name connected with Norse mythology, and occurs in the Dorset name Gillingham.

With this evidence before us, it is not surprising to find a Norse name used for the Wendish people settled on the western side of the Stour valley. It would have been strange, supposing such people had been settled there, if they had been called by any other name than the Scandinavian name for their tribe—viz., Winthr or Windr.

The use of the patronymic termination -*ing* in such names as Wintringa-tun[15] or Wintrington in Lincolnshire, and Wintrington in Dorset,[16] are clearly cases in which Wintr must have been used in a personal sense, as the name for the head of a family or clan. Similarly, -*inga* in Wintringa-tun denotes the descendants of a Wintr. In such instances the name can have no reference to winter, the season. There were other Wintr place-names in Dorset and Wilts in the Saxon period which had no reference to bourns: Winterburge geat,[17] Wilts; Windresorie, Windelhā, Windestorte, Winfrode, and Winlande—all Domesday names. The name Windelhā[18] clearly refers to a place that was named after a man called Windel at the time of its settlement. If, therefore, there were some places in Dorset called Wintr, Windr, or Windel after Wends, it is very probable that other Wintr place-names in this and other counties had a similar origin. In the West Riding of Yorkshire the old name Winterset[19] survived at a later period, and this may originally have denoted the settlement of Wends.

The name Winthr for Vandals, which was used by the Northern Goths and other Scandians in the sixth century, may have partly lost its significance as the dialects became blended into one speech. There is linguistic evidence of a great commingling of nations in the body of the English settlers.[20] The Anglo-Saxon, in its obscure etymology, its confused and imperfect inflections, and its anomalous and irregular syntax, furnishes an abundant proof of diversity of origin. It has the characteristics of a mixed and ill-assimilated speech, and its relations to the various ingredients of which it is composed are just those of the present English and its own heterogeneous system. It borrowed roots and dropped endings, and appropriated syntactical combinations without the inflections which made them logical.[21] There is no proof that Old English was ever spoken anywhere but on the soil of Great Britain.[22] The language grew as the tribal people who formed the settlers became fused. Anyone who will compare the oldest remnant of Anglo-Saxon poetry now extant, a few lines of Cædmon, and the same lines as they were modernised by King Alfred in his Old English version of Bede about 200 years after Cædmon's time, will have no doubt about the changes which time brought in the dialects and language of the Old English people. In this development, the Northern name Windr or Winthr for a tribe may have lost its original meaning, and have been confused with that of winter, the season; and there are other instances of names having a tribal origin, which subsequently had meanings attached to them which were foreign from their original ones.

The name Winterborne appears to have been used at first for considerable districts in Dorset and Wilts that were subsequently divided into manors. It is worth noting also that one of the manors called Wintreburne in Wiltshire was held at the time of the Domesday Survey by Godescal,[23] a man of the same name and perhaps a descendant of Godescalc the Wendish Prince, who was a notable person in England in the time of King Cnut, and who married that King's daughter. To the Norrena-speaking people this Wendish Godescalc was a Vintr.

Another fact which supports the evidence of Norrena-speaking settlers at an early date in Dorset is the name Thornsæta for the people of that district, corresponding to the Wilsæta and Sumersæta. This name Thornsæta is mentioned by Asser in his Life of Alfred, is repeated in some charters, and passed into Dornsæta or Dorsæta. As the word *thorn* is the name of one of the old Northern runes, it must have been familiar to the people whose name was connected with it. The inventors of the runes were certainly the Northern Goths, and the circumstance of the use of such a name supports the evidence of a settlement of Goths in parts of Dorset.

It is certain that during the later Saxon period Wends were connected with Dorset, for there is documentary evidence to that effect. In a charter dated 1033 King Cnut gave land at Horton in Dorset to one of his huscarls,[24] and, as is well known, these were originally a force of Wends. This was presumably a case in which Cnut, who was also King of Wendland, rewarded one of his Wendish subjects. Domesday Book tells us of payments from the boroughs of Dorchester, Bridport, Wareham, and Shaftesbury, which were annually made to the huscarls as late as King Edward's time. The Domesday record also tells us of a place in Dorset named Hafeltone.[25] This is of some weight, for it is difficult to see how such a name arose except from the settlement of a man so named because he was a man of the Wilte tribe, or Men of Havel, mentioned by King Alfred.

The old name Ruanbergh, which occurs in a charter of King Alfred,[26] also refers to an early settlement of Rugians, or people of a Wendish or Slavic descent, in Dorset. The similar name Ruwanbeorg survived in Wiltshire in the later Saxon period, and gave its name to the hundred of Rughe'berg in later centuries.

Among ancient names in Dorset that are probably of Wendish origin are Cranborne, Trent and Tarent, Luseberg and Launston. Crane, the name of a stream, and Cranborne, a boundary place-name, may be compared with the Slavic name Ukraine, from *crain*, a limit. Trent, a place-name in Rügen Isle, occurs also in the old Slavic part of the Tyrol. Luseberg, an ancient hundred name, reminds us of the Wendish tribe Lusitzes, and Launston may be compared with the Wendish Lauenberg. It is remarkable that in Germany the Trent name is only found where Slavic influence prevailed, and in England where Wendish settlers may be traced. Among names of old places in Wiltshire of similar origin are Semeleah, on the river Sem; Wilgi, a Domesday place; Launton, now Lavington; and the Ruan or Rughen names. There is a river Sem in the Ukraine. Launton was on the border of the hundred called in the Saxon charters Ruwanbeorg, and in later records Rughe'berg, which names correspond closely with those used in the old Germanic records to denote the Wendish people in Rügen.

As already pointed out, the name Wintr in Anglo-Saxon records is used in some instances for persons.[27] Wintra was an abbot in Wessex in A.D. 704. Another Wintra was a monk at Abingdon in 699, and a third so named was abbot of Tisbury in Wiltshire in 750. Wintred also was the name of several monks who are recorded in the later Saxon period, and Wintre was apparently the name of the head of a family who gave his name to the place called Wintreshleaw, now Winterslow, in Wiltshire.

The personal name Wintre was not confined to England, one who was so called having been physician to Charles the Great. It can also be traced in the form Wynther among people of Norse descent in the Shetland Isles[28] as late as the sixteenth century, and in England it can be traced from the Saxon age into the later mediæval period.

A considerable area in Dorset in the latter part of the Saxon period was held like the land in the Isle of Wight and the New Forest district, much of which, Domesday Book tells us, had been held collectively or in parage in the time of King Edward. At Wey, the Domesday Wai, there were three manors, which in the time of the last Saxon King were held collectively by nine, eight, and five thanes—a total of twenty-two landholders in parage in this place alone. At Hame the manor had been held by five thanes, at Ringstede by four, at Pourtone by eight, at Celvedune by nine, at Mapledre by seven, at Derwinston by five, at Horcerde by four, and at a place not named there were five hides held collectively by eleven thanes. At a place called Goda the land had been held by three free thanes, and the other places in which it had been held by brothers or by parceners are somewhat numerous. This system of land tenure, identical with that in the Jutish part of the south of Hampshire and the Isle of Wight, points to a connection in custom and probably in race between some of the original settlers in Dorset and the Goths and Jutes of the adjoining county.

One of the most remarkable peculiarities which any English county shows in Domesday Book is exhibited by Wiltshire in reference to those of its inhabitants who were called 'coscets.' These were evidently inferior tenants of the cottar class, but they were differentiated from the cottars. On some manors in Wiltshire there were at the time of the Survey both coscets and cottars, so that there can be no doubt that these coscets were different in some respects from the cottars. With the exception of five coscets who are mentioned in the Shropshire survey, all the others enumerated are found in Wiltshire, Dorset,

Somerset, and Devon. The numbers mentioned in these counties are, according to Sharon Turner's calculation: Wiltshire, 1,385; Dorset, 146; Somerset, 43; and Devon, 32; in addition to the 5 found in Shropshire.[29] Jones, in his book on the Domesday of Wiltshire, makes the total number rather larger than Turner, but substantially the two enumerations agree. Jones says: 'There are in the whole of Domesday but 1,750 registered, and of these more than 1,400 are found in the Wiltshire portion of the record.'[30] It is to be noted that, with the exception of the five mentioned in Shropshire, all these coscets are recorded in the survey of counties which were occupied by Gewissas at the time of the settlement, and even in Shropshire after the conquest by Ceawlin some may have migrated to that county. It is clear that Wiltshire was the home of the English coscets, and those found in neighbouring counties can easily be accounted for by their proximity to Wiltshire, and the migration of some of their descendants.

The existence in Wiltshire of two classes of inferior tenants of the cottar kind as late as the time of the Domesday Survey is a remarkable fact. The existence of both cottars and coscets in large numbers in Wiltshire—coscets alone being found on some manors, cottars alone on some, and both classes on some other manors—points unmistakably to a peculiarity in the customs of Saxon Wiltshire distinct from those which prevailed in other counties. This sharp distinction must have arisen from some ancient cause, and it is very difficult to see what it could have been except the attachment of people of different tribes to the immemorial customs of their race. If this is the explanation, the question arises whether we can identify any of these ancient Wiltshire people by their peculiar customary designations of coscets and cottars. The name coscets is spelt in Domesday Book in four ways—viz., coscets, coscez, cozets, and cozez.[31] The spelling is of little importance, the sound of the word is the same in each case. In Lower Saxony, near the old Wendish country, there exist, or have existed until modern time, tenants of a cottar kind who are, or were, known by the names kater, kotter, kotsass, and kossat, and these have been identified as the representatives of the cottars and coscets of our Domesday Survey.[32]

Those Wends who were known by the tribal name Wilte, or Men of Havel, and were located partly on the right bank of the Elbe below Magdeburg, could easily have sailed to England direct from their own territory. The evidence of the settlement of people of a non-Teutonic race with others in early Wessex is of a cumulative kind; any one part of it may be inconclusive, but the whole evidence proves the case. There is the statement of Bede that Rugians were one of the tribes from which the English of his time were known to have been descended. There are the old Rugian place-names in Hants, Wilts, and Dorset of the Saxon period. There is also the fact that as far back as historical references to Rügen and its people extend, or to the tribes on the coasts of Mecklenburg and Pomerania, they are found to be Wends and of Slavonic descent. Again, there is the historical name Gewissæ or Gewissas for the tribal settlers in Wessex, and the manifest interpretation of this name as confederates. There is, next, the settlement of Jutes in the Isle of Wight and South Hampshire, and the identification of these as Goths by the statement of Asser, and the discovery of a runic inscription on a relic found in the Isle of Wight. The alliance of Goths with Vandals, so potent elsewhere in Europe, could scarcely have been altogether absent in England, and particularly in Dorset and Wilts, where Vandal place-names survive. As the Northern Goths spoke a dialect of the Northern tongue, and had a custom of partible inheritance, we might expect to find traces of their Northern speech and of their customs in early Wessex, and of both the speech and custom of inheritance we find unmistakable traces.

The settlement of some part of Wiltshire by people of the Wilte tribe from the south of the Baltic or the right bank of the Elbe does not appear to be unlikely. Schafarik, a great authority on Slavonic antiquities, connects our English Wiltshire with this Slavonic tribe,[33] but some of our own philologists derive the name from Wilton, the town on the river Wiley.[34] The Wiltshire settlers are, however, mentioned by the name Wilsæte in the Anglo-Saxon Chronicle in the year 801, nearly 200 years before the name Wiltonscire occurs. The name Wilsæte long survived, and is mentioned in Ethelweard's Chronicle about A.D. 973. The name 'Wiltene weie' for the road from Damerham to Wilton is also used in a charter dated 946, and Wiltene, a variant of Wiltena, is the genitive plural of Wilte. Such being the facts, the derivation of the name Wiltshire from Wilton is clearly wrong. In a district that affords other traces of Wendish settlers the Wilte name may have been the origin of the Wilsæte name, and that of the Anglo-Saxon tribal people, the East Willa and West Willa, whose districts are mentioned in the Tribal Hidage.[35] The name Wilte Scira occurs in the Exon Domesday, and the name Wilsæte was probably at first only that of the settlers in the south of the county.

The traces that survive of a mythological or legendary kind in the counties that formed the early kingdom of Wessex find their parallels in similar survivals in Rügen and Pomerania. The most remarkable is that of Hertha, or Mother Earth, a goddess with somewhat similar attributes to the Norse Frige and the Saxon Frea. The name Frige survives in that of Freefolk in Hampshire, the Frigefolc of Domesday Book. In Wiltshire the mythological name which can be most clearly traced during the Anglo-Saxon period is that of Hertha.

Latham has pointed out that there is no word beginning with 'H' in any German equivalent denoting terra or earth.[36] The name Hertha, although mentioned by Tacitus, appears to have come from another source. Herkja and Herche are among its variants.[37] Hertha is still remembered in the folklore of North-Eastern Germany, the old borderland between the Teutonic and Slavonic tribes, where she goes by the name of Frau Harke,[38] the same as our Mother Earth, but in England she has lost her personality. In the old mythology the personified Mother Earth embodied also the attributes of Ceres,[39] and in that capacity Hertha was much honoured in the Wendish parts of Germany. Kine were yoked to her car, and her image was conducted through fields on her annual festival with much solemnity. We find that Hertha as the name for this goddess was used by the people of Rügen and the Baltic countries near it from time immemorial. The survival of the name and the folk-lore connected with it in Rügen and in Pomerania at the present day is important, in reference to the survival of the name in Wiltshire at the present time, and its wider existence in that county in the Anglo-Saxon period. Such a survival strongly supports the other evidence relating to Wiltshire settlers of Wendish descent. The original Wilsæte or Wilte settlers, being at least partly made up of Wends, would naturally bring with them to Wiltshire some of the mythology of Rügen. Adam of Bremen tells us that this island was opposite to part of the country of the Wilte. The names Hertha' and Heortha' are found in Domesday Book in three places in Wiltshire, and in one of these, Hertham near Chippenham, it still survives.

The Anglo-Saxon name Jerchesfont in Wiltshire is also found in Domesday Book, and leads us to the folk-lore of Hertha still surviving in the island of Rügen and in Pomerania. It brings us to one of the most ancient of legends, the Lady of the Lake. The lady was the goddess Hertha, who, it is believed, had her dwelling in the hill in Rügen still known as Herthaberg, where often yet, as people of that island believe, a fair lady comes out of the hill surrounded by her maidens to bathe in the lake at its foot.[40] Similarly, in a wood in Pomerania stands a round hill called Castle Hill, and at its foot is a small lake, called Hertha's Lake. Here, too, the mysterious lady is said to bathe. The home of the Hertha legends, consequently, must be allowed to be Rügen and Pomerania, where her worship has been described by historians and her legends survive more than elsewhere. The old Saxon name Jerchesfont connects her with a legendary bathing-place in one of our Wessex counties. Its modern name is Urchfont, and it is situated in the middle of Wiltshire, near the border of the old hundred of Rughe'berg, the Anglo-Saxon Ruwanbeorg. At this old settlement, named after Hertha, there are copious springs, where much water rises, and hence the termination -*font* in the name. Domesday Book tells us of three Saxon mills driven by this stream, not far from the springs. As copious chalk or green-sand springs never freeze, the water being uniform in temperature, and in winter much above freezing-point, such a pool may well have been associated in the minds of the Wilte settlers with the goddess Hertha.

These old Hertha-names leave but little room for doubt that some of the early settlers in Wiltshire were of Wendish extraction, and this conclusion is supported by other mythological names. Piriun and Pyrgean[41] are ancient place-names of the Anglo-Saxon period in this county, but now lost. Perun was the Wendish name for the god of thunder, the Scandinavian Thor, and the Frisian or Saxon Thunor, and place-names derived from both of these exist. The mythological names attached to the prehistoric dykes of Wiltshire, Wansdyke, Grimsdyke, and Bokerly dyke, tell the same story. Wansdyke, the Wodnesdic of the Saxon age, reminds us of Woden, Grimsditch of the Norse Grim, a Northern name for Woden, and Bokerly dyke, anciently Boggele or

Boccoli, reminds us of the circumstance that Boge is the name for a deity in every old Slavonic language or dialect. Another old Wendish name for a god was Kirt, or Krodo, which corresponded to Saturn,[42] and the name Creodan hylle, or hill of Creod, near Ruwanbeorg, Wiltshire, is met with in a charter of Egbert, A.D. 825.[43] One of the most remarkable legends of Rügen is that of the black dog which guards the treasure of an old heathen King in that island,[44] and a legend somewhat similar to this survives in that of the black dog at Winchester.

One of the most remarkable of the Celtic survivals during the early part of the Anglo-Saxon period, which can be traced anywhere in England, is that on the east of Somerset and the north-west of Wiltshire, and comprised the country which forms the valley of the Frome and that of the upper part of the Bristol Avon. The name Devizes may indicate the frontier of this British province, which extended from near Wells to Bredon Forest, north-east of Malmesbury. Guest recognises Devizes as having been situated on its eastern border, and traces the name to this circumstance.[45] It was a projecting strip of British territory extending northward, that was left under its native rulers for a considerable time after the West Saxon King Ceawlin had defeated the Britons at Deorham in south Gloucestershire. There must have been a commingling of race in and near to this district, and, as Beddoe's researches show, the result of this racial fusion may be traced at the present day in the darker complexion of the people in the north-west of Wiltshire.

In Dorset the darker hues of the people that have been observed in the Gillingham district may be due to descent from settlers of a darker race near the fairer people in the valley of the Stour. They were, no doubt, for the most part of Teutonic origin, but among them were others of the Wendish race who came into Wilts and Dorset among the Gewissas. The evidence of the black-haired Vikings of the ninth century is from contemporary records certain, and as the English place-names denoting settlers of a dark or black complexion are names which were in use in the Saxon period, there appears to be no reason to doubt that there were among the Anglo-Saxon settlers people of a darker race than the fair-haired Angles and Scandians, or the fair-complexioned Saxons and Germans. The anthropological researches of Beddoe and others have, however, shown the survival on a large scale of blondes in Dorset and Wilts. The valley of the Stour as far north as Somerset is marked at the present day by blondes. Some of the Baltic races, such as the Lithuanians, are as fair as Scandinavians. The recorded facts and existing ethnological characters evidently support the conclusion that Wessex was originally occupied by a mixed population.

The difference in the village shapes is of some interest. In the north of Wiltshire the isolated homesteads are more common than in the valleys of the Wiley, Avon, and Nadder, and the isolated homestead was the Celtic arrangement. The collected homesteads of South Wiltshire may be compared with those between the Elbe and the Weser—i.e., in the old Saxon country; and, allowing for variations, also with the collected homesteads east of the

Elbe—*i.e.*, in the former Wendish country. The villages of collected home-steads in England had large areas of open commonable land, including the cultivated fields, and it is of interest to note that, as late as a century ago, half the area of Berkshire was open land, and more than half of Wiltshire.[46]

The evidence which the features of the skulls from burial-places supply concerning the introduction of more than one race into Wessex has already been given, and there is further evidence of the same kind supporting the settlement in Dorset of people of Slavonic origin.

Among the skulls in West Saxon graves a small minority are of the broad-headed type, having an average cephalic index of 81, whilst the majority are long-headed, with an index of about 76. The reasons for concluding that this was due to the introduction of people of a broad-headed race with the Anglo-Saxon settlers, rather than to a fusion of the descendants of the remote Round Barrow men with Saxon immigrants, have already been stated.[47] The further point that skulls from Saxon graves in Wessex show a tendency to prognathism has been fully dealt with in the chapter on settlers from the Baltic coasts.[48] Fifteen skulls from the Saxon burial-ground at Winklebury, on the border of Wilts and Dorset, which was explored by General Pitt Rivers, were found to present differences in shape, showing that the interments could not have been those of people of homogeneous ethnological characters. Beddoe examined these skulls,[49] and found six to be elliptic, four ovo-elliptic, four ovoid, and one oblong-ovate. Some were thus much broader than the others, and he points out in his report that the skull which he finds to be oblong-ovate is the same as that called Sarmatic by the Continental anthropologist Van Hölder. The word Sarmatic was an older name for the Slavic race; and the Wends, who have been shown by other evidence to have settled among other tribal people in Wilts and Dorset, were Slavs.

[1] Cart. Sax., ii. 508, and iii. 43.

[2] Tax. Eccl. P. Nicholai, 179.

[3] Hutchins, J., 'Hist, of Dorset,' ii. 205.

[4] Cleasby and Vigfusson, 'Icelandic Dict.,' Preface.

[5] Monumenta Germaniæ, Script. xxix., 250. 'Ex Theodrici Hist. de Antiq. Reg. Norwagiensium.'

[6] *Ibid.*, 319, 'Ex. Hist. Reg. Danorum dicta Knytlinga Saga.'

[7] Hundred Rolls, ii. 265.

[8] Fergusson, J., 'Rude Stone Monuments,' 284.

[9] Codex Dipl., Nos. 470, 489, 658.

[10] Monumenta Germaniæ, River-names.

[11] Codex Dipl., Nos. 336 and 358.

[12] Dom. Bk., 143 *b*.

[13] Codex Dipl., Index.

[14] Cart. Sax., iii. 92-94.

[15] Codex Dipl., No. 953.

[16] *Ibid.*, No. 361.

[17] *Ibid.*, No. 436.

[18] Domesday Book, i. 82 *b*.

[19] Nomina Villarum, A.D. 1315.

[20] Marsh, G. P., 'Lectures on the English Language,' First Series, pp. 42, 43.

[21] *Ibid.*

[22] *Ibid.*, 43, and Latham, R. G., 'English Language,' 105.

[23] Domesday Book, 73 *b*.

[24] Codex Dipl., No. 1318.

[25] Dom. Bk., 83.

[26] Codex Dipl., No. 319.

[27] Searle, W. G., 'Onomasticon Anglo-Saxonicum.'

[28] *Proceedings Soc. Antiq. Scot.*, xxv. 189.

[29] Sharon Turner, 'Hist. of the Anglo-Saxons,' ed. 1852, iii. 219-224.

[30] Jones, W. H., 'Domesday of Wiltshire,' Introd., xix. and p. 201.

[31] Domesday Book, General Introd., xxxvi.

[32] Woodward and Wilks, 'History of Hampshire,' i., p. 335, quoting Garnet.

[33] Morfill, W. R., 'Slavonic Literature,' p. 3.

[34] *Ibid.*

[35] Cart. Sax., i. 416.

[36] Latham, R. G., 'The Germania of Tacitus,' Notes, p. 145.

[37] Grimm, J., 'Teutonic Mythology,' translated by Stallybrass, i. 253.

[38] *Ibid.*

[39] *Ibid.*, ii. 45.

[40] Hartland, E. S., 'The Science of Fairy Tales,' p. 71.

[41] Codex Dipl., Nos. 1263, 460, 479.

[42] Grimm, 'Teutonic Mythology,' i. 249.

[43] Codex Dipl., No. 1035.

[44] Hartland, E. S., 'The Science of Fairy Tales,' p. 236.

[45] *Journal Archæol. Inst.*, xvi. 116.

[46] Maine, Sir H., 'Village Communities in the East and West,' pp. 88, 89.

[47] Chap. VII., p. 117.

[48] Chap. VIII., p. 129.

[49] *Journal Anthrop. Inst.*, xix. 5.

# Chapter Fifteen - The Settlement Around London

BEDE tells us of battles in Kent between the Jutes and the Britons during the latter part of the fifth century, and it was probably these battles that opened the way for the settlement around London. He wrote from the traditional knowledge of these events, and his statement may be accepted as evidence of a series of conflicts that must have occurred before the British people abandoned London—a distinguished city, which during the later Roman period bore the name of Augusta. There were roads into it from all directions: from Canterbury, from Pevensey, from Chichester, from Silchester and the south-west parts of Britain; from Uriconium, or Wroxeter, and the Midland district; from York and Lincoln, and from Colchester. These roads and other less important ways radiated from London like the spokes of a wheel, thus proving the importance of the Roman city. They all existed at the time of the coming of the new settlers; many of them exist to this day, and the lines of others can be traced. The Romans made them, and our Anglo-Saxon forefathers wore them down, and here and there roughly repaired them.

The earliest Saxon records supply no evidence of the city in a ruined state. On the contrary, they show its continued existence as a port from the earliest date to which they relate. From its greatness in Roman time, Anglo-Saxon London probably declined, but there is no reason to doubt that it continued to be relatively a great commercial city. The Goths and Frisians, of whom the bulk of the settlers in Kent were composed, were the greatest navigators of Northern Europe. They, called Jutes by Bede, advanced on London. The Thames became their great waterway, and London for a time their chief port. The river by which commodities could be brought into the country and the Roman roads by which they could be distributed are sufficient to show the extreme probability of the continuous existence of London. Nowhere else in England did such a combination of advantages exist.

The city which the newcomers found was one of considerable importance. The great roads alone are sufficient to prove this, and the Roman remains which have been found attest it. It was protected by defensive walls, contained temples, elegant houses, and many other structures characteristic of a place that was the centre of a Roman province.

We must look on the forests around London, in both Roman and Saxon times, as necessities. To have cleared the land and settled a rural population on it, if a sufficient population had existed, would very likely have paralyzed the trade of the city. In an age when pit-coal for fuel was not available a great woodland tract near it was necessary for any great city, such as London was at the end of the Roman period, and continued to be during the Saxon era. We see the same connection of ancient forest land with a city in the Ainsty, which from very ancient time has been within the jurisdiction of York, and which was a great woodland. The forests around London supplied not only fuel for household purposes, but charcoal for arts and handicrafts. The smiths and metal—workers of all kinds required charcoal, and the charcoal-burners in the forests supplied it. Their occupation is one of the oldest, but has now almost disappeared from this country. In the New Forest, however, the charcoal-burners are not even yet extinct. Traces of them exist around London in such place-names as Collier's Wood, near Merton. The smiths in Saxon London must have been numerous, and, as the evidence points to settlements in and near the city of Northern Goths, who at that time were the greatest metal-workers in Northern Europe, they were probably also skilful.

The Romans finally left Britain about A.D. 430, and, although the settlement of Kent took place before the end of the fifth century, we have no records until the coming of Augustine, and no historical account until the time of Bede, who died in A.D. 735, or three centures after the Roman withdrawal. This early Anglo-Saxon age is the darkest period of our history, and yet it was this period that saw the beginning of the English race, and as such must always be a time of much interest to the people of the Anglo-Saxon stock. As history tells us nothing of this period on the evidence of contemporary writers, we may take what Bede and the writers of the various manuscripts of the Anglo-Saxon Chronicle wrote to be the traditional knowledge of this early Saxon period. We may supplement these accounts by information concerning the various tribes and races which are known to have taken part in the English settlement—or may reasonably be inferred to have participated—their customs, dialects, arts, weapons, race characteristics, and the relics which have been found.

In the Saxon records we first read of London in the year A.D. 457, in which year Bede and the Chronicle tell us the great Battle of Crayford in Kent was fought, and the British fugitives took refuge within the old Roman walls of London of which small parts may still be seen. There are no records of what happened in the city after this battle until the year 604, a century and a half later, when we are told that Augustine hallowed Mellitus as the first Bishop of London, and sent him to preach baptism to the East Saxons; but we know that it was Æthelbert, King of Kent, who gave him his Bishop's See. Bede also tells us that Æthelbert built the first church of St. Paul, and in the charter granted to it more than four and a half centuries later William the Conqueror specially mentions that the church was of Æthelbert's foundation. Thus, in the year 457 we lose sight of Roman London in connection with a great victory of the Kentish people over the Britons at Crayford, and when we get the next historical glimpse it is in connection with Æthelbert, King of Kent, founding a Bishop's See within the city. The inference to be drawn from these two historical statements is plain—viz., that some time between these two dates the Kentish people drove out the Britons, and took possession of the city. It may have been early or late, even as late as the early part of the time of Æthelbert himself, as Green supposes.[1]

It has been shown that the settlers in Kent must have been mainly Goths and Frisians, both maritime nations known to Bede under the general name of Jutes. It must have been the people of the Jutish race in Kent, assisted probably by emigrants from their former homes, who attacked and took Romano-British London. A great prize was theirs. We know nothing about its loot, but great loot there must have been—sufficient, no doubt, to attract a host of allies from the great shipping centre in the Baltic—Wisby, in the Isle of Gotland. The city became by conquest part of the Kentish dominion.

It would be out of place to discuss at any length how it was probably captured, but, considering that Goths, Frisians, and Wends were all maritime nations, and considering also how centuries later it was taken by the maritime Danes and Norwegians, there can be little doubt that a naval force on the Thames played an important part in its capture. Did the captors destroy it? There is no contemporary information, but, reasoning from archæological associations, their self-interest in preserving such a commercial prize, and the relatively vast importance of the city in the later Saxon period, there is sufficient reason to think that they did not destroy it. The continuous use of the Roman roads which crossed London from north to south and east to west is evidence of the continuance of ways through it. If the so-called Saxons destroyed it, they must have immediately set to work and have rebuilt it. Some buildings, repugnant to their religious and other ideas, particularly those in the continuance of which they might suspect evil influences, they very probably did destroy, but that the city continued without interruption there is every reason to believe. It probably grew as the Saxon conquest became more and more complete, and the country more and more settled. By the time of Æthelstan it had become so great and wealthy that it required a special code of laws of its own, and by the time of Cnut its wealth had become so vast that after his conquest he levied upon it a tax of ten and a half thousand pounds, equal to one-seventh of that levied on the rest of England, and this tax was paid.[2]

Another circumstance which points to the later wealth of Saxon London is that the laws of Æthelstan relating to the city are much concerned with regulations for the capture and punishment of thieves. It is clear that opportunities for thieves would be greater in a rich city filled with merchandise than in other parts of the country. We read of London first as a city controlled by Æthelbert, King of Kent. Whether it was or was not part of the kingdom of the East Saxons at that time is uncertain, but in any case Æthelbert was their overlord. We have no evidence that the neighbourhood of London was originally settled by people from Essex. Some may have come westward through the great forest, if the eastern part of Essex was occupied by Saxons at that time. On the other hand, there is considerable evidence pointing to this settlement around London having been made by people of the same races as the people of Kent—viz., Goths and Frisians, with probably some Wends. It is most improbable that the Anglo-Saxon people who conquered London could have been any other than those of the Kentish race.

It was not until the year 491, according to historical statements, that the second Saxon kingdom, Sussex, was founded. Whatever local settlements may have been formed on the Essex coast, there was certainly no kingdom of Essex until long after the Battle of Crayford; and when it does appear, it comes before us as a subordinate kingdom to that of Kent. History, therefore, if taken alone, points to Kent as the Anglo-Saxon State which first controlled London; but there is other evidence of a remarkable kind which leads to the same conclusion. There are the customs of inheritance which survived in the city for many centuries, and on the great manors that existed around London almost to our own time, which, with other customs, bear an unmistakable resemblance to those of Kent. It cannot be said that none of these have been found in Essex, but, as Essex was subordinate to Kent in the earliest period of its history, it is but reasonable to think that some settlers from Kent may have migrated across the Thames into it. The majority of the early people of Essex were probably of a different race from the Goths, the dominant race in Kent. The Essex people were called Saxons and those of Kent Jutes, and this distinction in names must have arisen through a difference in race. Some Wends, for example, can be traced as settlers in Essex more clearly than in Kent. The name Middlesex does not occur in Anglo-Saxon records until that district became a province of the East Saxon kingdom, and the distinctive name of Middle Saxons would be likely to have arisen from geographic considerations.

When we compare the condition of the people an customs of London and the manors around it with those of Kent, and still further with those that can be traced to ancient Gothland and Friesland, we find a remarkable similarity. Before customs of all kinds was personal freedom, and in Kent alone of all the English counties every man was from time immemorial personally free. Similarly in London, which was called the 'Free Chamber of the King of England,' every man was personally free.[3] The name Franklins of Kent has found a place in our literature, and all the native-born men of London, or those who had resided in it for a year and a day, were similarly accounted freemen. Kentish people, when they migrated, carried with them some, at least, of their own laws and customs, certainly their personal freedom.

The very remarkable custom of Kentish gavelkind may be considered in reference to the customs in and around London. Its nature has already been discussed. Its chief privilege was partible inheritance among the sons, and, failing sons, among the daughters. The gavelkind custom also provided for the inheritance of the homestead by the youngest son. The custom of partible inheritance among sons was the ancient custom of the City of London specially confirmed to the citizens in the charter of William the Conqueror. This charter runs as follows, in modern English: 'William the King greets William the Bishop and Godfrey the portreeve, and all the burgesses within London, French and English. And I grant you that I will that ye be all of your law worthy, that ye were in the days of King Edward. And I will that every child be his father's heir after his father's day. And I will not suffer that any man do you wrong. And God you keep.' As every child was to be his father's heir (not his or her father's), it is clear that the custom referred to was the old Kentish custom of partible inheritance among sons. This custom of dividing the property among the sons was also the custom of the ancient manors of Stepney, Hackney, Canonbury or Canbury, Newington Barrow or Highbury, Hornsey, and Islington.[4]

In view of the city's early connection with the Kentish kingdom, it is difficult to see any other satisfactory explanation of such a remarkable parallelism between its customs and those of Kent than a settlement of Kentish people in it and on the east and north of it; and when we take into consideration the early overlordship of Æthelbert, King of Kent, in relation to Essex, that explanation is strengthened. The Norman Kings, who desired to see a uniform system of primogeniture established, nevertheless respected these ancient customs of inheritance, so different from the rural primogeniture which prevailed in Normandy, or the feudal primogeniture which they established over almost the whole of England. We know that the partition of the lands, which was an ancient custom on some great manors in various parts of England, was allowed to continue in many instances, for cases have survived until our own time. In his general code of law, William I. expressly allowed it, but we know that the change from old customs of inheritance to primogeniture of the feudal type went on nevertheless, so that in a century or two after the Norman Conquest the survivals of customs of inheritance other than primogeniture became much rarer than they must have been during the Saxon period. Glanville, who wrote in the time of Henry II., tells us that partible inheritance was in his time only recognised by the courts of law in those places where it could be proved that the lands always had been divided.[5] Consequently, as the custom was allowed to continue on the manors to the north and east of London, it must have been proved to have been an immemorial custom to the satisfaction of the law in the twelfth century—*i.e.*, it must have been shown to have been the usage during the Saxon period. The custom of dividing the inheritance that prevailed among the German tribes in the time of Tacitus, which was of immemorial usage in Friesland, and can be traced further back to the Goths of Gothland, may, of course, have been brought into England, and to some of the manors on the north and east of London, by the settlers who originally formed colonies there; but there are other circumstances that connect early Kent and London. The custom of partible inheritance among the sons prevailed at Kentish Town, and it is a very remarkable circumstance that on this manor, which bears the Kentish name, a Kentish custom actually survived until modern times.

As in Kent, so in London, the people were not liable to the ordinary process of distress for debts.

Another custom which the citizens of London had in common with the people of Kent was the power of devising their property by will. Kent alone among the English counties had this privilege, which was a rare one possessed by the tenants of only a few isolated manors elsewhere. It was not until the reign of Henry VIII. that copyholds generally were made devisable by will. Another resemblance in custom between Kent and the City was the age at which heirs could inherit. Bracton, who wrote in the thirteenth century, tells us that the full age of heirs was twenty-one in the case of a military fief, and twenty-five in the case of a socman. In Kent a son could succeed his father at fifteen years, and the son of a burgher was understood to be of full age when he knew how to count pence rightly, to measure cloths by the ell, and to perform other like business of his father.[6]

There was yet another resemblance between the customs of London and Kent—viz., in the widow's dower. She was entitled to half her husband's estate, even if his goods should be otherwise forfeited for felony. This was the custom of Kent, and the Dooms of Æthelstan tell us that it was the custom also of Anglo-Saxon London.[7]

One of the privileged customs of the Frisians was their freedom from the wager of battle as a judicial proceeding. The custom of settling disputes of right or wrong by duel is among the oldest judicial customs that can be traced. We meet with it in England in the laws of King Alfred, in which it is stipulated what course a man has to take against his foe in order to obtain justice before he proceeds to judicial settlement by force of arms.[8] To a commercial people such as the Frisians there was an injustice involved in the merchant being liable to be challenged to wager of battle in order to settle a dispute with a possible swash-buckler, whose profession was that of arms, concerning the terms of a purchase or the price of a commodity. In the old Flemish charters, which apparently embody still more ancient privileges and customs, we find a law which exempts the Frisians of the early part of the twelfth century from duel in every market of Flanders.[9] Similarly, in London one of the oldest franchises was that none of the burgesses should be compelled to wager of battle, but that they might settle their disputes according to the custom of London; and although this privilege was subsequently granted to thirteen cities and boroughs,[10] such grants do not diminish the significance of it in London, where its origin is lost in antiquity, the custom being known as the 'Custom of London.'

The evidences of the early trade of London in the Anglo-Saxon period also point to its connection with the chief traders of Northern Europe at that time—the Goths and Frisians. That the maritime trade of London went on without any great break from the Roman period into that of the Saxons is extremely probable. In a charter dated A.D. 734, by which Ethelbald, King of Mercia, granted leave for a ship to pass into the port of London without tax, he speaks of the tax on shipping as his royal right and that of his predecessors. This appears to be the earliest notice of Saxon London in a contemporary document.[11] For maritime commerce there must have been regulations of some kind from the earliest time, and the earliest that can be traced in the North of Europe is 'The Maritime Law of Wisby.' At the time when Ethelbald granted a remission of his tax to this ship in the port of London, Wisby was the commercial centre of the North. In early London there was probably a maritime court, as there was in Ipswich. The court sat daily, as shown by the customary of that town, to administer the Law Marine to passing mariners.[12] This practice is referred to in the Domesday of Ipswich, and this is probably the earliest extant record of any court sitting regularly.[13] When and how the practice originated is uncertain, but it was a legacy of Imperial Rome that maritime causes should be heard without delay by competent judges in each province, and there is good reason for believing that mediæval Europe accepted this legacy and never allowed it to lapse.[14]

In the shipping trade of the Netherlands in the Middle Ages we meet with two codes of maritime regulations, one called the Rolls of Oleron, from a French source,[15] and another resembling what is known as the Maritime Law of Wisby. With these mediæval maritime codes we are only concerned so far as regards the antiquity of the Wisby code and its provisions in reference to 'lay days.' The Maritime Law of Wisby was first published at Copenhagen in 1505, under the name of 'The Supreme Maritime Law.'[16] The provisions of this code are similar to those of 'The Usages of Amsterdam,' with which those of the Frisian ports of Enchuysen, Stavern, and others on the Zuyder Zee, are identical. The extreme antiquity of Wisby as a port points to an early code of some kind necessarily connected with it as the original source of the Frisian regulations. By the Usages of Amsterdam and the custom of the Frisian ports, and by the Maritime Law of Wisby, the interval allowed as lay-days for a chartered vessel is fourteen days, the fortnight of English usage, whereas in the 'Judgments of Damme,' or regulations of West Flanders, derived from the Rolls of Oleron, the time is fifteen days.[17] There is thus a remarkable coincidence between the maritime usage of old Frisian and Gothic ports and those of England, of which London was the chief. It points to Frisian and Gothic traders in such numbers as to be able to introduce an important provision of their own marine customs into English ports, and this probably with people descended from their own races who traded with them, as was likely to have been the case in Anglo-Saxon London.

When we leave the consideration of the Goths and Frisians, and turn our attention to the remarkable customs which have come down from time immemorial on the south and west of the city, we are met by circumstances of another kind. Inheritance by the youngest son instead of the eldest, as in common law, prevailed unto within living memory on the manors of Kennington, Walworth, Vauxhall, Peckham Rye, Wandsworth, Battersea, Lambeth, Streatham, Croydon, Barnes, Shene or Richmond, and Petersham. On the north of the Thames it existed at Edmonton, Tottenham, Ealing, Acton, Isleworth, and Earl's Court.[18] Junior right prevails among some of the Frisians of Friesland. It can also be traced and still exists in parts of ancient Wendland—i.e., Pomerania—and, as already pointed out, is found sporadically in isolated districts of Germany, North-Eastern France, and Belgium, where isolated colonies of Wends existed. Since junior right has prevailed until modern times at Wandsworth, and at that place we have the custom associated with the ancient Vandal name Wendelesworth, the origin of the custom around London must, apparently, be traced to Frisians or Wends, or to people of both races.

On the manor of Earl's Court the youngest son inherited; at Lambeth the youngest son, and in default of sons, the daughters equally; and at Tottenham the same custom prevailed. At East Sheen the youngest son succeeded, and in default of sons, the youngest daughter, brother, sister, or nephew; and at Croydon the youngest son, and if no sons, the youngest in every degree. At Vauxhall the youngest son, and failing sons, the youngest daughter, was the heir. At Islington, on the Sutton Court and St. John of Jerusalem manors, the strict borough-English custom prevailed. At Isleworth, Sion, Ealing, and Acton, the borough-English custom extended to brothers. At Fulham, Wimbledon, Battersea, Wandsworth, Downe, Barnes, and Richmond, the inheritance, in default of males, passed to females lineally and collaterally.[19]

In tracing this custom, as far as we are able, from what appears to have been its home in Continental lands to England, we have to take into consideration the provision which the English custom shows for female rights. In it the widow had her dower; she held the land for her life, and the youngest son succeeded after her. Also, if there were no sons, either the youngest daughter or youngest female succeeded, or the land was divided among the female heirs. Whatever may have been the provision for females among the ancient Wendish tribes, we know that the right of dower was a custom among the Teutons, and is mentioned by Tacitus. We know, also, that inheritance by females as well as males prevailed among the Frisians, and was a custom of the Northern Goths. We may perhaps, therefore, see a Gothic influence in the junior right custom in England, by which dower for the widow is secured and succession by daughters provided for in the absence of sons. The growth of such provisions would be easy to understand on the supposition of a fusion of Goths with a Vandal tribe which had junior inheritance. The result would be a compromise, as may possibly have been the case in Kent, where, on the supposition that Wends, or some Frisian clans which had the same custom, were among the Kentish settlers, we find partible inheritance, not on the strict lines of the Gothic, but with daughters coming after sons, and the youngest son having the homestead.

The territory south of London and Middlesex, which afterwards became known as Suthereye, appears, from the custom which survived in it and its ancient topographical names, to have received as settlers Goths and Frisians, Norwegians and Wends. Some reference has already been made to them. Junior inheritance survived until modern time on many manors in Surrey, as mentioned in the chapter on Sussex. This points either to colonization from Sussex, where the same custom has survived more widely than elsewhere in England, or to the settlement of people of the same racial descent as those in the Rape of Lewes. It is not difficult to believe that colonists crossed the forest land of the Weald and settled on the lands which form the slopes of the chalk downs of Dorking and Reigate. This country of the North Downs must at an early period of the Saxon settlement, as now, have been more free from wood than the forest land of the Weald. As this same custom also prevailed at Wandsworth, Battersea, Lambeth, Walworth, Vauxhall, Peckham Rye, Barnes, Richmond, and Petersham, all of which are on or near the river, it is probable that Surrey was colonised, in part at least, by settlers who arrived by water. We may thus, perhaps, reasonably conclude from these survivals that the country was settled partly overland from Sussex and partly by other colonists who came up the Thames. Surrey thus appears to have received among its settlers some Goths of the same Northern stock as those who settled in Kent. From Kent to Surrey migration was easy. A great forest area separated these parts of Southern England during the period of the settlement, but there were two natural routes by which people from Kent could reach even the western parts of Surrey—viz., by the Thames and along the ridge of the chalk downs which extended from east to west, and, being incapable of growing trees, must always have afforded an open route.

The Æscings is one of the names by which the early Kentish settlers were known, and a place called Æscing, now Eashing, part of Godalming, is mentioned in King Alfred's will. On the boundary of Hampshire and Surrey, to which the ancient limit of Godalming extended, there is a hill still called Kent's hill. The name Godalming appears to have been derived from the descendants of one or more Goths, its old form being Godelming, and the old popular form being Godliman or Godlimen.

There are two remarkable entries in Domesday Book that point directly to an ancient connection of some of the settlements in Surrey with Kent. Under Waletone, now Wallington, we are told that its woods were in Kent; and under Meretone, now Merton, we are told that two solins of land in Kent belonged to this manor, as the men of the hundred testified.[20] We can trace Kentish place-names here and there through Surrey.

The survival of the custom under which the eldest daughter inherited the father's property in default of sons at Chertsey, Beaumond, Farnham, Worplesdon, and Pirbright, shows that the west of Surrey must have received some settlers who were neither Goths, Frisians, Wends, nor of any mixed race which clung to the custom of inheritance by the youngest son. The Goths and Frisians had not this eldest daughter custom. Saxons and Angles had none of it, for their customs were strongly marked by male inheritance. As mentioned elsewhere, there is only one old race to which it certainly can be traced, and that is the Norwegians. We may, consequently, conclude that Norse colonists, at some time or other, settled at these western parts of Surrey. This part of the county adjoins the north-east of Hampshire, where a similar custom prevailed, and in Surrey, on the east of Aldershot, the old place-name Normandy survives.

There is an early charter relating to the grant of land at Batrices-ege, or Battersea, to St. Peter's, Westminster, dated A.D. 693, in which Wendles-wurthe and Ceokan-ege are mentioned in the boundaries.[21] This mention of Wandsworth shows that the name is an early one, and shows also that it could not have originated from a settlement in the eleventh century during the time of Cnut, who introduced Wends from Jomberg into England as his huscarls.[22] The settlement at Wendles-wurthe was probably one of the early settlements of Surrey, and as junior right survived there, the settlers appear to have brought it with them. The name Ceokan-ege may refer to a man who was a Chaucian, or a settler of that race. It appears to point in any case to the only tribe who had such a name, the Chauci, settled between the Weser and the Elbe.

In the Middlesex settlement the old name for the people who lived around Harrow was 'Gumeninga hergae.' This word *gumeninga* can be traced through the Anglo-Saxon to the Gothic word *guma*, denoting a man, and thus appears to have come into the Old English language from the Goths. The words, *gumeninga hergae* denote the children or descendants of the men of Harrow, and occur in a charter of Offa dated 767.[23] This is important, as it points to an old settlement of people of Gothic extraction around Harrow, possibly a migration of some of the men of Kent, and we find close to Harrow a place still called Kenton.

Harrow was a great domain that belonged to the See of Canterbury from a very early date. The Archbishop's lands, apart from the monastic at Canterbury, were only separated in the time of Lanfranc,[24] just before the Norman Survey, and Domesday Book tells us that Harrow was held by the Archbishop. It was a great estate, and possessed privileges which placed it outside the jurisdiction of the county. What we are concerned with is the probability of the district around Harrow having been settled by Kentish people of Gothic extraction. We cannot trace the custom of partible inheritance, such as prevails in Kent, as having survived at Harrow, but we can point to a time when the Archbishop was permitted to change his estates, or some of them, from gavelkind tenure into knight's fees. This was in the reign of John, when a license was granted to Hubert, Archbishop of Canterbury, to that effect.[25] The non-survival of the custom of partible inheritance on the ancient estates of the Archbishop of Canterbury in Middlesex, that were apparently settled by Kentish or Gothic people, can thus be accounted for. The settlement around Harrow was probably an early one, before the invaders had become Christian; for the most ancient name of the place—Hearge, or Hearh (genitive, Hearges)—denotes a heathen temple, and we cannot think that after their conversion to Christianity any settlers would have given the place this name. Harrow was clearly a sacred heathen site, and there was probably a significance in the early grant of this estate to the Archbishop, and in the subsequent erection on the highest site in Harrow of a church by the Anglo-Saxon prelate.

The other estate of the early Archbishops of Canterbury in Middlesex was Yeading, or, as the manor was called later on, Hayes. It is first mentioned in a charter of Ceadwalla dated 678, in which that King granted Gedding and Wudeton to Archbishop Theodore. As Ceadwalla was a West Saxon King who had succeeded a Mercian as the overlord, this was probably, a confirmatory grant. The name Gedding, modified in spelling to Yeading, still survives in the parish of Hayes. These grants of lands to monasteries and Bishops by the early Anglo-Saxon Kings were colonization grants. All that they had in their power to give was the land, certain services from the people already settled on the land, or who might become settled on it, and the fines and forfeitures falling to the lord from the administration of the law.

Kent, of all the Old English kingdoms, had probably the least room for the expansion of its people. As they increased in number, they were necessarily obliged to seek new homes and migrate. We can hardly imagine any more likely circumstance in relation to the settlement of Middlesex than that some of the surplus population on the Archbishop's land in Kent should have been allowed to settle on his lands in Middlesex, to the advantage of both the settlers and their lord. In considering this probability, we should also remember the clause in the laws of Wihtræd, drawn up about 685, which refers to the Kentish freedman, his heritage, wergeld, etc., not only in Kent, but elsewhere, the words used being, 'Be he over the march, wherever he may be.' It is quite clear from these words that some of them had gone over the march at that early time.

A considerable proportion of the people who settled in Middlesex appear to have come from Kent, and to have retained privileges which their ancestors had also possessed. This is shown as probable by the Domesday records concerning the cottars. They were the labouring class of manorial tenants, but had land of their own, and had also more freedom as small tenants than those called borderers in many other counties. Cottars are only mentioned in Domesday Book in considerable numbers Kent, Sussex, Surrey, Middlesex,

Berkshire, Wiltshire, Dorset, Somerset, Herefordshire, and Cambridge-shire.[26] We can trace them from Kent up the Thames valley. Whatever the privilege of the cottar may have been (and it is generally agreed that he had a cottage and a few acres of land, which he cultivated himself when not working for his lord), it is certain that the man in this position, by whatever name he was called, was more free in Kent than in any other county, and probably better off in other respects. It is of interest, therefore, to trace the existence of the cottar in other counties into which Kentish people may have migrated, or people of the same races as those from which the Kentish people were descended may have settled. These were mainly the freedom-loving Frisians and Goths, collectively called Jutes. The cottar was a freeman subject to certain manorial customs. He paid his hearth penny—*i.e.*, his Rome scot or Peter's pence—on Holy Thursday, as every freeman did; he worked for the lord one day in the week and three days in harvest time, and he had five acres more or less.[27] This class of manorial tenants was relatively large in Middlesex and Surrey at the time of the Domesday Survey. If they existed in Essex, they are not mentioned, and this circumstance alone points to Kent rather than to Essex as the State from which colonists settled in Middlesex—*i.e.*, rather to Frisians and Goths than the so-called Saxons of Essex. The cottars of Middlesex lived at Fulham, St. Pancras or Kentish Town, Islington, Drayton, Staines, Hanwell, Harmondsworth, Sunbury, Greenford, Shepperton, Enfield, Tottenham, and other places. These Middlesex cottars, like the Middlesex villeins, the next class of manorial tenant above them, were more important persons and more free in their holdings than villeins and borderers in other counties usually were. This, again, points to early migrations from Kent, and to the influence of the great city on the country round it.

[1] Green, J. R., 'Making of England,' 109.

[2] Anglo-Saxon Chronicle, A.D. 1018.

[3] Stow, J., 'Survey of London,' A.D. 1598.

[4] Elton, C. I., 'Robinson on Gavelkind,' 34, 36.

[5] Glanville, R. de, 'Tract, de leg. et cons. Angliæ,' lib. vii., chap. iii.

[6] Bracton, H. de, 'De legibus et consuetudinibus Angliæ,' edited by Twiss, ii. 5.

[7] Æthelstan's Dooms, vi.; Judicia Civitatis Lundoniæ, i.

[8] 'Ancient Laws,' edited by Thorpe, i. 91; Maine, 'Early Hist. of Institutions,' 303.

[9] 'Saxons in England,' by Kemble, edited by Birch, ii., Appendix, 528, quoting 'Flemish Charters of Liberties.'

[10] Ballard, A., *English Historical Review*, xiv. 94.

[11] Cott. MSS., Chart, xvii. i; also Codex Dipl., No. 78.

[12] Black Book of the Admiralty, edited by Twiss, ii., Introd., vii., viii.

[13] *Ibid.*

[14] *Ibid.*

[15] *Ibid.*, iii., Introd., xx.

[16] *Ibid.*, iii., Introd., xxi.

[17] Black Book of the Admiralty, iii., Introd., xix.

[18] Elton, C. I., *loc. cit.*, and Corner, 'Custom of Borough-English.'

[19] Elton, C. I., *loc. cit.*, 238.

[20] Dom. Bk., p. 30 *a.*

[21] Cart. Sax., i. 116, 117.
[22] Adam Bremen, ii. 59, quoted by Kemble, 'Saxons in England,' ii. 120.
[23] Cart. Sax., i. 284.
[24] Elton, C. I., *loc. cit.*, p. 18.

[25] Lambarde, W., 'Perambulation of Kent.' Ed. 1596, p. 531.
[26] Maitland, F. W., 'Domesday Book and Beyond,' p. 39.
[27] *Ibid.*, 327.

# Chapter Sixteen - Settlements in the Thames Valley

As we proceed up the Thames from Middlesex, we meet with evidence of settlements by people of different races. This is apparent in the eastern part of Berkshire and the adjoining part of Buckinghamshire. The name Windsor, anciently Wendlesore,[1] is similar to that of Wendleswurthe, and can scarcely have been derived from any other source than the settlement of a Wend and his family, or a community of these people. When we consider that there are Wendish place-names in the south of Essex, it is not surprising to find them higher up the Thames. Wendlesore and Wændlescumb, also in Berkshire, are examples. The old place-name Wendlebury, a few miles north-east of Oxford, may have had its origin in the settlement of a family or kindred of Wends. Isaac Taylor, in reminding us of the statement by Zosimus of Vandals settled in Britain by the Emperor Probus, mentions this Wendlebury, near Bicester, in Oxfordshire, as a place that was likely to have been a Vandal settlements.[2] It may, of course, have got its name from an early settlement in the time of the Roman Empire, or a later one in the time of the Anglo-Saxon settlement, such as that of the Rugians, who were Wends, and whom Bede tells us were among the many tribes from which the English in his time had their origin.

In a charter assigning the boundaries of land at Waltham, near Maidenhead, given to Abingdon Abbey the name 'Godan pearruc' occurs.[3] This charter is dated 940, but the name was apparently an older one, and occurs in another charter. It denotes the enclosure of Goda, and Goda denotes a Goth, so that we may take it to have been derived from the settlement of a family of Goths.

There can be no doubt that the ancient names Goda and Geat denote a Goth and Jute, and if we note the old names of this kind as we proceed up the Thames, we find Goddards tything, Reading; Godstow and Godefordes Eyt, near Oxford;[4] Godeslave, in Oxon;[5] 'terram Gode,' the name of land belonging to the church at Culham;[6] Geatescumbe, in the boundaries of the land of the Abbey of Abingdon, near Oxford,[7] and others.

These names suggest that there was a migration into the Thames valley of people called by the race-names of the Goths, Geats, or Jutes, from Kent up the river. If we similarly trace the Kentish name itself up the valley, we meet with very old examples of it: Kenton, now Kempton, in Middlesex; Kentes, in

East Berkshire;[8] Kentswood, near Pangbourn; and Kentwines treöw, at Shefford, near the Thames above Oxford.[9]

When we look for other confirmatory evidence of a Kentish migration up the Thames, we find it in the Hengist place-names near Oxford. Hengist is a name common in the early history of Frisians as well as Jutes, and these names near Oxford may have been given them by Frisians or Goths. People of both these races settled in Kent, and it was apparently from Kent that the people came into the country near Oxford. The name Hengistesege is mentioned in a charter of Eadwy,[10] and refers to Hinksey. Hengesthescumb also occurs[11] among the boundaries of Scypford, now Shefford, not far from Oxford.

At Bray, in this same part of Berkshire, and at Wycombe, in Buckinghamshire, not far from it, we find evidence of settlements of some Scandinavians; for the ancient custom survived by which the eldest daughter inherited the whole of the father's estate in default of sons.[12] This identifies the settlers at these places, whenever they may have come, as Norwegians, for in no country but Norway, where the eldest daughter still has her birthright, can the custom, so far as known, be traced.

The evidence that Norse settlements existed in this part of the Thames valley is confirmed by the discoveries in a mound at Taplow overlooking the river. The objects found included two shield bones; a sword, and fragments of others; a bronze vessel; a wooden bucket with bronze hoops, like those common in graves in Scandinavia; two pairs of glass vessels, green in tint, and similar to one found with a burial ship in Void in Norway; silver-gilt ornaments for drinking-horns; a green glass bead; and a quantity of gold thread belonging to a garment, the triangular form of the pattern still remaining.[13] These objects have been recognised as apparently belonging to the later Iron Age of Scandinavia. The name Wycombe, in a charter of Offa in 767, is written Wicham,[14] by which it was known as late as the thirteenth century; and it is well known that the prefix *wick-* in place-names is often a sign of a Norse settlement. In the case of Wickam the significance of the name is confirmed by the survival of the Norse custom. At this place there appear to have been settlers of two races—viz., those in which the eldest daughter took the whole estate in the absence of sons, and those who held land called 'molland,' which was divided,[15] thus pointing, perhaps, to settlements there at two periods.

At Bray the original custom, which was probably inheritance by the eldest daughter in default of sons, appears to have been modified at some later time. In the thirteenth century Bracton tells us that the jurors of that place say the custom is that if a man have three or four daughters, and all marry out of the tenement of the father except one, she who remains in the father's house succeeds to all his land.[16] This is clearly only a modification of the custom of Norway.

A considerable part of East Berkshire, stretching from the river to the border of what is now Surrey, was occupied in the seventh century by people known as the Sunninges.[17] Their name is mentioned in several Saxon charters—in the words Sunninga-wyl bróc,[18] and survives in that of Sonning on the river, Sunninghill and Sunningdale on the border of Surrey. Their district is mentioned as 'the province that is called the Sunninges,' so that it must have comprised a considerable area of country. The name is an interesting one, and may have been that given to these settlers by their neighbours about Wycombe and Bray, for the Sunninges were Southerners to the people near Wycombe; but there is no evidence to show of what race they were. In this district there was, however, a place called Swæfes heale, which is named as a boundary of the land at Waltham given to Abingdon Abbey in 940. As mentioned elsewhere, Swæfas is a Northern name denoting the Suevi, which is used as an equivalent for Saxons. Swæfes heale, therefore, may refer to a boundary which was the limit of the settlement of a Saxon, as Godan pearruc, mentioned in the same charter, was that of a Goth. If this interpretation is the correct one, Swæfes heale points to Saxons settled in East Berkshire, with Scandians, Wends, and Goths as their neighbours.

In this part of the country we also find the significant name of Cookham, mentioned in an Anglo-Saxon charter[19] as Coccham, in Domesday Book as Cocheham. As already pointed out, a similar name—Ceokan-ege—occurs in an early charter relating to Battersea. There are many examples which show that the sounds *g* and *k* were interchangeable in names of the Anglo-Saxon period. Higher up the valley we find similar names—viz., Cuxham, Coxwell, and others. These apparently have a common source, in the tribal name of the Chaucians, the Frisian tribe near the mouth of the Elbe. The Chaucians, as previously mentioned, were also called Hocings, and both forms of their name are probably met with in place-names in the Thames valley. Hocheston, now part of London, is the Domesday name for Hoxton, and may denote the settlement of a Chaucian. In the eastern part of Berkshire we find separate hundreds mentioned in the Hundred Rolls for Sonning, Bray, Cogham or Cookham, and Windsor. This Cogham hundred of the thirteenth century may be a survival of a more ancient separate local administration, as the hundreds of Bray, Sunninges, and Windsor may be, of the original settlers at these places. Another entry under the name Cocheham occurs in Domesday Book in Burnham hundred in Buckinghamshire, not far from the Berkshire place of this name, so that some of this family or kindred appear to have lived on both sides of the river.

In the north of Berkshire there is a river called the Ock, written in Anglo-Saxon charters in the inflected forms Eoccen and Eoccene, the nominative form being Eocce. Close to the west of Oxford there was a ford which is called Eoccen-ford in part of an early charter of Ceadwalla which has been preserved in a later one. There was also land or a place close to this ford which in this charter is named Eoccene, and centuries later, in a charter of Eadwy, is called Occene. The river Ock flows into the Thames at Abingdon, but the Eoccene, or Occene, mentioned in these last-named charters was certainly close to the west side of Oxford. The proof of this is seen in following a set of boundaries of land given to Abingdon Abbey by Ceadwalla. These boundaries are passed as we proceed up the river from Sandford to the lower or old mouth of the Cherwell, up that river a short distance, round an old river island, down the other side of it again into the Thames, then up the river again, and further up the east side of a triangular or forked island which still exists on the west of Oxford, and down with the stream on its northern side into the main stream of the Thames again, and so on again up the river past Eoccene, the later Oseney, to Eoccen-ford. As there was only one river Cherwell, there can be no doubt that these boundaries lay close to Oxford. The mouth of the Cherwell is now changed by a new cut, but we can still stand on the west bank of the Thames north of the gasworks at Oxford, and see the water flowing along the north side of the forked island into the river, as described in Ceadwalla's charter at the end of the seventh century. This subject has been fully discussed by the present writer[20] in a series of articles on the origin of the place-name Oxford. Eoccen-ford is the earliest form of that name. The charter of Ceadwalla in which it occurs contains internal evidence of its authenticity, and that Eoccen-ford was on the west side of Oxford is proved independently by the later charter of Eadwy. Many instances have been referred to in which streams have been named, both in Germany and England, after people settled along them. The supposition is that in North Berkshire and part of Oxfordshire there was a colony or tribe of people who bore the name Eocce, after whom the Ock River, the stream called the Oke at Hook Norton, and the ford at Oxford, were named. The question which concerns us is this: Is there any evidence to be gathered from the old place-names around Oxford or from other sources of the existence of people who may be identified with the supposed colony or tribe of people called Eocce? The only tribe whose name appears possible in this respect is the Chaucians, a nation in alliance with the Frisians, who are believed to be the same people as the Hocings mentioned in Beowulf,[21] in which an account is given of Hnæf, Prince of the Hocings, and Hengest the Jute, vassals of the Danish King Healfdene, who were sent to invade the Frisian territory at that time governed by Fin, son of Folcwalda, and husband of Hildeburh, the daughter of Hoce. Whatever the name Eoccen-ford, the earliest name for Oxford, may mean, it should not be forgotten that in the old Frisian land, close to that in which the Chaucians lived, there was a place called Occenvorth.[22]

Latham, as already mentioned in Chapter V., says: 'In Beowulf we read of the Hocings. Word for word, this is held to be the Chauci by all or most who have written upon the subject.[23] Hocing means, not so much a Chaucus or Chaucian as of Chauch blood.' As regards the first syllable of Cuxhaven being derived from Chauc or Chauci, Latham says this has been suggested, and, he believes, adopted. As regards the variation in Anglo-Saxon spelling, Sweet quotes ch as equivalent to c, and this as passing into h.[24] Thorpe quotes the Hetware tribe as the same as the Chatuarii mentioned by Strabo.[25] Latham tells us further that ch in Old Frisian is equivalent to h Anglo-Saxon.[26] Maetzner tells us that the aspirated ch was completely foreign to Anglo-

Saxon before the eleventh century,[27] and he quotes the words *cild, cêce, ceafor, ceósan,* for the later English words child, cheek, chafer, and choose, as examples. These authorities will probably be held to be sufficient on this point. In dealing with the evidence of place-names in the Upper Thames valley which possibly may refer to the Hocings or Chaucians, there remains to be considered briefly the use of the aspirated *h,* or its omission. The Anglo-Saxon language was marked by the use of the aspirate, but there are examples which show its omission. Skeat attributes the modern English misuse of the *h* sound to French influence after the Norman Conquest, the French *h* being certainly weaker than the English, and hardly sounded.[28] He admits, however, that a few sporadic examples may be found in Anglo-Saxon.[29] He gives as an example *ors* for *hors* (horse), found in an unedited Anglo-Saxon manuscript. The following also appear to be examples of its omission or misuse: *ymen, ymn,* for hymn;[30] *Ybernia* for Hibernia;[31] Wulfhora and Wulfora[32] and Ockemere for Hokemere.[33] There are other examples, such as Elig and Helig for Ely. The misuse of the *h* among the Anglo-Saxons may have been due partly to Wendish influence or that of settlers from other Baltic lands. The pastor Mithof tells us that a peculiarity of the Wends in his day was that whenever they spoke German they were in the habit of putting an *h* before words in which it did not exist, and leaving it out where it did.[34] Morfill says that the same confusion is found in Lithuania.[35] The misuse of the letter and its sound which is occasionally met with may therefore have had its origin in settlers from the Baltic, and we have seen that there are Wendish place-names not far from Oxford. It is worth noting also, in reference to the aspirate *h,* that an old Frisian Chronicle of the thirteenth century has Engist for Hengist.[36] From what has been said, it will perhaps be admitted that the Anglo-Saxon aspirated *h* may not always have been sounded by all the Old English people, and that the *h* sound was used as an equivalent of that represented by the old *ch.*

We may now go back to consider what evidence the place-names in the Upper Thames valley afford of a possible settlement of Chaucians or Hocings. On the west of Oxford, near Farringdon, we find Coxwell, the Cocheswelle of Domesday Book. South of Witney, in Standlake parish, is Cokethorpe, the Cocthrop of the Hundred Rolls, and east of Oxford, near Watlington, is Cuxham, the Anglo-Saxon Cuceshámm.[37] Coccetley Croft is also an old name near Abingdon.[38] Hóchylle[39] is a name in the boundaries of Sandford-on-Thames, mentioned in Saxon time, and Hócsléw is another mentioned in the boundaries of Witney.[40] Hocan-edisce was the name of a place in Berkshire on the Thames in the tenth century.[41] Hockeswell is mentioned in the Hundred Rolls,[42] and is apparently the same place as that now called Hawkswell, in the northern suburbs of Oxford. Hokemere is an ancient name at Cowley,[43] near Oxford, the same, apparently, as the Anglo-Saxon name Ockemere,[44] which occurs in an early charter relating to St. Frideswide's Abbey. Hochenartone, which had flowing from it the stream called by the old name Oke, is the Domesday name for Hook Norton, and in one of the manuscript copies of the Anglo-Saxon Chronicle, under the date 914, it is written Hocceneretune. There was a place in Buckinghamshire called Hocsaga in Domesday Book, and the tribal name of the Chaucians may have survived locally, like that of the Gewissas, until after the Norman Conquest; for the Hundred Rolls relating to Oxfordshire show a greater number of inferior tenants entered under the names Choch, Cocus, Coc, and Hok than in any other county.

The evidence of the settlement of Kentish people or others of the Frisian or Gothic race that is supplied by the relics which have been found in the Upper Thames valley is very strong. At Iffley and at Abingdon brooches of the peculiar Kentish pattern have been found, and are now shown in the Anglo-Saxon collection in the British Museum. The relics discovered at Brighthampton and Wittenham, where Anglo-Saxon cemeteries were explored, show a strong resemblance to those found by Kemble at Stade in North Germany.[45] The ornamented pattern of a mortuary urn containing cremated remains found at Brighthampton closely resembled one found at Stade, where a very large number were discovered, all apparently containing cremated remains. Urns containing calcined human bones were also numerously found at Wittenham, and were of a similar pattern to those found at Stade.[46] In considering these resemblances, we must remember that Stade is near the lower course of the Elbe in the middle of the country anciently inhabited by the Chaucians.

All these circumstances which indicate a settlement of Chaucians around Oxford among other Frisians, Goths, and Kentish people, cannot be mere coincidences.

There remains one other point—viz., the probability of some connection of the Chaucians with the Jutes. Möller[47] identifies the language of the Jutes and Kentish people with that of the Chaucians. There is, also, mention of a people named the Eucii in alliance with the Saxons, and that they settled in Kent. These may be a tribe of the Chaucians, for Hengist and Horsa are said to have come from Engern, which at that time extended over the land of the old Chaucians on the Lower Weser.[48] The reference, whether traditional or otherwise, to a tribe known as the Eucii cannot but be of interest in considering the evidence which points to the existence of a tribe of Eocce in North Berkshire, of which some of the surviving traces may be the names of the river Ock, the Oke stream at Hook Norton, and that of Eoccenford, the earliest name for Oxford.

The personal freedom of all the people of Kent assists us in tracing the probable colonization of parts of the Upper Thames valley by migrations from that county. The manorial tenants called cottars, who are mentioned in Domesday Book, were freemen in some respects, and, as already stated, are found in considerable numbers in Middlesex. They occur still more frequently in parts of Berkshire near the river, and are also mentioned numerously in parts of Oxfordshire in the Hundred Rolls. The Berkshire cottars enumerated in the Domesday Survey lived in certain hundreds and not in others. These hundreds were Benes or Cookham; Heslitesford, near Wallingford; Blewbury, adjoining it on the west; Wantage; and Gamensfeld or Ganfield, which lay between the Wantage Hundred and the Thames. Five Berkshire hundreds close to, or not far from, the river were thus specially characterised by cottars. That they were the descendants of an original class of free settlers is probable from their number in various places. Cholsey had 98 of them, and Blewbury 65. In Heslitesford Hundred, which included Cholsey, there were altogether 144, and in Blewbury Hundred, anciently known as Blitberie, there were 166. They thus appear to have been too numerous as a class in these localities for their origin to be explained otherwise than as probable descendants of original free settlers. From the other evidence already stated, the migration up the river of colonists from Kent can scarcely be open to doubt, and the existence, centuries later, of these numerous cottars settled collectively in parts of the county near the river leads to the same conclusion.

One of the significant statements in Domesday Book relating to Oxfordshire is this: 'If any shall kill another in his own court or house, his body and all his substance shall be in the King's power, except his wife's portion, if she has any.' This refers to a privilege which corresponds to that of the Kentish tenants in gavelkind—viz., that a gavelkind tenant's land was not forfeited if he should be convicted of felony. The custom in Oxfordshire was not general, as will be seen by the Domesday extract. If the widow was entitled to dower, her share of the husband's estate could not be forfeited, but there were some people in Oxfordshire at that time whose widows had no dower, as may be inferred from the words 'if she has any.' This Domesday entry points to the custom having been an old one, and indicates the probable migration of people up the Thames from Kent, where the widow was entitled to half her husband's estate for her life, and from the manors in Surrey and Middlesex where, by the custom of borough-English, she was entitled to the whole for her life. The Hundred Rolls for Oxfordshire confirm the probability of such migrations, for they contain some entries which show that widows held a virgate of land each among other virgate-holding tenants, and others showing widows holding only half a virgate[49]—i.e., half the customary holding. The Hundred Rolls also show, in the occurrence of the personal name Franklin in Oxfordshire, the probability of the migration of Kentish freeholders called Franklins from their homes in Kent.

Similarly, in the Upper Thames valley we find examples of parcenary tenure or partible inheritance that resembled in its main features the gavelkind custom of Kent. Domesday Book tells us of brothers holding land jointly at Burfield in Berkshire, Hook Norton in Oxfordshire, Hevaford (Hatford) in North Berkshire, and at Cerney, near Cirencester. It is not improbable, also, that the many instances in Berkshire and Oxfordshire in which manors were held in the time of Edward the Confessor collectively by thanes or freemen are examples of the same kind, such as that of Brize Norton, which was held by fourteen thanes, who were probably of the same kindred. These instances, which are numerous, are apparently examples of manors that were taxed as a whole, but held collectively, as in Kent, by brothers, uncles, and other kinsmen.

The custom of junior inheritance is known to have prevailed at Binsey,[50] near Oxford; Garford,[51] near Abingdon; and Crowmarsh,[52] close to Wallingford. These examples are probably the only survivals of a custom that prevailed in a larger number of places in the Anglo-Saxon period, but which were changed under the feudal system. They show, in any case, an identity with the borough-English custom that existed on so many manors around London, and point to probable migrations from Sussex or Surrey.

The early settlers who came from the south into the valleys of the Upper Thames and of its tributary streams, the Evenlode, Windrush, and others, whose sources are in East Gloucestershire, probably travelled along the great Roman road that extended from Southampton Water through Winchester to Cirencester. This road can be followed at the present time for the greater part of its course, so that there can be no doubt whatever of the facilities it offered for a migration from the south coast. At Cirencester it joined the Fosse Way that connected Bath with Lincoln. By proceeding along this latter road colonists could pass to north-east Gloucestershire, where the observations of Beddoe upon the present ethnological character of the people show that the original settlers were probably fair people of the so-called Saxon type.[53] The ancient place-names along the border of Oxfordshire and Gloucestershire are of much interest, and point to settlers of various tribes and races, as will be discussed in a subsequent chapter. From Cirencester, also, the road known as Akeman Street passed eastward, through the middle of Oxfordshire, and thence into Buckinghamshire and the country that was brought under the West Saxon rule in the time of Ceawlin. The east and south of Berkshire were connected with Southampton Water by the great road from Winchester through Silchester, although its course beyond the north gate of Silchester cannot now be followed. A way of less importance also passed from Hampshire northwards through Speen, near Newbury, so that there were three roads which led directly into the Thames valley from the south.

The available evidence relating to the dialects that have survived also points to migrations from the south-Eastern counties up the Thames. The researches made on English dialects by Prince Lucien L. Bonaparte[54] and A. J. Ellis agree in the conclusion that the dialect of the south-eastern part of England extends up the Thames valley into Oxfordshire.[55] The dialect of east Gloucestershire, however, has been classed with that of parts of Hampshire and Dorset, with which counties, as shown, it was in direct communication.

As regards the villages, those of Oxfordshire and Berkshire for the most part consist of collected homesteads. The old maps of both counties, made before the enclosures of the great areas of common land, show this in a remarkable way. If, therefore, we may draw a conclusion from the resemblance which the shape of the old villages of Oxfordshire, especially those in the northern half of the county, bear to those in Germany east of the Weser and north of the Elbe, it is probable that a considerable proportion of the settlers in that county came from these Continental areas.

The conclusion in regard to the actual settlement which appears to be most probable is that the valley of the Upper Thames was first occupied partly by a migration of Gewissas from the South, and partly by Kentish people or Goths and Frisians, with some Wends, who came up the river.

[1] Codex Dipl., No. 816.

[2] Taylor, Isaac, 'Words and Places,' 1873 ed., p. 180.

[3] Chron. Mon. de Abingdon, edited by J. Stevenson, i. 98, and i. 420.

[4] Wood, A. A., 'Antiquities of Oxford,' edited by Clark, i. 430.

[5] Domesday Book, i. 159.

[6] Chron. Mon. de Abingdon, edited by J. Stevenson, ii. 58.

[7] Codex Dipl., No. 1171.

[8] Cal. Inq., p. m., iv. 394.

[9] Codex Dipl., No. 714.

[10] Codex Dipl., No. 1216.

[11] Ibid., No. 714.

[12] Elton, C. I., 'Law of Copyholds,' 134; Hale, W. H., 'Domesday of St. Paul's,' Notes.

[13] du Chaillu, P. B., 'The Viking Age,' i. 318, 319.

[14] Cart. Sax., i. 284.

[15] Cart. Sax., i. 284; Hale, W. H., 'Domesday of St. Paul's,' p. lxxv.

[16] Bracton, H. de, Note-book, ed. by Maitland, Case 988.

[17] Cart. Sax., i. 56.

[18] Codex Dipl., 208, 441, 1202, etc.

[19] Cart. Sax., i. 405.

[20] Notes and Queries, Ninth Series, vols. iii., iv., v., and vi.

[21] Lappenberg, J. M., 'Hist. of England under the Anglo-Saxon Kings,' i. 276, note, quoting Zeuss.

[22] Annales Egmundani: Monumenta Germaniæ Script., xvi. 464.

[23] Latham, R. G., 'English Language,' 5th Ed., 243.

[24] Sweet, H., 'Dictionary of Anglo-Saxon,' Preface, xix.

[25] Thorpe, B., 'The Poems of Beowulf,' Glossarial Index, p. 319.

[26] Latham, R. G., loc. cit., p. 93.

[27] Maetzner, E., 'English Grammar,' i. 151.

[28] Skeat, W. W., 'Principles of English Etymology,' 359, 360.

[29] Notes and Queries, Seventh Series, vi. 110.

[30] Bosworth, J., Anglo-Saxon and English Dictionary.

[31] Anglo-Saxon Chronicle, edited by Thorpe.

[32] Codex Dipl., 1093 and 1164.

[33] Cartulary of St. Frideswide, edited by Wigram, i., p. 4.

[34] Morfill, W. R., 'The Polabes,' Transactions Philolog. Soc., 1880-1881, p. 85.

[35] Morfill, W. R., loc. cit., p. 85.

[36] Bosworth, J., 'Origin of the English, German, and Scandinavian Languages,' p. 52, quoting Spiegel.

[37] Codex Dipl., Nos. 311, 691.

[38] Hundred Rolls, ii. 19.

[39] Codex Dipl., Nos. 793 and 800.

[40] Ibid., No. 775.

[41] Cart. Sax., iii. 560.

[42] Hundred Rolls, ii. 35.

[43] Wood, A., 'Antiquities of Oxford,' edited by Clark, ii. 507.

[44] Cartulary of St. Frideswide, edited by Wigram, i., p. 4.

[45] Akerman, J. Y., Archæologia, vol. xxxvii.

[46] Ibid., vol. xxix.

[47] Möller, H., 'Das Altenglische Volksepos.'

[48] Meitzen, A., 'Siedelung und Agrarwesen der Westgermanen,' ii. 101.

[49] Hundred Rolls, ii. 700, 717, 724, 739, 740, 742, etc.

[50] Wood, A., 'Antiquities of Oxford,' edited by Clark, i. 323.

[51] Bracton's 'Note-book,' edited by Maitland, No. 779.

[52] *Ibid.*, No. 1005.

[53] Beddoe, J., 'Races in Britain,' 257.

[54] *Philological Soc. Transactions*, 1875-1876, p. 570.

[55] Ellis, A. J., 'Early English Pronunciation,' Map of Dialect Districts.

# Chapter Seventeen - Settlers in Essex and East Anglia

ONE of the most interesting circumstances connected with the settlement of Essex is the old Kentish colony which was formed in the north-east of the county, and was part of the territory belonging to St. Paul's Cathedral.

Æthelbert, King of Kent, was the overlord of Essex in the beginning of the seventh century. He was also the founder of St. Paul's, and endowed it and the Bishopric of London with its earliest estates. Three centuries after his time Æthelstan, King of Wessex, confirmed its possessions to the Church. The date and authenticity of the charter in which Æthelstan is said to have done this is perhaps doubtful, but it is not doubtful that the landed estates of the See of London had been held beyond the memory of man in Æthelstan's time. The estate of this church in the north-east of Essex comprised Walton-on-the-Naze and the adjoining parishes of Kirby-le-Soken and Thorpe-le-Soken. These parishes were known as the 'Liberty of the Soke' for many centuries, and comprised several later manors within them. The name for this district in the Anglo-Saxon period was Ædulfness or Æduves-nasa.

That this district on the north-east coast of Essex was a Kentish colony is proved by its customs, which were identical with the gavelkind customs of Kent in the following particulars:

1. The lands in Ædulfness, or the later Liberty of the Soke, were divisible among sons, and failing these, among daughters, as in Kent. The evidence of this is found in the record known as the 'Domesday of St. Paul's,' in which a list of tenants is given. In some of these entries the sons are named, and in others the daughters, as holding their father's land in the year 1222, according to ancient custom.

2. The services due from the tenants are laid on the hides and not on the actual tenements. This was the case in Kent. Each hide, or, as in Kent, each sulong—the distinction being only in name—included a great number of plots. Some of these plots were very small, and in many instances the same person held plots in several hides. The system in the Essex soke was in this essential particular the Kentish system.

3. The widows of tenants had their dower lands, as in Kent, many entries of such lands being mentioned in the 'Domesday of St. Paul's.'

4. The tenants paid gafol, or small money rents, as in Kent.

5. They could pull down their houses or lease them, as in Kent, without their lord's license, and in other ways act with a degree of freedom unknown on other manors in Essex, but common in Kent.

Within this ancient soke are Horsey Island and Peutie, or Pewit, Island, identical in name to Horsey and Peutie, or Pewit, Islands in the north of Portsmouth Harbour, and within the territory of the Jutes in Hampshire, who were themselves closely connected with the people of Kent.

There is no record relating to the settlement of East Anglia and Essex similar to those concerning Kent, Sussex, and Wessex. All we know is that attacks on this part of England were many and often by people from Germany, who settled in these counties and in Mercia.[1] The East Anglian State was probably formed in the sixth century, for Bede tells us of its King Rædwald, son of Tytilus, whose father was Uffa,[2] and Rædwald is certainly historical.

The East Anglian people in the ninth century do not appear to have been regarded as different in designation from those of Essex, for Asser, in his 'Life of Alfred,' says, under the year 866, that 'a large fleet of pagans came to Britain and wintered in the kingdom of the Eastern Saxons which is called in Saxon East Anglia.' The important later ethnological circumstance in Norfolk and Suffolk is the large settlement of Danes, who appear to have been, according to Malmesbury, the ancestors of the free tenants or sokemen who were so numerous at the time of the Domesday Survey. Ethelweard, in his Chronicle, tells us that after the peace between Alfred and Guthrum the Danes went into East Anglia and reduced all the inhabitants of those parts to subjection. Malmesbury also tells us that they held East Anglia in subjection during their later invasions, and that in the early part of the eleventh century—i.e., in the time of Cnut—they distributed themselves as best suited their convenience in the towns or in the country.

Among the Essex place-names apparently derived from those of known Germanic tribes is Ongar, which appears to have come from the Old Saxon Angarian tribal name. Its old forms in Domesday Book are Angra and Angre. In a Saxon charter[3] a stream called Angrices-burne is also mentioned.

The name Coggeshall may possibly have been derived from a settler of the Chaucian tribe, and Amberden or Amberdon from the Old Saxon Ambrones. In the north-west corner of the county we find old places named Radwinter and Quendon, and these words, Wintr and Quén, are Old Danish or Norrena for Wend and Fin.

In this district, also, there are names such as Wixhoe, Duddenhoe, Farnham, Haverill, Wicken, and others, pointing to Norrena-speaking people. There are several groups of names in Essex, such as Roothings and Raines, which have been derived from clan settlements. The eight places called Roothing are all near each other, and Braintree, anciently Rayne Magna, was a centre of the settlement of people called by the clan-name Rayne. Dengy, also called Danesey, near the coast, points to Danish occupants.

The Old English place-names[4] in Essex that are suggestive of settlements of families or communities of Wends are important. They are Wenesuuic, Wendena', Weninchou, Wenesteda', and the hundred name Wensistreu. These names appear to have been chiefly those of localities in the south and west of the county, and Wanstead, the ancient Wenesteda', survives. There is also an old place in Essex close to the Thames called Wenington.[5] When we remember the evidence of settlements of Wends, whether named from heads of families or communities, which exists in the place-names and surviving customs in the higher parts of the valley of the Thames, there can be little doubt that these old place-names in Esssex point to people of the same race. The name Wendena in the genitive plural appears to denote a kindred of them. The modern name is Wendens, south of Chesterford, where the custom of borough-English survived, and this confirms the Wendish origin of the name. From the evidence of probable Wendish settlements in Essex, Sussex, and parts of Wessex, it would appear that the Saxons at the time of the settlement of these parts of England were in alliance with some tribe or tribes of Wends, as the Continental Saxons were with the Wendish Wiltzi in the time of Charlemagne. These Wend names in Essex and elsewhere in England can be compared with similar names in the old frontier lands in the East of Germany, and even to this day the Fins call Russia Wennalaiset, or the land of the Wends.[6]

There are in Essex other traces of Wendish settlements. Of these, Hauelingas, which is the Domesday name of places in two hundreds, is remarkable, in view of the statement of King Alfred that the Wendish tribe known as the Wilte or Wiltzi were also called the men of Havel.[7] It is direct evidence of the settlement of people called by the tribal name Havel.

The Essex Domesday names Ruuenhala and Ruenhale may also reasonably be connected with settlers who were Rugians. These names are similar to those found relating to Rugians in old Germanic records, and with those in the Saxon charters relating to Wiltshire, Dorset, Somerset, and Hampshire.

In East Anglia there is sufficient evidence that Frisians, including Chaucians and Hunsings, and Wends, including Wilte, must be regarded as among the settlers. These people were certainly not of the Anglian race as known to Charlemagne, or of the Angli as known in the time of Tacitus. There are still remaining in East Anglia traces of Saxon settlers. The earliest record we have of Teutonic people on the shores of the eastern counties is that of Saxons. The name was, no doubt, sometimes used for Frisian, and Frisian for Saxon. The Frisian ports were Saxon outlets to the sea, and it would thus be likely that some Saxons would be called Frisians, and *vice versâ*. Domesday Book tells us of Saxon place-names—Saxalinghaham and Sastorp in Norfolk, Saxmondeham, Saxham, and Saxteda in Suffolk, some of which remain at the present time. Among the early Continental Saxons was the pagus or tribe known as the Bucki, of whom records exist as far back as A.D. 775-776,[8] and in Norfolk we find Bucchesteda, Buccham, Bucham Regis, Buchestuna, Buchenham, and other names derived from settlers recorded in Domesday Book.

The name East Anglia which was applied to the country of the North folk and South folk is misleading to some extent, for it seems to imply that the settlers were chiefly Angles. If they were all Angles from Danish and Scandinavian lands we might expect to find in these counties some traces of their runic letters. Runes have been found in the Anglian districts north and south of the Humber. They have not been found in Norfolk or Suffolk except in one eleventh-century inscription, which is of much later date. This is an important fact, especially when considered in reference to the absence of any fixed runic monument or inscription in Friesland, Old Saxony, or any part of Germany. 'The monuments might have been destroyed and disappear,' says the greatest writer on runic monuments, 'but if they had ever existed in German or Saxon lands they would have left some trace behind them.'[9]

This at once establishes a sharp line of distinction between the Goths, Swedes, and Norwegians of Scandinavia, the Danes, Angles, and Goths or Jutes of England, on the one hand, and the Saxons, Frisians, Wends, and other nations and tribes of Germany on the other hand. As the latter have left no monuments with runic inscriptions in their original homes, and as certain parts of England which are supposed to have been mainly colonized by them are also marked by the absence of such monuments, the runic inscriptions on fixed objects in England help to prove the settlement in some parts of the country of Goths and other Scandinavians, whether called Anglians or Jutes, or by their later names of Norse and Danes. Similarly, the absence of such inscriptions appears to point to the colonization mainly of those parts of the country which are wanting in them by settlers of other races.

The absence in East Anglia of fixed runic inscriptions, except a late example about A.D. 1050 in the church at Aldborough,[10] therefore suggests the inquiry whether East Anglia was not originally occupied partly by settlers of Frisian and German origin rather than exclusively by colonists of the Anglian race. It is evidence also that its early colonists came mainly from north German lands rather than from the original homes of the people known as Angles. Viewed in this light, the original settlement of the eastern counties must be regarded as more Saxon than Anglian, more Frisian than Gothic or Scandian. As regards the Goths, Beddoe[11] has, however, pointed out that the name of Tytila (A.D. 586), son of Uffa, King of East Anglia, is very like that of Totila, King of the Ostrogoths.

In the eastern counties, as elsewhere, the place-names derived from people are probably as old as the settlement. The places must have been the abodes of men after whom they were named, and where they were designated by tribal names it probably was because their occupants were of these tribes.

When we think how few must have been the original places of settlement in any county compared with the total number of inhabited places at the present time, the survival of even a few place-names which may be referred to clan or tribal names must be regarded as remarkable. Many very old tribal or family names have, however, survived, of which only a few of each type can be quoted, such as Hunn and Finbo. Hunn is a family name at the present time at Old Hunstanton in Norfolk, which derived its name, apparently, from one or more settlers that were called Hunn. Finbo also survives in the same neighbourhood. These names point to the settlement in this part of England of some individuals of the Hunsing and Fin tribes. The survival, also, here and there in these counties of customs of inheritance that are different from the common customs point, probably, to different tribal usages of a very remote origin which were brought by early tribal settlers.

Many years ago some remarkable burial urns of the Anglo-Saxon age were found at Eye in Suffolk, and at Little Wilbraham in Cambridgeshire. Another large collection was found at Stade in the old Chaucian country of North Germany. Kemble says of these collections: 'Generally the urns in sepulchres of North Europe are not of a complicated character. The urns found at Stade, as well as those from Eye and Little Wilbraham, are, however, beaten out and embossed, the raised parts most likely pressed out with the thumb.' 'The urns embossed like those at Eye, at Wilbraham, and at Stade stand by themselves.'[12]This is a remarkable coincidence, for it is near Eye that we find such old place-names as Fressingfield and Hoxne, names that are probably traces of Frisians and Hocings—*i.e.*, Chaucians. Stade is in the old Chaucian county, and Hoxne is written in Domesday Book in the genitive plural form Hoxna.

Among many places which have old tribal names in Norfolk, we find both Wendling and Winterton, and these not improbably refer to settlers of the same race, who were called Wends by German tribes, such as the Frisians, and Winthr by the Scandians. The names Wendling and Winterton, which were probably given to these places by the neighbouring settlers, may, perhaps, point to people mainly of Frisian descent near Wendling, and to people mainly of Scandinavian descent near Winterton. The name Somerton, which occurs close to Winterton in Norfolk, is probably of later origin, and arose after the word Wintr had ceased to be understood as a race name. The name Wintretuna or Wintretona occurs in nine entries in that part of Domesday Book which relates to Norfolk.

King Alfred, in his 'Orosius,' says that Wendland was also called Syssele, and in the old name Syselond in the Norfolk Hundred of Launditch we probably have a trace of it. This hundred, named Lauuendic in Domesday Book, may be compared in name with Lauenberg, a province and city on the Elbe, in part of the Wendish area of North-East Germany. The river Wensum flowed on the east of the hundred of Launditch, and among the Anglo-Saxon place-names on its banks are Wenlinga, Lawingham, Leccesham, Goduic, and Elmenham.

It is not suggested that settlements of Wends in the eastern counties, or, indeed, in any part of England, were relatively numerous, but the collective evidence concerning such settlers appears to be great.

Owing to the later Danish settlement, Lincolnshire and Norfolk have an abundance of names of Danish origin. These counties and the East Riding are marked by the -*bys* and -*thorpes*, which will be considered under Lincolnshire. The country of the Danes was small, and the parts of England they colonized were large. It is certain, therefore, that they must have had allies who came in with them. There are historical references to their alliances or political connections with Swedes, Esthonians, Livonians, Kurlanders, and Wends.[13] Some of these probably settled in England. In the country to which the Wash is the entrance from the sea there are old place-names still surviving which appear to point to the Wilte, one of the Wendish tribes. In Lincolnshire we find Wilinghā, Wilsthorp, Wilgesbi; in Cambridgeshire, Wandlebury; in Northamptonshire, Wilaveston, Wendlingborough, now Wellingborough; and in Huntingdonshire, Wansford and Wintringham. Frisians are denoted by many such names as Friston in Lincolnshire, Hunston or Hunstanton in Norfolk, while Swaffham in Cambridgeshire and in Norfolk may reasonably be connected with settlers who bore names derived from the Swæfas or Suevi, a tribe of, or closely connected with, the Saxons. The significant old place-name Wynter-worda occurs in the early records of Ely,[14] and may possibly be a survival of a Norrena or Northern Gothic name for a worth that was the home of a man named Winthr—*i.e.*, a Wend.

Among the Domesday places mentioned in Suffolk are Wellingaham, Humbresfelda, Scadena, Scadenafella, and Elga. The name Wellingaham denotes the home of a community known as Wellings, and the only known people of this name are the Weletabi or Wilte. Humbresfelda apparently refers to settlers of the tribal Ambrones or Old Saxons from the country along the ancient Ambra or Ems. The Scadena name may point to Scandians, and Elga probably to a clan or ga different from those near it. Most of these names so closely resemble tribal names that it is very difficult to see what their origin could have been other than tribal. The English race in all parts of the country appears to have resulted from the blending of people of the same nations or tribes, but in varying proportions. In the eastern counties the later Danes formed a large proportion, and the racial characters of the English of Norfolk and Suffolk must have been modified greatly by the later Danish admixture. In the old record known as the 'Liber de Hyda' we find what is apparently a reference to this. The writer says that Offa first reigned in East Anglia, the people of which 'were called Offingas, but now they are called Fykeys.'[15] A fusion of race had apparently occurred.

As regards old customs of inheritance in the eastern counties, that which prevailed in Ipswich was the partible custom between all the children, male and female. The old book called 'The Domus Day of Gippeswich' says: 'Alle tenementz in the foreseid toun ben partable as weel betwixen heires male, as betwixen heyres female, and zif they be not forclosed by zifte or be devis of her antecessourys.' 'And zif the heritage be parted betwixen hem by her comoun assent, thanne have the eldere parcener avauntage to chesyn which part that he wil.'[16] This custom points to the Frisians or Goths, and that Frisians largely settled in the eastern counties there can be no doubt. The general custom of inheritance among the Frisians was the partibility of the property equally among all the children, males and females. It will be noted that the burgesses of Ipswich had the same privileges as those of London and the people of Kent in regard to devising their estates or conveying them to others, and the evidence is strong that both Kent and the neighbourhood of London was partly settled by Frisians.

In the eastern counties there are a considerable number of manors in which some form of the custom of borough-English or junior right survived as the customary mode of inheritance. Corner, who investigated this subject, tells us that he found it on eighty-four manors in Suffolk.[17] He also states that there were fourteen in Essex and twelve in Norfolk known to him.[18] Among the Norfolk manors are Kenninghall, Gessinghall, Herling Thorp, Semere Hall, and Thelton. Among the Suffolk manors are Sibton and its members, Yoxford and its members, Aldborough, Hoxne, Brockford near Woodbridge, Fressingfield, Elmswell (Framlingham), Geslingham, Pakenham, Middleton, and Mendlesham. The members of the Court Leet of Clare were called Headboroughs, a similar name to that in use in Sussex, where borough-English largely prevailed. Among the Essex manors are Maiden, Chesterfield, South Berstead, Tony Walthamstow, Wivenhoe, Wikes, Wrabness, and Woodford. It is not likely that this custom originated on these several manors. It is more probable that it was introduced by communities of settlers who brought it from the Continent, and it is not necessary to look for its origin entirely to Wendish tribes, for it is known to exist in some parts of Friesland, whence in some instances it may have been introduced by Frisian tribal settlers, and as their descendants formed new colonies or new rural settlements, the custom may have spread with the growth of the population. Although the custom of junior right, by which the youngest son in the partition of the father's possessions retained the homestead, was followed in some parts of Frisia, the prevailing general custom among the Frisians, as already stated, was partible inheritance, and if Norfolk and Suffolk received Frisian settlers, as there is reason to believe they did, we may look for survivals of that custom as well as the custom of junior succession. We find that customs of partible inheritance in these counties are mentioned by Bracton in the early law cases. He quotes cases at Altingeham, Fisinges, and Hecham in Norfolk, and at Gipewico or Ipswich, Illegha, Lillesheya, and Sproutona in Suffolk.[19]

The records of the Court of King's Bench, Hiliary Term, 20 Edward III., also show that the lands within the Fee of Pickering were partible among males.[20] The old manor of Clipsby in Norfolk was alleged to be within this fee and had this custom. The Marshall's Fee and Billockby in the same county had a similar custom,[21] as had also the lordship called Perting Fee, at Saxham in Suffolk.[22]

In Cambridgeshire there are two names of hundreds mentioned in Domesday Book of much interest—viz., Wederlai and Flamindic. The first so much resembles the name Wederas,[23] which was that of the Goths of the Weder-mearc east of Lake Wetter in ancient Gothland, that it is difficult to see a more reasonable origin of the name, especially in a county which affords so many other traces of settlements of Northmen. The name Flamindic, similar-ly, appears to point to some of the people who were among the earliest to be known as Flemings. The survival of the old name Wendlebury for the earth-work on the Gog Magog Hills near Cambridge may be compared with the similar old name Wendlebury north-east of Oxford, and with Wendel Hill in the Elmet district of Yorkshire, all apparently referring to settlers who were called by this name. Among other significant Cambridgeshire place-names is Hinxton, which is certainly a contraction of Hengesteston, the town of Heng-est. Leverington, written Liuerington in 1285, probably represents a tribal name, as also do Hockington, the town of the Hockings, and Haslingfield, written Haslingefeld in Domesday Book, the field of the Hæslings.[24]

The chief circumstances we can discover in the records of Cambridgeshire concerning the classes of tenants within it and their customs point more clearly to the later settlement of Danes than to the earlier one of Anglians and their allies. There was at the time of Domesday Survey a considerable number of cottars in this county, and in the Hundred Rolls, in which the ac-tual holders of the land are stated in detail, a large number of small free ten-ants are mentioned by name. The presence of numerous holders of crofts, tofts, or other small tenements is a striking character of the records in the Hundred Rolls relating to this county. The very large number of small hold-ings of various sizes—12, 10, 7, 3, 2½, 2 acres, also 1½ acres and 1 acre—which were held in many places in Cambridgeshire proves that the custom-ary and small free tenements were divided on inheritance, as in Gothland and in Kent.

Another feature is the number of widows holding land, and in some in-stances it is expressly stated that they hold their tenements for life, so that it must have been by customary right. These circumstances point to small ten-ants who were free and, as mentioned in many instances, paid small rents, in lieu of personal services. On some manors parceners are mentioned. In the town of Cambridge, Domesday Book tells us of lahmen, which shows that officers originally Danish survived there. The burgesses also had the power of devising their tenements by will. These customs indicate that in the earlier or later Scandinavian or Danish settlements a large number of free tenants were located in this county, and retained their personal freedom and privi-leges. In Cambridgeshire the frequency of the lordless village type is a prom-inent feature of the Domesday record, as pointed out by Maitland.

As regards the dialect of the eastern counties, one of the most interesting circumstances is that stated by Ellis, who says: 'It is remarkable that in the American colonies, afterwards the United States, a distinctly East Anglian character was introduced.'[25] There was, as is well known, a large emigration from East Anglia. Ellis also says: 'In intonation, the "drant" of Norfolk and the "whine" of Suffolk are well known, but, like other intonations, are difficult to understand, and practically impossible to symbolize.'[26] The Suffolk is the broader and more drawling intonation, the speaker's voice running up and down half an octave of sharp notes. Whatever may be the origin of these intonations, we may probably conclude from their variations that there were some tribal differences in the original settlers from whom the people of the two counties are descended.

Mackintosh, half a century ago, expressed his opinion that 'a considerable proportion of the inhabitants of the East of England present the Dutch physical and mental characteristics, but the more influential inhabitants of Norfolk and the neighbourhood are Danes.'[27] This is what might be expected from a settlement of ancient Frisians, and the subsequent domination of the Danes is perhaps indicated by the records of the tenure of land in Domesday Book, in which it is shown that there was in Norfolk a much larger proportion of freemen or sokemen than in any other part of England. These latter were presumably descendants of the Danish people, who supplanted or partly enslaved the descendants of the previous settlers. Beddoe says: 'A remarkable tall blonde race occupies the hundred of Flegg in the north-east of Norfolk, where the local names are Danish.[28] The same physical characters have been observed around Debenham in Suffolk. People of a blonde complexion form the prevailing type in both Norfolk and Suffolk.' 'In Cambridgeshire and the north-west of Essex,' says Mackintosh, 'there would appear to be mainly Saxons, but in the east and south of Essex the mass of the people show very few signs of Teutonic descent.'[29] The natural entrance open to settlers in Cambridgeshire and north-west Essex would be by way of the Wash and up the valleys of the Cam and its tributaries. The survival of various tribal names among the place-names of those districts appears to point to a mixed population of much the same tribes as those indicated by the names of Sussex and Wessex, among which Frisian, Jutish, or Gothic, and some of Wendish origin, can certainly be traced. In the same districts customs can be recognised which certainly prevailed among these tribal people.

[1] Henry of Huntingdon, 'History of the English,' edited by Arnold, p. 48.
[2] Beda, 'Hist. Eccl.,' ii. 15.
[3] Codex Dipl., No. 104.
[4] Domesday Book, Index to vol. ii.
[5] Morant, P., 'History of Essex,' vol. i. 85.
[6] Morfill, W. R., 'Slavonic Literature,' 35.
[7] King Alfred's 'Orosius.'
[8] Monumenta Germaniæ, Script, i. 155.
[9] Stephens, G., 'The Old Northern Runic Monuments,' i., p. viii.
[10] Stephens, G., *loc. cit.*, i. xxiii.
[11] Beddoe, J., 'Races of Britain,' p. 42.
[12] Kemble, J. M., *Archæologia*, xxxvi. 273.
[13] Saxo Grammaticus.
[14] Inquisitio Eliensis, Index.
[15] Liber de Hyda, edited by Edwards, E., p. 10.
[16] 'The Black Book of the Admiralty,' edited by Sir T. Twiss, ii. 121-123.
[17] *Bury and West Suffolk Arch. Inst. Proceedings*, vol. ii., pp. 227-235.
[18] Elton, C. I., 'Robinson on Gavelkind,' quoting Corner's list.
[19] Bracton, H. de, 'Note-book,' edited by Maitland.

[20] Elton, C. I., *loc. cit.*, 33.
[21] *Ibid.*, 34-36.
[22] *Ibid.*, 40.
[23] 'The Scop, or Gleeman's Tale,' edited by B. Thorpe, Glossarial Index.
[24] Skeat, W. W., *Cambridge Antiquarian Soc., Oct. Pub.*, xxxvi.

[25] Ellis, A. J., 'English Dialects, their Sounds and Homes,' p. 87.
[26] *Ibid.*, p. 59.
[27] Mackintosh, D., *Transactions of the Ethnological Soc.*, i. 221.
[28] Beddoe, J., *loc. cit.*, 254.
[29] Mackintosh, D., *loc. cit.*, i. 221.

# Chapter Eighteen - Tribal People in Lincolnshire

IT is to Scandinavia and Denmark mainly that we must look for any gleams of light in reference to the successive settlements of tribal people in Lincolnshire.

This county was the country of the Old English tribes known as the Lindisware, or the Southumbrians, the Gainas and the Gyrwii, or Marshmen. There appears to have been much that was similar in the settlement of Norfolk and Lincolnshire. There is a similarity in their coast, with the same sand-dunes and gently-sloping reaches. As we stand on the cliff at Hunstanton on a clear day we see as far as the eye can reach the low sand-hills stretching away towards the east, and across the Wash on the Lincolnshire coast We see them lying before us for many miles towards the north-east. These coasts must have appeared to the ancient Angles and Danes very homelike, and similar to those they had left behind them in parts of Denmark. The country was open to them by the wide estuary of the Humber on the north, giving access to the valley of the Trent, and by the Wash, past Boston and Lynn, to the great fens. The physical features of the coast must have been attractive to a people who had been accustomed to similar surroundings in their old homes, and who would be able to make settlements with environments resembling those of the Danish lands they had left. Fen, heath, and forest made up a large proportion of the area of Lincolnshire at the time of the coming of the Angles and Danes. The great freshwater swamp formed by the confluence of the Don, the Went, the Ouse, and the Trent, in which the Isle of Axholm rose like a beacon, was the barrier that divided it from Northumbria.[1] Lincolnshire was the early Southumbria of Anglo-Saxon records, and is mentioned by this name in 702.[2]

On the south was the great fen that reached from the coast along the course of the Witham almost as far as Lincoln, also westward almost to Sleaford, and from the north, near Horncastle, southwards into Cambridgeshire. West of this was the great heath between Sleaford and Lincoln, on which no ancient settlement could be made owing to the poverty of the soil, and on which, in later centuries, it was a pious work to erect a land lighthouse to guide travellers at night across it. Lincolnshire was not wanting in woodlands and forests, a necessity for all primitive settlements. That of Bruneswald covered a large extent of country south of Bourn, and part of the south of the county was also called the Forest of Arundel as late as the time of King John.[3].

In our endeavour to trace the character of its early colonization, careful attention must be given to the fact that Lincolnshire is pre-eminent among English counties as the land of the *-bys* and the *-thorpes.* These *-bys* were not domains of lords with their serfs, but were the characteristic communities, in their origin at least, of freemen come from Northern lands, living under tribal conditions similar to those they had left behind them. The *-by* place-names in Lincolnshire end where the old tens began. The settlement of this county is typical of settlements of people of the Old Anglian, Danish, and Northern races. Some Saxons and Frisians there must have been among them, as the old place-names indicate, but the villages which the Danes established were clearly part of a State or States in which the prevailing type of settlement was Scandian and not Germanic. Nothing is more remarkable in considering the evidence which the Domesday Book affords of the different classes of tenants who cultivated the land on which they lived than the far greater proportion of freemen or socmen settled within the old Dane-law, as compared with those parts of Mercia to the west of it or with Wessex. The *-ing* place-names which are characteristic of the Saxon State are not conspicuous in Lincolnshire, but the *-bys* and *-thorpes* abound. These *-bys* apparently mark the Old English homes of men among whom the German system of village life was not the prevailing one, and on looking for their analogies in Continental lands, we must turn to Denmark and the Scandian peninsula. As already mentioned, the ancient kingdom of the Danes about A.D. 880 included the provinces of Skane, Halland, and Blekinge.[4] It will be seen, therefore, that emigrants from these provinces who in the ninth century would be called Danes were probably also called by their tribal names.

If we study the settlement of England by the light of the very scanty historical records alone which have come down to us, without reference to that which may be derived from the archæology and anthropology of the districts from which our forefathers came, we shall not be able to arrive at any conclusion more satisfactory than that which satisfied the chroniclers who copied from Bede. They tell us nothing of runes or of the parts of the Continent where the people lived who wrote in these old characters, and where they did not, which we now know from archæological inquiry; nor do they tell us anything of the different shapes of the skulls or the complexion of the Anglo-Saxon people in various parts of England, but we now know from anthropological discoveries that there were important differences. We gather very little from the chroniclers concerning the Anglo-Saxon courts and judicial procedure, but we can learn much about these from the codes or collections of primitive laws which have been preserved, and by a comparison of them with those that have come down to us in other countries from which some of the Old English came. Similarly, the local customs which have survived on many manors, and in some cases in wide districts, are but legal curiosities until they are compared with similar systems of local jurisprudence elsewhere, in the Continental countries from which our remote fore-fathers came. It is by such a comparison we should study the Lincolnshire -*bys*. These -*by* place-names are commonly regarded as Danish, but they are also Northern Gothic, as the numerous places-names ending in -*by* to this day in Swedish Gothland prove. This shows that some of these places may have got their names from so-called Anglians. The strongest evidence as to what these -*by* places really were is found in ancient Gothland, the old country from which we derive so much other information that throws light upon the origin of the Anglo-Saxon race.

The oldest legal code of any part of Sweden which has been preserved is the Westgota-lag, and this contains some references to the administration of local law in the early time among the Goths. It has already been pointed out that Anglo-Saxon legal procedure was local, that the Hundred Court was a very important institution, and that the right of proof between litigants, as to which of them it might be given, was a most important advantage. If the disputant to whom the right of proof legally belonged could bring forward the required number of oath-helpers, to declare on oath that they believed in his oath and the justice of his cause, he won his case. This right of proof is mentioned in the Westgota-lag under the name of the 'vita.' This old Gothic legal code contains much information concerning the parties to disputes, and to which of them by ancient custom, apparently from time immemorial, the right of proof belonged. Thus, in a dispute between the Bishop and a bondi, or peasant proprietor, the right of proof belonged to the bondi. He had also the right of proof in any dispute between himself and the King, which circumstances may perhaps be explained by the fact that the bondi as a class existed before either Bishop or King.[5] The value of this ancient local code in considering the original nature of the different kinds of English villages is in its reference to the by, the primitive village or rural community of Gothland. Between the bondi and anyone else, the bondi had the right of proof. This points to the ancient rights of the people, to an old democracy. Disputes might, however, arise between communities. Between the hæræd, or hundred, and the by, the hundred had the right of proof; Between the by and the thorp, the by had this right, a circumstance which leads to two conclusions— viz.: (1) That the right of proof given to the by was assigned practically to a number of freemen acting collectively as a community; and (2) that the community of the by, having the right of proof in a dispute with the thorp, was the more important, and probably the earlier institution.

All this is both interesting and important in considering the settlement of bys and thorpes in England, and more especially in Lincolnshire and the East Riding. The people of Lincolnshire came from Anglian, Danish, and Scandian lands, where communities of this kind existed. They established settlements which they called bys and thorpes on English soil, after the types of rural life to which they had been accustomed in their old countries, and unless we are to believe that the English bys and thorpes were different from those of West Gothland—and of this there is no evidence—we must arrive at the conclusion that a by was a community, and a thorpe a member of it or an offshoot from it or some similar community. We must remember also that it is not to the Saxon laws of Wessex, or even to the laws of Kent, that we should naturally look to find the early prototype of some ancient institution in Lincolnshire, but to laws of Danish or Scandian lands, such as the ancient laws of West Gothland, which, happily, have been preserved. In these laws the vita, or right of proof, belonged as here stated:

1.   Between the asserter of common proprietorship and the asserter of individual ownership, to the former.
2.   Between the King and the Bishop, the Bishop.
3.   Between the lænder (occupant of the spare lands of the by) and the Bishop, the lænder.
4.   Between the bondi (or peasant proprietor) and anyone else, the bondi.
5.   Between the by and the thorp, the by.
6.   Between the alleged heritor and the alleged purchaser, the heritor.
7.   Between the owner of the bol (homestead) and the owner of the utskipt (close), the owner of the bol.
8.   Between the land (the province) and the hæræd (hundred), the land.
9.   Between the hæræd and the by, the hæræd.[6]

It should be noted also in reference to these rights to having the proof that the disputant who asserted the common proprietorship of anything in dispute had the right of proof before the asserter of individual ownership of the same. The rule in regard to communities, large and small, was in the following order: (1) The province; (2) the hundred; (3) the by or village; (4) the thorp. In Lincolnshire there were all these organizations. Lindsey, Holland, and Kesteven were its provinces; its hundreds and wapentakes were numerous, and its bys and thorpes also numerous within these larger areas. In Domesday Book we find some of the hundreds, such as Hazebi, Alesbi, Fenbi, and Walesbi, named after some of the bys, apparently from the places where the Hundred Courts met. We find also in the Domesday account of Lincolnshire instances in which wapentakes are mentioned, and also the hundreds contained within them.

The -bys are much more common than the -thorpes in the wold district—a circumstance which appears to indicate that the open parts of the county were first settled, the thorpes having probably had their origin as offshoots from the bys.

Lincolnshire contains about sixty places whose names have the -by termination, and are of Scandinavian origin, but it also contains fifty-six places[7] whose names have the -ham ending, and these must be traced to Anglian and Frisian or other Germanic settlers. It is probable that the early place-names ending in -burh, -berh, and -berge denoted places where the people had common rights and privileges; i.e., the places were folk villages, more or less free, rather than estates belonging to a lord, and the inhabitants more or less

184

subject to him. A curious survival of the early *burh* has apparently come down in the name burley-men, birla-men, or by-law-men.[8] The burley-men were inhabitants of certain manors who were appointed annually, with the object of settling disputes among the inhabitants. In some old records the name is spelt bye-law-men, and they existed in various places in Yorkshire in the seventeenth century. The ancient by-law was derived from the old common-law power to make by-laws that belonged to parishes and manors. The difference between burly and by-law, says Skeat, 'is merely one of dialect. In Iceland people say *bær*, in Norway *bö*, in Sweden and Denmark *by*. Thus, burly-men and by-law-men are etymologically identical.'[9] As the *-by* place-names in the Danish districts of England must be regarded by their parallelism to the bys of ancient Gothland to have been folk villages, we may reasonably conclude that those places known by the equivalent names *berk, berge,* etc., had similar common privileges. In Lincolnshire, at the time of the Domesday Survey, there were 11,503 socmen to 7,723 villeins. This very large number of socmen points to the existence of folk villages in that county containing numerous freemen. As regards the people at the present time, the broad fact at which we can arrive connected with the settlement of this county is that they are in complexion fairer than those of Leicestershire and Northamptonshire.

If we were to confine our attention in Lincolnshire to the historical name Angles, that of the people by whom the county is usually supposed to have been originally settled, and to the Danes, by whom it was afterwards overrun and again presumably settled, we should necessarily look only for traces of these two nations or races. If, however, apart from these names and the history, more or less traditional, connected with their invasions, we proceed on inductive lines, and consider the old topographical names of the county, we shall have no difficulty in finding about a dozen groups which are apparently tribal or national names, and these neither Anglian nor Danish. It is very likely, indeed, that the people of various tribes or nations who migrated to Lincolnshire came under the general names of Angles in the former period and Danes in the latter, but they gave their tribal names or personal names derived from their tribes, in many cases, to the new homes they formed. Domesday Book tells us of a group of three names—Frisebi, Frisetorp, and Fristune. These evidently refer to Frisian settlements. Among the Frisian pagi, or tribes, were the Hunsings, and the Domesday account of Lincolnshire tells us of places named Hunbia, Hundebi, and Hundintone. Among the Frisians were the Chaucians, also called the Hocings; and at the time of the Norman Survey we find there were places in Lincolnshire called Cocrinton, Cocrintone, Hoctun, and Hochtune, probably after individuals who bore such names. Among the Frisians were also the Brocmen, or East Frisians; and among the Domesday names of Lincolnshire are Broxholm and Brochelesbi, as if apparently named after people of this tribe. That there were brown people of some race settled in this county appears probable from the names Brune, Brunebi, Brunetorp, Dunesbi, Dunebi, Dunestune, and Dunetorp.

There are seven entries in Domesday Book of places called Normanebi, three of Normanesbi, and others of Normaneston and Normenton. These must refer to Northmen, and not necessarily to either Angles or Danes. In the Lincolnshire Domesday record, we find also eight references to a place or places called Osgotebi, and two to Osgotesbi. It is difficult to understand to what people these can refer, except to persons or families so called because they were of the Eastern Goths from that part of Sweden east of Lake Wetter. Some settlers from Skane, on the Scandinavian mainland of old Denmark, are probably indicated by the Domesday names Scantune and Scantone.

The Sweons or Swedes are perhaps represented by the Domesday names Suauitone, Suinhope, Suinhamstede, and Suinhastede. In the Orkney nomenclature, Suin or Swin is a form of Suion or Sweon. The name Svin Kunugr for one of the Kings usually called Swein occurs in early northern literature.[10] People of Saxon descent are probably represented by the Domesday names Sassebi, Saxebi, and Scachetorp, and the Swæfas by Svavintone and Svavetone. When we look among the Domesday names in the county for some evidence of people of Wendish descent, we find Wintringehā and Wintrintone, of which there are four instances; and there are also four entries of places called Wilingeham. The tribal Goths are apparently also to be recognised by the people who named their settlements in Lincolnshire after the city of Lund in the South of Sweden. Of these Domesday names, there are Lund, Lund alter, Lundertorp, and Lundetorp. These names suggest, at any rate, that the Lincolnshire people at the time of the Norman Survey must have been a more mixed race than is usually supposed. Lund, in Sweden, is a city of great traditions. It is called also by the Latin name of Lundinem Gothorum, and is said to have been so great as to have had 200,000 inhabitants. One of the traditions relating to its antiquity is that when Christ was born Skänor and Lund were already in harvest, meaning that they were already prosperous. Lund was called the Metropolis Daniæ, and was the place of residence and coronation of many Kings[11] of early Denmark.

We must bear in mind the words of King Alfred in describing the voyage of Othere from the Cattegat into the Baltic, when he had Denmark on the bæcbórd (the left), and the Danish isles and Jutland on the starbord (the right). 'In these lands dwelt the Angles ere they to the land came.' The Lund people from Southern Sweden may have been genuine Angles; the Wends, Wilte, Frisians, Hunsings, Brocmen, Chaucians, and Saxons of Lincolnshire could not have been, strictly speaking, either Angles or Danes. If we knew the many alternative names, ekenames or nicknames, employed by our remote fore-fathers to designate people of various races and tribes, or to distinguish persons, we should probably be able to read more of the settlement of Lincolnshire in the early names of its -bys and -thorpes. This much we do know, that some of the -bys, -hams, and -tons had -thorpes presumably named after them as local colonization went on. Thus we find among the Domesday names Alesbi and Aletorp, Endreby and Endretorp, Frisebi and Frisetorp,

Saxebi and Scachetorp, Berchehā and Berchetorp, Barnetone and Barnetorp, Lund and Lundetorp.

It does not appear unreasonable to adopt the view that many of these ancient place-names came into use through settlements of families of people who, or whose heads, were known by tribal names. Even if the original place-name was derived in most cases from the name of a man, who bore some such name as Hun, Osgod, Suen, Saxe, or Broc, it is difficult to see how during the settlement the name became attached to the place, except through being that of a man so called by his neighbours because he was of the tribe denoted by this name. An ancient name for the Danish islands was Withesland and Withesleth,[12] and it is possible that such Lincolnshire names as Withern and others may be traced to this source. There is certainly documentary evidence of the existence of a tribe in England in the early Anglo-Saxon period known as the Witherigga.[13] In reference to the -by names, there is one of more than ordinary significance still surviving in Lincolnshire—viz., that of Bonby, written in Domesday Book Bondebi. The name bondi for the yeoman or peasant proprietor still survives in Norway and also in Gothland, where his ancient legal status is shown in the old laws of West Gothland, already mentioned. Lincolnshire contains also some old place-names of much interest relating to fields, such as the old name Waringwang,[14] *wang* being an old Northern name for field or plain. The name Waring may have been that of a man of the Waring tribe.

The Trent name, whose Wendish significance has already been stated, found in Lincolnshire close to Winterton and Winteringham, is remarkable. The name of this river probably had its origin in its lower course. The name Wintringa-tun, which occurs in a Saxon charter, is of more than ordinary interest. It is similar to many others, such as Billinga-tun (the town of the Billings) or Wæringawic (the wic of the Wærings). Wintringatun is thus a word made up of *Wintringa*, gen. plural (of the Wintrings), and *tun*, the town—i.e., the settlement of the sons or descendants of Wintr; and Wintr is the old Danish word for Wends. The modern name is Winterton, but the old form of the word shows that it was derived from people. The district in which it is situated was subjected to great Scandinavian influence, and the old Norræna dialects were spoken by all the Scandinavian races—Norse, Swedes, Danes, and Goths[15]—and this name Winthr for Wends may thus have come down to us from its use by Northern Goths, as well as by Norse, Swedes, or Danes. As already mentioned, it survives in the form of Winter in several English counties, notably Dorset and Wiltshire, where we know Gewissas or the confederate tribes settled; and among these were numerous Northern Goths or Jutes, or others of northern speech.

In Lincolnshire, also, the custom of inheritance by the youngest son survives at Long Bennington, Thoresby, Kirton-in-Lindsey, Keadby in the Isle of Axholm,[16] and other places close to Winterton—a relic, probably, of an old Wendish custom brought in by allies of this race among the Danes or Angles.

Lincolnshire people have always been regarded as more distinctive than other parts of England in regard to their Danish descent. All the people who in ancient time were called Danes did not, however, come from Denmark, nor even that greater Denmark which included part of Sweden. There were so-called Danes in the Danish hosts who did not come either from Scandinavia or Denmark and its islands, as the evidence already brought forward shows.

Bearing these facts in mind, it will not be surprising to note that, according to Mackintosh's ethnological observations in Lincolnshire, the Danish type there appears to present two varieties: the Dane with convex profile and prominent mouth, and the Dane with sunk mouth and prominent chin. Both have high cheek-bones and a sinking in above the cheek-bones at the sides of the forehead, long face and high nose, ruddy complexion, and red or sandy hair, the skull being rather narrow and elongated, the body tall, and the figure rather loosely made, with long legs and arms.[17] Beddoe tells us that in Lincolnshire, as far as the borders of the Fens, the Danish element in the physical appearance of the people is particularly strong.[18]

The Roman road, which is part of Ermine Street, passing through the length of the county from Stamford in the south to Winteringham on the Humber, affords evidence of the manner in which part of that county was originally settled, and we can scarcely see so good an example in any other part of England. It is interesting to observe in connection with this ancient road that there are very few villages actually on it, but that there are many near to it on either side. When the Angles and their allies, whoever they were, first came to Lincolnshire, this road was in existence. The roads running irregularly in a north and south direction, which connect the chain of villages and extend more or less parallel to this old Roman way, are evidently of a later date. Their irregularity shows that they were originally made for local communications to connect villages with each other, but in time became more or less continuous. Almost all these villages, however, have branch roads running east or west to the Roman road, which thus appears to have been used as the main highway by the original settlers.

[1] Pearson, C., 'Historical Maps,'. p. 3.

[2] Freeman, E., 'English Towns and Districts,' 198.

[3] Saunders, J., 'History of the County of Lincoln.' p. 281.

[4] Otté, E. C., 'Denmark and Iceland,' p. 69.

[5] Jenks, Edward, 'The Problem of the Hundred,' *English Hist. Review*, xi. 512.

[6] 'The Westgota-lag,' quoted by Jenks, *English Hist. Review*, xi. 512.

[7] Peacock, E., 'Scotter and its Neighbourhood,' p. 6.

[8] Smith, L. Toulmin, *Athenæum, August 9, 1879, p. 176.*

[9] Skeat, W. W., 'Etymological Dictionary.'

[10] Mémoires de la Soc. Royale des Antiq. du Nord, 1850-1860, p. 405.

[11] du Chaillu, P. B., 'Land of the Midnight Sun,' ii. 463.

[12] Latham, R. G., 'Germania of Tacitus,' Epileg. cxxv., quoting Chron. Erici.

[13] Cart. Sax., edited by Birch, i. 416.

[14] Streatfeild, G. S., 'Lincolnshire and the Danes,' 152.

[15] Cleasby and Vigfusson, 'Icelandic Dictionary.'

[16] Peacock, E., 'Glossary of Words in the Wapentake of Manley,' p. 66.

[17] Mackintosh, D., *Transactions Ethnological Society*, i. 220.

[18] Beddoe, J., 'Races in Britain,' 252.

# Chapter Nineteen - Settlers in Northumbria

THE early settlers in the kingdom of Bernicia, which included the country from the Firth of Forth to the Tees, were known as Beornicas, and those who occupied Yorkshire were called Deiri or Deras. These latter, like the Jutes of Kent, adopted the name of the Celtic tribe they displaced. There is strong evidence that Frisians settled numerously in Northumbria under the Anglian name, and evidence also that among the Anglian and Frisian settlers in Yorkshire there were Goths and others known by various tribal names. That some of the Angles were of Gothic or Scandinavian extraction is proved by the early runic inscriptions on fixed stone monuments still existing in ancient Northumbria. That some of the settlers on the north-east coasts were also known as Jutes is probable from early references to them.

The descendants of these early colonists in the North of England and the South-East of Scotland were, in the seventh century, brought within the kingdom of Northumbria, which in subsequent centuries was conquered and recolonised by the Danes, Northmen, and their allies. The descendants of the earlier stock who survived these wars were absorbed among the later colonists of a kindred race, and the Anglian kingdom became merged into an Anglo-Danish kingdom. It is, consequently, hard to find survivals distinctive of the earlier tribal settlers in the northern counties apart from those of the later Scandinavian colonists who had so much in common with them in ethnological characteristics, customs, and even in language. The Old English people of the northern counties had, at the close of the Saxon period, well-marked characters, closely approaching to the Scandinavian, owing to the large immigration from Norway, Denmark, Sweden, and probably also from the other Baltic coasts, which differentiated them from the people of the southern and midland counties. There is little historical evidence concerning these counties to assist us in an inquiry into the successive immigrations, except the facts that Anglians and their allies came first, and that they were followed by a larger immigration of Scandinavians and their allies.

In the evidence which the survival of old customs of inheritance or traces of them may supply, the existence of an early system of primogeniture is perhaps the most important. The custom of the eldest son having some preference or birthright existed in the North of England in the time of Bede, and is mentioned by him.[1] As already stated, it exists still in Norway, where it has come down in its essential features from a remote antiquity. Two ancient laws relating to the succession of land exist in that country, so old that their origin is lost. These are the asædesret, or homestead right, and the odalsret, or allodial right. The asædesret is the right of the eldest son to inherit the farm after his father, he, however, being obliged to pay the other heirs their share of the estate, the value of which is given by the father, or else it is estimated below its valuation. If the father has left no son, his eldest daughter inherits.[2] Odalsret, as previously mentioned, is the right when a farm has to be sold of any member of the family to buy it, or if sold to a stranger, to redeem it within ten years at the price paid, with the additional cost of any improvements that may have been made. We are only concerned at present in the consideration of the first of these laws—the right of the eldest son to inherit the farm. This early custom of primogeniture could not have been first introduced into the North of England by Norwegian settlers of the ninth century, for as it is mentioned by Bede, who died in 735, it is clear that it existed there before they came. That the north-eastern counties of England and the Lowlands of Scotland were chiefly occupied by Anglian tribes is generally admitted. The Regiam Majestatem, or ancient laws of Scotland, tell us that succession by the eldest son was the custom in the case of knights, but among socmen the custom was to divide the heritage among all the sons, if from ancient time it had been divided. These considerations point to the probability that some of the Anglian tribes must have introduced both customs into ancient Bernicia. Northern tribes, who were afterwards called Norwegians, but perhaps earlier by some tribal name, may have brought in primogeniture. In considering this we should remember that King Alfred tells us the Angles came from the lands on both sides of the passage into the Baltic. It is necessary to remember that there was a custom of rural primogeniture existing in England centuries before the feudal system prevailed. Our early chroniclers who tell us of Angles and Saxons say little of their customs, but the information they give can be supplemented by the traces of the customs which still exist, or which are known to have existed, in parts of England and parts of Northern Europe from which the settlers came. The rural primogeniture such as survives now in Norway so clearly resembles the old rural primogeniture of which traces remain in the North of England, especially in that it secures the succession to the eldest daughter in default of sons, that it cannot reasonably be doubted they had a common origin among the early tribes of Norway or adjacent parts of Scandinavia. It is unreasonable to suppose that a body of colonists, whether in ancient or modern time, would settle in any particular locality and afterwards proceed to invent their customs. We know how in the case of modern colonies the settlers take their laws and customs with them. So it must have been in regard to the customary law of rural primogeniture, with a reversion to the eldest daughter, among some of the early Anglian or Scandian colonists in the North of England. What the tribal names of these people were it is perhaps now impossible to discover.

As we stand on one of the higher mountains south of Keswick, a great part of the ancient lordship of Derwentwater is spread out before us. In this region, which still retains so many characteristics of its Norse settlers, traces are found, in the extensive districts of Castlerigg and Derwentwater, of this Norwegian custom of rural primogeniture, under which, in default of sons, the eldest daughter succeeds to the inheritance.[3] The same rule survives, or did within recent times, in other lordships in Cumberland, Westmoreland, the Isle of Man, at Kirkby Lonsdale, and in Weardale in the county of Durham. The evidence of Norwegian settlements on the north-western coasts of England is so widely spread that the custom no doubt formerly prevailed on many manors of these districts, where its traces are now lost. Something almost identical with it existed in the city of Carlisle under the name of cullery tenure. The cullery tenants of this city were seised of certain customary estates of inheritance, consisting of houses and shops, etc., which they held of the mayor, aldermen, and citizens as the lords of the city. They were admitted to these estates and paid a small annual quit-rent. On the death of a cullery tenant, in the absence of sons, his eldest daughter succeeded him as sole heiress of his customary tenement,[4] instead of, as in the case of a freehold, all his daughters as coheiresses. The surviving names of places around Carlisle point strongly to their Norwegian origin, and there can be no doubt that this curious tenure which prevailed in the city is a primitive one, which, like others in Cumberland, can be traced to Norway.

In considering its origin and survival, we must remember that customs were the laws of our Teutonic forefathers. To alter a custom which had come down from a remote antiquity was so great an innovation that it may reasonably be concluded such a change would not be made except under the pressing needs of altered conditions of life. Between the custom of rural primogeniture and those of equal division and of succession by the youngest son there is so great a difference that they must have had separate origins among different races of people. In the North of England, as elsewhere, there can be little doubt that in many cases all traces of these early customary laws, which at one time prevailed in certain districts or manors, have now been lost. We can, however, trace the partible custom as having existed among the ancient socmen of South Scotland, and rather extensively in Yorkshire, and in Tynedale and Reedsdale in Northumberland,[5] while that of junior right prevailed at Leeds, [6] and was not, apparently, unknown in ancient Bernicia over the border.[7]

It is not difficult to imagine that when a place was occupied at an early time by people of more than one race having their own different systems of inheritance, these customs would in the course of time become blended as the population became mixed in descent. This may, perhaps, have been the origin of the ancient system of inheritance which prevailed at Tynemouth. It was an old port to which ships of Angles, Goths, Frisians, and Northmen would all be likely to have come, and not improbably early merchants or others of these nations settled there. Those who were Frisians or Goths, having a custom of partible inheritance in their own lands, would naturally follow the same, and those who were Northmen, having some form of primogeniture and succession by the eldest daughter in their land, would naturally continue to follow this custom. In process of time these customs, which may be supposed to have prevailed at Tynemonth, apparently became blended, and that of the Goths and Frisians, who, perhaps, were the more numerous section of the inhabitants, became the more prominent. The custom of descent in Tynemouth is, or was, partible inheritance among sons only; in default of sons, the eldest daughter came into the inheritance for her life, and afterwards the next heir male who could derive his title through a male.[8] In considering this curious succession it is necessary also to remember that the custom of inheritance among the Angles was marked by a strong preference for the male line, such as that which has survived at Tynemouth shows.

In addition to those places in Yorkshire where the custom of partible inheritance has survived to modern times, as at Pickering, Domesday Book supplies us with information concerning the land in Holderness and other parts of the county which was held in parcenary at the time of the Survey. By the old general law of the country land could only be held in parcenary by females, but by the custom of gavelkind males might hold their lands collectively by descent to all the males equally.[9] Whether in Kent or elsewhere, the title of parceners accrued only by descent.[10] To hold land in parcenary was, therefore, an ancient custom, and that land was held by this custom in many parts of the East Riding and elsewhere in Yorkshire at the end of the Saxon period is a circumstance which assists us in endeavouring to discover traces of ancient settlers of different races. In the South of England, as we have seen, a great deal of the land in the Isle of Wight and in the New Forest which was colonised by Jutes was held in parcenary at the time of the Norman Survey, and Jutes are admitted to have been Goths or Frisians, or both. Among the Goths, but interspersed by a diversity of local usages, the custom under which estates were administered by a single heir for all the heirs grew up and spread through parts of Germany and countries where Gothic influence prevailed.[11]

The survival of the custom in England points, therefore, to people of Gothic or Frisian descent, or to German people of some other tribe or nation. It may, however, have been Danish, for among Saxons and Danes the ordinary course of descent was to all the sons.[12] As, therefore, we can trace Norwegian settlements in parts of Berkshire, Buckinghamshire, Surrey, and Hertfordshire in the custom of succession by the eldest daughter in default of sons, so by this parcenary system in Yorkshire we can trace people of Gothic extraction and others who were Frisians or of some German race. In addition to the cases recorded in Domesday Book where holdings in parcenary were found in Yorkshire, the custom of partible inheritance, more or less resembling gavelkind in Kent, prevailed on at least some of the lands which formed the fees of Richmond, Pickering, and the great fee of the Archbishop known as that of St. Peter's, York.[13]

Pickering is mentioned in Domesday Book by the ancient clan-name of the people living in the district round it, Picheringa. On this great manor the evidence of Gothic settlement is supported by another custom which also existed there, that of freedom from distraint.[14] It has been mentioned that this was incidental to gavelkind in Kent. The custom in that county, as already stated, was not merely partition among all the sons equally, but comprised several subsidiary privileges of great interest. Freedom from distress for debts was one, and this can be traced to the laws of the ancient Goths.[15] By the records of the Court of King's Bench, Hiliary Term 20 Edward III., it is shown that the lands within the Fee of Pickering were partible among the males,[16] and Pickering also had freedom from distraint. The old name of Goathland, anciently written Gothland, still survives on the north of Pickering Moor, and was perhaps a boundary name. It is marked Gothland on an old map of Pickering of the seventeenth century, published in the first volume of the North Riding Record Society. In the case of Pickering we thus have three circumstances pointing to a settlement of Goths—viz., the custom of partible inheritance, freedom from the general law of distress, and the survival of the name Gothland. Early records, both English and those of kindred nations, point to a time when distress was almost the universal form of civil remedy. The laws of the Visigoths, however, prohibited this remedy, and in Kent, in London, and in Pickering the people enjoyed by custom freedom from it in the recovery of debts or rents. They were probably all of Gothic descent; and here reference may be made to what has been said of the -by places which abound in the East Riding. These are Gothic as well as Danish, and some of them in Yorkshire may have been derived from settlers who were Goths.

The earliest of all the settlements in the northern counties, if we may trust the account concerning it, was that of people of the same race or races as the people of Kent, who are said to have formed settlements on the north-eastern coast under their Kings Octa and Ebissa[17] in the fifth century. There certainly were early settlements made by the Angles, and later ones by the Danes and Norwegians. That of the Norse in the north of Cumberland was probably one of the latest, for the northern parts of Cumberland and Westmoreland were still occupied by the Celts, while their southern parts and the districts of Furness and Cartmel had passed to Teutonic settlers of some kind, using the word Teutonic in its widest sense as including Scandinavians. The name Ulpha in the valley of the Duddon, and another Ulpha in Cartmel, near the mouth of the river Kent, appear to be of Gothic origin. Ulph is a Gothic word, and appears in the name of Ulphilas, the Bishop who translated the Gospels into Mœso-Gothic. The customs of Kendal also point to Goths among its early settlers, and as there were Goths in Kent, and they were skilled in navigation, there appears nothing improbable in a Kentish migration, which would account for the ancient name of Kentmere. Kendal is the name of the most extensive parish in Westmoreland, comprising twenty-four townships or constable wicks, among which are Kentmere and Helsington.

This name Helsington in a district where there is other evidence of the settlement of Goths may be considered in connection with the Helsings, the name of the people of Helsingja-land in Sweden. The manorial tenants of Kendal held their lands by military obligation and on payment of certain rents, but, like the ancient Visigoths, they were not liable to distraint for the recovery of them.[18] Partible inheritance cannot be proved to have been the custom at Kendal, but in the will of Henri Fissher of that place, dated November 5, 1578, we appear to have a trace of it. He says: 'Mye evidences to be safflie kepte under twoo locks and kyes in my studye at Helssington, and at the full aige of my sonnes to be divided accordinge to their rights.'[19]

The customs relating to the widow's dower that prevailed in South Westmoreland and North Lancashire are varied. In the Barony of Kendal the widow of a customary tenant was entitled to the whole of her husband's customary estate during widowhood.[20] In some other parts of the south of Westmoreland she received half the estate. Similarly, at Much Urswick, Kirkby Irleth, Lowick,[21] and Nevill Hall in Furness, the widow was entitled to half the estate during widowhood. By the old common law of the country she was entitled to only a third share, and at Clitheroe to a fourth, as was the custom among the ancient Lombards. The Kendal dower custom is the same as existed so largely in Sussex and on manors elsewhere, as in the vale of Taunton, where junior inheritance prevailed. The half dower custom is the same as that of Kent, and points to settlements of Goths or Jutes.

The north of Lancashire and south of Westmoreland were included in the West Riding at the time of the Domesday Survey, and apparently had been considered a part of the kingdom of Deira, or Yorkshire, since the seventh century. In 685 'the land called Cartmel and all the Britons there' was given to Cuthbert by one of the early Kings, from which record it may be considered certain that Celtic people survived there among the early Teutonic settlers. The early church dedications to St. Wilfrid at Standish, Preston, and Ribchester, and to St. Cuthbert at Kirkby Irleth, were received from their Yorkshire connection.[22] The colonists of North Lancashire and South Westmoreland appear to have come partly from Yorkshire and partly by the sea. Some of them would probably be Northumbrian Anglians, and others of Jutish extraction. The remains of early stone crosses at Whalley and at Burnley, of the same style as those found in other parts of ancient Northumbria, are traces of the early Anglian connection of these parts of Lancashire, and the runic inscription found at Lancaster supplies confirmatory evidence of this connection.

Close to Lancaster there are distinct traces of a later settlement of Norse, for around Heysham and Halton the hills are called fells, the pools are tarns, the streams becks, the farms are thwaits, and the island rocks are skears.[23]

As regards the early customs of partible inheritance which prevailed over large districts of Yorkshire, Glanville's remarks in the time of Henry II. must be remembered—viz., that partible inheritance was only recognised by the law-courts of his time on those manors where it could be proved that the

194

land always had been divided. Consequently, as this custom was allowed to continue on many manors of the great lordships of Richmond, Pickering, and St. Peter's, York, it must have been a custom of immemorial usage, and proved to the satisfaction of the law in the twelfth century. This points to the conclusion that these areas were originally occupied by Goths and Frisians among the Anglian settlers of Yorkshire. The proof lay in an actual inspection of the subdivided lands, which must have borne their testimony, as well as in the sworn evidence of witnesses. The partible lands of the Dalecarlian people of Sweden, who are descendants of the Northern Goths, show at the present day similar evidence of this immemorial usage. The custom could not have been general throughout England, because it was allowed to continue in comparatively few places. If it had generally prevailed, its antiquity could have been proved, and the custom preserved by appealing to the evidence of partition on the surface of the fields themselves.

The old place-names in the northern counties point to people of many tribes as having taken a part in its settlement. If we confine our attention to old Anglo-Saxon names of places, which had their origin in all probability from people bearing tribal names who settled there, we shall be able to make a considerable list. Such a name as Hunmannebi clearly points to a settler and his family or kindred who was a Frisian of the Hunsing tribe—*i.e.*, he was a man of the Hunni race mentioned by Bede. In the same way, other names indicate Frisians, called by their national name; others who were either Frisians of the Brocmen tribe, or of the German tribe of Boructers, who are also mentioned by Bede as among the tribes from which the Old English were descended. Such a name as Boructer might easily be shortened by use into Broc. The Chaucians or Hocings are probably represented by the survival of a number of *Choc-* or *Hoc-* names of places. Here and there we meet with the Engle name, and a few which appear to have been derived from people known to their neighbours as Saxons. Among other places bearing names derived from settlers of various ancient races are those in Dan or Dene, which point to Danes; Norman, which points to Norse; Suen, which points to Swedes; Goth, or Goda, which indicate Gothic people; and Wend or Winter names, which indicate Vandal settlers. Among the old place-names in Northumberland are the fifteenth-century names Waringford and Wynt'ingham, denoting a Waring and a Wendish settlement.[24] Winterset is an old place-name in the parish of Wragby.

Borough-English or junior right is known to have prevailed at Leeds,[25] the only place in the northern counties where it has been traced. Its prevalence there in the midst of a kingdom such as Yorkshire was, settled at first by people called Anglians, and largely occupied later on by people commonly called Danes or Norse, is a very remarkable circumstance, for, so far as known, none of these had such a custom. Leeds is in Airedale, and was apparently the chief place in the old district known in Saxon time as Elmet. This district is mentioned by Bede as the ' Regio Loidis,' or the region of Leeds, Elmet being mentioned by the same early writer as a silva or woodland.[26] If from the occurrence of the custom of junior right at Leeds we may consider that it prevailed elsewhere in this region, then, as the custom is an old one, and it could not have been that of Anglians or Danes or Norwegians, it probably was brought by a fair race of people. Seeing that succession by the youngest son to the whole inheritance is not a Welsh custom, it is not probable that the junior right which prevailed at Leeds could have been derived from a survival of the old British stock. Moreover, the racial characters of the Airedale people, as described by Beddoe, point to descent from a fair race. This subject takes us back to the time when Elmet was first brought under subjection by Edwin in the seventh century. Beddoe considers it probable that new settlers of a fair stock were introduced, and it is remarkable that an old name, Wendel Hill, for an earthwork at Berewic, in Elmet, still survives.[27] There are some old place-names in addition to this one in the northern counties which may have had their origin from Wendish settlers, relatively few in number, but still significant. Wendesbery[28] and Wandesford[29] in Yorkshire, Windleton near Darlington, Wensley, Wendeslowe,[30] Wenslawe, and Wendeslaghe,[31] are names of this kind. Wensleydale aid Old Wennington, in the north of Lancashire, may also be of the same origin.

There is evidence of the survival in Northumbria of people of Celtic descent, who were subsequently absorbed among the English race of the northern counties. The historical information on this point concerning Cartmel has been mentioned. The probability of a mixture of Celts among the Scandinavian settlers of Cumberland is also great. The Northumbrian Priest-law, which mentions the penalty for the practise of heathen rites by a King's thane, affords evidence of the survival of people in Yorkshire of British descent, who were known as Wallerwente. Heathenism in some of its rites survived long in the North. A thane who was accused of heathen practices was fined according to the Priest-law ten half-marks, unless he could prove his innocence by thirty oath-helpers, ten of whom must be named by himself, ten by his kindred, and ten others must be Wallerwente.[32] These Wallerwente, as their oaths were taken in evidence, must have been freemen. They were apparently men of another race, and chosen for this legal process on that account, as native Celtic inhabitants living among others of Teutonic descent, and whose testimony as native Christians would be specially acceptable in such cases. This recognition of descendants of a remnant of the old Celtic people is of interest, seeing that the oldest name for what is now Yorkshire—viz., Deira—is Welsh, and derived from its Celtic inhabitants, the Deiri, or their country.[33]

It is well known that two very remote successive immigrations of Celtic people into Britain can be traced—viz., those of the Round Barrow period, who are also known as the men of the Bronze Age; and the later Brythons, from whom in the main the Welsh are descended. From the examination of the bones of the men of the Bronze Age, which are met with but sparingly—for cremation was their common mode of disposing of the dead—they are known to have been a broad-headed and large-limbed race. The later Celts are not characterised by this head form. The survival among living people here and there of representatives of the broad-headed type is an interesting ethnological circumstance. As might be expected, it is chiefly in the most mountainous part of England—viz., in the remote parts of Cumberland—that traces of this race may still be met with. The type is, according to Beddoe and Ripley, marked by being 'above the average in height, generally dark in complexion, the head broad and short, the face strongly developed at the cheekbones, frowning or beetle browed, the development of the brow ridges being especially noticeable in contrast with the smooth, almost feminine softness of the Saxon forehead.'[34] In Cumberland there had been going on a fusion between the descendants of the Norse and those of these more ancient Cumbrians, some of the descendants of whom are now fair in complexion.[35]

[1] Beda, 'Life of St. Benedict,' s. xi.

[2] du Chaillu, P. B., 'The Land of the Midnight Sun,' ii. 289.

[3] Elton, C. I., 'Law of Copyholds,' p. 134.

[4] Nanson, W., *Cumberland and Westmoreland Antiquarian and Archæol. Soc. Transactions*, vi. 305, 306.

[5] Gray, W., 'Chorographia; A Survey of Newcastle, 1649,' p. 26.

[6] Elton, C. I., 'Robinson on Gavelkind,' 243.

[7] Regiam Majestatem.

[8] Elton, C. I., 'Law of Copyholds,' pp. 128, 134.

[9] Reeve's 'History of English Law,' edited by Finlason, ii., 587.

[10] *Ibid.*, ii. 589.

[11] Cecil, Evelyn, 'Primogeniture,' p. 114.

[12] *Ibid.*, 27, quoting Hale.

[13] Elton, C. I., 'Robinson on Gavelkind,' p. 157.

[14] 'Honor and Forest of Pickering,' vol. iii.

[15] Maine, Sir H., 'Early Institutions,' 269, 270.

[16] Elton, C. I., 'Robinson on Gavelkind,' p. 33.

[17] Nennius, edited by Gunn, W., p. 183, notes.

[18] Ferguson, R. S., 'History of Westmoreland,' 118-122.

[19] 'Wills and Inventories of the Archdeaconry of Richmond,' edited by Raine, J., p. 284.

[20] Nicholson and Burns, 'History of Westmoreland and Cumberland,' 24.

[21] Harland and Wilkinson, 'Lancashire Folk-Lore,' 281-284.

[22] Fishwick, H., 'History of Lancashire,' 185, 200, 201.

[23] March, H. C., *Lancashire and Cheshire Arch. Soc.*, ix. 50, 51.

[24] Placita de quo Warranto, 586, 591.

[25] Elton, C. I., 'Gavelkind,' Index.

[26] Beda, 'Hist. Eccles.,' lib. ii., chap. xiv.

[27] Whitaker, T. D., 'History of Leeds,' 152.

[28] Cal. Rot. Pat. (Henry III.), p. 96.

[29] Cal. Inq. Post-mortem, ii. 18.

[30] *Ibid.*, ii. 125.

[31] *Ibid.*, ii. 72.

[32] Seebohm, F., 'Tribal Custom in Anglo-Saxon Law,' 399.

[33] Rhys, J., 'Celtic Britain,' 112.

[34] Ripley, W. Z., 'Races of Europe,' 309.

[35] *Ibid.*

# Chapter Twenty - Settlers in Northumbria— *continued.*

THE settlement of Frisians in Northumbria is probable from the historical evidence of Procopius, who says that 'three very numerous nations possess Brittia, over each of which a King presides, which nations are named Angeloi, Phrissones, and those surnamed from the island, Brittones.' Some of these Phrissones must have settled in the northern counties of England and in the south of Scotland, for the Firth of Forth is called by Nennius the Frisian Sea, and part of its northern coast was known as the Frisian shore.[1] The name Dumfries appears also to afiord a trace of the same people.

It is reasonable to conclude that in the settlement of the coasts of the North-east of England and the South of Scotland by the Angles their neighbours the Frisians took a large part. Even at the present time the resemblance between the Frisian dialects and Lowland Scotch is in some respects very close. As we have seen, Octa and Ebissa, with whom as leaders the early settlements in Northumbria are connected, have characteristic Frisian names ending in *a*. The early kingdom of the Beornicas included the Lowlands, and these people had a Frisian name. Halbertsma refers to the name Beornicas as having been derived from the Frisian word *bearn*, denoting men, used possibly in the sense of descendants.[2]

There are in Yorkshire old place-names which point directly to Frisians, such as Fristone in the West Riding, mentioned in Domesday Book; Freswick, an old place in the North Riding; and Frismarsk, or Frysemersh, a lost place that formerly existed in Holderness.[3] It is probable there was a very early colony of Frisians in this district, for Ptolemy mentions a race of people resident there whom he calls the Parisi.[4] The Teutonic equivalent of Parisi is Farisi, and the probability is that these were a colony of Frisians from the opposite coast. This identification of the Parisi of Ptolemy as Frisians is supported by some remarkable circumstances pointing to a Frisian migration to the country of the Humber. Holderness had an alternative name, that of Emmertland, and among the ancient river names of the northern part of Old Saxony or Frisia was the Emmer or Ambra,[5] which we now call the Ems. Along the course of this river the tribal Ambrones, or people of the Emisga pagus, lived.[6] These Ambrones are mentioned by Roman writers. From the consideration of all the circumstantial evidence connected with them and with Holderness, the settlement of Frisians of this old tribe at an early date near the mouth of the Humber is practically certain. It was from this tribe that in all probability the Humber received its name, after that of the Ambra in their old country. It should also be remembered that Paulinus is said to have preached for forty days among certain old Saxons. We know he did carry on this mission among the people south of the Humber, and these may have preserved their old tribal designation of Ambrones, or old Saxons, until that time.

The Holderness dialect, which has probably come from more than one source, is one of the most interesting in Yorkshire, for it shows variations in vocabulary in different parts of the district. It has usually only one form of the verb for the three persons, many participles ending in -en or -in, many adjectives ending in -ish or -fied, and no possessive case.[7] The pronunciation of the place-names in some of the northern parts of England at the present time strongly points to Frisian settlements. In Northumberland there are many places whose names end in -ham, but, with the exception of Chillingham, they are all pronounced as if ending in -um, like the terminal sound so common in the present place-names of Friesland. In the Cleveland district of Yorkshire, also, examples of the same kind occur, in which the local pronunciation making names ending in -um is very marked. Thus, Yarm is pronounced Jarum; Moorsholm, Morehusum ; Acklam, Achelum; Lealholm, Laclum or Lelum; Airsome, Arusum; and Coatham, Cotum, and so on.[8] A similar pronunciation of names in Sussex has been referred to in the chapter relating to that county.

There can be no doubt that Frisian was one of the dialects used by the settlers in the northern counties, and that many Frisian words passed into the Anglian speech. As late as 1175 we find a Frisian dialect separately mentioned by Reginald, a monk of Durham.[9] In referring to the eider-duck, he says these birds are called lomes by the English, but eires by the Saxons and inhabitants of Frisia.

The dialect of Northumberland and on Tyneside shows important differences from that in the middle and south parts of Durham and Yorkshire.[10] This helps to prove that when the Danes overran and conquered Northumbria it was chiefly in Yorkshire they settled. The country north of the Tyne was left, apparently, more in the occupation of the descendants of the original colonists. The old Northumbrian dialect was the language of the Anglian and Frisian settlers from Aberdeen to the south of Yorkshire. When Yorkshire was recolonised by Danes and their allies, a modified dialect arose. The evidence of the place-names affords striking testimony to the extent of the Danish settlements. North of the Tyne the terminations -ham and -ton are conspicuous, while -by, which abounds in the East Riding, does not occur. The streams in Northumberland are called burns, and not becks, as in the Scandinavian districts of the northern counties. The pronunciation of the word 'the' is not clipped in Northumberland into 't,' as it is in the Danish districts of Yorkshire and Lancashire. The contrast in this respect between Northumberland and Tyneside on the one hand, and the south of Durham and East Riding of Yorkshire on the other, is very marked.[11] There are, however, some traces to be found in Northumberland of Norse colonists of a kind different from those of the Danes in the East Riding, although traces of Angles and Frisians are most in evidence.

The Firth of Forth, mentioned by Nennius as the Frisian Sea, and a part of its northern shore known as the Frisian shore, must have had an early connection with the Frisians, although, as Skene says, 'the great bulk of immigrants are Anglians.'[12] This is of interest in reference to the people of Northumberland, a county in which traces of Frisian occupation are strong. It is known that Frisians came to Britain among the Roman military, and Skene says that 'of the Saxons who settled in Britain before the year 441, the colony which occupied the northern district about the Roman wall were probably Frisians.' This may well have been the case, and the traces of people of this race which the Northumberland place-names supply may therefore be of older date than the time of Hengist and Horsa. There may, indeed, have been settlements in the time of the Roman Empire of both Frisians and their allies the Chaucians. This view possibly receives support from the discovery in Northumberland of a Roman altar,[13] bearing the inscription 'Deo Cocidi'—a reference, perhaps, to a supposed Chaucian divinity.

The name of the river Coquet and others, apparently connected with Chaucians, may be traces of a settlement before the end of the Roman rule in Britain. A garrison of Frisians was certainly located on Hadrian's Wall early in the fifth century.[14]

The Roman place-name Hunno[15] has been identified with Sevensdale in Northumberland, and that named Cocuneda civitas[16] with Coquet in the same county.[17] In the Boldon Book relating to the tenancies held under the Bishop of Durham in the eleventh or twelfth century we find old place-names that are apparently traces of settlers who had Frisian names, such as Hunwyk and Hunstanworth. The same record also affords instances in which brothers held land jointly, and of other parceners more or less resembling the holdings in Kent. In connection with these *Hun* names, it is of special interest to note the existence of a Roman station called Hunnum in Northumberland. As an old tribe called Phundusii is mentioned by Ptolemy living near the mouth of the Elbe, not very far from the later Frisian districts, inhabited by the Hunse or Hunte, the name Hunnum may have been one used in Roman time in connection with the Frisian garrison.

If further proof were wanted of Frisians among the Angles of this part of England and the adjacent coast of Scotland, the remarkable inscribed stone found at Kirkliston, Edinburghshire, would supply it. Stephens describes it as a heathen stone of the fourth or fifth century, bearing Roman letters and words to commemorate a fallen chieftain, with a name so rare that it has only been found three times in English literature and once in Northern. It has also his father's name, a rarer one still. Both these names are Frisian, and are still found among modern Frisian personal names.[18] The inscription, by dividing the letters into words, reads: 'In oc tumulo iacit Vetta f(ilius) Victi.' The name Wyttenham in Northumberland, apparently derived from a similar name Witte, is mentioned in the Hundred Rolls. Sweet has pointed out another linguistic connection of the Anglians of Northumbria with the Frisians. He says that the Anglian dialect was characterised by a special tendency to throw off the final *n* in names.[19] Of this many examples may be found among old place-names of the Northern counties, and the early personal names connected with them, some of which have been referred to. It was also a Frisian characteristic.

In his 'History of Cleveland,' Atkinson tells us of four places whose ancient names were Englebi, of two whose old names were Wiltune, and of two named Tollesbi. They may have been so named after heads of families who bore tribal names. The Tollenzi on the Tollensee were a Wendish tribe.[20]

In considering the evidence relating to the settlement of people of different races in the North of England, that afforded by the runic monuments is of the first importance. The Anglian runes are the older Gothic with modifications, and their modifications were made on English soil. This points to Goths among the so-called Anglian settlers, or Angles from Swedish Gothland. In any case, the knowledge of runic writing must have been brought into Northern England by early settlers from Gothland or the countries near it. The Frisians who formed settlements in Northumbria, on the contrary, had no knowledge of runes.

In one of the old Norse records we are told of Old Northumbria, that 'Nordimbraland is for the most part inhabited by Northmen. Many of the names are in the Norræna tongue Grimsbær (Grimsby), and Hauksfljot (Hawkflot), and many others.'[21] This refers to the older and larger Northumberland, and includes, apparently, part of South Humberland or Lincolnshire. The earliest runic inscriptions of old Northumbria are not within the limits of the present county, but are within the kingdom of the Northumbrian Anglians. Among them are those on the Bewcastle column in north-west Cumberland, and on the Ruthwell cross in Dumfries. The date of the Bewcastle[22] monument is about A.D. 670, and the words used in the inscription on the Ruthwell cross show that it cannot well be later than the middle of the eighth century,[23] The inscriptions on the Collingham cross in Yorkshire, and on a slab found at Lancaster, have been assigned to the seventh century.[24] All these and others are inscriptions of the Anglians, and not of the later Danes or Norse, whose runic letters differed in some instances from those of the earlier Anglian.

One of the Old English tribes that can be clearly recognised in Northumbria is that of Lindisfarne. This name was not originally given to the island off the Northumbrian coast, but to a strip of country along it. Lindisfaran was part of the mainland along the courses of two rivers—the Lindis, which was the old name for the Low, and the Waran, that ran into the sea a little north of Bamburgh.[25] This island was the island of the Lindisfarne people or territory, as mentioned by Bede. This small Anglian tribe is one of the most interesting of which any trace has come down to us. Its rulers derived their origin from Woden, through a line of mythological ancestors of their own,[26] and it is not improbable that their island was known as Hälig or Halige, the Holy Isle, before they became Christians, for the Continental Angles and Frisians had a Holy Isle off their coast, and it still retains the name of Heligoland. The Wends of the Baltic coast also had their sacred island—viz., Rügen—where their chief pagan temple was situated. The possession of a sacred or holy isle for their pagan rites was, therefore, probably considered by the pagan Angles who settled in Northumberland as part of their religion; and after their conversion the sacred isle of the pagan time was selected for the site of the Christian monastery.

Some of the old shire and district names in the northern counties were apparently derived from Scandinavian and other tribal names. Hallamshire appears to have got its name from a manor mentioned in Domesday Book as Hallun. As this district is called a shire, and this as a designation for a district is Scandinavian, Hallun may not improbably have been connected in its origin with people from Halland, in the South-west of Sweden, and within the limits of Old Denmark. Gillingshire, also, for Gilling Wapentake in Yorkshire, appears to be a Scandinavian name. Gylling, an island in Halogaland, is mentioned in the Northern Sagas.[27] One thing, therefore, is certain in reference to old settlements in the northern counties, that we find districts which contain many traces of Norse near others in which traces of Anglians have survived. There may have been a connection between the name Rossendale in Lancashire and the Wrosn tribe of the Pomeranian coast. As the settlement of Norse and their allies in Lancashire was probably late, the possibility of such a connection is strengthened by the known association of Danes and Norse with the Jomberg Wends of Pomerania.

The Yorkshire Domesday names Scotona, Scotone, Englebi, and Engleston, point to family settlements of people who were Scots and Engles. Similarly, there can be little doubt that the Domesday names Danestorp, Danebi, Wedrebi, Leccheton, and Lecchestorp, point to settlers who were Danes, Wederas or Ostrogoths, and Lechs, who were their allies. Traces of Swedes are met with in the old names Suanebi in Yorkshire and Suenesat in Agremundreness in Lancashire,[28] and other names similar to those of tribal allies of the Danes may be traced.

The name Wensleydale and the old Semer names which it contains suggest some connection with Wends, and this is strengthened by the folk-lore. A special characteristic in the folk-lore of the Northern Slavs is that of magic horses, of which many examples occur in Russian folk-tales.[29] In Wensleydale folk-lore the kelpie or water-horse comes up occasionally out of the water,[30] and, like the Russian horses, is a wonderful beast. The place-name Semer also occurs in Cleveland, near Stokesley,[31] and Domesday Book tells us of Semser in the North Riding and Semers in the West Riding, these names being, apparently, of old Wendish origin, from *zieme*, the land. Their parallels may be found in Slavic countries, and other examples of their occurrence in Wiltshire and Sussex have already been mentioned.

The earliest frontier between the kingdoms of Northumbria and Mercia on the west of the Pennine Range, along the Mersey, appears to have been subsequently altered to the Ribble. There is some documentary evidence relating to this later boundary. In 923 King Edward ordered a body of Mercians to take possession of Manchester, and to repair and fortify it.[32] We read, also, that the northern limit of Mercia was Hwitanwylles geat,[33] which may be identified with Whitwell in the upper part of the valley of the Ribble. Whitaker's researches point to the Ribble as having been an ethnological frontier.[34] The Fylde, between the mouths of the same river and the Lune, exhibits evidence of Scandinavian settlements. Its name may be compared with the Norse Fjelde, the name for the Norwegian wastes. The Lancashire Fylde consists even at the present time of a great extent of more or less peaty soil, commonly called moss. Danes pad, or path, the name for an old road across it, Angersholm, Mythorp, Eskham, and other place-names in the district, are distinctly Scandinavian.

When we remember that the Anglian kingdom of Northumbria was conquered by Northmen, and was a Danish kingdom for about 200 years, until reduced in status to one of the great earldoms of the later Saxon period, we naturally expect to find more characteristic remains of Danes and Northmen than of the earlier Anglians. Some interesting evidence of the agricultural customs of Northmen connected with the old farmhouses called onsteads survived in Northumberland as late as 1827, and may still survive in part. The customs may be ancient, even if the farms are comparatively modern. They are scattered over a large part of that county, at a distance of two or three miles from each other, and from the villages or towns. In these onsteads the farmers resided with their dependents. Immediately adjoining them a number of cottages were situated, proportionable in some degree to the size of the farms. They are, or were, inhabited by the steward, the hinds, and in some instances by the bondagers, who have, or had, their cottages at a small rent, and are entitled to a certain quantity of potatoes. The wages of the steward and hinds were chiefly paid in kind, and they had their cottages rent free, with hay or grass for one or two cows and other privileges, and a small sum of money.[35]

The system in Norway is very similar to this. The farms have houses for housemen, with enclosed land to each, that extends to the keeping of two cows and six sheep all the year round, and to the sowing of a certain quantity of corn and potatoes. A small general rent is paid for these holdings. In this system the main object provided for is that the labourer may be able to live on the produce of the land.[36]

We may recognise the Scandian or Danish influence in the northern counties in some of the ancient designations of the tenants mentioned in the Boldon Book of Durham, such as Cotmanni and Malmanni, the former corresponding to the cottars of southern counties. The Danes commonly used the word manni[37] in names of this kind. The characteristic Scandinavian termination -hope or -op in place-names is found in many instances in the west of Northumberland—Bowhope, Ramshope, Wickhope, Blenkinsop, Killhope, and Hawhope being examples. The significance of these -hope names will be discussed in the chapter relating to the Welsh border. The word -side, also, which is a characteristic in the Cumberland names, is found in the western parts of Northumberland, such as Hesleyside, Whiteside, Wheelside, and

Monkside. These point to a similarity in dialect, and hence probably in race. The place-names originally derived from shelter names, such as booth, shield, and scale, are more frequently met with in the northern counties than elsewhere. They had their origin, probably, in summer huts, commonly erected by pastoral people among the hills or on the upland wastes, for temporary abodes while pasturing their cattle away from their permanent homesteads, as is the custom in Norway at the present time.

The descendants of Danish or Norse settlers may be distinguished in Lancashire as late as the time of Domesday Survey by the statements that some of them paid their rents in the Danish computation. Thus, in many places between the Ribble and the Mersey each carucate of land paid a tax or tribute of two ores of pennies.[38] The ore was a Danish coin of the value of sixteen pence, and later of twenty pence. Similarly, it may be noted in the ancient Northumbrian Priest-law that the fines mentioned are in half-marks, also of old Northern origin.

People of the same descent may be recognised in the land register of the monastery of Hexham, which tells us of 'husbands' and 'terræ husband.'[39] These husbands were no doubt descended from Northern settlers known as bondi, a name still used for the peasant proprietors of Scandinavia.

The race characters shown at the present time by the people of Northumberland are, according to Beddoe, strongly Anglian, and can be well seen in the rural population around Hexham.[40] The Northumberland people are, in the main, above the average English size. It is on evidence that a regiment of men of that county standing in close formation occupies more space than an average regiment of the same number. The old race in north Durham is also Anglian in the main. The North and East Ridings of Yorkshire have an Anglo-Danish population, the prevailing types being Anglian and Danish. Phillips describes these people as tall, large-boned, and muscular, with a visage long and angular, fair or blonde complexion, blue or gray eyes, and light-brown or reddish hair.[41] In the more elevated districts of the West Riding he describes the people as robust in person, of an oval, full, and rounded visage, with a nose often slightly aquiline, a complexion somewhat embrowned or florid, brown or gray eyes, and brown or reddish hair. This brown, burly breed Phillips thought to be Norwegian, but Beddoe considers it to be a variety of the Anglian race, as it abounds in Staffordshire, which is a very Anglian county.

In the plains of Yorkshire, Durham, and Northumberland the old agricultural arrangements of the townships appear to have been largely those of the nucleated villages or collected homesteads. This system corresponds to that now prevailing in Holstein, part of Schleswig, which was within part of the Anglian country, a circumstance that points to the plan of collected homesteads having been introduced into these parts of the northern counties by people of that race. On the other hand, on both sides of the Pennine Range isolated homesteads have largely survived in both west Yorkshire and east Lancashire, and these are probably traces of ancient Celtic occupation. The homestead arrangements in these districts have much in common with those found in Cumberland and in Wales.

[1] Skene, W. F., 'Celtic Scotland,' i. 192.

[2] Halbertsma, J. H., 'Lexicon Frisicum.'

[3] Cal. Patent Rolls, 1340-1343, p. 449.

[4] English Dialect Society, 'Glossary of Holderness,' p. 2.

[5] Monumenta Germaniæ, i. 166, 167.

[6] Ibid., ii. 386.

[7] English Dialect Society, 'Glossary of Holderness,' p. 6.

[8] Atkinson, J. C., 'Glossary of the Cleveland Dialect.'

[9] Reginaldi Monachi Dunelm. Libellus, chap, xxvii.

[10] English Dialect Society, 'Glossary of Northumberland,' viii.

[11] English Dialect Society, 'Glossary of Northumberland,' ix.

[12] Skene, W. F., 'Celtic Scotland,' ii. 192.

[13] Ferguson, R., 'The River-names of Europe,' 85.

[14] Notitia Imperil, and Wright, T., Lancashire and Cheshire Historic. Soc., viii. 141.

[15] Notitia Imperil.

[16] Ravennas.

[17] Pearson, C. H., 'Historical Maps,' quoting authorities.

[18] Stephens, R. G., 'Old Northern Runic Monuments,' i. 60.

[19] Sweet, H., 'Dialects and Prehistoric Forms of Old English,' PhiloL Soc. Transactions, 1875-6, 560, 561.

[20] Latham, R. G., 'Germania of Tacitus,' Prolegomena, xvii.

[21] 'The Heimskringla' by Sturluson, trans, by Laing, ii. 6.

[22] Stephens, G., loc. cit., vol. i., 398.

[23] Sweet, H., 'Oldest English Texts," 125.

[24] Ibid., 124-130.

[25] Proceedings Soc. Antiquaries, Newcastle-on-Tyne, iii., p. 401.

[26] Grimm, J., 'Teutonic Mythology,' iv. 1711.

[27] 'The Heimskringla,' by Sturluson, trans, by Laing, ii., 180.

[28] Dom. Bk.

[29] Ralston, W. R. S., 'Russian Folk-Tales,' 243-258.

[30] Gomme, G. L., 'Ethnology in Folk-Lore,' 78.

[31] Abbrev. Rot. Originalium, vol. i., 181.

[32] Anglo-Saxon Chronicle.

[33] Ibid., A.D. 941.

[34] Whitaker, T. D., 'History of Whalley,' 4th Ed. i. 52.

[35] Mackenzie, E., 'View of the County of Northumberland,' ii., pp. 52, 53.

[36] Laing, Samuel, 'Journal of a Residence in Norway.' ed. 1851, pp. 101, 102.

[37] du Chaillu, P., 'Viking Age,' i. 23.

[38] Domesday Book, quoted by Fishwick, H., 'History of Lancashire,' 54.

[39] Nasse, E., 'The Agricultural Community,' translated by Oudry, p. 71.

[40] Beddoe, J., 'Races in Britain,' 249.

[41] Beddoe, J., 'Races in Britain,' 250.

# Chapter Twenty-One - Settlements in Mercia

IN some of the counties which were comprised within the kingdom of Mercia we meet with remarkable traces of old tribal customs. There is a charter relating to the borough of Leicester granted by Simon de Montfort, and dated October 25, 1255. In this document he ordered, apparently as Earl of Leicester, that the burgage tenements of the people of that town which by custom descended to the youngest son should thereafter follow the course of common law and go to the eldest. This charter never received the King's ratification, but its validity does not seem to have been questioned.[1] By similar arbitrary measures changes were probably made in other places. Junior right is known to have existed in Derby, Nottingham. Stamford. and Stafford, in addition to a considerable number of rural manors in the Midland counties. It could not have been spontaneously developed in these towns, not at the other more numerous places in which traces of it can be found, and was probably brought in by the early settlers.

Partible inheritance, more or less resembling the gavelkind custom in Kent, as well as junior right, can be traced unmistakably in the counties of Leicester and Nottingham. To what extent they prevailed originally it is not possible to say, for in some places customs may have been changed and all traces of them lost, either by the later settlements of Danes or by compulsory orders like that made at Leicester. In Leicestershire, partible inheritance is known to have been the rule in the soke of Rothley.

This place is situated in the north of the county, and at the time of Domesday Survey included twenty-one members or subordinate manors, among which were Allexton, Baresbi, Segrave, Markfield, Halstead, Frisby, Saxelby, Bagrave, and Gaddesby.[2] It comprised at that time 204 sokemen, 157 villeins, and 94 bordiers, who together formed an administrative district apart from the hundreds of the county. In this liberty the lands held by a sokeman, and presumably also by the other tenants, were on the death of the holder parted between his sons, or in the absence of sons, among his daughters. If he left only one son and one daughter, the son took the whole. If he left a widow, she held the land for her life, provided she remained single, but if she married again she kept only a third as her dower, and the rest passed to the heirs.

There is much similarity between this custom and that of Kent. There can thus be little doubt that Leicestershire received among its Anglian colonists some settlers who migrated from Kent or came from Gothland and Frisia. It should be noted that Frisby and Gaddesby are among the names of ancient places which were included within the Soke of Rothley. The early Anglo-Saxon inhabitants of Leicestershire were known as the Middle Angles, but the laws of the Angles of the Continent were especially marked by preference for male inheritance in the time of Charlemagne. If we may assume that this was an earlier custom characteristic of the race, as it was among the Continental Saxons, it would not be likely that the Angles of Leicestershire brought in a custom which recognised daughters such as prevailed at Rothley. To account for it we must conclude that there must have settled among these Middle Angles people who had a custom of female inheritance—at least, in default of sons. As the burgesses of Leicester had another custom—that of junior inheritance—which was different altogether from what prevailed generally among the Saxons or Angles, we are led to the conclusion that the original settlers at Leicester must have come from some other part of the Continent where this custom prevailed; and there is reason to believe it did prevail among the Burgundians of the Baltic or people of Slavic or mixed Slavic descent. Such tribes may have been allies of the Danes who settled in Leicester, Nottingham, and other towns before the end of the ninth century.[3]

The evidence that the five Danish towns of Leicester, Lincoln, Nottingham, Stamford, and Derby, were permanently occupied by Northmen of some kind during the earlier Danish conquests, in or before the time of Alfred, appears conclusive from the reference to these places in the Saxon Chronicle in the year 941. This was the time when Eadmund succeeded Æthelstan, and his various territories are stated. We are told that he subdued Mercia and the five towns 'that were ere while Danish under the Northmen.' This statement places the antiquity of the Danish settlement in these towns beyond doubt, and the custom of junior right which is known to have prevailed in four of them, but not in Lincoln, is significant, as pointing to people who had different tribal usages having probably settled in them, although all called Danes. There is, indeed, some evidence that under the pressure of population which urged them to the west, Slavs 'established themselves in parts of the southern isles of Denmark, Laaland, Falster, and Langeland, where their traditions and place-names bear witness to their settlements.'[4] If this migration took place at an early date, as is probable, some of these Danes of Wendish descent may well have come into England with other Danes during their earlier as well as their later incursions.

Beddoe tells us that as a result of his observations on the people of Leicestershire and Northamptonshire, compared with those of Lincolnshire and Nottinghamshire, he found a considerably higher percentage of dark hair and eyes in the two former counties than in the two latter. From observations on 540 persons in Leicestershire and 300 in Northamptonshire, he found the index of nigrescence to be 20·8 in the county of Leicester and 31·2 in that of Northampton; while of 500 persons observed in Lincolnshire, it was only 12·3; and of 700 observed in Nottinghamshire, it was 14·1. Regarding Leicestershire and Northamptonshire, he says: 'There is, if I may judge by the colour of the hair and eyes, a strong non-Teutonic element.'[5] In order to account for this darker character of the people we must assume either a survival of people of a darker British race, or that a considerable proportion of brown or dark people settled in these counties with the fairer Angles and Scandinavians. It has already been shown in reference to similar observations in Hertfordshire and Buckinghamshire that there are Continental areas within the parts from which Anglo-Saxon settlers came where people of a darker complexion still live, and apparently have from time immemorial.

The original Mercians formed a comparatively small State, which absorbed the Gyrwas, or Fen people of Lincolnshire, Northampton, and Huntingdon; the Lindisware of north Lincolnshire ; the South Humbrians, or Ambrones, in the north of Nottinghamshire, Derbyshire, and part of Lincoln; the Middle Angles of Leicester; and the Pecsetena of Derby. The Mercians acquired the southern part of their territory around Bedford and westward from the West Saxons. The Hwiccii of Gloucestershire and part of Worcestershire were also originally under Wessex. The Hecanas of Herefordshire, the Mægasetas of west Gloucestershire and part of Hereford, the Wrocensetnas and other tribes of Shropshire, were probably always Mercian. The Derbyshire people appear to have been annexed from Northumbria, as later on were the Lancashire people south of the Ribble. Under the year 941, as already mentioned, the Saxon Chronicle describes the Mercian boundaries as extending from Dore to Whitwell's Gate and the Humber—*i.e.*, from Dore Valley, in Herefordshire, to near Whitwell, north-east of Clitheroe, in Lancashire, and thence south and east to the Humber. The ancient Diocese of Lichfield, which also extended to the Ribble, appears to confirm this identification of the northwest extension of Mercia.

The river Trent was apparently a boundary between people of different tribes at the time of the settlement, and even at the present time a fairer population is found in Nottinghamshire and Derbyshire than in Leicestershire. The most probable view of the settlement of these parts is that the British people in the country north of this river—as far westward, at least, as Staffordshire, the Derbyshire mountains, and Cannock Chase—were expelled or enslaved by an extension of the settlers from what is now Yorkshire, or an extension up the Trent valley of the Gainas and Lindiswaras from North Lincolnshire. In this way it is probable that a compact Anglian State, which was at first dependent on Deira, was formed.[6] In any case, anthropological research has shown that both Derbyshire and Nottinghamshire have a population at the present time which is distinctly fairer than that of Leicestershire. Beddoe says of Derbyshire: 'The type of the population is certainly Anglian. My own observations, the military statistics, and those of the Anthropometric Committee, all agree in representing the Derbyshire people as having lighter hair than all but very few English counties. East Staffordshire is also very Anglian, but no wise Danish.'[7] It is in Staffordshire and the parts of other counties adjoining it on the west and south, of all the counties in England, that traces of any Danish or Norse settlements are the least.

One of the most interesting of the old frontiers in England is that between Northamptonshire and Oxfordshire. The former county was within the later Danelaw, the latter was not. The Danish territory, as settled between Alfred and Guthrum, had Watling Street for its boundary north of Stony Stratford. As extended a century later, it included the counties of Northampton, Buckingham, Middlesex, and Hertford. There must have been a reason for this extension of Danish law over the parts of Northampton and Buckingham which are west of Watling Street, and this probably was the settlement of Danish subjects in these counties between the time of Alfred and the end of the Danish rule in England. They were forest counties, and Danes were probably given settlements in them. The old place-names in the south parts of Northamptonshire bear witness to this. We find Aynho, Farthingho or Faringho, Furtho, Grimsbury, Overthorp, Astrop, Warkworth, Thorpe, Byfield, Abthorp, Wicken, Badby, Barby, Farendone, Ravensthorp, Kingsthorp, Catesby, Kilsby, and other characteristic Scandian names. On the Oxfordshire side of this frontier names of this kind are scarcely met with. The names ending in -o may be compared with those still in use in Norway, where they are very numerous. This Scandian settlement in the south-west of Northamptonshire was probably a late one. This extension of the Danelaw frontier is significant of a change in the general population, as is also the circumstance that as late as the time of the Domesday Survey payments to the royal revenue from this county were made in Danish money, twenty silver pennies being reckoned to the ora. The survival of the custom of inheritance by the eldest daughter in the absence of sons at Middleton Cheney,[8] in the south-west of the county, is confirmatory evidence of Norse colonists.

In Northamptonshire we find also a trace of the Frisians, under the Northern name Hocings, in the name of the Domesday hundred Hocheslau.

There are reasons for believing that Northamptonshire was partly occupied by immigrants into it from the north-east, as well as others from the south-west. Sternberg, who wrote many years ago on its dialect and folklore, says that two distinct and opposite modes of speech may be observed among the rurul population of the two extremities of the county.[9] This immigration from two directions would probably be up the river valleys from the Wash, and along the Roman roads from the south and west. Among its immigrants, earlier or later, some Wends must have been included. It has already been pointed out that in the old place-names Wendlingbury, or Wendlesberie and Wansford, also called Wandlesworth,[10] in the Nen valley, we have traces of Wendish settlers, and these people have also apparently left other traces in the folk-lore. The most remarkable instance is that of the May-trees, which at the present time are such a characteristic custom in Russia. In Northamptonshire a young tree ten or twelve feet high used to be planted in some villages before every house on May Day, so as to appear as if growing.[11] This custom does not apparently prevail except in Slavonic counties, and where old Wendish settlements were made.

Another example of Northamptonshire folk-lore which points to Wendish influence is that concerning Bogie. This name in reference to a ghost is common, but in this county the word was used in a somewhat more personal sense. 'He caps Bogie' was a proverbial expression, often amplified to 'He caps Bogie, Bogie caps Redcap, and Redcap caps Nick.'[12] Boge is the Wendish equivalent for a god, and the word is common in Slavonic languages for a deity. Northamptonshire being within the later Danelaw, the old dialect, in common with that of the East Midland counties, points to a Danish influence. In these counties the Southern expressions 'I be,' 'we be,' etc., are not heard; but 'I are' for 'I am,' analogous to the Danish *jeg er*, is not uncommon. Sternberg says that 'he are' for 'he is,' analogous to the Danish *han er*, was used in north and east Northamptonshire.[13] When Sternberg wrote, the legend of

209

the Wild Hunt had not quite died out in this county. In Pomerania and Mecklenburg, Wode (Woden) is said to be out hunting[14] when stormy winds blow through the woods, and formerly the wild huntsman was heard along the gloomy avenues of Whittlebury Forest.[15]

As mentioned in a previous chapter, the county of Buckingham shows traces of settlements by Northmen, Danes, and their allies, including Wends, in various parts of it. One of the historical facts bearing on this settlement is the Wendish connection of Cnut.[16] He was King of Vindland, as well as of Denmark, and Vindland was the name of Mecklenburg and Pomerania in the Old Norræna language. In the early part of the eleventh century, consequently, when England had a King who was also King of the Wends, it is certain that a considerable immigration of Danes and Wends into England took place. The formation by Cnut of the body of huscarls, many of whom were Wendish exiles from their native land, is historical. In the north of Buckinghamshire the name Wendover, which still survives, is suggestive of some Wendish connection with that part of the county, and Domesday Book contains other similar names, among which are Weneslai, now Winslow, and Wandene. The same record tells us that in the time of King Edward the manors of Senelai, Achecote, Stanes, Hamescle, Haiscote, and Lauendene, had all been held by huscarls of King Edward, who had continued the body of men Cnut had established. The land they occupied appears to have been held by huscarl service, for in one instance Domesday Book tells us it was held by one described as son of a huscarl. It is worth noting also that the name Lauendene, now Lavendon, closely resembles the Wendish name of Lauenberg, and that Lauendene was held by a huscarl in King Edward's time.

In the Anglo-Saxon Chronicle, Buckingham is written Buccinga-ham, a name clearly referring to a kindred called Buccings. A pagus of a similar name is also known, that of the Bucki in Saxony, mentioned in the time of Charlemagne.[17] This or another pagus of the same name is mentioned as the 'Bucki, pagus Angariorum' in the eighth century.[18] The Angarians of the Carlovingian period are the same as the Angrivarii mentioned by Tacitus, who pressed upon and well-nigh exterminated the Boructarii in the Engern district, which lies between Westphalia and Hanover—i.e., the country anciently known as Ostphalia.[19] By looking at a map of Germany, we shall see that this 'Bucki, pagus Angariorum' must have been located not far from Brunswick, and near the western border of the more extended Saxony of the eighth century. Tacitus says the Angrivarii were an intrusive people, and as the advance in his time was from the east, they probably came from that direction, as their name still lingers in the old Wendish parts of Germany. The places whose names begin with the word *Buk-* are almost all, as far as Germany is concerned, found in its eastern or ancient Slavic parts.[20] Some are also found in the Slavic parts of Austria. West of the Elbe, Buchau is the name of a suburb of Magdeburg in Prussian Saxony, a district which was close to, or within, the ancient Slav frontier. It must therefore be allowed that the evidence, both ancient and modern, which connects the name of the people known as the Bucki with the old country of the Wends in Eastern Germany is by no means slight.

The traces of people of different tribes which the Domesday names in Hertfordshire and Buckinghamshire exhibit are of interest. Danais and Daneslai, in Hertfordshire, point in all probability to Danish settlements, while Wenriga and Wenrige probably denote Wendish people.

The fact already mentioned that there is in Buckinghamshire a higher percentage of brunettes at the present time shows that there was some unusual element among the people.

In Bedfordshire there were at the time of the Survey two hundreds which had the significant names Weneslai and Wilga. It is difficult to see how they could have arisen except from settlements of people with Wendish names. The name Wilga seems to denote a community of the Wilte or Wiltzi, the largest known tribe of the Wends.

Among the old Mercian shires, Bedfordshire and Buckinghamshire are remarkable for the various kinds of land tenure which prevailed in them at the close of the Saxon period. In the former there were land-holders who could let their land to whom they pleased, others who could sell their land, others who could both let and sell, and others who could neither let nor sell without license from the superior lord. Some tenants in these counties were very differently circumstanced in other respects in regard to the land they held, the privileges they enjoyed, or the obligations they were under, and these facts point to differences in tribal custom extending back to an early period.

The Anglo-Saxon names Huntandune and Huntedune,[21] for Huntingdon, like that of Buckingham, were probably given to it from the name of the head or chief of its original family community. There was a pagus of the Huntanga known in Frisia in the eighth century.[22] The eastern part of Gröningen in Holland appears to have been its western boundary, and the river Hunte, a branch of the Weser, to be a survival of this tribal name. As the evidence of the settlement of Frisians in England is unshakable, and the Huntanga were a Frisian tribe, the old name Huntandun may reasonably be connected with it, as derived from a settler of that tribe with his family or kindred.

There are traces of Frisians to be found in Hertfordshire and the valley of the Lea. Such names as Broccesborne (now Broxbourne), Brockhall, and Brockmans, an ancient manor connected with North Mimms,[23] suggest the settlement of Frisian Brockmen; and those of Cockernoe, Cochehamsted, an old part of Braughing, and Hockeril, close to Bishop's Stortford, suggest similar settlements of Chaucians or Hocings; while Honesdon, or Hunsdon, is suggestive of a settler of the Hunni tribe. The parish of St. Margaret, near Ware, was formerly known as Theele,[24] which, like Mimms and others, are manorial names suggestive of Frisian origin. Like the custom on the Theellands in part of Frisia, that of inheritance by the youngest son has survived until modern time at Much Hadham and at Cheshunt in this county.[25]

Although we cannot trace the survival of junior inheritance over any considerable districts in the Midlands, as we can in Sussex, and some counties on the eastern or south-western coasts, yet examples of its existence have been found in a few manors of nearly all the old Mercian shires. It may have existed among copyholders in other manors only known locally. Elton says that although in the Midland counties it is comparatively rare, yet it has been found at the rate of about two or three manors to a county.[26] From its survival on a comparatively large scale in some of the maritime counties and on numerous manors around London, and its rarity in the Midlands, we appear justified in drawing the conclusion that this custom, as it existed in England, was brought by maritime settlers, and that, as some of their descendants migrated farther inland, they carried it with them. In Huntingdonshire borough-English was the customary law of inheritance at Gumecester, or Godmanchester,[27] and at Eynesbury.[28] The name Gumecester, or Gumycester, may be traced to the Gothic *guma* (a man), so that the settlement of northern Goths at Godmanchester, close to Huntingdon, appears to be shown by both its ancient and modern names. Some of their allies who settled there with them may have brought in the junior right.

In the custom that prevailed at Godmanchester we appear to have an example of the blending of those of two races—viz.: (1) That in favour of the youngest son, which was not Anglian; (2) that in favour of males in preference to females, which was Anglian. By the laws of the Continental Anglians, males were preferred to females as far as the fifth generation. The custom of Godmanchester provided 'that if a man have two sons by his wife, and one of these have an heir masculine and the other an heir feminine, and if after these sons do depart and die, the father of them being alive, and after it chances the father of them do die, then the same heir masculine shall be the heir, and not the heir feminine, though she be of the younger son.'[29]

In the manor of Liddington-cum-Caldecot, in Rutland, the junior inheritance custom that prevailed was that the land descended to the youngest son, and if no son, to the daughters in parcenary.[30]

At Kimbolton the custom in regard to succession was division among the sons, the whole estate being kept together under one, as the nominal head. This was a family or tribal arrangement, the parage or parcenery tenure. The Domesday account tells us that the manor was held by six socmen—Alwold and his five brothers[31]—and the entry probably points to descendants of Northmen of some tribe who had retained a custom of their forefathers. Two of the hamlets at Kimbolton bore the names of Wormedik and Akermanni, as shown by the Hundred Rolls, both apparently of northern origin.

The chief districts in the midland counties where partible inheritance prevailed were the soke of Rothley in Leicestershire, and the soke of Oswaldbeck[32] in Nottinghamshire. The continuance of the custom to modern time shows that it must have been of immemorial usage to have satisfied the courts of the twelfth century, when primogeniture had become the general law. Oswaldbeck soke comprised the area of country in the north-east of Nottingham between the river Idle and the Trent. The soke was a separate administration, and apparently was bounded on the south by places now called

East and West Markham. It comprised the old Domesday manors of Sutton, Lound, Madressi, Crophill, Laneham, Ascham, Bolun, Bertun, Waterlege, Leverton, North Muskham, and Scrobi. Most of these old manors can still be identified, but the district contains at the present time many newer villages and hamlets. The old list shows which places in the district were probably settled first. The custom of partible inheritance in Oswaldbeck was limited to males,[33] whereas that of Rothley in Leicestershire provided for the inheritance to be divided among daughters in default of sons.[34] This latter custom points to Goths and Frisians, while that of Oswaldbeck points to Angles or Saxons, among whom male inheritance was the rule. The country of the South Humbrians, or Ambrones, a tribe of Old Saxons, may have included Oswaldbeck.

In reference to the missionary works of Paulinus or one of his contemporaries among these people, Nennius tells us that he was engaged for forty days in baptising the Ambrones.[35] As they were in all probability a tribe of Old Saxons, the statement must refer to some of them who had settled in England, and had brought their tribal name from the borderland of Frisia and Old Saxony. The old name for the river Ems, as already mentioned, was Emmer or Ambra; the country near the Humber was Ymbraland, and an old Continental tribe called the Ymbre is mentioned in the 'Traveller's Song.'[36] Under the year 697, there is a reference in the Anglo-Saxon Chronicle to the South Humbrians, and there are traditions of Paulinus baptising in the river Trent. In Derbyshire there is, or was, a river named the Amber, from which Ambergate takes its name.[37] The thirteenth-century records show also that there was a place named Ambresbur' in Derbyshire, and another of the same name in Nottinghamshire.[38] These old names and the circumstances mentioned appear to denote that the settlements of the tribe called Ambrones extended to some parts of these counties.

In the borough of Nottingham two ancient customs of succession at one time prevailed, those connected with its English and French inhabitants, respectively called by the Norman-French names Burgh Engloyes and Burgh Frauncoyes. The borough-English custom by which the youngest son succeeded also prevailed at Southwell,[39] which was a soke having twelve berewicks, or subordinate manors, belonging to the Archbishop of York, at the time of the Domesday Survey. Its connection with that See was very ancient, going back to the early days of Christianity in York. Here it should be noted that the custom at Southwell was different from that of Oswaldbeck, the Archbishop's extensive district in the north of the county. It also differed from the general custom which prevailed on that prelate's Yorkshire land. It could not, therefore, have been owing to uniformity of tenure on those lands that junior right prevailed and survived at Southwell. The custom was continued probably because it was the custom of the early settlers at that place, and if so, it points to people of a different race or tribe to those in the soke of Oswaldbeck—to some tribal allies of the early Angles or later Danes.

In Leicestershire the Domesday place-name Brochesbi may refer to the by or settlement whose chief was one Broche, so named from being either a Frisian of the Brocman tribe, or possibly a Boructer of the tribe of the Boructware, from whom, Bede tells us, some of the English of his time were known to have descended. In Leicestershire, also, the Domesday place Frisebi must have been the settlement of a Frisian, as Hunecote probably was of a Hunsing named Hune; Osgodtorp was the thorp of Osgod—i.e., an Eastern Goth; Suevesbi that of one of the Suevi, and Saxebi that of a Saxon, the early settlers from whom the places originally derived their names being probably so named in each case after the name of their tribe or nation. The Domesday name Cuchenai, in Nottinghamshire, points to one or more settlers of the Chaucian tribe, and may be compared with that of Cuxhaven at the mouth of the Elbe, which has come down to us in the old Chaucian country itself.

Such old place-names as these in parts of the old kingdom of Mercia show that among the so-called Angles that settled in the Mercian States there must have been people of other tribes. The Angles of these States may have been more Germanic than those of Northumbria. That there were differences is certain from the large number of runic inscriptions on monuments in the northern counties, while only two appear to have been discovered in the Mercian shires—viz., at Bakewell in Derbyshire,[40] and at Cleobury Mortimer in Shropshire.[41]

The old Mercian counties present a remarkable contrast in the manner in which the original homesteads of the settlers were arranged. In the east midland counties villages of collected homesteads must have very largely prevailed, for this is the common type of village met with in these counties. The old villages with the homesteads more or less collected always was the system in these shires since the coming of the Anglo-Saxon people. They are especially noticeable in Northamptonshire, Leicestershire, Huntingdonshire, Bedfordshire, and Buckinghamshire, and they may be commonly seen to have roads leading to them from various directions, originally the ways from the villages to the common fields that lay around them. At the beginning of the nineteenth century 130,000 acres in Huntingdonshire, out of a total of 240,000, were open commonable lands,[42] chiefly pasture. On the other hand, in the west midland counties, such as Gloucestershire, Worcestershire, and Shropshire, the old Celtic arrangement of isolated homesteads has survived much more largely, especially in the vale of the Severn, and more particularly in the parts east of that river. The collected homestead system which now prevails over so large a part of Holstein is probably due to the survival of the Anglian type of village in one of the homelands of the Angles, and so many of the collected villages of the East Midland counties are probably survivals, in plan, of the Anglian immigrants.

As regards possible British survivals among the Anglo-Saxon people of the old Mercian shires, we must look for any traces of them, apart from the country along the Welsh border, in those districts which were chiefly characterized by forests and fens. In the fen district of Huntingdonshire we meet with traces of people of British descent as late as the beginning of the eleventh century, for the early historian of Ramsay alludes to 'Britones latrones,' or Welsh robbers, as still possible in that part of the country as late as the time of King Cnut.[43] The Fen country was long a stronghold of Britons, as of Anglo-Saxons after them.

There are incidental traces showing that during the Anglo-Saxon period some Wilisc men—*i.e.*, Welsh or British—lived in Mercia, as well as in Northumbria and Wessex. These were treated as strangers, and their wergeld was only half that of others of the same class. They were outside the kindred organization, so that in the case of crime being imputed to them they could only prove their innocence by the ordeal, the oaths of their family relations not being acceptable, as they were not accounted freemen.[44]

[1] Elton, C. I., 'Robinson on Gavelkind,' p. 66.

[2] Domesday Book, and Maitland, F. W., 'Domesday Book and Beyond,' 114.

[3] Anglo-Saxon Chronicle, A.D. 941.

[4] Réclus, E., 'Nouvelle Géographie Universelle,' v. 25, quoting Schiern, 'Om Slaviscke Stednavne.'

[5] Beddoe, J., 'Races of Britain,' p. 24.

[6] Beddoe, J., *loc. cit.*, p. 66.

[7] Beddoe, J., *loc. cit.*, p. 253.

[8] Elton and Mackay, 'Law of Copyholds,' 134.

[9] Sternberg, T., 'Dialect and Folk-Lore of Northamptonshire, ix.

[10] Camden, W., 'Britannia,' 1722,, Ed. by Gibson, 192.

[11] Frazer, J. G., 'The Golden Bough,' 1890 Ed., i. 75.

[12] Sternberg, T., *loc. cit.*, 128.

[13] Bonaparte, Prince Louis L., 'English Dialects,' *Philol. Soc. Transactions*, 1875-1876, p. 573.

[14] Wagner, W., 'Asgard and the Gods,' 71, 72.

[15] Sternberg, T., *loc. cit.*, 131.

[16] Seebohm, F., 'Tribal Custom in Anglo-Saxon Law,' 34.

[17] Monumenta Germaniæ, Scriptores i. 155.

[18] *Ibid.*, 154, 155.

[19] Latham, R. G., 'Handbook of the English Language,"24-26.

[20] Rudolph, H., 'Orts Lexicon von Deutschland.'

[21] Codex Dipl., 575, 579.

[22] Monumenta Germaniæ, Annales Weissem., A.D. 781.

[23] Chauncy, Sir H., 'Historical Antiquities of Hertfordshire,' p. 530.

[24] *Ibid.*, p. 284.

[25] *Notes and Queries*, Seventh Series, ix. 206.

[26] Elton, C. I., 'Origins of English History,' p. 184.

[27] Fox, R., 'History of Godmanchester,' p. 92.

[28] Hundred Rolls, ii. 669.

[29] Fox, R., *loc. cit.*, p. 94.

[30] Elton, C. I., 'The Law of Copyholds,' 130.

[31] Domesday Book, i. 206.

[32] Elton, C. I., 'Gavelkind,' 32.

[33] Elton, C. I., 'Gavelkind,' 32.

[34] *Archæologia*, xlvii. 97.

[35] Nennius, 'Historia Britomim,' i. 117.

[36] Latham, R. G., 'Germania of Tacitus,' Epil. cix.

[37] *Derbyshire Archæol. and Nat. Hist. Soc.*, ii. 33.

[38] Placita de quo warranto, pp. 154, 659, Calendar.

[39] Elton, C. I., 'Gavelkind.'
[40] Stephens, G., 'Old Northern Runic Monuments,' i. 373.
[41] *Ibid.*, iii. 160.

[42] Maine, Sir H., 'Village Communities,' 88, 89.
[43] Freeman, E. A., 'Norman Conquest,' i. 477, note.
[44] Seebohm, F., *loc. cit.*, 403, 499.

# Chapter Twenty-Two - Settlements in the South-Western Counties

WE can trace the expansion of the older settlements in the south-western counties. Somersetshire obtained its name from its original settlers, the Sumersætas. These, as the name implies, probably first formed summer settlements on its marshes, hill pastures, and in its forests. To have used these parts of the county for summer purposes at first the Sumersætas must have come almost wholly from Wiltshire and Dorset. Their pasturage places were probably of the same kind as the Scandinavian sæters or summer pasture houses, often many miles from the permanent homesteads, are at the present time. As the population increased the summer settlements became permanent, and in various portions of the country, as in the Vale of Taunton, immigrants from more distant parts were no doubt located. Somerset was not conquered by the West Saxons until after their conversion to Christianity, or at least until subsequently to the conversion of the royal house. This probably explains the continuous existence of Glastonbury and its abbey from the British period into that of the Saxons. A fusion of some of the British people with the Saxons went on in this county, and in this the influence of the abbey, whose estates were apparently—at least,in part—confirmed to it, must have been very considerable. This fusion probably explains Beddoe's conclusion that 'almost everywhere in Somerset the index of nigrescence is greater than in Wiltshire or in Gloucestershire east of the Severn.'[1]

It is of some interest to note that among the early settlers in Somerset there were colonists from Sussex. In the great manor of Taunton Dean the customs which prevailed were almost identical with those in the Rape of Lewes. This great liberty in Somerset resembled in its constitution a Sussex rape in containing hundreds within it. These hundreds were Holwey, Hull, Nailsborne, Staplegrove, Taunton Borough, and Taunton Castle.[2]

The chief customs of the tenants within the barony of Lewes and within the manor of Taunton Dean may be compared under the following heads,[3] in which they were practically the same:

1. The tenants were able to alienate their land, and so to dispose of it by a process of surrender in court, and this privilege extended in both districts to parcels of the land as well as the whole.

2. The lands passed from a tenant to his heir at his death.

216

3. By the custom both at Lewes and at Taunton the widow inherited the estate for her life. She was admitted for life by the court.

4. On both manors if the husband made a surrender in favour of some other person than his wife, even if done on his deathbed before legal witnesses, the widow lost her right to succeed.

5. The guardianship of infant heirs, at Lewes and at Taunton, was, by the custom of both places, entrusted to one or more of the next of the infant's kindred, to whom the land could not descend.

6. By the custom of both manors the youngest son succeeded to the estate, and if there was no son, the youngest daughter. If there were no children, the estate was similarly inherited by the youngest relative collaterally.

7. The customary tenants on both manors had to keep their houses and other customary tenements in repair.

8. The tenants on both manors were unable to let or farm their copyholds for a longer time than a year and a day without license from their lord's court.

9. The customary tenants both at Lewes and Taunton were required to do their suit at the lord's court held from three weeks to three weeks. There were also similar regulations by which defaulters were essoyned or fined.

10. A reeve was appointed in every manor of the barony of Lewes and in every hundred of the manor of Taunton Dean to collect the rents and to act as the lord's immediate officer.

When we consider that junior inheritance and the other customs incidental thereto were not part of the common law of the country, but prevailed only in certain districts, having apparently come down from very ancient time, the similarity of these customs must be allowed to be very remarkable indeed.

The earliest historical references to Taunton connect it with Sussex. The conquest of the country around it was effected by Ine, King of Wessex, in alliance with his kinsman Nunna. This, the Anglo-Saxon Chronicle tells us, took place in the year 710, when Ine and Nunna fought against Gerent, King of the Welsh. In a charter of a later date Nunna styles himself 'King of the South Saxons.'

The Chronicle tells us also that in the year 722 Queen Æthelburh, wife of Ine, destroyed Taunton, which her husband had built. It was probably owing to disloyalty or rebellion by the colonists from Sussex that this destruction was necessary. This event agrees exactly in date with that of Ine's war against his former allies the South Saxons. It is difficult to see why it became necessary to destroy Taunton during a South Saxon war unless there had been a South Saxon colony in and around it. On the very probable supposition that the people in and around that town took part against Wessex in the South Saxon war its destruction becomes intelligible. It is difficult to see how the remarkable similarity in the customs of the people around Lewes and Taunton can be explained except by a South Saxon migration. It is difficult also to see why Taunton should have been destroyed in 722 except as part of the military operations of a South Saxon war.

The evidence which appears to connect the settlers around Lewes with the Wendish Lutitzer or Wilte tribe has been stated, and whether a coincidence or not, we find a place named Wilton was an old suburb of Taunton.[4] The Saxon charters[5] also tell us of a stream named Willite and of a place named Ruganbeorh, or Ruwanborg, apparently named after one or more settlers of Rugian descent, in the Vale of Taunton. The old place-names of Somerset afford traces of settlers of various races: Godeneie[6] and Gateneberghe[7] are apparently old names denoting Goths or Geats—i.e., Jutes. Godeworth,[8] Godecumbe, Guttona,[9] and Godele[10] point also to settlers of the same name and probably the same race.

The hundred of Winterstoke, named after a decayed village so called, was one of the old hundreds of the county extending along the coast from Clevedon to Weston-super-Mare, and inland to Axbridge. On the north this hundred adjoined that of Portbury, which contained the district known now as Gordano. In the north-east of Somerset a range of hills extending generally from east to west finds its western termination near Clevedon. From this place another hilly ridge stretches along the coast in a north-easterly direction and ends at Portishead. The intermediate country between these ranges has been known for many centuries as Gardinu' or Gordano. The name appears in the records in the thirteenth century, where it is stated that certain land in Gardinu' was held at a quarter of a knight's fee.[11] Later on we find a record of Edmund Mortimer, Earl of March, holding the manor of Easton in Gordon in the time of Henry VI.,[12] and others stating that Emma Neuton held the manor of Walton in Gordano, and that Richard Percyvale held Weston in Gordano, both in the time of Edward IV.[13] This district is separated by the river Avon from Gloucestershire, and among the thirteenth-century list of land-holders in that county was Thomas de Gardino, who held a knight's fee in Side and Gardino.[14]

As we stand on the hills near Weston in Gordano the Steep Holme and Flat Holme may be seen rising above the water of the Bristol Channel, and on the coast near by are places called Blacknore and Capenore. All these are certainly Danish place-names. When we consider the strong evidence which exists of Scandinavian settlements on the Somerset coast and up the Wye and Severn, it does not appear unreasonable to connect this Gordano district with the Danes, and more particularly with that tribe of them known as the Gardene or Gardanes mentioned in Beowulf. Four places at the present time— viz., Easton, Weston, Walton, and Clapton—have 'in Gordano' attached to their names, the district name being evidently an old territorial one.

The name Winterstoke may have been connected with this Danish settlement, and derived from Winthr or Windr settlers, or Wends, who were allies of the Danes. In such a settlement some dialect of the Old Danish tongue, in which Wends were called Windr, would certainly be spoken.

The country around Glastonbury was not added to the West Saxon kingdom until the time of Cenwealh, who in 658 extended his frontier as far as the Parret. He, a Christian King of the Gewissas, began to build at Winchester the old church of St. Peter on the site probably of the present cathedral. His successor, Centwine, drove the Welsh to the sea in 682, and added the Quantock district to his kingdom. Thus, before the end of the seventh century Saxon Christians were settled in parts of Somerset. We cannot doubt that the profession of a religion common to both races must have had a great influence in preventing a war of extermination in this county. Then, no doubt, began that blending of the two races which can be traced by ethnological observation in the county at the present day. Fair and dark haired people may be observed among the natives in almost every village.

The dialect of Somerset, and particularly that of the western part of the county, points to a commingling of different tribal people among the original settlers. In the west, Elworthy has found eight forms of plural terminations, and in a small district containing two or three villages, among which is Kingsbury, the word *utch* for *I* is still used.[15] The use of this word *utch* or *itch* as a survival of the Anglo-Saxon *ic* for *I* was formerly common in the dialect of various parts of the county. The dialect of west Somerset thus clearly points to colonists of various origins.

The ancient ports of Somerset were Watchet and Portlock, and through them we may trace the immigration of early settlers, among whom probably came the colony from Sussex. One of the peculiarities of the settlement of the south-western counties is the evidence pointing to the establishment of colonies on the coasts before the occupation of the interior of these counties or the subjugation of the whole British population within them. Beddoe's researches have shown that a population much fairer than that in the interior exists along the Devonshire coast.[16]

At Exeter the custom of partible inheritance prevailed, the estate of the father being divided among both sons and daughters. This might well have been brought there by a colony of Goths and Frisians, as the custom can be traced among both these ancient races. This could not have been a British survival, for in Wales daughters had no share in the paternal estate.

There are in Cornwall traces of Norwegian settlements in the survival on some manors of the custom by which in default of sons the eldest daughter succeeded to the whole estate. In Cornwall, also, the ancient divisions were called shires instead of hundreds, corresponding to the names used in those parts of the northern counties where Scandinavians settled, and to the names of ancient divisions in Norway itself, which were also called shires.

The settlements that were formed on the south-western coasts of England resembled on the one hand those early colonies of Teutonic people on the southern and eastern coasts in the earliest Anglo-Saxon period, and on the other the later settlements of maritime people, including Danes and Northmen, on the coasts of Wales. The existence of colonies of Saxons on the eastern coasts before the end of the Roman rule can scarcely be open to doubt, from the historical mention of the Saxon shore and the ethnological evidence afforded by the people of the maritime parts of north-eastern France at the present time, the coast of which had a similar name. Similarly, some of the coast settlements of the south-western parts of England were probably of the nature of migrations from Kent and Sussex, in association with people of the same racial descent from Northern Europe. It must be remembered that the maritime skill of the people of the east coast of Kent and East Sussex appears always to have been great. They were the ancestors of the people of the Cinque Ports, and by them communications with the Continent during the Saxon period must have been largely maintained. When a migration became necessary for such a population, a maritime colony would naturally suggest itself, in which people of the same races would also probably take part. At the time of the Domesday Survey the burgesses of Dover by old custom supplied the King with twenty ships for fifteen days in the year, each with twenty-one men, and they did this because he had released to them his sake and soke.[17] The maritime facilities of the Kent and Sussex ports must have been formerly relatively great.

In the west of England we can trace the probability of Kentish settlers by the survival here and there of the custom of dividing the lands among all the sons, although the divided parts were taxed collectively, and by the survival here and there of the name Kent. Kent is written in Domesday Book as Chent, and in the same record we find Chent, now Kenn, Chentone,now Kenton, and Chentesbere, now Kentisbear in Devonshire. In the Exon Domesday, Kenn on the Somerset coast, is also written Chent,[18] and Kentisbere is written Chentesberia. Caninganmærsces is mentioned as an old name for the Kentish marshes, and Caninganmærsces in Somerset as an old name for Cannington Marshes.[19]

It is difficult to see how these coincidences can be explained except on the supposition of Kentish settlements. Among other Kent names in Devon are those of Kent's Cave at Torquay, and Kentsmoor, near Honiton. The place-name Hengestecote, in the parish of Bradford,[20] Devon, occurs in Domesday Book, and Kentish people, or Jutes and Frisians, are the only races whose history and traditions tell us of Hengist, or among whom the personal name of the hero would be likely to survive. There was probably an early settlement at Crediton, as shown by the birth of Winfrith, the missionary Bishop of Germany, better known as Boniface, at that place in the seventh century.

That the early colonies of Teutonic people on the south Devon coast appear to have been either migrations from Kent or settlements of people of the same race as the Jutes—*i.e.*, Goths and Frisians—is supported by the survival of the custom of gavelkind in Exeter and Totnes,[21] by the names of settlers in the district around Honiton, of the Hunni tribe of Frisians, mentioned by Bede as among the ancestors of the English race, and by the survival of the Kentish name in certain places along the Devon coast. As regards the custom of partible inheritance at Exeter, it was the Kentish custom, under which daughters divided the patrimony if there were no sons, and not the Welsh, under which they had no inheritance. This is a remarkable fact, and the prevalence of the gavelkind custom also at Totnes adds to its significance. The custom of the Goths and Frisians in respect to inheritance extended the shares to daughters as well as to sons, as previously mentioned.

In a grant by King Æthelstan in A.D. 938[22] to Earl Æthelstan of land at Lyme Regis, which is not far from Honiton, the name Huneford occurs as one of the boundaries. The Saxon names Hunespil, Honelanda, Honechercha, and Honessam, also, are met with in the Exon Domesday record. The Domesday name Hunitone for Honiton can scarcely have come from any other source than the head of a family named Huni, of the Hunni tribe, or from a kindred of Hunni or Frisian Hunsings. Another Domesday name in Devon is Frisehã, or Friseham, which appears to have been derived from the home of an original Frisian settler. Similarly, the names Brocheland and Godescote probably denote a family of the Brocmen or Boructers and of Goths. Galmentone points to British people, Danescome to Danes, and Essemundehord[23] possibly to one or more Eastmen. There are also names in the Exon Domesday which point to the settlement in Devonshire of other Danish allies from some of the tribal people of the Baltic. Weringehorda and Wereingeurda appear to be named after one or more families of Warings, and the place-name Wedreriga, which is found in the same record, similarly denotes people from the Wedermark—*i.e.*, Ostrogoths from the east of Lake Wetter in Sweden. The Anglo-Saxon Curi names in Somerset—Curi and Curesrigt, and Curylond, and Curymele, as well as others of the same kind in Cornwall, derived, apparently, from settlers' names, are peculiar among English place-names, and may reasonably be connected with the Curones or Curlanders, who were allies of Danes and Northmen[24] in some of their wars, and may have had representatives among Danish settlers in England.

The earliest settlements of Devonshire and Cornwall were probably all formed from the sea. In this they differed from Somerset, where the parts adjoining to Wilts and Dorset most likely received their earliest permanent colonists from the Wilsætas and Thornsætas of Wilts and Dorset. The Devonshire settlements began on the coast like the earlier ones of Kent, Sussex, and Wessex. It is no doubt owing to this that the Devon people along the south coast and banks of the navigable rivers are of fairer complexion at the present time than the people of the interior.[25]

Of all the south-western counties, Devonshire and Cornwall afford perhaps the best example of the blending of the Teutonic and Celtic races. Herefordshire and Shropshire afford similar examples on the border of Wales. The old Cornish people differed from the Welsh in being probably of a darker complexion, owing to their descent more largely from an ancient darker stock. The same process that went on in Devon and Cornwall went on, apparently, in South Wales, but with a difference. In the south-western counties the Teutonic element absorbed the Celtic to a great extent. In South Wales the Teutonic element was to some extent absorbed in the Celtic. There is a considerable percentage of people in Cornwall who have red hair, and among the country people of South Wales there are some with red hair. It is certain that this is not a common characteristic of either the Cornish or the Welsh. It probably came in through settlers of another race in each case.

The custom of junior right prevailed on the three manors of Braunton, near Barnstaple. The place was no doubt originally one settlement, and the Domesday name Brungarstone may refer to it. In the mediæval period it became parcelled out, apparently, into three manors, all having the same custom of inheritance. The widow of a tenant had her customary dower of the whole of her husband's land for her life, if she remained chaste and single, and the youngest son succeeded. If there were no sons, the daughters shared equally.[26] This custom was not Welsh; it was not Saxon or Jutish; it was not Anglian. Unless the settlers at Braunton invented it—a most unlikely proceeding—they must have brought it with them, and as it did not prevail among the Britons or Scandinavians, or generally among the Frisians, it must have been brought into Devonshire by Wendish settlers, or perhaps in this instance by settlers from the hinterland of Frisia, or by a migration from the vale of Taunton. The common name, used locally, of Barum for Barnstaple,[27] points, in reference to the common Frisian termination -um, to Frisian settlers in this neighbourhood.

Of all the counties in England at the present time, Cornwall has the darkest people. Its pre-Saxon inhabitants do not appear to have been all of one race. Some were descendants probably of the Neolithic or old Iberian stock, and some of the people of the Bronze Age. The former were long-headed; the latter were broad-headed. Beddoe recognises three race types among the Cornish people: (1) The Neolithic or Iberian; (2) the British or bronze broad-headed; (3) the Saxon or other Teutonic invaders. The physical type which struck his eye most in Cornwall was the first crossed by the second.[28] Topinard, who also made observations in Cornwall, found there many people of a fair, tall type, with blue eyes, blonde hair, and a reddish complexion.[29] These are clearly descendants from Teutonic or other settlers. A reddish complexion of some kind is, according to Ripley, one of the most general characters of the Slavs of Russia.[30] Beddoe says also of the blue eyes: 'I am not ready to admit that pure blue eyes are more common in the Teutonic than in the Slavonic or any other race.'[31] There is, however, another trace of this racial character among the Cornish people, which is locally connected with a settlement of Danes, and survives to the present time. In all the western parishes of Cornwall there has existed time out of mind a great antipathy to red-haired families, who are popularly supposed to be descendants of Danes, and, much to their own disgust, are often called Danes or Deanes. As late as 1870 this local prejudice came out in a magisterial inquiry at Penzance.[32]

The possibility that the Danes and Northmen who settled in parts of Cornwall had some Wendish allies among them finds support in the folk-lore of the county. Lach-Szyrma[33] has drawn attention to the remarkable resemblance that exists between Slavonic and Cornish folk-tales, and has mentioned instances in which practically the same superstitions and omens prevail. Some of these relate to witches, omens connected with luck, storm

222

myths, transfixing the fiend in mid air, the enchained spirit neither saved nor lost, the mermaid and the lady of the lake, the river claiming its yearly tribute of a life, etc. It is not improbable that these Cornish tales may have been introduced when the Scandinavians, who formed settlements on the coast, were in alliance with the Wends, as they were both before and during the time of Cnut. West Cornwall has apparently some traces of the mythology of these Wendish allies of the Danes. The Wendish word for Thursday is Perün-dan, after Perun, the thunder god, corresponding to the Norse Thor, and the Cornish place-name Mên Perhen and others may be traces of him.

Near Penzance, also, the Cornish black spirit of evil omen called Bucca, Bugga, or Buccaboo, is still remembered, and he may probably be traced to the old Slavic Boge, the general name for a deity, which after the Christian conversion became degraded to that of a hobgoblin. The most notable of the folk-tales common to Scandinavia and Pomerania on the one hand and to Cornwall on the other is probably that of 'Jack and the Beanstalk,' which is found with but slight variations, and does not appear to have been a native folk-tale in intervening countries. In Norway, the Cornish Jack the Giant-killer is also known.

The common personal names ending in -o among Cornish family names, such as Pasco, Jago, also point, apparently, to Scandinavian colonists.

The very old place-name Ruan, near the Lizard, is, of course, commonly derived from the saint so called, but, like some old names found in Anglo-Saxon charters, it is identical with the Latin Ruani used in old German records for the people of Rügen. The name of the Scilly Isles is Scandinavian, as is Grimsby, one of the places in the islands. St. Agnes, also, may not improbably be traced to Hagenes, a common name among the Norsemen.[34] The Devonshire names ending in -beer, such as Rockbeer, Houndsbeer, Aylesbeer, Lungabeer, are perhaps of Norse origin, derived from the Old Norræna word byr, corresponding to by, the ending so common in the Lincolnshire place-names.

Those tenants who are entitled to common rights on Dartmoor are known as Venville tenants. The ancient form of this name was Wengefield or Venge-field, and it was applied to those free settlers in the villages around Dartmoor who had summer pasture rights upon it. In Lincolnshire there are many fields known as the wong, the older form of which was wang, such as War-ing-wang and Quenildewang.[35] The Old Norse word 'vangr,' or 'vengi,' appears to denote an enclosure.[36] The word 'wang' or 'wong' for a field or plain may not improbably be traced to an old Northern dialect, and so be another trace of Scandinavian settlers in Devon.

The settlement of Danes and Northmen, probably in alliance with Wends or Frisians, in parts of Cornwall is shown by evidence of several kinds: (1) The Scandinavian place-names along the coast. Among these are Helston, which may have had some connection with a settler from Helsingland. All the chief harbours in Cornwall are or were anciently called havens, from the Danish havn—viz., Falmouth Haven, Helford Haven (leading to Helston),

Bude Haven, and Fowey Haven. (2) The survival here and there in Cornwall of certain customs of inheritance which are not Celtic. On the manor of Blisland the tenant's land, in default of sons, was inherited by the eldest daughter, a custom pointing to Norwegian settlers. On the other hand, at Helston the tenant's customary heir was the youngest son, which points either to Wendish settlers or some of the tribal Frisians. Frisic is an old place-name near the Lizard. (3) There is also the evidence of the remarkable parallelism between some of the folk-lore of Cornwall and that of Pomerania, which points to Wendish allies among the Norse settlers. (4) The existence of fair people at the present time among those descended from old Cornish families.

The ancient circles of stone in Cornwall have no counterpart in the purely Celtic districts of Wales, but very much resemble those in Scandinavia and the parts of Britain occupied by the Northern race. The remains of numerous small camps or earthworks for defensive purposes along the coasts of Devon and Cornwall, close to those rivers which might afford protection to the ships of an invader,[37] point to enemies by sea, as do similar earth-works on the coasts further eastward. The most remarkable of these in Devon is Grimspound, in the parish of Manaton, which is a curious amphitheatre having within it no fewer than twenty circles, none of them more than 5½ yards in diameter. At the present time two of these circles have stones set up as pillars on their circumferences—thirty-five in one and twenty-seven in the other.[38] All the circles appear to have originally had similar erect stones. The area of the whole enclosure is only 4 acres. This remarkable monument may mark the site of a Scandinavian battlefield. A battle is commemorated by a number of similar stone circles on Bravella Heath in Östergothland in Sweden.[39] At Mortura in Ireland, also, two battles in which Northmen, called in the Irish records Tuatha de Dananns, are said to have been engaged, are similarly commemorated by stones arranged in circles spread over a large area.[40]

There is evidence of early Scandinavians in Devon and Cornwall in the stones which have been discovered marked with ogham characters.[41] There is further evidence of these settlements in Cornwall in inscriptions in the Northern language which have been found. The discovery of a block known as a pig of tin, now in the Truro Museum, with a runic figure stamped on it, proves that among the metal-workers in that county during the Anglo-Saxon period there must have been some to whom the runic letters were known. The figure on this block is, Stephen says, a well-known character of the English type, and has the equivalence of the letters *st.*[42] It must be remembered, as already mentioned, that the Goths of Scandinavia, who first wrote in runic letters, were the most skilled metal-workers in Europe during the centuries immediately after the fall of the Roman Empire. Runic letters similar to those on the block of tin now at Truro have lately been discovered in an inscription found at Ödemotland in Norway, the identification of which was one of the last made by Stephens before his death.[43] Another discovery pointing to Scandinavians or their descendants in Cornwall is that of the inscribed slab found at Lanteglos between Bodmin and Camelford, and now, or lately, in the rectory grounds at Lanteglos. It is not in runic letters, but in an old dialect resembling a Scandian dialect, and identified by Stephens as about A.D. 1100 in date.[44]

There can therefore be no doubt that people speaking dialects of the Old Norræna or Danish language were settled in isolated colonies at an early period on the coasts of the south-western counties, or that in the tenth century, when King Edgar ordered his laws 'to be common to all the people, whether English, Danes, or Britons, on every side of my dominions,' he had in view these maritime settlements in the south as well as the great Danish settlements in the north and east.

The arrangement of the homesteads over a great part of the south-western counties, more particularly in the hilly parts, is even at the present time largely that of isolated farms and hamlets. This is probably a survival of that of the Celtic tribesmen,[45] who had both permanent and temporary homesteads, feeding their herds in summer on the higher ranges of the hills and in winter in the villages, as is the case in the Highlands of Scotland and in Switzerland. The same homestead arrangement prevails in Scandinavia.

The settlement of the south-western counties was accompanied by a migration of some British people, and perhaps by a reflux of descendants of the same race. As Wales was the refuge of those who were driven from the old homes in the midland counties, and Cumberland their refuge in the north, so there is both historical and archæological evidence that Brittany received Celtic refugees from probably the south-western parts of Britain. We are told that 'Britons who dwelt as early as the sixth century beyond the sea were passing over into Lesser Britain'—*i.e.*, Brittany.[46] At that time Armorica, although diminished from its ancient extent, still existed as a separate State, extending as far south as Nantes.[47] There is evidence in relation to South Wales, as will be stated in the next chapter, to show that some very early Teutonic settlements were established in Pembrokeshire, and equally early colonies may have been formed on the south-west coast of England. Ermold, a French monk who wrote in the early part of the ninth century, records the arrival in Brittany of Britons fleeing from their Teutonic enemies,[48] and he lived sufficiently near to the time in which this migration is said to have occurred for the traditions concerning it to have been local history when he visited Armorica in 824. In connection with this migration, we must consider also the interesting contemporary statement of Asser, that in King Alfred's time Armoricans were among those people of foreign birth who voluntarily placed themselves under his rule. In Alfred's time some of the descendants of the former British refugees may well have returned, and if so, the south-western counties probably received them.

[1] Beddoe, J., 'Races in Britain,' 258.

[2] Shillibeer, H. B., 'History of the Manor of Taunton Dean,' Appendix, xxvii.

[3] *Ibid.*, pp. 31-67, and Horsfield, T. W., 'History of Lewes,' 178, 179.

[4] Collinson, J., 'History of Somersetshire,' iii. 294.

[5] Codex Dipl., Nos. 1052, 1083.

[6] *Ibid.*, Nos. 73 and 567.

[7] Collinson, J., *loc. cit.*, iii. 61.

[8] Taxatio Eccl. P. Nich., 179.

[9] Testa de Nevill, 416.

[10] Domesday Book.

[11] Testa de Nevill, 159*b*.

[12] Cal. Inq. Post-mortem, iv. 85.

[13] *Ibid.*, iv. 311, 374.

[14] Testa de Nevill, 82

[15] Elworthy, F. T., 'Grammar of the Dialect of West Somerset,' p. 34.

[16] Beddoe, J., *loc. cit.*, p. 258.

[17] Maitland, F. W., 'Domesday Book and Beyond,' p. 209.

[18] Exon Domesday, p. 132.

[19] Camden, 'Britannia,' edited by Gough, i. cx.

[20] Cal. Close Rolls, 1323-1327, p. 597.

[21] *Devonshire Association, Report and Trans.*, vol. xii., 193, quoting Hoker's MS.

[22] Cart. Sax., ii. 438.

[23] Dom. Bk., Index.

[24] Saxo Grammaticus.

[25] Beddoe, J., *loc. cit.*, p. 49.

[26] *Devonshire Association, Report and Transactions*, xx. 278, 255.

[27] Gribble, J. B., 'Memorials of Barnstaple,' pp. 1, 2.

[28] Beddoe, J., *Journal of the Anthropological Inst.*, New Series, i. 328.

[29] *Ibid.*, i. 329, quoted by Beddoe.

[30] Ripley, W. Z., 'Races of Europe,' 346, 361.

[31] Beddoe, J., 'Races of Britain,' p. 76.

[32] Bottrell, W., 'Traditions of West Cornwall,' 148.

[33] Lach-Szyrma, W. S., *Folk-Lore Record*, iv. 52.

[34] Streatfield, G. S., 'Lincolnshire and the Danes,' 28.

[35] *Ibid.*, 152.

[36] *Ibid.*

[37] Polwhele, R., 'History of Cornwall,' iii. 20.

[38] *Devonshire Association, Report and Trans.*, v. 41.

[39] Fergusson, J., 'Rude Stone Monuments,' 281.

[40] *Ibid.*, 176-183.

[41] Taylor, I., 'Greeks and Goths,' 110.

[42] Stephens, G., Old Northern Runic Monuments,' i. 372,

[43] *Ibid.*, iv. 25.

[44] *Ibid.*, iv. 102.

[45] Seebohm, F., 'Tribal Custom in Wales,' 46, 47.

[46] Boase, W. C., 'The Age of the Saints,' 165, quoting 'Chron. in Morice,' i. 3

[47] *Ibid.*

[48] Ermoldus, Nigellus, Monumenta Germaniæ, ii. 490.

# Chapter Twenty-Three - Settlements on The Welsh Border

AT an early time in the Saxon period the district which is now Gloucestershire became a frontier country. It was opened to settlement on the east of the Severn by the victory of Ceawlin, King of Wessex, at Deorham in 577. The Severn then became the boundary between the Britons and Saxons, and the county was down to a late period considered to be within the Marches of

Wales. The Gloucestershire country east of the Severn, which was originally part of Wessex, became later on separated from it under the rule of Ceolric of the West Saxon royal house, and was subsequently absorbed by Mercia. This is of interest in pointing to the direction from which this county probably received its earliest Saxon settlers. The early administration of this district appears to have been connected with Gloucester, Berkeley, Tewkesbury, and Cirencester. There was an extensive administrative area attached to Tewkesbury as late as the Norman survey. The Berkeley administrative area was also large, and was known for many centuries as Berkeley-herness. This name appears to be Scandinavian, and, like those of Inverness in Scotland, Agremundreness in Lancashire, and Holderness, the Berkeley district as a separate area may have had a Scandinavian origin.

In Gloucestershire, as in the northern counties, the evidence of earlier Scandinavian settlers is much mixed with that of the later, so that it is not possible in some localities to distinguish the earlier from the later.

The evidence of Northern settlers, whether of earlier or later date, is remarkable. Near Bristol is a place called Yate, the Geate mentioned in several Saxon charters. Another old name, probably denoting the settlement of a Goth, is Mangotsfield; Hacananhamme, or Hacon's ham, the old name[1] for Hanham, near Bristol, is clearly Scandinavian. In Gloucestershire, and close to it along the Wye, there were small areas called shires, corresponding to hundreds similar to the shires in the northern counties, and to the shires of ancient Norway. There are old records relating to Blakeborneshire and Pignocshire, near the Severn and the Wye. Huntishamshire was the name for a detached part of Monmouthshire, near Welsh Bicknor. In the south of the county, also, is an old hamlet called Kendalshire. The name Scir-mere occurs in a Saxon charter, and the modern name Shirehampton, nee Bristol, may be a survival of one of these old names.

The name Berkelai-erness, as already mentioned clearly corresponds to those of Holderness and Agremundreness, both of which received Northmen among their colonists. The termination -ærnes is common among the place-names of Scandinavia. The tidal bore in the Severn at the time Camden wrote still retained its Scandinavian name Hygre, derived from the Norse mythological name Oegre, the Neptune of Northern tribes. The Scandinavian name Brostorp is a Domesday name near Gloucester, south of which place are also Brookthorp and Calthorp.

The dialect of the vale of Berkeley differs both in words and pronunciation from that of the vale of Gloucester, higher up the river.[2] As already noted in relation to Somersetshire, the Scandian name Holm appears in the names Great Holm and Flat Holm for islands at the mouth of the Severn. It occurs also in Holm Lacy, near Hereford. Some remarkable Scandinavian names are found along the lower course of the Severn. Sanagar, anciently written Sevenhangar, is that of one of the old tythings of Berkeley, and Saul, also near the river, reminds us of the Saul district and the Saulings, whose name is mentioned in a runic inscription at Glavendrup in Scandinavia.[3] The forest district of Dean between the Severn and the Wye was, apparently, named after *Dene*, for Dane, and not *den*, a wood. Giraldus Cambrensis, writing in the twelfth century, tells us that the Dean Forest was known in his time as Danubia and Danica Sylvia, or Danes' Wood.[4] The name Danube for the country of the Danes is an old one. Asser, in his 'Life of Alfred,' says that in the year 866 a large fleet of pagans came to Britain from the Danube. The old name Dene for this forest district appears thus to be that of Dene, the Danish name, and it is still called Dane in the local pronunciation. The language of the ancient Northmen has survived to the present day in the name Aust, anciently Austrecliue,[5] or Aust cliff, on the east side of an ancient ferry across the Severn, near Bristol, *austr* being the Old Northern word for east.[6] Mona is a variation of the name of the stream called Monow, which joins the Wye at Monmouth, and Mona is the latinised form of the name of the Danish island Moen, or Mön.

Ethelweard tells us in his Chronicle that in 877 the Danes made a settlement of some kind in Gloucester. The custom of borough-English still survives there, as it did at Stamford, Nottingham, Derby, and Leicester, all of which were Danish towns, and we may reasonably connect the custom at Gloucester with some of the so-called Danes who may have settled there. The custom was probably brought by some allies of the real Danes, perhaps people of the Wendish or a mixed race. The custom of the real Danes of Old Denmark was that of partible inheritance.

Gloucestershire had a custom that resembled one of those of Kent—viz., that under which the lands and tenements of condemned felons were not forfeited. They were only held by the Crown for a year and a day. In this we may see a resemblance both to the custom of Kent and that of the Archenfeld part of Herefordshire.

The settlements in the lower parts of the valleys of the Severn and the Wye appear to have been effected by direct maritime migrations. The ships of the period could ascend these rivers by aid of the strong tide which flows up them to the neighbourhood of Gloucester and Monmouth. Goths or Kentish colonists on the Wye have not only left a trace of their name in that of Goderich, now Goodrich, but also in some of their customs in the district known as Ircingafeld[7] or Archenfeld. It comprised the south part of Herefordshire, having the Wye on the east and Monmouthshire on the south. Some remarkable old Kentish place-names can be traced within or near it, such as Kentchurch, Kenchester, Kentyshburcote,[8] and Kenthles.[9] These names, together with the customs which prevailed, show that the Herefordshire province of Archenfeld must have received Kentish people among its Gothic or Jutish settlers, who had no doubt inferior Welsh tenants under them. The local customs of Archenfeld closely resembled those of Kent. That of partible inheritance, of the same nature as Kentish gavelkind, survived in the district until it was abolished in the reign of Henry VIII. This Kentish custom differed from the partible custom that prevailed in Wales in three essential particulars, which will bear repetition: (1) By the Kentish custom in Archenfeld only legitimate sons inherited the paternal estate. By the Welsh custom all sons, legitimate or otherwise, had their shares, or in early centuries fought for them. Giraldus, writing in the twelfth century, tells us of the contention of legitimate and illegitimate sons for shares of the paternal estate. (2) By the custom of Archenfeld, like that of Kent, daughters inherited if there were no sons. Under the Welsh custom they did not. (3) By the custom of Archenfeld, like that of Kent, widows were entitled to their dower of half their husbands' customary estate. Under the Welsh custom they had no dower.

The resemblances between the other local customs are also remarkable. In Kent, if a tenant in gavelkind was convicted of crime and executed, his land was not forfeited, but went to his heirs. This was known as 'the father to the bough, the son to the plough' custom,[10] and was a rare privilege,[11] which the people of Archenfeld also had. In Kent, a tenant in gavelkind had the power of bequeathing his land to whom he pleased, and the people of Archenfeld had a similar privilege in respect to land they acquired.

The most remarkable of these parallel customs is, however, that under which the men of Kent claimed as their immemorial right the privilege in war of being marshalled in front of the King's army, a claim that was recognised.[12] The men of Archenfeld claimed and had allowed to them the same honourable distinction.[13] These remarkable coincidences clearly indicate a Kentish colony.

This district of Herefordshire appears to have been in any case occupied by Teutonic settlers at an early period, and to have become an outlying part of Mercia by the end of the seventh century. Ceolred, King of Mercia, dated a charter 'in loco Arcencale,' probably only a variation of the name, early in the eighth century.

The Scandinavian evidence already mentioned points to a later settlement between the Severn and the Wye, and also in the north of Monmouthshire. This country and that near the west of Herefordshire was part of the district of the Dunsetas, where English settlers of some kind lived side by side with the Wealas or Welsh. In Ethelred's ordinance relating to the Dunsetas[14] provision is made for diffusing among them a knowledge of the laws they were required to obey, and it is expressly stated that twelve lahmen shall explain the law to both the Wealas and the English, of whom six shall be English and six Welsh. The significance of this ordinance is in the legal terms used[15] *lahcop*, Old Norse *lögkaup*, and *witword*, Old Norse *vitorth*. The term lahmen is also Danish, and is mentioned in Domesday Book in connection with the administration of the Danish towns, such as Stamford. The names lawrightmen and lawmen survived in Shetland until comparatively modern times.[16] There is also a reference to the twelve lahmen in the 'Senatus consultum de Monticolis Walliæ,'[17] who were, apparently, the successors of those appointed for the Dunsetas a century earlier. If the English people among the Dunsetas had not been of Danish or Northern descent, Norrena or Danish names for legal officials and legal terms would not have been used in this ordinance. Sweden and Gothland in olden time were the land of lagmen or lahmen, for the whole territory was a confederation of commonwealths, each with its assembly of freemen, law-speaker and laws.[18]

From the evidence relating to Archenfeld there can be little doubt of an early settlement of Kentish colonists or Goths in that district, as there was, perhaps, in other parts of the same county, and a later settlement of North-men. The only record of any political connection between Kent and Here-fordshire occurs in the seventh century, when Merewald, viceroy of the Hecanas, or tribal people of that county, and brother of Wulfhere, King of Mercia, married Eormenbeorh, a princess of Kent. She was a granddaughter of King Æthelbert, and a cousin of Eormengild, who married King Wulfhere. Between the royal houses of Kent and Mercia there was by these marriages a double alliance. Merewald was also called ealdorman of the West Angles. In the eighth century we read of Arcencale as apparently part of Mercia, and by that time it had perhaps already received its Kentish or Gothic settlement, of which Goderich became the administrative centre. It is probable also that before the time of Ethelred II., King of Wessex, there had been a further set-tlement of Danes or Northmen along this Welsh border, seeing that officials with old Danish titles were appointed to explain the laws to the Dunsetas.

One of the proofs of Scandinavian settlements in the border counties is the *hope* place-names. Among the names on the coasts of Scotland and in the parts occupied by Scandinavians in that country are a large number of *hope* names. There were sea-shelters so named by them, such as Long Hope, Kirk Hope, Pan Hope, and St. Margaret's Hope, in the Firth of Forth, another in the Orkneys, and Gray Hope in Aberdeen Bay. The Norse settlers in the south of Scotland also gave the name *hope* to inland places which were shelters be-tween hills. There are sixty *hopes* in the counties of Peebles and Selkirk alone, and many more in Roxburghshire and the Cheviot country.[19] The der-ivation from *hóp*, Icelandic, an inlet of water, is clear for the sea *hopes*, and in the sense of land havens in exposed hilly regions for the inland places so named. The termination *-hope* is often pronounced *-op* and *-up*. The place-names along the Welsh borderland show some remarkable examples of this kind—*i.e.*, places with names ending in *-op* and *-hope*. In the east of Radnor-shire we find old places named Cascop, Augop, and Hope; in Shropshire, Hope Bagot, Hope Bowdler, Hope Hall, and Hope Sey; in Herefordshire and along the Gloucestershire border, Hopend, Faunhope, Woolhope, Hope, Hope-Mansel, Longhope, Arcop or Orcop, Brinsop, Seller's Hope, and the Domesday name Gadreshope.

Wigmore, Wormsley, and Ross appear to be names of Northern origin. The old district shire names already referred to are also remarkable. The Scandi-an termination *-ore* appears in the names of English and Welsh Bicknor, Yasor, Eastnor, and Radnor.

The Herefordshire Domesday hundred names include those of Radelau, Thornlau, and Wermlau, which appear to be of Northern origin, and at Marden in this county the old Norse custom survived by which in default of sons the eldest daughter succeeded to the whole inheritance.[20]

The Teutonic colonies on the coast of South Wales have been commonly ascribed to the Flemings settling there in the late Norman period. The dialect of Gower and Pembrokeshire, which resembles the West Saxon, shows, however, no trace of Flemish influence. A. J. Ellis, who investigated this subject, says that at most there could only have been a subordinate Flemish element, which soon lost all traces of its original but slightly different dialect, while the principal elements must have been Saxon, as in Gower and the Irish baronies of Bargy and Forth, in the south-east corner of Ireland.[21] A Flemish settlement in South Wales is historical, but the loss of all linguistic traces of it shows that the descendants of these settlers were absorbed among the much larger population of Saxon and Scandinavian descent previously located there. This view is supported, first, by the place-names which are of the West Saxon and Scandinavian types; and, secondly, by the customs of a large number of manors in Glamorganshire, which are different from the Welsh, and bear a close resemblance to those in west Somerset, to which locality the dialect also points. There must have been a connection between the settlers on both sides of the Channel, as the dialect, customs, and general character of the old names show.

There is also evidence which shows that the coast of Wales and its border near the sea was occupied by Anglian settlers at an earlier period than that of the main settlements by Northmen, and this may be summarised as follows: The topographical name Angle survives on the coast, and can be traced also in old records on the north-east border of Wales. There are Anglesea on the north-west, Angle and Angle Bay in Pembroke Harbour, and Pen Anglas, a promontory west of Fishguard Bay. In the Patent Rolls 9 Edward I. and other documents we read of the cantred of Ross and Englefeld, in or very near the county of Chester. It may be considered certain that these Angle place-names were not given to the districts to which they refer by the Welsh. Their name for Angles, Saxons, and Jutes alike was Saxons, similar to the popular Irish name for the English at the present time. These old place-names must have originated at a time when Angle was in use as a distinctive name for people who migrated from England or for settlers from the North of Europe. During the Viking period such settlers would be known as Northmen and Danes. It is not at all probable that the Angles of Northumbria or parts of Mercia formed new settlements on the Welsh coast while the Danes were establishing others on their own, and it must be remembered that after the Danish period the name Angle or Engle passed out of use, and the English name became solely used. It is difficult, therefore, to avoid the conclusion that these Angle names on the Welsh coast must have arisen some time before the earliest Danish inroads.

The probable Anglo-Saxon occupation of parts of the coast of South Wales before the period of settlements by the Northmen is confirmed by the prevailing dialect. Ellis says: 'The south-west of Pembrokeshire, or two peninsulas at the south-west, form an old English colony.'[22] He points out that the character of the dialect of this part of Pembrokeshire is decidedly southern, having such examples as *dr* for *thr* in three, through, and threaten; having *v* for *f* in fair, farm, fast, feel, fiddle, fox, flail, from, and furrow; having *z* for *s* in say, self, seven, sick, six, soon, and Sunday; while *s* remains with less regularity in sad, sand, saw, so, and sweet. He likewise says: 'The peninsula of Gower is also a very old English colony, consisting of seventeen English parishes.' He remarks that the reverted *r* is inferred from the word *drou* for *through*, and that there is an occasional use of *z* as an initial sound for *s*, and *un* as an unaccented word for *him*. These examples are distinctly southern English, but the dialect in Gower seems to have much worn out. With this evidence, side by side with the English place-names, and the prevalence of manorial customs in the vale of Glamorgan identical with those in the vale of Taunton, the supposition that the English characteristics of the people in these parts of South Wales are due to the Flemings entirely breaks down.

One of the most interesting of all the English district names is that anciently given to Pembrokeshire, Anglia Transwalliania, or 'England beyond Wales.' That it must have been a very old designation is probable from the surviving Angle place-names in this county, which clearly point to early settlements.

Isaac Taylor says: 'The existence of a very early Scandinavian settlement in Pembrokeshire is indicated by a dense cluster of local names of the Norse type which surrounds and radiates from the fiords of Milford and Haverford.'[23] There is other evidence pointing strongly in the same direction, which the same author has mentioned. This refers to the inscriptions known as oghams. The ogham inscriptions which have been found in Wales are about 20. Of these, 17 have been discovered in the counties of Pembroke, Cardigan, Carmarthen, and Glamorgan, 9 out of the 17 having been found in Pembrokeshire. In Devon, 2 ogham inscriptions have been discovered, and 1 in Cornwall. In Ireland they are much more numerous, 155 having been found, but of these, 148 belong to the four counties of Kilkenny, Waterford, Cork, and Kerry—*i.e.*, roughly speaking, they fringe the line of coast which stretches between the two Scandinavian kingdoms of Waterford and Limerick,[24] thus clearly showing their Scandinavian origin. Oghams are, indeed, a variation of runic writing.

The custom of borough-English is certainly not a relic of Welsh law.[25] In parts of South Wales it prevailed, with similar privileges to widows as in the vale of Taunton and on so many manors in Sussex. This custom of some manors in Glamorganshire and Pembrokeshire, by which the youngest son succeeded to the whole of the father's land, must have been introduced by settlers of another race. It prevailed on many lands in Gower;[26] it was the custom of the manors of Llanbethan,[27] Merthyr Mawr,[28] Coity Anglia,[29] and others. It was also the custom on some of the manors of the Bishop of St. David's.[30] The resemblance between this custom as it prevailed at Coity Anglia and the many manors of Taunton Dean in Somersetshire is very close— practically identical. The name Anglia attached to this manorial name is of special significance, for here we find a name with a special Old English designation, having an Old English custom. The custom points to Somersetshire,

232

the dialect of Pembrokeshire and Gower point to the same part of southern England, and there are traditions which indicate this locality as the district whence the Old English colonists of South Wales largely came. Gower is visible in clear weather from the West Somersetshire coast looming in the distance across the Severn Sea. Rhys has drawn attention to a tradition[31] in connection with the Welsh Arthurian legends, which makes Melwas king or lord of a winterless glass island. This he identifies with Glastonbury in the Æstivo regio, or summer region—*i.e.*, Somersetshire. Another and a different tradition makes Melwas king of Goire, or the peninsula of Gower seen from the Somerset coast. Thus, by mixing the two versions of the myth, the writers of romances came to speak of the kingdom of Melwas as Goire, and of his capital as Bade or Bath. The curious aspect of these traditions is that there may have been a basis for connecting Gower with Somerset; and, as Max Müller says on the growth of myths, there may have been circumstances or words, 'understood, perhaps, by the grandfather, familiar to the father, but strange to the son, and misunderstood by the grandson.'

As regards the settlement of north-east Gloucestershire, Beddoe has observed the blonde character of the population in the country around Moreton-in-the-Marsh, and considers it evidence of West Saxon colonisation northwards.[32] He notes that the distribution of colour of hair and eyes in this district resembles that found in other Saxon districts in England, and also in parts of Flanders, Holland, Friesland, and Westphalia, with the same tendency to the conjunction of hazel and dark eyes with lightish hair, rather than of light eyes with dark hair. The head form also he judges to be mostly of the two types found at Bremen, which are also those commonly found in Anglo-Saxon graves. He says that the West Saxons appear to have settled numerously in the Upper Thames districts before they began to interfere with the inhabitants of the valley of the Bristol Avon—*i.e.*, they pushed their settlement northwards at first rather than westwards.

In the same district, near Bourton, in north-east Gloucestershire, the Anglo-Saxon place-names Cwéntan[33] and Cwénena-broc[34] occur, referring to Quinton and to a stream which is named as a boundary.

The name Cwénena-broc brings us to a curious difficulty—viz., to determine whether Cwénena is the genitive plural of Cwén, a Fin, or Cwén, a woman. It has been explained as the women's brook,[35] but the name Cwéntan, now Quinton, mentioned in a Saxon charter, is in the same locality. There is a well-known story of Adam of Bremen being present at a conversation during which one of the old Scandinavian kings spoke of Quénland, or Quéna-land, the country of the Quéns or Quains. As the stranger's knowledge of Old Danish was very imperfect, he supposed the king had said Quinna-land, the country of women or amazons. Hence arose the absurd story of the terra feminarum, or amazons' country, which spread through the whole of Europe, through mistaking the name for that of a woman.'[36] The name Cwénena-broc must mean either the brook of the Quéns or Fins, as allies of Scandinavia and their descendants, or that of a community of women. Which is the more probable? It is a boundary name, apparently a boundary of Cwéntan, and we must either recognise a settlement of Fins or a settlement of women. During the period when the dialects of many tribal people were being assimilated into one form of speech it is not difficult to suppose that Cwénena may have been written for Cwéna, the usual form of the genitive plural of Cwén, a Fin.

In east Gloucestershire there were also two distinct places called Quénintune at the time of the Domesday Survey—one near Fairford, the Domesday Fareford, and the other in the north-east, apparently the Cwéntan of the Anglo-Saxon period, of which Cwénena-broc was a boundary. It thus appears probable that there were two settlements of Quéns. That there were Scandinavian settlers with whom they probably came as allies, and in whose language Fins were called Quéns, also located on this borderland of Gloucestershire and Oxfordshire, is certain from the old place-names of the district. There are, or were, not less than nine places with the characteristic -thorp or -throp names in this locality. In Domesday Book, Dunetorp, Duchitorp, and Edrope, now Heythrop, are mentioned on the Oxfordshire side. In Gloucestershire there are Addlestrop, Hatherop, Southrop, and Wiiiiamstrop. Tadilsthorpe, the Domesday Tedestrop, and Burdrop, are also old place-names. Among others of Scandinavian origin in the district are Wickenford or Wickhamford; Meon, the Domesday Mene, which may be compared with the Jutish places called Meon in Hampshire; Fareford, Wormington, Guiting, and Sclostre, now Slaughter. Rollright, the Domesday Rollendri, also occurs on the Oxfordshire side of the border, and at this place there is a rude circle of stones of the Scandinavian type. These names, together with that of the Domesday hundred name Salemanesberie, apparently derived from the Salemen or Salings of one of the Danish islands, in which hundred Bourton, Broadwell, and Slaughter were situated, are evidence that there must have been in this district of north-east Gloucestershire many settlers who spoke the old Danish or Norrena language, in which Quén is the name for Fins. Moreover, at Sclostre, now Slaughter, at the time of the Domesday Survey, the rents of two mills were paid in Danish money computation. When King Eadgar promulgated his laws in these words, 'Let this ordinance be common to all the people, whether English, Danes, or Britons, on every side of my dominions,' he must have had in mind settlements of Danish-speaking people in the south and west of England, such as this in Gloucestershire, as well as the greater Danish settlement in the northern and eastern counties.

There is evidence, in addition to that of existing place-names, which points to the settlement of some Hunni or Hunsings in the valley of the Worcestershire Avon. There are two Saxon charters relating to grant of land at Hampton, close to Evesham, which in the eighth century bore the name of Huntena-tun, the -tun of the Hunte or Hunsi, the name being mentioned in the genitive plural in both charters—one a grant by Aldred with leave of King Offa, dated 757-775[37]; the other a grant by King Acgfrid, dated 790.[38] In a charter of Eadgar, dated 969, relating to land at Witney,[39] there is a reference to the same settlement in the boundaries, the name 'huntena weg' being mentioned—*i.e.*, a road that led to the Huntena district, or Huntena-tun. A few miles east of the Anglo-Saxon Huntena-tun is Church Honeybourne, with its hamlets Cow Honeybourne and Honeybourne Leasows. These surviving names and the reference to the Huntena show that there was a settlement of people who bore that name in this district, and it should be remembered that in the old country of the Hunsings and Frisians there is a river called Hunte, as well as the Hunse.

Reference has already been made to the fair aspect of the people of east Gloucestershire at the present time. The circumstantial evidence of the place-names points to the settlement of tribal people of various blonde races in this district. Among such races are the Fins, concerning whose aspect the prover-bial expression 'as blonde as a Fin' is in use among the Russians of the parts adjoining Finland at the present day.[40] The Fins that settled in England must have come as allies of the Danes, and it is interesting to note that by the Ro-man road east Gloucestershire was in direct communication with Lincoln-shire.

One of the peculiarities of the topography of Shropshire and Worcester-shire is the considerable number of old names we can trace that apparently denote tribal settlements, as if a number of different people were settled on this borderland in large communities for defensive purposes. Among these, the following are mentioned in the Anglo-Saxon charters[41]: Wrocensetna and Scrobsetan in Shropshire, and the Tonsetan or Temsetan somewhere west of the Severn. The latter may be the settlers on the river Teme, whose name can still be traced in that of the ancient manor of Tempsiter, which in-cluded twenty-three townships of the Honour of Clun, and through which Off as Dyke passes.[42] The river Clun is the longest tributary of the Teme, the latter name being now applied to the stream only after its junction with the Onny near Ludlow. The Tonsetan or Temsetan appear to have been the set-tlers on the Welsh border near Clun. Another Worcestershire settlement which is described as a province was that of the Usmére people,[43] whose name appears to have been lost. In Herefordshire and a part of north Gloucestershire the tribe known as the Magesætas were located. We read of a grant of land at Hay 'in pago Magesætna' as late as A.D. 958.[44] This tribe must have been a large one, and Maisemore near Gloucester may have been its eastern limit. May Hill near Ross, and another May Hill near Monmouth, are probably places where the name survives.

The settlements of Gewissas, by the victories of Ceawlin in the Severn Val-ley, extended not only over parts of East Gloucestershire, but probably fur-ther northwards. Ceawlin's victories opened the country more or less as far as Shropshire. The earliest colonists into this part of England must have come either up the river or along the Roman roads, the Fosse way from the north-east, the Watling Street from the south-east, or from Wessex by the road from Winchester to Cirencester, and thence by the Fosse way to the north-east of Gloucestershire, and northwards by the Ryknield Street. It was probably about A.D. 583 that the Roman city of Uriconium was destroyed. It was situated where Wroxeter now is, close to the lowest ford across the Severn, south of Shrewsbury, where Watling Street crossed the river. Its remains show its importance, and probably many buildings of the Saxon time in its neighbourhood were constructed from its ruins. In the Severn Valley there is historical evidence of the settlement of West Saxons, and that about 590 an independent State of Gewissas was formed in Gloucestershire under Ceolric, a nephew of Ceawlin.[45] The dialect also points to its settlers having largely come from Wessex. Ellis groups it with Wilts, Berks, and parts of Hants and Dorset, as districts having much in common.[46]

Anglian settlers from Mercia or others who had a knowledge of runic letters appear to have reached the south-east of Shropshire by the end of the sixth century, for a runic inscription discovered at Cleobury Mortimer has been assigned by Stephens to that period.[47]

It may have been from the circumstance of the ruined condition of the Roman city Uriconium that the Saxon colonists near it got their name of Wrocensetna, as Camden suggested. It may, perhaps, have arisen partly from the settlers having made a quarry of the ruins. Almost all the stones in the walls of Roman Uriconium were removed, as well as the ruins of its buildings, and from the wrecked city there can be no doubt many a house, or even in later centuries a church, was partly built, as may be traced around Silchester, where the destruction was less complete. The Wrocensetna have either left their name in that of Wroxeter, the village on the site of Uriconium, or derived their name from it, the wrecked ceaster. The name survives also in those of Wrockwardine and the Wrekin. The pagus or province of the Wrocensetna is mentioned in a charter of Burgred, King of Mercia in 855,[48] and in one of Eadgar, dated 963.[49] The survival of the word 'wrocen' or 'wrekin,' as probably a reference in Saxon nomenclature to the ruins of a Roman city, is unique among English topographical names.

The ancient name Ombersley in Worcestershire, whose early settlers are called the Ombersetena, is as old as the Saxon period.[50] These people, whose name has come down to us in the genitive plural, are probably the same as the Ymbras or Ambrones—i.e., the tribe of Old Saxons south of the Humber. This colony of them in Worcestershire was probably a migration from their district on the Amber River in Derbyshire, from Nottinghamshire or Lincolnshire, along the Roman roads that passed from Chesterfield through Lichfield into Worcestershire. They apparently gave their new settlement the same name, which some of the tribe had brought from the Ambra River in Old Saxony.

In Shropshire an interesting peculiarity has been observed in the country dialect. This, according to Prince L. L. Bonaparte, is the verb plural ending in n, as 'we aren' for 'we are,' and also the form 'we bin' for 'we are.' This he points out as an interesting instance of the shading of the southern dialects, in which 'I be' and 'thou bist' are common, into the north-western.[51] That some settlers in Shropshire came up the river is probable from the dialect and from some of the customs. Borough-English, which still survives at Gloucester, prevailed in the English part of Shrewsbury.[52] In this county also there were, at the close of the Saxon period, tenants called coscets, few in number; but as coscets are peculiar to Wiltshire, these may have been descendants of Gewissas who had migrated.

Along the border counties of Wales there was necessarily going on during the Anglo-Saxon period some racial fusion between the tribal people respectively of the Teutonic and Welsh races. As the Welsh were driven westward from the Midland counties, their agricultural system of isolated homesteads appears to have been commonly adopted. Villages of collected homesteads, like those between the Elbe and the Weser, or east of the Elbe, and such as are found in Northamptonshire and the adjacent counties, are comparatively rare along the Welsh border. Giraldus tells us that in the twelfth century the houses of the Welsh tribesmen were not built either in towns or villages. Like other pastoral people, they had two sets of homesteads, feeding their herds in summer on the higher ranges of the hills and in winter in the valleys. The Old English settlers along the border counties adopted this system, or brought it with them, and many of the isolated hamlets on the higher slopes of the hills were probably in their origin only summer shelters.

The original settlement of Cheshire must have been, at least in part, a direct one, and not wholly an extension of local colonies from the Staffordshire side. A similarity has been noted between the Cheshire dialect in some respects and that of Norfolk, while the intervening counties differ.[53] This may have arisen from Danish influence, and be a result of direct settlements on the coast. The maritime parts of North Wales have many old place-names to attest their settlements, and Chester appears to have been largely a Danish town during the later Saxon period. It was governed by twelve judges or lahmen, who were chosen from among the vassals of the King, the Bishop, and the Earl.[54] As the institution of lahmen is Scandinavian, it is clear that there must have been a population of that race at Chester. Other circumstances that point to Northmen are the prevalence of family names ending in -son, corresponding to the Norse -sen, which survive in Cheshire, and the mention in Domesday Book of certain fines in the city of Chester being paid in oræ or by Danish money computation. The place-names of the Wirral district between the Mersey and the Dee show that it was occupied by the later Northmen. The discovery, however, of a runic inscription, which Stephens assigned to the seventh century,[55] at Overchurch in the Wirral, proves that Anglians advanced into this district soon after the Battle of Chester in 613. Among the Domesday place-names that were apparently derived from those of early tribal settlers in Cheshire are Englefeld, Englelei, Inglecrost, Wareneberie, Leche, and Cocheshalle.

The Cheshire dialect, as spoken in different parts, shows certain well-marked differences in respect to vocabulary, pronunciation, and grammar.[56] In the formation of place-names in the south of the county there was apparently little or no Danish influence. The speech in this part is broad and rough, differing in pronunciation from that of the northern part, and approaching more to that of north Staffordshire and Derbyshire. These are the counties in which the descendants of the early Anglian settlers were least disturbed by subsequent Danish inroads, and south Cheshire appears somewhat to resemble them. On the other hand, there is a clear line of difference between the local talk in south Cheshire and Shropshire, where the highly-pitched tone, the habit of raising the voice at the end of a sentence, the sharp and clearly-defined pronunciation, probably marks a Welsh element among the Shropshire people which is absent in south Cheshire.

As the settlement proceeded from east to west in the Mercian States, some of the Welsh people must have been allowed to exist among the newcomers. As far east as Buckinghamshire there was in the Anglo-Saxon period a place called Wealabroc, and in the south-west of Northamptonshire there exists still an old way called the Welsh Road. These names probably imply old frontier lines. As the advance was continued towards the present Welsh border, it is certain that here and there small areas inhabited by Welsh people in the midst of Old English settlements were left. Beyond the present border, as around Radnor, settlements of Old English or Scandian folk surrounded by Welsh people were formed. Offa's Dyke, thrown up in the eighth century to divide the Welsh from the English, was not a strict ethnological frontier. There were some English to the west of it at the time it was made, or soon afterwards, and some Welsh to the east of it, as at Clun, Oswestry, and Cherbury, at which places early Welcheries existed, which were not governed by English customs.

It was along this border that the customs of the Old English settlers were brought into contact with the tribal customs of the Welsh. The various English customs of inheritance derived from tribal settlers have been described. In some important respects the Welsh differed from all of these. The land of the Welsh tribesmen was held by families and allotted to members of the family. On the death of the head of the family, it was first divided among all the sons. This, however, was not a final division. On the death of the last of these brothers, the land was again divided among all their sons *per capita*, each first-cousin taking an equal share. On the death of the last of these first-cousins, the land was again divided as before, each second-cousin taking an equal share. Land could be inherited, consequently, only by direct descent.[57] There was no inheritance by daughters. There was no widow's dower. No man was his brother's heir. If a man left sons, they inherited; if he left none, the land was shared according to the tribal custom. This is of interest in reference to the custom of Dymock in west Gloucestershire, which was apparently left as an ethnological island of Welsh people. Its name is Welsh, and its custom was Welsh, for the land at Dymock passed on the death of the holder to the heirs of the body only; otherwise it reverted to the community or the lord.[58]

The place-names Welsh Hampton, east of Ellesmere, and Welsh Bicknor and Welsh Newton, near Monmouth, tell the same story of mixed settlements. There was both an Englecheria and a Walecheria, of ancient origin, at Clun and at Cherbury in west Shropshire.[59] There were English landholders and Welsh subtenants of ancient date in the great district of Archenfeld, west of the river Wye. It was owing to such conditions as these that the blending of race between the Old English and Old Welsh people went on. Then, as generations passed, English folk arose along the Welsh border who were partly of Welsh descent, having complexions somewhat darker than their forefathers—a physical characteristic they have transmitted to their descendants at the present day.

[1] Cart. Sax., ii. 588.
[2] English Diaelct Society, 'Glossary,' by D. Robertson, 194.
[3] Stephens, G., 'Old Northern Runic Monuments,' ii. 1009.
[4] *Archæological Journal*, xviii. 342.
[5] Domesday Book.
[6] Cleasby and Vigfusson, Icel. Dict.
[7] Anglo-Saxon Chron.,
[8] Testa de Nevill.
[9] Cal. Inq. p.m., ii. 34, 196.
[10] Elton, C. I., 'Gavelkind,' p. 176.
[11] *Ibid.*, p. 192.
[12] *Ibid.*, p. 229, quoting Camden and Gervase.
[13] Hazlitt's ed. of Blount's 'Tenures,' p. 173.
[14] Laws of Ethelred.
[15] Worsaae, J. J., 'Danes and Norwegians in England.'
[16] *Proceedings Soc. Antiq. Scot.*, xxvi. 189, 190.
[17] Domesday Book, General Introduction, by Sir H. Ellis.
[18] Cleasby and Vigfusson, 'Icelandic Dict.,' see *lög-mathr.*
[19] Christison, D., 'Place-Names in Scotland,' *Proceedings Soc. Antiq. Scot.*, xxvii. 269.
[20] Elton, C. I., 'Law of Copyholds,' 134.
[21] Rhys, J., 'The Welsh People,' p. 29.
[22] Ellis, A. J., 'English Dialects,' p. 23.
[23] Taylor, Isaac, 'Greeks and Goths,' 110.
[24] *Ibid.*, 111.

[25] Cobbett, J. A., *Journal Cambrian Arch. Assoc.*, vi. 76.
[26] *Ibid.*, Fifth Series, x. 5.
[27] *Ibid.*, vi. 76.
[28] *Ibid.*, Fourth Series, ix. 20.
[29] *Ibid.*, Fourth Series, viii. 13, 14.
[30] *Ibid.*, Fifth Series, ii. 70.
[31] Rhys, J., 'Studies in the Arthurian Legend,' 330, 346.
[32] Beddoe, J., *Journal of the Anthropological Inst.*, xxv. 19.
[33] Codex Dipl., No. 244.
[34] *Ibid.*, Nos. 426, 1359, 1365.
[35] Bosworth and Toller, 'Anglo-Saxon Dict.'
[36] *Ibid.*, and Latham, 'Germania of Tacitus,' 174, 179.
[37] Cart. Sax., i. 306.
[38] *Ibid.*, i. 369.
[39] *Ibid.*, iii. 520.
[40] Réclus, E., 'Nouvelle Géographie Universelle,' v. 334.
[41] Codex Dipl., Index.
[42] *Shropshire Archæological and Nat. Hist. Soc. Trans.*, xi. 244.
[43] Codex Dipl., Nos. 127, 143, 1251.
[44] Cart. Sax., iii. 242.
[45] Anglo-Saxon Chronicle.
[46] Ellis, A. J., 'English Dialects,' 24.
[47] Stephens, G., *loc. cit.*, iii. 160.
[48] Codex Dipl., No. 277.
[49] *Ibid.*, No. 1246.
[50] *Ibid.*, Nos. 637, 1366.
[51] *Transactions Philological Soc.*, 1875-1876, p. 576.
[52] Bateson, M., *English Hist. Review*, 1901, p. 109.

[53] Beddoe, J., 'Races of Britain,' p. 70.
[54] Lappenberg, J. M., 'History of England under the Anglo-Saxon Kings,' ii. 354; and Domesday Book.
[55] Stephens, G., *loc. cit.*, iv. 53.
[56] Darlington, T., 'Folk-Speech of South Cheshire.'

[57] Rhys, J., and Jones, D. B., 'The Welsh People,' 221, 222.
[58] Pollock and Maitland, 'History of English Law,' ii. 272.
[59] Plac. de quo warr., 681.

# Chapter Twenty-Four - Conclusion

ONE of the conclusions to which the evidence that has been brought forward leads us is that the Old English or Anglo-Saxon race was formed on English soil out of many tribal elements, and that the settlers who came here were known among themselves by tribal names, many of which still survive in those of some of the oldest settlements, where they lived under customary family and kindred law. Under the general names Jutes, Angles, Saxons, Danes, and Northmen, came numerous allies. It appears certain that Frisians of various tribes were, in regard to number, as important as any settlers, and that they came among the Angles as well as among the Jutes and Saxons. Under the Saxon name there can be very little doubt that colonists were settled on the east coast of England before the withdrawal of the Romans.

In reference to Danes and Scandinavians, it appears from the evidence adduced that they brought with them many allies from various countries on the Baltic coasts on which they had previously formed settlements, or which they had brought under subjection. The evidence appears conclusive that there was a Wendish, and consequently a Slavonic, element among the earlier tribal immigrants as well as among the later. It has also been shown that some Celtic people must have been absorbed into the Anglo-Saxon stock.

The Old English race grew by the absorption into it of tribal people descended from various ancient races. It assimilated to a great extent their dialects, and the Old English speech, as it prevailed in various parts of England, was formed by this process. No example of an Anglo-Saxon language has even been found out of Britain itself.[1] It arose here, like the race itself, by the blending of tribal dialects, of which those of northern origin are important. From the traces we find of Danish or Scandian settlements in nearly all parts of England it appears that the Scandinavian influence in the origin of the Anglo-Saxon race has been underestimated.

In tracing the assimilation of the dialects, as far as it is possible to do so, we trace the formation of the race. As regards those of Scandinavian origin, Stephens says: 'Manifold dialects were in continual growth and change through the Northern lands, though in the oldest time they all agreed in their bolder features. But local developments and fluctuation of population and settlement went on unceasingly both on the Scandian main and in the English colony. . . . In Scandinavia itself, as in England, the languages and dialects differ. The spoken dialects are many in each Scandian land, and the folk of one district often cannot understand the natives of another. But the Scandian talks in general, especially the Danish, greatly liken the English (especially the North English), and a farm labourer from Jutland, for instance, can after a couple of days be hob-a-nob with the peasantry of northern England and southern Scotland. In the Old Northern Runic Age all these folkships could get on very well together, while they were also very closely allied in speech and blood with the Frisic and Saxon clans, some of which took part in the settlement of England.'[2] In the Old English speech, as it has come down to us, there are as many as ten words, more or less synonymous, for the word man, and as many for woman.[3] The language abounds in synonymous words, thus showing a commingling of elements from many sources. Its obscure etymology, its confused and imperfect inflections, and its anomalous and irregular syntax, point to the same conclusion, and indicate a diversity of origin.

It does not appear that the Old English, as the speech of a nation, existed until towards the later Anglo-Saxon period. 'We are all weary,' says the distinguished author of the great work on the Old Northern Runic Monuments, 'of an Anglo-Saxon language that never existed. The Old English in its many dialects we know, and if we know anything we are aware that it is of a distinctly Northern character, whenever Northern writings as old as the Old English can be found to be compared with it.'[4] The oldest remains of Old Saxon, says Marsh, 'are not Anglo-Saxon, and I think it must be regarded, not as a language which the colonists or any of them brought with them from the Continent, but as a new speech resulting from the fusion of many separate elements.'[5] There is, says the same American philologist, 'linguistic evidence of a great commingling of nations in the body of the intruders.'

All the available evidence, the dialects of the period, the surviving customs, or those known to have existed, and the comparison of place-names with those of ancient Germany and Scandinavia, point to the same conclusion, that the English race had its origin in many parent sources, and arose on English soil, not from some great national immigration, but from the commingling here of settlers from many tribes.

The many traces that remain of the mythology of the early settlers in England point in the same direction. As York Powell has said,[6] 'There is one fact about Teutonic mythology as we have it which has never been brought out quite clearly. The mass of legend in more or less simple condition that has come down to us is not the remains of one uniform regular religion...but it is the remains of the separate faiths, more or less parallel, of course, of many different tribes and confederacies, each of which had its own several name for each several mythic being, and its own particular version of his or her adventures and affinities.' The old German world, with its secrets and wonders, and the views of its ancient people regarding their gods and heroes, were, as Wagner says, formerly lost in the darkness of the past, and are now visible in the light of the present.[7] The same may be said of the old Scandinavian world, and the modern light in which we may view their mythology is due to the long labour of German and Scandinavian scholars. The results of their researches point to the existence of many tribes having differences in their mythological names, beliefs, and practices.

It is to the Old English race more than any other that we must look for the most remarkable examples of the absorption within it of people of many various tribes and nations. It is probably largely owing to this absorption within itself of people of other descent that the race owes much of its vigour. In all ages of the world and in all countries it is and has been the strongest and ablest of a tribe or nation that has been selected by natural circumstances or political considerations for conquest and colonization. Those who have gone to the wars, or have become successful colonists, have been among the ablest of the race. England, during the centuries in which her settlement went on, received and absorbed into the Anglo-Saxon stock immigrants from probably almost all the tribes of Northern Europe. As the newer and greater Anglo-Saxon stock in Britain, America, and the British colonies is at the present time constantly absorbing into itself people of all European races, so during the centuries of its growth tribal elements were constantly becoming blended and assimilated in the old English nation.

As it was in the Old English time, so it has been more or less continuously throughout the course of our national life; streams of immigrants, now many, now few, have found in England a refuge from oppression, or homes when driven from their own lands. They have been absorbed among the people of England. Streams of colonists for more than three hundred years have gone out from our shores, and have formed new nations in the Westen and Southern hemispheres, and these, repeating the old story, have absorbed and are absorbing into the newer and greater Anglo-Saxon race immigrants from all European countries.

[1] Marsh, G. P., 'Lectures on the English Language,' First Series, p. 43.
[2] Stephens, G., 'Old Northern Runic Monuments,' iii. 396.
[3] Turner, Sharon, 'History of the Anglo-Saxons,' ii. 379.
[4] Stephens. G., *loc. cit.*, ii. 516.
[5] Marsh, G. P., *loc cit.*, pp. 42, 43.
[6] Saxo Grammaticus, translated by Elton, introduction by York Powell, cxv.
[7] Wagner, W., 'Asgard and the Gods,' p. 2.

www.ingramcontent.com/pod-product-compliance
Lightning Source LLC
Chambersburg PA
CBHW030006290326
41934CB00005B/241